FREEDOM FOR OBEDIENCE

FREEDOM
FOR
OBEDIENCE

Evangelical Ethics
in Contemporary Times

Donald G. Bloesch

1817

Harper & Row, Publishers, San Francisco

Cambridge, Hagerstown, New York, Philadelphia, Washington
London, Mexico City, São Paulo, Singapore, Sydney

FIRST EDITION

Library of Congress Cataloging-in-Publication Data

Bloesch, Donald G., 1928–
  Freedom for obedience.

  Bibliography: p.
  Includes indexes.
  1. Christian ethics.   2. Evangelicalism.   I. Title.
BJ1241.B56   1987   241   86-42998
ISBN 0-06-060804-8

87 88 89 90 91 RRD 10 9 8 7 6 5 4 3 2 1

To Walter F. Peterson
President of the University of Dubuque Theological Seminary

Contents

Acknowledgments

I am deeply grateful to my wife, Brenda, for her painstaking copyediting and research that have helped to make this book possible. I also acknowledge my indebtedness to my former teacher James Luther Adams for introducing me to Paul Tillich and Ernst Troeltsch; to my colleague Arthur Cochrane for sharing the wealth of his insights on Karl Barth's theological ethics; to Mark Noll of Wheaton College for his copyediting of chapter 12; to Daniel Bloesch for his assistance in German translation; to Deborah Fliegel and Mary Anne Knefel, reference librarians at the University of Dubuque library, for their invaluable help in procuring needed information; and to Peg Saunders, our seminary faculty secretary, for the cheerful diligence and expertise with which she typed the third draft of the manuscript.

An abbreviated version of chapter 13, "The Ideological Temptation," has appeared in *Christianity and Conflict,* edited by Kevin Perrotta and Peter Williamson (Servant Publications, 1986). The brief section on James Gustafson in chapter 10, "Alternatives in Ethics Today," was published in a slightly different form as a book review in *TSF Bulletin,* November-December 1986.

The material in a number of these chapters was originally presented in a somewhat modified form at the following events: Christian Reformed Pastors' Conference, Calvin College, Grand Rapids, Michigan (June 1979); Great Rivers Presbytery, Monmouth College, Monmouth, Illinois (March 1982); Hugh Th. Miller Lectures, Christian Theological Seminary, Indianapolis (April 1982); Greenhoe Lectures, Louisville Presbyterian Seminary (October 1982); Conference on American Evangelicals, Billy Graham Center, Wheaton College (March 1985); Allies for Faith and Renewal Conference, Eastern Michigan University, Ypsilanti (May 1985); and the Founders Lectures, Trinity Evangelical Divinity School, Deerfield, Illinois (February 1986).

Abbreviations

Scripture references are from the Revised Standard Version, unless otherwise indicated by the following abbreviations:

NIV   New International Version
NEB   New English Bible
GNB   Good News Bible
JB   Jerusalem Bible
KJV   King James Version
NKJV New King James Version
LB   Living Bible

Preface

Among my reasons for writing this book is the desire to present an evangelical alternative to the situationalist and naturalist ethics that presently dominate the discussion in this field. While the primary focus of the book is on theological ethics, frequent references are made to current social issues; the last chapter is devoted to the intractable problem of war.

Besides the traditional issues of law and gospel, love and justice, and the role of principles in ethics, I discuss the mission of the church, the insidious power of ideology in shaping ethical decision, and the work of God as Civilizer as well as Redeemer. From my theological perspective God's civilizing work is to subdue human passions, whereas his redeeming work is to transform these passions into the service of the kingdom. God not only restores us to his family as his sons and daughters, but he also restores us as fit instruments for a new society. But this restoration is dependent on the work of regeneration by his Spirit.

I also examine the perplexing question of how to discern the will of God. In contrast to Paul Tillich, who sees the will of God as the law of our own being, I understand God's will in terms of a divine command that comes to us from the beyond but ordinarily in conjunction with the witness of Holy Scripture. The will of God is not "the silent voice of our own nature" (Tillich) but the living voice of the God who stands over against us as our Creator, Judge, and Redeemer. The will of God is not a call to realize our essential selves but an invitation to become what we are not—saints of the Most High.

I believe that this book is somewhat distinctive in the field of theological ethics because it combines a number of features. First, it seeks to be evangelical in the classical sense, meaning that it finds its basis in the gospel of reconciliation and redemption as attested in Holy Scripture. Second, it views ethics as a creative response to God's free grace rather than either a servile conformity to an inflexible moral code on the one hand or an ongoing discovery of abiding values on the other. Third, it affirms both an absolute norm and the need to relate to the concrete situation or cultural context in which people find themselves. Finally, in contrast to much traditional ethics, it conceives of the way of the cross as a morality beyond the morality of code and convention. I do not claim that these emphases are original, but a good case can be made that they contravene much of what is being said in theological ethics at the present time.

This book is intended for all college-educated people, both in and outside the churches. It should be of special interest to teachers of theology and ethics in seminaries and colleges, theological students, ministers, and full-time lay workers, including missionaries. It might also have a certain appeal to teachers and students of philosophy. It is a book in spirituality as well as in ethics in that its focus is on the Christian life.

Many of the chapters in this book were originally given as lectures in courses, pastors' institutes, renewal conferences, and seminary convocations. It is through creative interaction with lay people as well as clergy on the decisive issues in theological ethics that I have been able to forge a position of my own—one that draws on the theological heritage of the church universal but at the same time is integrally related to the existential and cultural situation of our day.

Oh, that you were not so proud and stubborn! Then you would listen to the Lord, for he has spoken.

JEREMIAH 13:15 LB

I will live in perfect freedom, because I try to obey your teachings.

PSALM 119:45 GNB

The love of Christ leaves us no choice. . . . His purpose in dying for all was that men, while still in life, should cease to live for themselves.

2 CORINTHIANS 5:14, 15 NEB

Our return to obedience is indeed the aim of free grace. It is for this that it makes us free.

KARL BARTH

Obedience without freedom is slavery; freedom without obedience is arbitrary self-will. Obedience restrains freedom; and freedom ennobles obedience.

DIETRICH BONHOEFFER

CHAPTER 1

Introduction

My light will shine out for you just a little while longer. Walk in it while you can, and go where you want to go before the darkness falls, for then it will be too late for you to find your way.

JOHN 12:35 LB

The will of God is the supreme rule of righteousness, so that everything which he wills must be held to be righteous by the mere fact of his willing it.

JOHN CALVIN

The taking of the cross means the death of self, of personal ambition and self-centered purpose. In the place of selfish attainment, however altruistic and noble, one is to desire alone the rule of God.

GEORGE ELDON LADD

God's requirement is holiness. Now the accumulation of all the virtues in the world, all the good works, all the high ideals, all the honest intentions, does not constitute holiness.

JACQUES ELLUL

I have endeavored in this study first of all to present a viable alternative to legalistic ethics on the one hand and situational and relativistic ethics on the other and, second, to arouse the wider Christian community in general and the evangelical community in particular to explore anew the theological foundations for both personal holiness and social justice.

This book is the fruit of many years of reflection and reading on the paradoxical and enigmatic relationship between law and grace, the divine command and the divine promise. It has its basis in an ever-deepening conviction that ethics is an integral part of dogmatics, that the Christian life is inseparable from the Christian creed.

I am no less convinced of the need to recover the dualistic motif in ethics and theology—not a metaphysical but a moral dualism: heaven and hell, righteousness and sin, the kingdom of God and the kingdom of the world, love and justice, gospel and law. Yet even this dualism is not ultimate, for the power of heaven overwhelms that of hell; righteousness advances despite and paradoxically sometimes through the folly of sin; the kingdom of God triumphs over the kingdoms of this world; love radically transcends but at the same time fulfills justice; the gospel transforms rather than annuls the law. The dualities often prove to be polarities that complement rather than oppose one another. This is not true of sin and righteousness, where the opposition is implacable, but it is true of love and justice and gospel and law. I see not so much a disparity between a purified human righteousness and divine righteousness, creative justice and sacrificial love, as a correspondence—one that is broken but nevertheless real.

At the same time, the morality that Christ embodied in his life, death, and resurrection is qualitatively different from the morality of code and convention. I have called it a morality beyond morality.[1] Whereas the common morality urges a fair adjudication between competing claims, the higher morality bids us surrender our claims for the good of our neighbor. While the common morality upholds the integrity and authority of the family, the ethic of the cross frees us from the tyranny of the clan. While the common morality relies on the sword to enforce justice, the ethic of the cross relies on the power of suffering love.

It is not true to say, as John Macquarrie does, that "Christian moral teaching is an unfolding of the 'natural' morality of all men."[2] On the contrary, the way of the cross sharply questions natural morality without negating it in any absolute sense. In the perspective of Christian faith, morality is not a disposition conformable to duty (Kant) but an exercise in compassion that goes beyond moral decorum and social obligation.

Yet this theological stance must not be confused with that of philosophers who might use similar language but with different meanings. Nietzsche declared that whatever is done for love always occurs beyond good and evil. But for Nietzsche, love is divorced from law so that the distinction between good and evil no longer exists. Likewise, I cannot go along with Berdyaev's "morality of creativity," which stands in contrast with a "morality of obedience." By describing the creative impulse as "absolutely unique, unbidden and lawless," he overlooked the fact that grace does not cancel the law but sets it on a new foundation.[3] He was correct in his perception that there is an element of heedlessness in pure love, but he went too far when he separated law and love.

My position is much closer to that of Barth and Bonhoeffer, both of whom appealed to the divine commandment over codified law.[4] Yet the divine commandment does not overthrow law but transforms it. In the divine commandment law and promise are united so that God's word is seen as an empowering to obey and not simply a command to obey. It is a word of grace and hope that rids the law of its tedious aridity and fills it with promise. In this perspective the gospel opposes the misunderstood law, the law of works and condemnation, but it affirms and ratifies the law of spirit and life, the law that is now in the service of the gospel.

I reject the existentialist view that the divine commandment has no definite conceptual content. It is surely difficult to reconcile the biblical testimony with Bultmann's claim that "man does not meet the crisis of decision armed with a definite standard; he stands on no firm base, but rather alone in empty space."[5] We must not make a disjunction between God's commandment in the here and now and the summary of the commandments and ordinances of God in Scripture. The Spirit brings not a new revelation but a clarification and deepening of the one revelation in Holy Scripture. Our criterion is not the Spirit alone but the Spirit united with the written Word of God. Yet when the Spirit acts upon the commandments in Scripture, they are seen no longer as the moral codes of a people in the past but as directives to service that apply to peoples in all times and places.

What I am proposing is not merely a theocentric ethics (as in the attenuated neo-Calvinism of Gustafson),[6] but a Christocentric ethics. This is an ethics in which Jesus Christ is central, not only his teachings and commandments, but also and above all his life, death, and resurrection. Fidelity to the high and holy God involves the imitation of Christ not in the sense of trying to copy the details of his life but in the sense of seeing in his self-sacrifice the paradigm for our discipleship. But the Christian ethic is even more a demonstration of our gratitude for what God has done for us in Jesus Christ, for his act of reconciliation and redemption that makes all things new.

The Christocentric ethics delineated in this book is also to be contrasted with an anthropocentric ethics as this is found in existentialism, with its emphasis on gaining authentic selfhood, and in eudaemonism, where the focus is on self-realization. We are called not to satisfy our dreams and desires nor to realize a destiny to greatness but to serve the glory of God. But we serve the glory of God precisely by upholding Christ as Savior and Lord and following Christ as our Teacher and Example.

Finally, as people who are called to the higher righteousness of the kingdom of God, we need to be constantly alert to the threat of ideology, the cultural self-understanding that is shaped and warped by the biases of class, race, and clan. We need to realize our vocation to be ambassadors and witnesses of Jesus Christ in the conflicts and discords of social existence. We need to take stands on controversial social and political issues, but we must make sure that in so doing we never play into the hands of self-serving vested interests. Christians should always be on the side of the poor, but when the poor are no longer poor and when the rich are dethroned, our task is then to side with those who were formerly oppressors but are now the oppressed.

The Christian ethic is an ethic that always goes against the stream of popular opinion. It is an ethic that cannot be assimilated into the moral consensus of the wider community. It is an ethic that contravenes rather than ratifies and confirms cultural wisdom. The way of the cross cannot be reconciled with the way of the world, just as the gospel cannot be conjoined with the laws that give stability to social order.

At the same time, the spiritual righteousness of the kingdom of God does not annul law but transforms it. As people delivered from the condemnation of the law, we are no longer under the prohibitions of a legal system but now under the imperatives of the gospel or the law united with the gospel. In the new light and power that come to us from Christ, we are free even to break the commands of moral tradition, but only in order to give effect to these commands anew (Bonhoeffer). We are free to realize the intention of the commands in strikingly new ways. We do not become our own masters and saviors, as in Nietzsche, but we are under a new Master, the living Christ, who interprets the law for us by the Spirit, who shows us how to obey in the concrete situation in which we find ourselves. We are no longer under law but are now directly under the Lawgiver, who grants us the power to live in the spirit of the law, the joy of serving beyond the obligation of the law, the hope of realizing a vocation that fulfills and transcends the letter of the law. The morality beyond morality in evangelical perspective is not an ethic that annuls the moral but one that affirms the supremely moral—the perfection of love that exceeds the limits of moral propriety but at the same time fulfills the deep-seated yearnings of all people for truth, beauty, and goodness.

The thesis of this book is that human justice can never be a substitute for divine justification (William Stringfellow), but it can be a sign and witness of the justifying grace of God in Jesus Christ. Humanitarian works can never reach the heights of deeds of sacrifical love and mercy, but they can point to this higher righteousness and awaken a thirst for it. The codified law of religious tradition can never duplicate or reproduce the divine commandment, but it can prepare us to recognize this commandment when it is given.

We must always be on guard against two perils: the Scylla of legalism and rigorism and the Charybdis of antinomianism. An ethics of the divine commandment, by uniting law and grace, the imperative and the indicative, shows how we can live the authentic Christian life in obedience to the highest, which is not a law but a person, not an ideal but the reality of the New Being, the power of crucified love, as we see this in Jesus Christ.

Notes

1. Reinhold Niebuhr uses this phrase (citing Berdyaev as his source) in arguing that forgiveness finally stands in contradiction to punitive justice. *Christian Realism and Political Problems* (New York: Charles Scribner's Sons, 1953), pp. 164–65. With both Niebuhr and Berdyaev, I see a qualitative gulf between the morality of redemption and the morality of code and law. Yet with Niebuhr I contend that even at the pinnacle of grace as unmerited forgiveness, law is not completely transcended.
2. John Macquarrie, *Three Issues in Ethics* (New York: Harper & Row, 1970), p. 110.
3. Nicolas Berdyaev, *Dream and Reality*, trans. Katharine Lampert (New York: Macmillan Co., 1951), p. 218.
4. The divine command theory of Barth and Bonhoeffer was anticipated already in the late Middle Ages and is indeed in accord with the position of the Reformers, Luther and Calvin. Where Barth and Bonhoeffer differ from some of the schoolmen who tended toward voluntarism is that the former generally avoid speaking of God as absolute power; instead, God is depicted as the power to love or the will to love. For an illuminating introduction to the divine command theory in the history of theology and philosophy see Janine Marie Idziak, *Divine Command Morality: Historical and Contemporary Readings* (New York and Toronto: Edwin Mellen, 1979).
5. D. Rudolf Bultmann, *Jesus and the Word*, trans. Louise Pettibone Smith and Erminie Huntress (New York: Charles Scribner's Sons, 1934), p. 85.
6. See James M. Gustafson, *Ethics from a Theocentric Perspective*, 2 vols. (Chicago: University of Chicago Press, 1981–1984).

CHAPTER 2

Law and Grace in Ethics

Keep falsehood far from me and grant me the grace of living by thy law.

PSALM 119:29 NEB

Hence it comes that faith alone makes righteous and fulfills the law; for out of Christ's merit, it brings the Spirit, and the Spirit makes the heart glad and free, as the law requires that it shall be.

MARTIN LUTHER

In order to fulfill the commonest law . . . we must rise into a loftier region altogether, a region that is above law, because it is spirit and life and makes the law.

GEORGE MACDONALD

The point of departure for Christian ethics is not the reality of one's self, or the reality of the world; nor is it the reality of standards and values. It is the reality of God as He reveals Himself in Jesus Christ.

DIETRICH BONHOEFFER

Beyond Legalism and Relativism

The noted French Reformed theologian Jacques Ellul has complained, "All ethical systems are either in ruins or empty—empty when they come down to the mere repetition of ancient and obviously outdated rules."[1] When ethical theory lapses into relativism or reverts to legalism, Christians are presented with two equally unpalatable alternatives. William Blake, who is celebrated in our day by Thomas Altizer, Theodore Roszak, and various other neomystics, has made the outrageous statement that "no virtue can exist without breaking these ten commandments. Jesus was all virtue, and acted from impulse, not from rules."[2] But antinomianism (living without the law) was certainly not the teaching of Jesus nor of his apostles. Yet it cannot be denied that Jesus challenged the moral code of his day with a higher righteousness that did not annul but instead fulfilled the Old Testament law.

In contradistinction to both legalism and relativism, I propose an ethics of the divine commandment in which the law and gospel are united in the voice of the living Christ, who speaks to us in the here and now, even as he has spoken in the past. The divine commandment cannot be reduced to rules or principles, for it signifies the act of God speaking and people hearing in the divine-human encounter.

What I am advocating is not relativism and certainly not situationalism, as this is understood in contemporary ethics. As Christians, we have a reliable road map that gives us some idea of the path we are to follow in our cultural and temporal situation. This road map is the Decalogue, the Sermon on the Mount, the Pauline injunctions, and similar commands in both the Old and New Testaments. These criteria provide an ethical parameter for the people of God, but they do not give specific guidance. They indicate where God might lead us, but they do not tell us precisely what God is now requiring of us. They point to the way God would have us walk, but they do not reveal the concrete steps we must take here and now. This is provided only by God's commandment, which we hear in conjunction with the Decalogue and the Sermon on the Mount as well as with the kerygmatic proclamation.

The Decalogue and Sermon on the Mount are foundational criteria, but neither is the absolute or irreducible criterion. They are relative criteria that nevertheless by the Spirit participate in the Absolute. The absolute criterion is the unity of the law and the gospel in the divine commandment as it is applied to a particular situation. These relative criteria direct us to the Absolute—God's self-revelation in the Christ of biblical history. They are the signposts that guide us to the narrow gate and keep us on the straight way (Matt. 7:13, 14; cf. Ps. 119:105). They serve to communicate the Absolute when they become transparent to their revelatory meaning by the action of the Spirit, when they are united with the living Word of God, Jesus Christ.

There is no eternal moral law in the sense of unchanging principles. But there is an abiding moral order. There is a consistent moral teaching associated with God's revelation in that what God commands at one time in history will be in harmony with what he commands on another occasion. For God is faithful to himself; he has integrity of being. (Barth speaks of the constancy of God). His will does not conflict with his nature. In this qualified sense we can speak of a moral law. But there is no moral law in the sense of a propositional formula that is in and of itself absolute and eternal, that is there waiting to be discovered.[3] Divine revelation provides moral direction, but it does not yield rules that are eternal and therefore directly applicable to every situation.

The divine commandment is never a general principle available for our inspection, a value judgment open to our consideration. It cannot be reduced to an abiding truth that may lend meaning to our lives. It is not so much an object of reflection as a call to action. It is not so much a moral possibility as a summons to obedience. For a commandment to be the very Word of God, we must hear it as the voice of the living Lord. Our hearing does not make it the Word of God, but if it is in fact this Word, it will so confront us that we will hear. If we hear rightly, we will hear it as a word of grace, a word that empowers as well as demands.[4]

According to Bonhoeffer, the divine commandment "is so comprehensive and at the same time so definite that it leaves no freedom for interpretation or application, but only the freedom to obey or to disobey."[5] This can be seen in Jesus' call to his disciples: "Follow me, and I will make you fishers of men" (Matt. 4:19). We read that "immediately they left their nets and followed him." This same pattern is evident when Paul was confronted by the risen Christ on the road to Damascus: "Rise and enter the city, and you will be told what you are to do" (Acts 9:6; cf. 22:10; 16:9, 10). Despite his temporary blindness, Paul obeyed through the power of the Spirit that had set him free for obedience.

Yet it is also possible to resist the divine commandment, to equivocate, which is already an act of disobedience. When the Lord confronted Moses at the burning bush and commanded him to tell Pharaoh to release the children of Israel from their captivity, Moses objected that they would not listen to his voice, that therefore another should be sent in his place (Exod. 3, 4). Although "the anger of the Lord was kindled against Moses" (Exod. 4:14), God nevertheless demonstrated his forbearance by permitting Aaron to go with Moses and speak for him. Jonah actually fled from the commandment of God, but he could not escape his responsibility. God pursued him as the hound of heaven. Jeremiah complained of the burden that God had placed on him, and yet he obeyed despite the persecution that came to him (Jer. 11:18–20; 18:18–23).

Reinterpreting the Ethical Task

The task that God has assigned his people is not only to heed the word of the Lord but also to wait for this word. It is not only to assess the implications of his commandment but also to prepare ourselves to hear it in the light that comes to us from Holy Scripture. In this light we come to see that his commandment is not simply law but grace, that it brings us freedom for obedience. Then we are enabled to bear witness to it in the abundance of joy.

Karl Barth, perhaps more than any other theologian, has pointed the way to a new understanding of the ethical task, one that finds its basis in God's gracious initiative. Ellul gives a terse summation of Barth's position: "The task of ethics cannot be to decide on the content of God's commandment, nor to judge man's action, but to describe the limits of God's commandment and of man's corresponding action."[6] What Barth means is that we cannot decide in advance what God's commandment is. Nor can we judge a person's action before the commandment is revealed. To describe the limit of God's commandment means to see it in its context, to perceive that it applies to a particular situation.

Yet although the church cannot claim to know God's commandment for all time, it must act on the light that God has given it for our time. While we cannot presume to know God's command before he gives it, we can have some intimation of what he might command because of the biblical revelation, which his Spirit illumines but never contradicts. We can prepare ourselves to hear God's commandment by reflecting on the commandments and ordinances of Holy Scripture, which give us an undeniable indication of God's will and purpose for his people. Above all, we ought always to keep before us the gospel of reconciliation and redemption in which God's law is fulfilled and transformed.

It is the Spirit of God working in conjunction with sacred Scripture that determines the content of God's commandment, but once the Spirit speaks, the church must then endeavor to translate this imperative to its constituency and to the world. The word that the church is called to proclaim has its origin not in its own consciousness nor in the self-understanding of the culture but in divine revelation, which is both gospel and law, promise and command (cf. Gal. 1:11–12).

Ethics in this theological perspective is no longer a submission to law but instead a response to divine grace. Grace, unlike law, gives us the power to obey. God's command is not so much an order as an invitation. Here we see the ineradicable difference between theological ethics and philosophical ethics, which thinks mainly in terms of principles or rules but rarely, if ever, of grace.

In the evangelical ethics I propose, law as such is not a dependable standard for faith and life; instead, it is law united with the gospel that becomes our sure foundation. Situational ethics appeals to the law of love. Legalistic ethics upholds the laws of moral and ecclesiastical tradition. A bona fide evangelical ethics directs us to the living Christ, who speaks to us through the law and the gospel. George MacDonald declares, "In order to fulfill the commonest law . . . we must rise into a loftier region altogether, a region that is above law, because it is spirit and life and makes the law."[7]

Law is not overthrown or discarded but is now seen in a new perspective—as a word of grace as well as of judgment, as permission as well as command. Instead of a law of sin and death, it is now "the law of the Spirit of life in Christ Jesus" (Rom. 8:2).[8]

Theological Mentors

My principal mentors in this area of theological reflection are Karl Barth, Jacques Ellul, Reinhold Niebuhr, and Dietrich Bonhoeffer. The first two are Reformed and the last two Lutheran, though not in any narrow or sectarian sense.[9] Despite their often severe criticisms of latter-day Pietism, all these men drew upon the Pietist heritage of the church, which emphasized the practice of the Christian life over adherence to an external creed.[10] Kierkegaard, one of the luminaries of nineteenth-century Pietism, had a decisive impact on all four thinkers.[11]

Barth has helped me see that in the biblical panorama there is a sense in which the gospel comes before the law. God's grace, indeed, is manifest not only in his judgments and after his judgments but also prior to his judgments. Ethics is based on God's commandment, but this is always a word of grace as well as of judgment. Our appeal is not to the law as such but to the law transformed and fulfilled in the gospel. Ethics therefore is fundamentally a response to divine grace, not conformity to a sometimes stifling and rigorously exacting moral code.

I am indebted to Ellul for showing me that there are two moralities.[12] The common morality must be respected and supported wherever possible, because social order depends upon it. At the same time, the Christian is called to a higher morality, a righteousness that manifestly transcends social mores.

Reinhold Niebuhr has done much to remind me of the paradox in Christian life, that the command of love can be fulfilled only by the gift of grace. He has also made a noteworthy contribution by recognizing the qualitative distinction between love and justice, though he has obscured a more fundamental polarity—that between God's holiness and human justice.

Ellul can help us to redress an imbalance in Niebuhr's theology, which is evident in his treatment of love. At least one aspect of Niebuhr's theology tends to make love too transcendent and ahistorical. Ellul, by contrast, insists that love is realizable and demonstrable in the history of the redeemed people of God.

On the other hand, Niebuhr's view is a salutary corrective to a disquieting tendency in Ellul to give up on the political enterprise, to see "all of faith's 'constructive' extensions in politics and morality," as "nothing more than so many forms of betrayal."[13] Niebuhr can be appreciated for his insistence that even proximate solutions in the political arena are better than no solutions at all, that even a modest stride toward justice is better than no stride at all.

Bonhoeffer is important for his emphasis on the costly character of Christian discipleship. God's grace is free, but it is also demanding. The gospel includes an imperative—the call to discipleship by which we bear witness to the grace given to us in Jesus Christ.

I also appreciate Bonhoeffer for his high view of the church and the sacraments. Where Bonhoeffer corrects Barth is by reminding us that the kingdom of God is realized at least partly through human instrumentality. We are to be not only witnesses to God's grace but also instruments of his grace in bringing the message of salvation to others.

All of the above theologians, who are associated with neo-orthodoxy, need to be assessed in the context of the historical orthodoxy of the Reformation. Even though they combated misconceptions endemic to Reformation teaching (such as double predestination), their own positions need to be corrected as well as supplemented by the insights of the Reformers. It goes without saying that both the catholic tradition and above all the the biblical witness will also play a determinative role in any appraisal of contemporary thinkers.

While neo-orthodoxy recovered the dualistic motif in Christian ethics—divine and human righteousness (Barth) or love and justice (Niebuhr)—it failed to give adequate recognition to the deeper moral dualism of the New Testament—the kingdom of God versus the kingdom of the devil. Barth did acknowledge a kingdom of darkness or chaos but would not allow that this kingdom is directed by an overarching personal spirit bent on a strategy of world conquest. He also insisted that this kingdom has already been overcome and belongs to the history of the past,[14] whereas in the New Testament this kingdom still works destructive power in the world. Both Barth and Bonhoeffer contended that there is now only one kingdom, that of Jesus Christ, who is lord of both church and state.[15] But this is to emphasize the "already" at the expense of the "not yet." The chess game is not over (as in Barth), for the devil still has a few remaining moves. He is mortally wounded, but just for this reason he becomes all the more dangerous. The great tribulation is not behind us but ahead of us.

Where neo-orthodox theologians are at one with the Reformers (Luther, Calvin) is in their conviction that Christian ethics cannot be reduced to a code of do's and don'ts. The new life in Christ must not be confused with conventional morality. Discipleship under the cross is not the same as moral respectability. The call to holiness cannot be confounded with humanitarian service.

Our salvation has already been enacted and fulfilled in Jesus Christ. But the fruits of our salvation need to be appropriated and manifested in a life of discipleship. Indeed, the purpose of our salvation is to enable us to live in freedom and responsibility in service to our neighbor for whom Christ died. The knowledge of God (dogmatics) is for the sake of the service of God (ethics).

The Way of the Cross

Obedience to the imperatives of the gospel will inevitably bring us into conflict with the principalities and powers that still strive to exercise dominion, desperate in the knowledge that they have been effectively dethroned in the cross and resurrection victory of Jesus Christ (Col. 2:15; Luke 10:18; Rev. 12:9, 10). Jesus reminded his disciples that a servant is not above his master (Luke 6:40; John 15:20). If they have hated him, he says, they will also hate those of us who are his disciples, for we do not belong to the world (John 15:18–19). Our obedience to Christ is the point of conflict with the secular state because our obedience calls attention to the scandal of the cross, which is a stumbling block to Jews and folly to Gentiles (1 Cor. 1:23). Christian obedience is a sign of offense because Jesus is a sign of offense. His claims relativize the claims of the world, and his commands contradict the expectations and hopes of the world.

One of the problems I wrestle with in this book is whether the way of the cross can ever be reconciled with the way of the sword. Although not a pacifist, I perceive that the righteousness to which Christ calls us goes beyond the morality necessary to maintain public order in society. The problem is exacerbated by the advent of weapons of mass extermination that can be used only in ways that make a mockery of the claims of Christ.

It seems to me that in our time the divine commandment has two sides: firm resistance to modern totalitarianism, including communism, and unequivocal condemnation of nuclear and biochemical weapons.

It might well be that Christians are called to demonstrate a new kind of resistance, one employing nonviolent methods. What is not possible for nation-states may be possible and even necessary for those who represent the kingdom of the new age, which is already dawning, an age in which peace and righteousness will reign.[16]

In the present time, when the powers of darkness are very much on the move, Christians may well be persecuted not simply for their social stands but also for their faith. Bishop Desmond Tutu's experience in South Africa has convinced him that "it is our Christian faith, it is the Christian churches . . . who are on trial. It is our Christianity, it is our faith and therefore our theology that are under scrutiny, and the central matters at issue are profoundly theological."[17] Tutu speaks as a black African cleric in a country ruled by a minority of whites, most of whom are dedicated to apartheid, the enforced segregation of the races. Though not an absolutist like Gandhi, Tutu upholds the way of nonviolence, but whether the protest of the black people can be kept within these parameters remains to be seen.

Ethics in the Christian sense is not simply promoting the ideal of social righteousness. Nor is its primary task the cultivating of moral and religious values. Instead, it means remaining faithful to the gospel in a culture that is becoming steadily more secularized and barbarized. It means taking up the cross and following Christ as a witness to peace in an age of violence and revolution. It means confessing Jesus Christ as the only Lord and Savior of the world in the face of the rising idolatries of class, nation, and race. It means giving praise to the One who stands in judgment over every worldly claim and presumption. Ethics involves obedience to the imperatives of the gospel of the cross, upholding the claims of this gospel before the world not only with our words but also with our lives.

Notes

1. Jacques Ellul, *Living Faith*, trans. Peter Heinegg (San Francisco: Harper & Row, 1983), p. 51.
2. William Blake, *The Marriage of Heaven and Hell*, in *The Complete Writings of William Blake*, ed. Geoffrey Keynes (London: Oxford University Press, 1966), p. 158.
3. Even the great commandment to love God and neighbor (Matt. 22:36–40; Mark 12:28–34; Luke 10:27) is absolute only as a commandment of the living Christ addressed to people personally and calling them to a concrete course of action. It is possible to agree intellectually with Jesus' interpretation of the great commandment and still not be grasped by the word of God as the truth and power of salvation. One of the scribes indicated his approval, and Jesus told him that he was not far from the kingdom (Mark 12:34). Yet he was still not in the kingdom because he did not have the Holy Spirit, who alone opens our inward eyes to Jesus' messianic identity. The

succeeding verses in the twelfth chapter of Mark indicate that the scribes indeed lacked a saving knowledge of the word of God. They may have claimed to have absolute truth, but they were not in communion with the One who alone is the Absolute, the living God who revealed himself in Jesus Christ. In the biblical view, one cannot have eternal truth unless one stands in a right relationship with the eternal God.

4. Those who lack faith will hear it wrongly and therefore invariably misunderstand it as a law of works and death rather than a law filled with promise and power.

5. Dietrich Bonhoeffer, *Ethics*, ed. Eberhard Bethge, trans. Neville Horton Smith (New York: Macmillan Co., 1965), pp. 279–80. Bonhoeffer goes on to say that the divine commandment sets one free for "unreflected doing," since we are allowed "to live and to act with certainty and with confidence" (pp. 280, 283). Yet he also sees the necessary place for critical understanding as we seek to live out our faith before God (pp. 37–42). Once we respond to the word of God in faith, we need to learn what is pleasing to God (Eph. 5:8–10); we need to discern what is the perfect will of God (Rom. 12:2); and we need to examine ourselves as to whether we are really living the life of faith (2 Cor. 13:5).

6. Jacques Ellul, *To Will & to Do*, trans. C. Edward Hopkin (Philadelphia: Pilgrim, 1969), p. 248. Cf. Karl Barth, *Church Dogmatics*, III, 4, eds. G. W. Bromiley & T. F. Torrance (Edinburgh: T. & T. Clark, 1961), pp. 26–31.

7. *George MacDonald: An Anthology*, ed. C. S. Lewis (New York: Macmillan Co., 1947), p. 37.

8. Even in the Old Testament, the law rightly understood is a law of grace. The Psalmist implores his God, "Turn me from the path of delusion, grant me the grace of your Law" (Ps. 119:29 JB; cf. Prov. 6:23). The Judaic misunderstanding was what occasioned the conflict between law and gospel.

9. Reinhold Niebuhr, it should be noted, was confirmed and ordained in the Evangelical Synod of North America, which had its roots in both German Pietist missionary societies and the Evangelical Union of Prussia of 1817, bringing together Lutheran and Reformed congregations. The Lutheran ethos was dominant in the American church as well as in its European counterpart. Interestingly, the Evangelical Synod, showing the influence of the Prussian Union Church, required formal adherence to the Augsburg Confession, Luther's Small Catechism, and the Heidelberg Catechism insofar as they agree and "where they disagree, we adhere strictly to the passages of Holy Scripture bearing on the subject, and avail ourselves of the liberty of conscience prevailing in the Evangelical Church." In 1934 the Evangelical Synod merged with the German Reformed Church to become the Evangelical and Reformed Church. The new body united with the Congregational Christian Churches in 1957 to form the United Church of Christ. See Arthur C. Piepkorn, *Profiles in Belief* (San Francisco: Harper & Row, 1978), 2: pp. 667–69; and Louis H. Gunnemann, *The Shaping of the United Church of Christ* (New York: United Church Press, 1977), pp. 167–95.

In a brilliant and insightful essay, Gabriel Fackre detects both Reformed and Lutheran motifs in Niebuhr, but gives more weight to the former. Gabriel Fackre, "Reinhold Niebuhr," in *Reformed Theology in America*, ed. David F. Wells (Grand Rapids: Eerdmans, 1985), pp. 263–79. In my opinion, Niebuhr was closer to Luther than to Calvin in his spirituality and probably closer to Augustine and Kierkegaard than to either Reformer in his anthropology. In his political theory he acknowledged his indebtedness to both Augustine and the Calvinist sectarians.

10. Barth freely acknowledges his indebtedness to the Blumhardts, Kierkegaard, Zinzendorf, and Bengel. See Eberhard Busch, *Karl Barth und die Pietisten* (Munich: Chr. Kaiser Verlag, 1978).

11. For the Pietist cast of Kierkegaard's life and thought, see Vernard Eller, *Kierkegaard and Radical Discipleship* (Princeton, N.J.: Princeton University Press, 1968).

12. Ellul, *To Will & To Do*, pp. 73–110.

13. Ellul, *Living Faith*, p. 180.

14. Barth asserts that "this kingdom is behind us and all men. We and all men are

released from . . . this prison." *Church Dogmatics,* IV, 1 trans. G. W. Bromiley (Edinburth: T. & T. Clark, 1956), vol. 4, 1, p. 503. At the same time, Barth acknowledges that the people of God still move within the sphere of the kingdom of unrighteousness, even though they now belong to another, and therefore they are summoned to fight against it. See Karl Barth, *The Christian Life,* trans. Geoffrey Bromiley (Grand Rapids: Eerdmans, 1981), p. 267.

15. Cf. Bonhoeffer: "The world is not divided between Christ and the devil, but, whether it recognizes it or not, it is solely and entirely the world of Christ." *Ethics,* p. 204.

16. What I am suggesting is an eschatological pacifism, but I do not regard this as absolutely normative for all Christians. Christians may still be true to the divine mandate if they engage in military service or assume positions of authority in government that relate to national security, so long as their primary purpose is to restrain the powers of the old aeon. This means always to work for a relaxing rather than a heightening of tensions between nations. Such persons nevertheless cannot willingly participate in a war that does not have the permission of God, and they are therefore committed to living in tension, if not in conflict, with their peers and superiors. For today's situation, I see the ordinary vocation of the Christian to be a witness for peace outside the military and national security establishments, but there may be an extraordinary vocation to work within these institutions as an instrument of God's will and purpose for truth, justice, and peace.

17. Desmond Mpilo Tutu, *Hope and Suffering,* ed. John Webster (Grand Rapids: Eerdmans, 1984), p. 154.

CHAPTER 3

Two Types of Ethics

I the Lord speak the truth, I declare what is right.

ISAIAH 45:19

To love is not . . . as the sophists imagine, to wish good for another person; it is to bear another's burden, that is, to bear what is painful to you and which you do not bear willingly.

MARTIN LUTHER

 Christianity did not come in order to develop the heroic virtues in the individual but rather to remove selfishness and establish love.

SØREN KIERKEGAARD

Do not desire to be strong, powerful, honoured, and respected, but let God alone be your strength, your fame and your honour.

DIETRICH BONHOEFFER

Christianity used to mean the ethic of atonement. Now it is but that of attunement or even attainment.

P.T. FORSYTH

The Radical Character of Christian Ethics

That Christianity radically transcends and contravenes all moralism and humanitarianism has been recognized by the fathers of the church through the centuries. The Christian ethic cannot be harmonized with natural wisdom because it finds the fulcrum of meaning in the crucified Christ, the one who conquered through suffering and death and thereby revealed the bankruptcy of the world's values.

Perhaps no one saw more clearly the radical character of Christian ethics than Friedrich Nietzsche, the nineteenth-century Romantic who was in some respects "a fool for Christ" even in his denial of God.[1] Nietzsche perceived that moderns no longer have "the sense for the terribly superlative conception which was implied to an antique taste by the paradox of the formula, 'God on the Cross.' Hitherto there had never and nowhere been such boldness in inversion, nor anything at once so dreadful, questioning, and questionable as this formula: it promised a transvaluation of all ancient values."[2] Yet Nietzsche could not accept this inversion of values exemplified in the cross of Christ because he felt that it led to the emasculation rather than the celebration of humanity.

While continuing for a time to hold Jesus in respect, Nietzsche complained bitterly of the distortion of this earnest and misguided figure in history by the New Testament church. As he saw it, "The Christian faith, from the beginning, is sacrifice: the sacrifice of all freedom, all pride, all self-confidence of spirit; it is at the same time subjection, self-derision, and self-mutilation."[3] "What is more harmful than any vice?" he sneered. "Practical sympathy for the botched and the weak—Christianity."[4] Yet in his strident attack on Christianity he continued to think highly of Jesus, though he finally chose Dionysus, the ancient Greek god, over Jesus. He saw Jesus as the herald of a new morality, beyond good and evil: "Jesus sided against those who judge: he wanted to be the destroyer of morality."[5] Throughout his life Nietzsche was haunted by the figure of Christ, but he was finally compelled to dismiss Christ as a vain dreamer whose teachings were misrepresented by his followers.

In place of the Christian ethic as well as the humanistic ethic of antiquity (which we see in Socrates), Nietzsche sounded the call for a new ethic—the will to power that is not bound to the taboos and restrictive codes of the past. What is required is a new morality—the morality of the masters, which sharply challenges the slave morality perpetuated by Christianity. The new morality is one beyond good and evil, since it summons people of foresight and valor to fashion a new world of meaning in face of the collapse of the values of modern civilization. It urges the "new man," or the "superman," to slay the God that has held humanity in captivity in order to open it to a new and glorious future. For Nietzsche evil is whatever springs from weakness. The good is whatever augments the feeling of power or the will to power.

Nietzsche called for a transvaluation of values that would honor the strong over the weak, celebrate the heroic over the ignoble, glorify the solitary individual over the herd. Whereas in his earlier years, Nietzsche saw the meaning of life in artistic achievement, his morality of the superman challenged even this conception, for all human values are overthrown by the will to power. To his credit he recognized that the Holy could not be identified even with the Beautiful, but he ended by denying the reality of the Holy. His struggle against the Holy was born out of a deep-seated awareness of the awesome reality and terror of the Holy, which he tried but utterly failed to extinguish.[6]

Critics have rightly pointed out that Nietzsche confused the biblical witness to Christ with the domesticated Christianity of his time and therefore saw in Christianity only weakness and vacillation. He did not realize that the meekness that Christ taught is utterly different from what the world discerns as weakness. Meekness is the strength to love, which is more powerful than the brute force eulogized by many of Nietzsche's followers. Christianity calls people to a revolutionary style of life that contradicts servility and self-pity. The subordination it upholds is a revolutionary subordination whereby one overcomes one's enemy by doing good (Rom. 12:14–21). Paul exulted in the fact that we as Christians are "more than conquerors" through the love of God that is more powerful than the stratagems of heroic, though misguided, souls who in their vain efforts to be as God end by being less than human (cf. Rom. 8:37–39).

Nietzsche saw that the authentic life points people beyond good and evil, but he failed to recognize that it is not the vision of the superman that overcomes the restrictions of code morality (for the superman can only create a new code of values) but the living God himself who alone declares what is good and right, thereby overturning the misconceptions of both ceremonial law and natural morality. It is the Bible that introduces us to the truly good, but this good is not an idea or moral axiom but the living God in action who both creates and destroys so that a new kingdom can come into being.

In the Christian perspective, the morally good is not something achieved before God but something returned to God. This is not an ethic of resignation to the divine order of things nor an ethic of attaining the supreme good. Instead, it is the ethic of vicarious, suffering love, which does not call us to heroic sacrifice as such but creates within us a new being enabling us to be a sign and parable of the perfect sacrifice for sin that we see in Jesus Christ.

Christ, we should remember, did not suffer as a tragic hero who exceeded his limitations in pursuit of glory and grandeur and who was finally cast down by the fates. On the contrary, he suffered as a divine Savior who limited himself in order to descend into ignominy and dereliction and who was raised up even in his humiliation. We cannot imitate or duplicate his atoning sacrifice for sin, but we can bear witness to it through a sacrifice of praise and thanksgiving.

What characterizes the really Christian life is not gaining the goods of this world, whether by diligence or piety, but dying to the world.

It is a life broken and thrown away, but God in the mystery of his providence may grace such a life with dignity and fulness so that even the world can discern an authentic or purposeful existence.

The disparity between the Christian ethic and worldly ethics was underlined by Bonhoeffer: "Do not desire to be strong, powerful, honoured, and respected, but let God alone be your strength, your fame and your honour."[7] The Christian lives outside of himself in the glory of God and therefore in the needs and travails of his neighbor. The "man of the world" seeks to find the good within himself as he tries to actualize powers resident within him. The Stoic philosopher Epictetus advised: "Seek not good from without; seek it within yourselves, or you will never find it."[8] Luther's counsel was quite different: "Go out of yourself, away from yourself to Christ."[9]

The Christian ethic was perhaps approximated in Gandhi's ideal of *satyagrapha*, the force of truth and love that is expressed through self-sacrifice and passive resistance. But even here there is an incontestable difference. For Gandhi *satyagrapha* is a method of securing our rights by personal suffering. For Christianity, love entails the sacrifice of our rights for the sake of the welfare of others. The ethic of the cross is not nonviolent resistance but nonresistance, as Reinhold Niebuhr so cogently discerned.[10] This is why this ethic can appropriately be called an "impossible possibility": its realization lies not in human capability but only in divine grace that enters history as a new reality.

Theological and Philosophical Ethics

It is fashionable in the circles of academia to divide ethics between the deontological (from the Greek *deon,* meaning duty) and the teleological (from *telos,* or end, where the emphasis is on goals and consequences). In my opinion, it is more helpful to differentiate between the theological and philosophical types of ethics. The former can also be called evangelical ethics and the latter humanistic ethics. I here acknowledge my affinity with Thielicke, Barth, Bonhoeffer, and Paul Lehmann.

Whereas philosophical ethics seeks to understand the good in light of a general metaphysic or world view, theological ethics appeals to a definitive revelation of God in the sacred history mirrored in the Bible.[11] Philosophical ethics is invariably anthropocentric, for its focus is on the possibilities resident within humanity. Theological ethics, on the other hand, is unabashedly theocentric and Christocentric, placing the emphasis on a divine intervention in human history that brings promise and hope to a despairing and lost humanity. More accurately, theological ethics might be described as theoanthropocentric because it sees the source of human hope in Jesus Christ, the God-Man, the Word made flesh.

According to Helmut Thielicke: "Evangelical ethics is completely different from all natural or philosophical ethics. Indeed, the two lie on wholly different planes and must be sharply differentiated from one another, however much the theme of 'obedience' may be common to both."[12] Thielicke goes on to say that ethics in the biblical sense "does not teach us what we are obliged to do; strictly speaking, it teaches us what we are permitted to do. It surveys the sphere of freedom."[13]

Karl Barth's position is remarkably similar. He warns against "the attempt to set up general ethics as a judge, and to prove and justify theological ethics before it."[14] This "can only disturb and destroy theological ethics."[15] Theological ethics, in contrast to all general ethics, is an ethics of grace, for it is only in grace that "the command of God is established and fulfilled."[16]

What makes theological ethics distinctive, according to Barth, is not "that it understands the command of the good as God's command. The same thing is done elsewhere with seriousness and emphasis. But its peculiarity and advantage consist in the name of Jesus Christ with which it can state the basis and right of the divine claim."[17]

Unlike his teacher Wilhelm Herrmann, who grounded theology in ethics, Barth grounds ethics in theology. In his view, ethics forms an integral part of dogmatics and is not to be regarded as either a prelude or supplement to the dogmatic task.

In theological ethics, the good is identified not with an idea or principle at the disposal of human reason but with the action of God that places human reason on a new ground and gives it a new goal. As Barth phrased it, the subject of ethics is not "the Word of God which man claims, but the Word of God which makes its claim on man."[18]

Although there are many different types of philosophy, there is only one type of genuine theology—the evangelical or biblical. Yet all philosophy has this in common: its appeal to human reason as the final authority in the determination of the good. Reason is here understood as any cognitive faculty within man—feeling, intellect, mystical insight, and so on. The appeal in theology is to the biblical revelation, which has its apex or culmination in Jesus Christ.

Whereas philosophy will often make a place for the idea of God in ethical construction, this is invariably a God who remains but an idea or principle. It lends meaning to life, but it is not itself the Giver and

Sustainer of meaning. God is there to help people to attain the *summum bonum* (the supreme good); God is not the end or goal of ethical endeavor. In theology, on the contrary, we seek to live the good life in order to glorify God, in order to witness to what God has done for us in Jesus Christ.

While philosophers may occasionally postulate a universal or natural law that becomes a criterion for the good, theology of the evangelical type has difficulties with this conception. Instead of a universal moral law, which connotes a certain independence from God, it is more biblical to speak of the personal law rooted in the very being of God, which is identical with his will to love. Our appeal is not so much to a general moral law as to the living voice of the Lawgiver. Our criterion is not law as such but God's Word, which signifies the unity of his will and his wisdom, his commanding and his truth.

Ethics in the general sense refers to the attempt to understand the meaning of the good. Christian ethics, on the other hand, means the attempt to live the Christian life, a life reflecting the passion and victory of Jesus Christ. Christian ethics is not a category under general ethics but a new kind of ethics that calls general ethics into question.

In Christian (or theological) ethics the indicative has priority over the imperative. It is what God does that sets the stage for the Christian life. We hear the divine command as something united with rather than separate from the divine promise, which we see in the life, death, and resurrection of Jesus Christ.

There is no revealed morality in the sense of divinely given moral principles that are accessible to natural reason and universally binding. But there is a revealed reality, the living Word of God, which shapes moral decisions and guides moral reflection. Scholasticism, which we find in both Roman Catholicism and Protestantism, sought a synthesis between theological and philosophical ethics by resting its case on universal principles. The only difference from the philosophical approach is that these principles were believed to be a product of revelation. Theology at its best speaks of the divine commandment, which is specific and concrete, rather than a universal principle, which is general and abstract.

Theological ethics calls us to the obedience of discipleship rather than to conformity with the idea of the Good. According to Bonhoeffer, ordinary moral deliberations are quite different from discipleship under the cross. Moral decisions generally result from reflection on problems and cases, rules and applications; Christian ethics is based on the simplicity of response to the Word of God.[19]

Christian ethics is neither utilitarian—appealing to the consequences of an action—nor deontological—appealing to a universal moral rule. Instead it is revelational—submitting to the divine commandment, which is always concrete and particular.

Whereas philosophical ethics speaks of virtues, the realization of human potentialities, theological ethics prefers to speak of graces, the ways by which the Spirit of God is manifested in our thoughts and actions. Alasdair MacIntyre restates the Aristotelian position: "A virtue is an acquired human quality the possession and exercise of which tends to enable us to achieve those goods which are internal to practices and the lack of which effectively prevents us from achieving any such goods."[20]

Evangelical Christianity acknowledges the reality of virtue but sees it as hopelessly deficient, for our moral effort is always tainted by sin. This is why we are called to repent of our virtues as well as our vices, since only by the alien righteousness of Christ apprehended by faith can we be restored to the favor of God.

Whereas in the Greek view to be a good person is also to be a good citizen, in the biblical view to be a righteous person often entails a break not only with the cultural but also with the religious establishment. On occasion the prophets in the Old Testament were considered "mad" (Isa. 59:15 NEB; Hos. 9:7) and Jesus and Paul were similarly accused (Mark 3:21; John 10:20; 1 Cor. 4:9, 10).

In theological ethics the appeal is not to the abstract good but to the concrete good—Jesus Christ. The basis for our moral decisions is not the idea of the good but the will to good, which we see in the sacrificial life and atoning death of Jesus Christ.

Yet against a philosophical voluntarism that views ultimate reality as blind, arbitrary will, I contend that God wills only what is in harmony with his nature.[21] He wills what he essentially is. Yet the paradox is that his nature is shaped or determined by what he wills. Both statements are true: He wills the good because he himself is the good; He is the good because he wills the good. In accordance with a long and venerable theological tradition, I affirm the paradoxical unity of act and being in God.

God is pure actuality, he is being in action, but he is not a perpetual becoming by which he changes into something other than he was. He eternally becomes what he himself is, and this is why we can speak of the constancy and faithfulness of God. He is the "I am who I am" (Exod. 3:14) or the "I shall be who I was."[22] He is not a static, immobile God, but neither is he a God in the process of self-realization. He is the infinite God in action, not the finite God who is involved in self-actualization, as process philosophy and theology would have it.

God's commandment is rooted in the very being of God as the irrepressible will to both love and holiness. Yet his commandment is ever new, for it is always related to the concrete moral situation in which we find ourselves. This is why his commandment might be spoken of as "eternal-temporal" rather than eternal in the abstract or general sense, for it has a specific focus and direction.

General Orientation in Ethics

From a purely philosophical point of view, ethics is basically concerned with the attainment of the good. The ground of ethics is the knowledge of the good. Life in its fulness is one in conformity to the idea of the good.

In theology, the emphasis is on the Christian life rather than the moral ideal. The focus is on discipleship under the cross. We are called not to the contemplation of the Good (as in Plato and Plotinus) but to obedience to the demands of the Holy.[23] Our task is not to know as God knows but to know what God wills. We are called not to be judges of the law but doers of the law (Bonhoeffer). Gaining perfect knowledge of the good is not our business; knowing the commandment of God is. We are to venture forth in obedience fortified in the assurance that our actions will always be judged by God's goodness. Adam, we should recall, strayed from God's commandment when he sought knowledge of good and evil (Gen. 3).

Philosophy is preoccupied with the fulfillment or well-being of the self rather than the glory of God. Some philosophers who are close to mysticism may speak of transcending the self, yet this is always for the sake of the self. Cicero voiced the humanistic tradition in philosophy when he declared that virtue is nothing but nature perfected and developed to its highest point.[24]

Theology speaks neither of self-fulfillment nor self-transcendence but instead of self-denial. It is not the realization of the self but its crucifixion and the birth of a new self that is expounded in the New Testament. At first glance, ascetic philosophies might appear to be close to evangelical theology in their emphasis on flesh denial and world denial. But their concern is the liberation of the self from the world for the sake of the perfection and fulfillment of the self. Theology in the evangelical tradition calls not for flight from the world but for bringing the world into submission to the Lordship of Jesus Christ. Moreover, its primary concern is not with the perfection of nature but with the creation of a new nature.

It is often alleged that the Old Testament, in contrast to the New, presses for the fulfillment of self, for gaining the goods of this world as well as trusting in God. Indeed, faith in God, so it is said, is considered a steppingstone to material well-being. This note is especially conspicuous in the electronic church. Walter Kaiser presents a much-needed corrective to this distortion of Old Testament piety: "Neither hedonism nor a quest for a 'this-worldly-success' is espoused in the Old Testament as a reward 'caused' by piety. The success, reward, or escape from disaster is instead a 'gift' accepted by the wise God-fearer from the hand of a gracious Lord."[25]

Philosophy, here understood as the creative thinking of the natural man, is concerned with gaining a place in the sun, even if this should entail self-denigration. The key phrases are "Be thyself" or "To thine own self be true" (Polonius in *Hamlet*). Being true to oneself, securing the self from harm, advancing the self—these are the motivating forces in life. Spinoza voices a viewpoint that resonates throughout the history of philosophy: "The more each person strives and is able *to seek his own profit*, that is to say, to preserve his being, the more virtue does he possess; on the other hand, in so far as each person neglects his own profit, that is to say, neglects to preserve his own being, is he impotent" (italics mine).[26] Hegel's "World-historical figure" realized himself at the expense of others: "So mighty a form must trample down many an innocent flower—crush to pieces many an object in its path."[27] The superman, whom Nietzsche saw as the climax of world evolution, wills not the salvation of the world (the masses are an obstacle to the creation of a new kind of man) but power over both the self and the world.

In contrast to philosophy, theology invites people to bear the cross for the sake of the world. The key phrase is not "Fulfill yourself" but "Overcome yourself."[28] This theme is conspicuous in the heritage of Christian mysticism and Pietism.[29] But this overcoming of oneself should not be understood in the Stoic sense of gaining mastery over one's passions for the sake of a disciplined life; instead it is bringing one's total self into submission to the Lordship of Jesus Christ. It is not the preserving of the self but the sacrifice of the self for the cause of the kingdom of God that is the Christian concern. When we are willing to let go of ourselves for the sake of our Lord and of our neighbor for whom Christ died, we will find ourselves in the end. That is, we will discover a life of authenticity and joy as a result of our endeavors. This paradox of faith is succinctly expressed by Jesus: "He who finds his life will lose it, and he who loses his life for my sake will find it" (Matt. 10:39).

The hallmark of the morally good life in the world of philosophy is inward satisfaction, peace of mind, happiness in the sense of well-being. In theology the hallmark of the truly good life is vicarious suffering born out of service to others. Kierkegaard never tired of stressing that "the distinguishing mark of religious action is suffering."[30] The apostle Paul could exclaim: "I will boast all the more gladly about my weaknesses, so that Christ's power may rest on me. That is why, for Christ's sake, I delight in weaknesses, in insults, in hardships, in persecutions, in difficulties. For when I am weak, then I am strong" (2 Cor. 12:9, 10 NIV). Calvin observed that "the more we are afflicted with adversities, the more surely our fellowship with Christ is confirmed! By communion with him the very sufferings themselves not only become blessed to us but also help much in promoting our salvation."[31]

In Greek and Roman philosophy those who pursue the moral life seek to detach themselves from suffering and pain. Christians, on the other hand, willingly take upon themselves suffering and pain—not in order to perfect themselves but in order to serve their neighbor for whom Christ died.

Self-love occupies a prominent place in most philosophy, whereas in theology it is generally condemned as a sin. For Aristotle eudaemonia, or happiness, which is the ethical goal, is an "enlightened selfishness." In utilitarian philosophy egoism is rendered powerless by virtue of the power of reason to transmute its anarchies into a higher harmony. For Adam Smith, egoism is innocuous because it forms a part of a preestablished harmony. In the view of Thomas Hobbes, egoism is the hallmark of all human existence. For theologian Reinhold Niebuhr egoism is always destructive and must be countered by the love of the cross.[32]

Philosophy generally makes a place for altruism, but it proves most often to be in the service of one's own happiness. Benjamin Franklin declared, "When you are good to others, you are best to yourself."[33] Nietzsche urged the love of others in order to better oneself. For Zoroaster, "doing good to others is not a duty. It is a joy, for it increases your own health and happiness."[34]

Christianity makes a place not for self-love in the sense of self-aggrandizement but for a paradoxical self-acceptance (Tillich). We can come to accept ourselves when we know by faith that we are accepted by God. We are not called specifically to love ourselves, but we are given the grace to accept ourselves through the knowledge of divine forgiveness.[35] In this perspective, the self is treated not as an object of admiration or worth in its own right but as an object of God's infinite love and therefore deserving of care and respect. Yet the self is never an end in itself but always a means to the work of the kingdom. We are called to accept ourselves as children of God in order to be instruments of the will and purpose of God in the world.

What characterizes the Christian life is a "selfless egoism" (Bonhoeffer) as opposed to both egoism and altruism, as the world understands these terms. The Christian way is not to denigrate or macerate the self but to commit the self into the hands of a loving God who will then crown us with glory so that we can be fit instruments in his service. The Christian motto is God first, neighbor second, and self last.[36] But the self is not a zero, as in some kinds of existentialism, but a unique individual—infinitely precious in the sight of God. Neither is the self a potential god (as in some types of idealism). Instead, the self is lower than divinity and higher than animality (Ps. 8:5–8), deserving only condemnation because of sin but receiving grace because of God's infinite compassion. The self has a glorious destiny, but only when its goals are subordinated to the needs and travails of other selves in Christian love and service.

Between the way of the cross and the way of the world there is indeed an infinite qualitative difference. Hedonistic utilitarianism says, "pleasure for the sake of pleasure." Hellenistic eudaemonism says, "virtue for the sake of happiness." Kantian morality says, "duty for the sake of duty." The new morality of Nietzsche says, "power for the sake of nobility." Evangelical Christianity says, "obedience for the sake of our neighbor for whom Christ died."

Criteria in Ethics

In a discussion of the criteria for ethics, we can expect to hear many discordant voices in the history of philosophy, since philosophy is not a monolithic system, though it can be an ideal type. One thing all philosophers have in common in this area, however, is the appeal to some cognitive capacity within humanity.

One significant strand of philosophy rests its case on intuition. Intuition may be a flash of insight, or it may be the inner light, the divine ground of the self. Or it may be practical reason or conscience (Kant). Thomas Reid of the Scottish Enlightenment was convinced that "the principles of morality are known intuitively by our moral sense or conscience."[37] Rousseau believed in a universal, innate conscience, that "immortal voice from heaven . . . infallible judge of good and evil, making man like to God!"[38] For Plotinus, the luminary of Neoplatonism, our knowledge of the good has its source in an ecstatic rapture by which we are lifted above ourselves in the experience of unity with the One. In Albert Schweitzer's philosophy, our highest moral insights have their origin in our dim perceptions of the unitary life force.[39]

Then there are those philosophers who argue their case on the basis of reason (deductive or inductive). The appeal is to the principles of logic, natural law, or empirically tested experience.[40] For the Stoics, reason is the "ruling principle" of humanity, and the active working of reason is critical to the health of the human soul. With a confidence bordering on idolatry, Kant declared, "Reason must regard itself as the author of its principles independent of extraneous influences."[41] In a similar vein, Erich Fromm argued that "valid ethical norms can be formed by man's reason and by it alone."[42]

Ethical rationalism can foster a relatively austere life in which we deny our passions and desires (as in Stoicism), but it can just as easily promote a life in which we assiduously pursue our own happiness and welfare. Such is the case with Socrates, who virtually identified knowledge and virtue and at the same time virtue and happiness. To act in conformity with reason is to insure a life free from misfortune. His formula was, "Nothing bad can happen to a virtuous man; nothing good can happen to a wicked man."[43] Yet his emphasis was on personal well-being (eudaemonia), not self-gain (as in egoism). If we follow Plato's interpretation, moreover, it would seem that Socrates' principal concern was not with the profits of virtue here below but with the opening of our inward eyes to a realm that transcends the senses.

Rationalistic egoism has a number of notable exponents in the modern period. Act in accord with your own interests, Thomas Hobbes advised, but always in the light of natural law.[44] In the view of Spinoza, acting virtuously is "nothing but acting, living and preserving our being . . . as *reason* directs, from the ground of seeking our own *profit*" (italics mine).[45] For the objectivist Ayn Rand, selfishness is the highest virtue, and rational selfishness is the ground for ethical decision. "Since reason is man's basic means of survival, that which is proper to the life of a rational being is the good; that which negates, opposes or destroys it is the evil."[46]

In still another strand of philosophy, the vitalities of nature loom much more significant. For the ancient Greek philospher Callicles, who appealed to the law of nature, righteousness consists in the superior ruling over the inferior. The Sophist Thrasymachus was even more extreme, blatantly arguing that righteousness is nothing other than the claims of those who prove to be stronger. Nietzsche disdained morality as the rationalization of the weak, of little interest to "the man of destiny," who rejoices in the possession and exhibition of power. For this philosopher, the question "What is good?" is easily answered: "All that heightens the feeling of power, the will to power, power itself in man."[47] The superman, of course, would not exploit the weak, Nietzsche assures us, but he would not permit the weak to thwart him in his pursuit of greatness.

What is valued most highly in hedonism is not power but pleasure. That which provides deepest pleasure is the greatest good. For Aristippus the moral good is to be found solely in the pleasure of the moment. Epicurus distinguished between the pleasures and ranked intellectual above physical enjoyment. While pleasure is ultimately reducible to the senses, he held that reason is the guide in regulating the life of pleasure. The highest good is the aesthetic self-enjoyment of the person of culture and refinement. For the English utilitarian Jeremy Bentham, right behavior is that which increases the amount and distribution of pleasure. In a similar vein, Herbert Spencer maintained that the desirable or ideal life is the one that brings a surplus of agreeable feeling.

Not all thinkers in the hedonistic tradition have been willing to preserve the delicate restraints calculated to insure some measure of order in the pursuit of pleasure. There are those who find pleasure primarily in the intoxication of the senses and the intensity of passion. This vitalistic or Dionysian note is evident in D. H. Lawrence: "My great religion is a belief in the blood, the flesh, as being wiser than the intellect. We can go wrong with our minds, but what our blood feels and believes and says is always true. . . . The real way of living is to answer one's wants."[48] The same theme is glaringly apparent in Carl Jung, whose aim was "to transform Christ back into the soothsaying god of the vine . . . and in this way absorb those ecstatic instinctual forces of Christianity for the *one* purpose of making the cult and the sacred myth what they once were—a drunken feast of joy where man regained the ethos and holiness of an animal."[49] His deep animosity to bourgeois values even led him to ask, "Must we not love evil if we are to break away from the obsession with virtue that makes us sick and forbids us the joys of life?"[50] No one would have agreed more than the Marquis de Sade, who identified pleasure with pain and saw the highest pleasure in acts of violence and degradation.[51] His ideal was the primitive savage, for the savage is most independent and closest to nature.

In Albert Schweitzer we encounter a vitalistic naturalism, though not hedonism. For Schweitzer the will-to-live is rooted in human nature, and indeed in the whole of creation, and this forms the basis for an ethic of reverence for life. While he understood the will-to-live as basically a will-to-love, he acknowledged that the creative and moral proclivities of life are mixed with the blind destructive forces of the world. Consequently, there are some things in nature that must be opposed.

In ethical relativism there is a denial of universal norms and criteria for determining right behavior. Hume contended that morality proceeds from our dislike of pain, our sympathy for others, and our feelings of benevolence. Sartre believed taste to be the final determinant for action. Drawing on Dostoevsky, he averred that when God does not exist, everything is permitted. For Machiavelli Fortuna, or chance, is ultimately responsible for guiding political and moral decision.[52] In Freudianism the only criterion for moral action is whatever serves to resolve the conflict between the id and the superego. In Marxism right action is that which advances the social revolution. For Lenin the sole norm is the "revolutionary consciousness."

When we turn to theology, the basis for moral judgment is radically altered, for the spiritual wisdom of the gospel is incommensurable with the worldly wisdom of speculative thought. For the theologian, the ultimate criterion for faith and morality is the living Word of God, Jesus Christ. We have this norm embedded and reflected in the Bible, conscience, and the church. While philosophy contends that "man is the measure of all things" (Protagoras), theology confesses that God is the standard for truth and justice. This insight can also be found in Plato, for example,[53] but when philosophers speak of God, they invariably mean the God conceived of by reason. For theologians, the ultimate standard is not the idea of God nor the idea of the Good but God in Christ, the Word made flesh. The criterion is divine revelation, not human reason.

From the theological perspective, the good is what God wills and declares, not what human beings can discover on their own. The Old Testament is here at one with the New Testament. We read in Isaiah, "I the Lord speak the truth, I declare what is right" (45:19). And in Micah, "He has showed you, O man, what is good" (6:8). To know the good is a gift of grace which can be sought but not assured through prayer. Solomon pleaded, "Give thy servant therefore an understanding mind to govern thy people, that I may discern between good and evil; for who is able to govern this thy great people?" (1 Kings 3:9).

Evangelical theology allows for the role of conscience in guiding moral action, but this is not an autonomous conscience (as in Kant) but a conscience illumined by the Word of God. Conscience is not an independent criterion in theological ethics. Paul recognized the limitations of conscience in providing moral guidance and assurance: "I am not aware of anything against myself, but I am not thereby acquitted. It is the Lord who judges me" (1 Cor. 4:4). This is a far cry from Kant's audacious assertion: "Even the Holy One of the Gospels must first be compared with our ideal of moral perfection before we can recognize Him as such."[54]

In theology reason is not annulled or forsaken, but it must be converted. When reason is brought into the service of faith, it becomes faithful reasoning or Christian thinking. Reason can be an instrument in moral decision, but it can never be the final authority.

The Word of God, as theology understands this, is neither an eternal principle nor a transcendental ideal but instead a divine command. The Word of God is the outstretched hand of God that seizes us rather than a timeless idea that is always available to us. As the Psalmist put it, "He sends out His command to the earth; His word runs very swiftly" (Ps. 147:15 NKJV). To know God is to meet God in the divine-human encounter in which our illusions are shattered and our hopes for success and happiness in this life are buried. To know God means to be given new hopes and expectations, new motivations for living, new goals that will forever remain alien to the mind-set of the world.

Motivations in Ethics

In philosophy the motivation for the morally good life is the advancement or fulfillment of the self. Whether the highest good be understood as virtue, power, or happiness, it is still seen as contributing to the enhancement of the self. Even the knowledge of God, even union with God, is a means to the perfection of the self. John Stuart Mill held that our motivation should be to seek the happiness of the greatest number, though he was quick to remind his hearers that we are all included in this greatest number. The greatest number is the collective self rather than the individual self, but this is still qualitatively different from an ethics dedicated to the glory of God, which cannot always be harmonized with what reason tells us is the general good.

Philosophical ethics, unlike theological ethics, is invariably anthropocentric and egocentric.

Selfism in ethics is especially prominent in the philosophers of the Renaissance and Enlightenment. Leibniz contended that all of our actions should be calculated with regard to the future of our being. His ethical stance is therefore properly described as enlightened self-interest. Spinoza is still more blunt: "As reason makes no demands contrary to nature, it demands that every man should love himself, should seek that which is useful to him."[55] According to Thomas Hobbes, any regard for the welfare of others is secondary to regard for one's own welfare.

Albert Schweitzer, who tried to make a place for altruism, nevertheless argued that the will to live involves the will to self-realization. Reverence for life is understood in terms of world-affirmation, which includes rather than annuls the self.

Immanuel Kant stressed moral duty over the quest for happiness, but he was convinced that happiness would be an invariable by-product of fulfilling the categorical imperative, the law of our being. We should therefore strive for virtue but also hope for happiness. Pardoning grace is simply the reward for virtue rather than the condition of it. Kant's emphasis was on being true to oneself, not on giving glory to God. God has a distinct place in his system, but only in order to help human beings to attain the summum bonum.

In the philosophy of Nietzsche, the primary motivation is the will to power, which means greatness of soul as opposed to weakness, cowardice, and vacillation. The will to power also brings intoxicating delight in the affirmation of the world in all of its sensuous beauty and vitality.

Greatly influenced by Nietzsche, Alfred Rosenberg, the philosopher of National Socialism, upheld honor and nobility as the prime motivations for conduct, sharply distinguishing them from what Christianity means by love. "Nordic people, conditioned by the concept of honor, could not be summoned in the name of a condescending love to extend communion to one in trouble; they would have to be summoned in the name of justice and duty. This would result not in submissive humility, but in an inner elevation; not in the shattering of personality, but in its strengthening, i.e., a reawakening of the consciousness of honor."[56]

For evangelical Christianity, the motivations for living an upright life include zeal for the honor of God, love for our neighbor, fear of God, and gratefulness for God's gift of salvation in Jesus Christ. A desire for one's own salvation is also permissible (cf. Phil. 2:12), though not as an end in itself but as a means to the glory of God and the extension of his kingdom. The life of bearing the cross will entail suffering, since the disciple is not above his master (cf. Acts 9:16; Phil. 1:29; Rev. 2:3).

Both John Calvin and Ignatius Loyola placed the accent on *soli Deo Gloria* (glory to God alone). The aim in life is not to gain a place in the sun, not to achieve fame or success, but to lose ourselves in the glory of God. Calvin put it this way: "We are not our own: in so far as we can, let us therefore forget ourselves and all that is ours. Conversely, we are God's: let us therefore live for him and die for him. We are God's: let his wisdom and will therefore rule all our actions. We are God's: let all the parts of our life accordingly strive toward him as our only lawful goal."[57]

The evangelical Christian does not believe that one can merit salvation by good works but that good works will flow spontaneously out of a joyful heart. Kierkegaard, who emphasized the costly character of discipleship, could nevertheless declare, "It is by no means man's effort which brings atonement, but it is the joy over the reconciliation, over the fact that atonement has been made, it is the joy which produces an honest striving."[58]

We are justified not by a holy life, not by sincerity or zeal, not even by good intentions, but only by the perfect righteousness of Jesus Christ that covers our sins and presents us blameless before the throne of God. But once justified we then are moved irresistibly to zeal for the honor of God and love for our neighbor for whom Christ died.

The way of the cross does not generally entail the crippling or maceration of the body, though it does call for a royal rule over the passions for the sake of kingdom service. Health of body as well as serenity of mind are permissible goals so long as they are sought in order to make us proper instruments of the will of our Lord. I here heartily agree with the Puritan theologian Richard Sibbes: "This is a sign of a man's victory over himself, when he loves health and peace of body and mind, with a supply of all needful things, chiefly for this end, that he may with more freedom of spirit serve God in doing good to others."[59] Sibbes displayed a biblical sense of priorities when he subordinated personal well-being to Christian service. How utterly different is the way of the world in which religious values are coopted to advance purely personal goals!

The disparity between the prophets and apostles of biblical faith and the sages of human culture is highlighted when we compare the two traditions on the subject of love. The former see love in terms of the vicarious identification of God with the travails of the human race. The latter understand love as the quest for union with the ground of the soul. Anders Nygren has given us a helpful and important work on the ineradicable differences between these two types of love, agape and eros.[60]

Eros is self-regarding love. It is the love that seeks its own fulfillment and perfection in union with God. It is born out of personal need and deficiency. It is the kind of love by which human beings strive to raise themselves to God, to climb the mystical ladder to heaven, as Plato put it in his *Symposium*. When this understanding of love entered Christian thinking, it was qualified to a certain extent by biblical motifs. For the Christian mystics, divine grace enables us to make the arduous climb to the gateway of divinity; yet the emphasis was still on the ascent to God, not on the descent of God to our level. Eros is acquisitive and egocentric. It seeks to gain possession of the supreme or highest good. For Aristotle, Spinoza, Fromm, and various other philosophical luminaries, self-love is a virtue. For Calvin and Luther self-love is a sin.

In contrast to eros, agape (the word for love used most often in the New Testament) is self-giving and sacrificial. It is the love that does not seek its own (Rom. 15:1–2; 1 Cor. 10:24; 13:5). Agape is not even mutual love but love for one's enemies, for those who persecute and hate us (Luke 6:27–29). It is invincible good will, which sometimes entails the sacrifice of our desires. Both Aristotle and Confucius advocated love for one's friends, but they drew the line at loving one's enemies. Agape means an infinite preference for our neighbor's welfare (Paul Ramsey). It is the vicarious, suffering love we see exemplified in the cross of Christ. It is unconditional, not dependent on the moral qualifications of the object of our love. It is the love that expects no payment or reward. Jesus said, "Freely ye have received, freely give" (Matt. 10:8 KJV). This is the love that impels the Christian to a life of sacrificial service on behalf of the poor and the oppressed (cf. 2 Cor. 5:14, 15). It is not an ascending but a descending love—a descending into the needs and travails of the world.

Some types of philosophy, particularly the mystic variety, seek to overcome crass self-seeking by disinterested love. At first glance, this appears similar to the sacrificial love of the cross, but disinterested love, unlike agape, is completely free from bias and passion, removed from the turmoil and pathos that disrupt the world. Christian love, on the other hand, is born out of sorrow in the heart of God for the sins of the world. It includes rather than excludes pity and grief. It also pre-supposes a bias for the poor in spirit, the lowly and contrite, and a bias against the proud and unloving. God's love goes out to all, but it raises up some and casts down others. It embraces the sinner but seeks to uproot the sin. It comes to us while we are still sinners (Rom. 5:8) but is not content to leave us in our sins.

Disinterested love in the traditions of mysticism and humanism has taken various forms. In Stoicism it appeared as apathy—love without emotion. Meister Eckhart regarded disinterestedness, understood as detachment from the world, as higher than love. For Spinoza, to say that God has disinterested love means that he does not love or hate anyone, since such love is devoid of any feeling of pleasure or pain. Buddhism upholds selflessness over altruism, passionless benevolence over compassion.[61] The perfect individual in Taoism is self-contented, indifferent toward all people and all things. One Hindu sage declares, "By ceasing to do good to one's friends or evil to one's enemies [one] attains to the eternal Brahman by the *yoga* of meditation."[62]

Christianity does not necessarily eradicate or exclude other loves, such as *philia* (friendship) and eros, but it sets out to transform and purify them.[63] Friendship becomes fellowship. Lustful desire becomes loving desire. The search for union with God is converted into the joy of communion with God.

Love is the foundational motivation in Christian ethics—love for God and for one's fellow human beings. This love is not the desire for union with God but the joy of knowing that our sins are forgiven, a joy that is expressed in sacrifices of praise and thanksgiving to God and loving service to our neighbor. Existentialism advises: Act as free-dom requires in the concrete situation. Christianity insists: Act as love requires in the situation of encountering your neighbor in need.

The Tragic Flaw

Every system of ethics posits a tragic flaw in human beings, a flaw that impedes them from heeding or fulfilling the moral requirement. In some types of philosophy, ignorance is the source of human misery. We do not do the good because we lack knowledge of the good (Pla-tonism). In others the tragic flaw is fate, which propels us in a certain direction because of our place in history (Sophocles). In still others the key to our undoing is matter or our animal nature (Gnosticism, Man-ichaeism). Or it is desire, which needs to be extinguished (Buddhism). Or it is karma accumulated in a preexistent state (Hinduism, Buddhism, Jainism, Theosophy). Or it is the inertia of nature (Plato, White-head). Or it is the oppressive character of social institutions (Marxism). Or it is hubris or immoderation (Greek tragedians). Or it is cultural and religious taboos (Nietzsche, Marquis de Sade).

For theology the tragic flaw is sin—revolt against the will of God. This is also understood as hardness of heart, the heart curved in upon itself (*incurvatus in se*). The core of sin is unbelief, and its chief manifestations are pride, fear, and sloth. Sin is not simply concupiscence, the inclination to sin, but a lust for power. It is not so much a deficiency of the good as an assault on the good. By *sin* theologians mean both acts of transgression and a state of alienation or estrangement from God. We are sinners not only because we do sinful acts but because we exist in a state of sin. The opposite of sin is not virtue but faith (Kierkegaard).

In the theological view, the seat of sin is in the human spirit. For the mainstream of Western philosophy, the seat of evil is in nature or human finitude. Christians of a biblical orientation envisage not an ontological fall—from being at one with God to being separated from God—but a historical fall—from being in fellowship with God to being in guilt before God. In philosophical mysticism the primal sin is individuation. In evangelical Christianity the primal sin is unbelief—doubting the Word of God. The antithesis in philosophy is between spirit and matter, freedom and necessity, knowledge and ignorance. For theology the antithesis is between the holy God and man the sinner.

Christian faith locates the source of our misery in the wickedness and corruption of the human heart, not in weakness or ignorance. Jeremiah lamented, "The heart is deceitful above all things, and desperately corrupt; who can understand it?" (Jer. 17:9). Socrates in Plato's *Protagoras* presents a quite different picture: "No man voluntarily pursues evil, or that which he thinks to be evil. To prefer evil to good is not in human nature; and when a man is compelled to choose one of two evils, no one will choose the greater when he may have the less."[64] The contrast with Paul's description of human life in Romans 7 could hardly be greater. Paul confesses that the evil that he would not do he does, and the good that he would do he fails to do (7:15–20).

For theology hate can only be replaced by love; for philosophy hate is replaced by enlightenment. Buddha, like Spinoza, did not preach the overcoming of hate by love but the overcoming of both love and hate by understanding.

The Greek tragedians approached the Christian doctrine of sin in their conception of *hybris*, the pride that drives men and women to seek greatness. But upon close examination this proves to be a kind of immoderation that is wholly natural, not unnatural (as is sin). It means to exceed the bounds given one by Fate. It springs from the vitalities of nature, not from a corrupted heart. The tragic hero is a victim of fate, not a willing accomplice in sin. Such a person is to be pitied, not reproached. The sinner, on the other hand, is deserving not of mercy (though he receives this through grace) but only of divine judgment.

Goals in Ethics

The contrast between these two ideal types—theology and philosophy—is also illumined when we consider ethical goals. In one important strand in philosophy, the goal is happiness or pleasure. Here we can list Epicurus, Thomas Hobbes, Jeremy Bentham, John Stuart Mill, Herbert Spencer, Herbert Marcuse, D. H. Lawrence and many others. Epicurus upholds the ideal of *ataraxia*, a state of repose and equilibrium, undisturbed by the discords and agitations of life. In his thought pleasure is the greatest good and pain the greatest evil.[65] For both Bentham and Mill the right course of action is what is conducive to the happiness of most people, and happiness is defined in terms of pleasure. Mill, unlike Bentham, tries to make a qualitative distinction between pleasures, giving priority to intellectual enjoyment. Marcuse sees "libidinal pleasure" as the "permanent fountainhead of human existence."[66] For Herbert Spencer, "happiness signifies a gratified state of all the faculties."[67] Bertrand Russell also shows an affinity to this general position: "The good life, as I conceive it, is a happy life. I do not mean that if you are good you will be happy: I mean that if you are happy you will be good."[68]

Philosophical humanism upholds as the goal in life not pleasure but well-being (*eudaimonia*). This, too, is often described as happiness, but it means not the gratification of the senses but the fulfillment of human potentiality.[69] It is true happiness as opposed to pleasure. Here we can list Socrates, Plato, Aristotle, Cicero, Francis Hutcheson, Thomas Jefferson, Whitehead, Erich Fromm, Mortimer Adler, and many others. Eudaemonia means a life in conformity to virtue, a fulfilled or well-regulated life. For Aristotle, virtue by itself cannot guarantee eudaemonia. There must be a right ordering of the virtues. Virtue is therefore a means to eudaemonia.

Another variation of philosophical humanism was Stoicism, which also strenuously objected to the equation of happiness and pleasure.[70] Real happiness lies in *apatheia*, the complete control of one's passions. This is a peace of mind that is independent of the circumstances of life. The way to find happiness is to strive to live a virtuous life, one of rigorous self-discipline in accordance with reason. As in Plato and Aristotle, virtue and happiness are inseparable. Cicero, an eclectic philosopher who drew upon both Platonism and Stoicism, declared, "Neither can the virtues exist without a happy life, nor a happy life without the virtues."[71]

As Catholicism developed into a social institution with growing power and responsibility, it began to seek support from classical sources as it endeavored to fashion a new civilization. Not surprisingly, an attempt was made by well-meaning theologians to incorporate the valid insights of Greco-Roman philosophy into a universal rational system. In the resulting biblical-classical synthesis, the Hellenistic life goals of both happiness and pleasure were sometimes unwittingly accepted with only slight modifications. Augustine confessed, "When I seek you, my God, I seek the happy life."[72] Indeed, Karl Holl maintains that for Augustine, "conversion is basically only a change in taste, the desire for earthly goods is replaced by the sweeter desire for heavenly goods."[73] Leslie Dewart detects a similar accommodation to the Hellenistic perspective on life in Thomas Aquinas, whose doctrine "in the last analysis, rests on the hellenic principle that man's perfection *is* happiness. Though man may 'know not in what thing the general notion of happiness is found,' it remains true that 'to desire happiness is nothing else than to desire that one's will be satisfied.' "[74]

This appeal to cultural values, born basically out of an apologetic concern, has been prominent in the modern church as well. Pascal hastened to assure his readers: "We must not believe that the life of Christians is a life of sadness. We give up pleasures only for greater pleasures."[75] The will of God, insisted the Anglican divine William Paley, can be known not only from Scripture but also from the light of nature, which tells us that the rightness of an act is determined by whether "it produces more happiness than any other act possible at the time."[76]

Many other ethical goals have been entertained in the history of philosophy. For Confucius the goal is social harmony; for Kant it is eternal peace; for Marx it is social justice and equality; for Fromm it is humanization; for Buddhism it is equanimity;[77] for Schopenhauer it is nothingness; for the Gnostics it is knowledge; for Plotinus it is the reunion of the soul with the ground of being; for L. Ron Hubbard, founder of Scientology, it is survival.

In theology, on the contrary, the goal of the moral life is the glory of God, the advancement of his kingdom. Whereas Catholics place the emphasis on beholding the glory of God, evangelical Christians stress conformity to the will of God. This has priority even over personal fulfillment and salvation. So fervent was Paul's missionary zeal that he declared himself ready to be "accursed and cut off from Christ for the sake of my brethren, my kinsmen by race" (Rom. 9:3; cf. Exod. 32:32). He was willing to let go even of salvation for the sake of the salvation of the Jews. Yet the paradox is that personal salvation is precisely what gives glory to God, and so long as the divine glory is our primary goal the other has a rightful place. Philip Spener had his priorities right: "Next to God's glory my great object is that God shall save my soul and those whom he has entrusted to me."[78] C. S. Lewis shows that the two belong together: "The glory of God, and, as our only means to glorifying Him, the salvation of human souls, is the real business of life."[79]

Besides personal salvation, Christianity calls us to pursue other worthy, albeit subordinate, goals: perfect love, the fellowship of the saints, social holiness, the extension of the kingdom, glorification.

Can happiness be included as a legitimate goal for Christians? It is well to note that *makarios* (blessed), the word used in the beatitudes in Matthew and Luke, is not the same as *eudaimōn* (happy). Gollwitzer defines blessedness as "delight in seeing the face of the gracious God."[80] According to Barclay, human happiness is something dependent on the circumstances of life, something that life may give and take away, whereas *makarios*, or blessedness, describes joy "serene and untouchable, . . . independent of all the chances and changes of life."[81] Aristotle insisted that *makarios* belongs to the gods alone, for it is a blessedness that "does not require ease and comfort; it is independent of circumstances."[82] Blessedness in this sense can be an object of hope for the Christian, but it should be seen basically as a by-product or fruit of a living faith in the Lord Jesus Christ. It is the gladness at knowing that our sins are forgiven, and is to be contrasted with all self-gratification or self-contentment.

Biblical faith by no means promises a life free from discord and tension. God often fills his people with a divine discontent. One Old Testament prophet complains, "My soul is bereft of peace, I have forgotten what happiness is" (Lam. 3:17). Luther observes that the highest thing people want is "to have joy and happiness and to be without trouble," but "Christ turns the page and says exactly the opposite; He calls 'blessed' those who sorrow and mourn."[83] Indeed, the "highest stage of faith" is "when God punishes the conscience not only with temporal sufferings, but with death, hell and sin and refuses grace and mercy, as though it were His will to condemn and to be angry eternally."[84]

God gives the higher peace, the peace that passes all understanding (John 14:27; Phil. 4:7). This peace is the presence of God in the midst of tension, not the absence of tension or conflict. He brings the deeper joy, the joy of knowing that God is an ever-present help in trouble, that there is a refuge for the sinner that is unshakable and eternal.

For the Christian, pain is not the greatest evil, and pleasure is not the greatest good. Obedience to God's commandment is the highest good, and disobedience is the greatest evil.

The Ground for Ethical Action

In philosophy the ground for moral action is the will, power, or freedom of man. Or it is rational or mystical insight, which then moves the will in a particular direction.[85] According to Aristotle, the way to become virtuous is through the practice of virtue. Kant's axiom was "I ought, therefore I can." By way of countering this, the evangelical Christian might say, "God commands, therefore I must."

All philosophical ethics proves upon close examination to be a form of autosoterism (self-salvation). For Cicero, the "noblest" is the one "who has raised himself by his own merit to a higher station."[86] Fichte announced to the German people, "Man has no need of a Mediator, since he has the divine spark within himself."[87] When still a comparatively young man Bertrand Russell concluded that through philosophy "the mind is rendered great, and capable of that union with the Universe that constitutes its highest good."[88] The key word here is "capable," for philosophy presupposes a capacity within the human soul for moral excellence and spiritual fulfillment. Montaigne argued, "Life in itself is neither good nor evil; it is the scene of good or evil, as you make it."[89] This resonates with William Henley's celebrated aphorism, "I am the master of my fate; I am the captain of my soul."[90]

Against the above claims, theology insists that the ground of ethical action is the free grace of God revealed and fulfilled in Jesus Christ. This grace, moreover, goes out precisely to the undeserving. The Pauline and Reformation doctrine of the justification of the ungodly contravenes the thinking of the "natural man," which supposes that human worth merits divine pardon but chafes at the idea of pardon being freely bestowed to the unworthy. In his famous debate with Erasmus, Luther maintained that human beings are helpless to help themselves in a moral or spiritual way until the grace of God turns their will completely around.[91] The hope of humanity rests not on free will, which is in bondage to sin, but in a liberated will, a will set free by the grace of God to know and obey the good.

Jesus said to Nicodemus, "Unless a man is born again, he cannot see the kingdom of God" (John 3:3 NIV). The key to a reformation in character lies in a regeneration of the human spirit. We cannot pull ourselves up by our own bootstraps, but we can be lifted up by free grace. It is not the mystical ladder to heaven that is the root metaphor for Christian salvation but instead the lift, or elevator, of free grace. We need only enter by a simple act of faith, and this itself is to be attributed to the grace of God drawing us irresistibly to the one way out of the human dilemma.

According to P. T. Forsyth, "The Stoic says in strength, 'I must, therefore I can'; the Christian says in grace, 'I can, and therefore must.' "[92] Once grace has come to us, we recognize that we can now say yes to the great invitation extended by our Lord to sinners, and if we *can*, we *must*, if salvation is to be real in our lives. For the Stoic, moral obligation presupposes moral capacity, but this is precisely what Christian faith denies.

For the Christian, our righteousness is anchored not in ourselves but in Jesus Christ by whose perfect righteousness, accounted to us in faith, we are placed in the favor of God. We can and do begin to make progress in the moral life, but because our good works are always mixed with less than the highest motivations, our personal holiness can never merit the eternal salvation prepared for us. The Psalmist rightly confessed, "You are my Lord, My goodness is nothing apart from You" (Ps. 16:2 NKJV).

It is to be acknowledged that the concept of grace is present in various world religions, but it is a far cry from the doctrine of grace found in evangelical Christianity. In Bhakti Hinduism grace is emphasized, though not as divine pardon for sin but as a vision of life, as enlightenment. A notion of grace is found in Amida Buddhism, but it is understood not as the forgiveness of sins but as unmerited illumination. In Mahayana Buddhism we encounter the bodhisattva, a figure of grace. This is a person who, although reaching the acme of perfection, willingly forgoes Nirvana in order to help his less fortunate brethren. Yet as one Buddhist scholar observes, "Strictly speaking, even a Buddha cannot help another being to salvation unless the latter's karmic merit is already ripened to such a degree that he can respond to a Buddha's teaching and influence."[93]

Plato said, "Virtue of herself is sufficient for happiness." Evangelical theology says, "Grace alone is sufficient for holiness." Here we see a drastic alteration affecting both the ground and goal of moral endeavor. For biblical Christianity it is not human virtue but the free grace of God that gives us the incentive and power to live the right kind of life. And our goal is not happiness or well-being but holiness—nearness to God, conformity to the will of God.

The Christian could not say with Cicero that "virtue is its own reward." It is not the actualization of human potentiality (the meaning of virtue, or aretē) but the transformation into a new creation that is the hope of humanity. The crown of glory is not a reward for virtue but a prize given to those who continue to struggle, despite the fact that they forever fall short of the perfect virtue that God commands.[94] In 2 Peter we are called to supplement our faith with virtue and virtue with knowledge (1:5). But the apostle goes on to say that both virtue and knowledge must be fulfilled in love (v. 7). Moreover, this injunction is addressed to those who have already been granted "the divine power . . . that makes for life and true religion, enabling us to know the One who called us by his own splendour and might" (2 Pet. 1:3 NEB). Our task is to confirm our adoption and election, but there is no hint that we could ever merit these things.

Nowhere is the disjunction between philosophical speculation and theological reflection more apparent than in their conflicting understandings of freedom. In the tradition of classical humanism, freedom means the ability to go one way or another, to choose good or evil, God or the devil. In evangelical theology, freedom means the capacity to realize our divinely appointed destiny to be ambassadors and heralds of our Lord Jesus Christ. True freedom signifies true obedience. The possibility of disobedience is canceled when we meet the One who makes us free. To be sure, there is the ontological impossibility of forfeiting this freedom in pride and folly, but this involves the loss, not the exercise, of our freedom.

Humanistic philosophy asks people to become what they essentially are, to realize their potential as human beings, to fulfill their humanity through the practice of virtue. Both Augustine and Calvin called us to "become what we are not."[95] The hope of mankind rests upon a new creation, the creation of a new heart that gives us new motivations and expectations, a new horizon and a new destiny (cf. Ezek. 11:19; 36:26; Jer. 31:33; Ps. 51:10–12; 2 Cor. 5:17). It is the power of transforming love and not simply the performance of good action (as in Aristotle) that enables people to live lives of freedom and victory over the powers of darkness.

In our discussion of the tensions between these two types of faith-orientation, theology and philosophy, it is well to keep in mind that we are finally speaking of two types of persons. In the Fourth Gospel 9:39 our Lord days, "For judgment I came into this world, that those who do not see may see, and that those who see may become blind." The man who was born blind and who was healed by Jesus at the pool of Siloam was able to see because of his unfailing trust in the word of our Lord. The Pharisees, who were righteous in their own eyes and despised others, curtly asked Jesus, "Are we also blind?" The reply of our Lord was clear and cutting: "If you were blind, you would have no guilt; but now that you say, 'We see,' your guilt remains" (v. 41). Those who think they see or are capable of seeing by their own power are the Pharisees of this world. They are those who believe themselves to be wise and good in the eyes of God and the world. These people will be made blind, for they refuse to throw themselves on the mercy and wisdom of God. On the other hand, those who admit that they do not now see as they ought to see and who make the venture of trust in the One who alone can give them true sight and understanding will be made to see truly at the end. It is the pure in heart who will see God (Matt. 5:8; Heb. 12:14), not those who are pure or wise in their own eyes. Pascal summed up the situation: "There are only two kinds of men: the righteous who believe themselves sinners; the rest, sinners, who believe themselves righteous."[96]

For Plato, "the perfection of man stands in the imitation of God."[97] For evangelical Christianity, the perfection of humanity lies in the crucifixion of the God made man. Through his grace we are enabled to walk in his steps, but it is not what we can do for God but what God has done for us that ensures our eternal salvation. This is why we can take up the cross and follow Christ in freedom and joy, knowing that our sins are already forgiven, knowing that sin now lies behind us and before us is the road to glory.

Notes

1. On this dimension of Nietzsche see Jaroslav Pelikan, *Fools for Christ* (Philadelphia: Muhlenberg, 1955), pp. 118–44.

2. Cited in Gordon D. Kaufman, *The Theological Imagination* (Philadelphia: Westminster, 1981), p. 97.
3. Friedrich W. Nietzsche, *The Philosophy of Nietzsche*, intro. Willard Huntington Wright (New York: Modern Library, 1927), p. 432.
4. Nietzsche, *The Antichrist*, trans. H. L. Mencken (New York: Alfred A. Knopf, 1924), p. 43.
5. Cited in Karl Jaspers, *Nietzsche and Christianity*, trans. E. B. Ashton (Chicago: Henry Regnery Co., 1961), p. 89.
6. Pelikan, *Fools for Christ*, pp. 141–144.
7. Cited in Eberhard Bethge, *Dietrich Bonhoeffer: Man of Vision, Man of Courage*, trans. Eric Mosbacher et al (New York: Harper, 1970), p. 197.
8. Epictetus, *Discourses* 3, 24, in *The Works of Epictetus*, trans. Thomas W. Higginson (Boston: Little, Brown & Co., 1918), p. 108.
9. Luther, *Tischreden* 5, 5624. Cited in Fred Berthold, Jr., *The Fear of God* (New York: Harper, 1959), p. 43. Cf. "And this is the reason why our theology is certain: it snatches us away from ourselves and places us outside ourselves, so that we do not depend on our own strength, conscience, experience, person, or works but depend on that which is outside ourselves, that is, on the promise and truth of God, which cannot deceive." *Luther's Works* ed. Jaroslav Pelikan (St. Louis: Concordia, 1963), 26: p. 387. Also cf. Bonhoeffer: "Our salvation is 'external to ourselves.' . . . Only he who allows himself to be found in Jesus Christ, in his incarnation, his Cross, and his resurrection, is with God and God with him." *Life Together*, trans. John W. Doberstein (New York: Harper, 1954), p. 54.
10. See Reinhold Niebuhr, *An Interpretation of Christian Ethics* (New York: Seabury, 1979), pp. 113, 114.
11. It should be kept in mind that these generalizations (theological and philosophical ethics) are ideal types, and no particular representative of either type completely embodies the ideal. Theology is here understood as the systematic explication of the biblical revelation, seeking to interpret the whole of experience in the light of this revelation. Philosophy is the attempt to understand the totality of experience on the basis of human reason, here indicating any cognitive capacity within man.
12. Helmut Thielicke, *Theological Ethics* (Philadelphia: Fortress, 1966), 1: p. 51.
13. Ibid., p. 456.
14. Karl Barth, *Church Dogmatics*, II, 2. ed. G. W. Bromiley and T. F. Torrance (Edinburgh: T. & T. Clark, 1957), p. 524.
15. Ibid.
16. Ibid., p. 539.
17. Ibid., p. 565.
18. Eberhard Busch, *Karl Barth*, trans. John Bowden (Philadelphia: Fortress, 1976), p. 182.
19. See Robin W. Lovin, *Christian Faith and Public Choices: The Social Ethics of Barth, Brunner and Bonhoeffer* (Philadelphia: Fortress, 1984), pp. 126–58.
20. Alasdair C. MacIntyre, *After Virtue* (Notre Dame, Ind.: University of Notre Dame Press, 1981), p. 178.
21. For a discussion of voluntarism and actualism see chap. 4, note 48.
22. See Adrio König, *Here Am I!* (Grand Rapids: Eerdmans, 1982), pp. 67–68.
23. On the Holy as an experienced reality in Christian life see Rudolf Otto, *The Idea of the Holy*, trans. John W. Harvey (New York: Oxford University Press, 1958).
24. See Peter Gay, *The Enlightenment* (New York: Alfred A. Knopf, 1966), vol. 1 p. 108.
25. Walter C. Kaiser, Jr., *Toward Old Testament Ethics* (Grand Rapids: Zondervan, 1983), p. 302.
26. Baruch Spinoza, *Ethics*, trans. W. Hale White (London: Oxford University Press, 1927), vol. 4, prop 20, p. 195.
27. Georg Wilhelm Friedrich Hegel, *The Philosophy of History*, trans. J. Sibree (New York: P. F. Collier & Son, 1900), p. 32.
28. One could also say that the key phrase is "Lose yourself," since as Christians we

are called to forget about our own fears and vexations in meeting the agonizing needs of our neighbor.

29. See Thomas à Kempis, *The Imitation of Christ*, trans. Leo Sherley-Price (Harmondsworth, Baltimore: Penguin Books, 1952), pp. 30, 31. In Thomas à Kempis we see a curious blend of Neoplatonic mysticism and biblical prophetic religion.

30. Søren Kierkegaard, *Concluding Unscientific Postscript*, trans. David F. Swenson (Princeton, N.J.: Princeton University Press, 1941), p. 387.

31. John Calvin, *Institutes of the Christian Religion*, ed. John T. McNeill, trans. Ford Lewis Battles (Philadelphia: Westminster Press, 1960), 3, 8, 1, p. 702.

32. Niebuhr, *An Interpretation of Christian Ethics*, pp. 23, 38, 53, 69–71.

33. Quoted in Dale Carnegie, *How to Stop Worrying and Start Living* (New York: Simon & Schuster, 1953), p. 163.

34. Ibid.

35. Bultmann reminds us of the abysmal gulf between the biblical and humanistic perspectives on self-love: "It is therefore meaningless to say (what can only be said on the basis of a humanistic ideal of man), that neighbourly love must be preceded by a legitimate self-love, a necessary degree of self-respect, because we are told 'Thou shalt love thy neighbor as thyself.' Self-love is thus presupposed. And it is in fact presupposed, but not as something that man must first learn, something that must be expressly required of him, but as the attitude of the natural man, which has simply to be overcome." *Jesus* (Tübingen: J. C. B. Mohr, 1951), p. 100. Cited in Anders Nygren, *Agape and Eros*, trans. Philip S. Watson (Philadelphia: Westminster, 1953), p. 101.

36. A legitimate self-love is indicated in Eph. 5:21–33, where Paul says we should nourish and cherish our own bodies (v. 29). At the same time, husbands are called to lay down their lives for their wives as Christ laid down his life for the church (vv. 23–27).

37. William Kelley Wright, *A History of Modern Philosophy* (New York: Macmillan Co., 1941), p. 243.

38. Jean-Jacques Rousseau, *Émile*, trans. Barbara Foxley (New York: E. P. Dutton & Co., 1957), p. 254.

39. See Jackson Lee Ice, *Schweitzer: Prophet of Radical Theology* (Philadelphia: Westminster, 1971).

40. Cf. Cicero: "Following Nature as our guide, we shall never go astray, but shall be on the road to keen perception and understanding (which is wisdom), and to an ardent and courageous spirit." *Selected Works of Cicero*, intro. Harry M. Hubbell (New York: Walter J. Black, 1948), p. 360.

41. Immanuel Kant, *Metaphysical Foundations of Morals*, in *The Philosophy of Kant*, ed. Carl J. Friedrich (New York: Modern Library, 1949), pp. 193, 194.

42. Erich Fromm, *Man for Himself* (New York: Holt, Rinehart & Winston, 1947), p. 6.

43. Cf. Socrates: "Living or dead, to a good man there can come no evil." Plato, *Apology*, in *Plato on the Trial and Death of Socrates*, 5th printing, trans. Lane Cooper (Ithaca, N.Y.: Cornell University Press, 1977), p. 77. Socrates was convinced that the knowledge of the good is sufficient for a life of virtue and therefore also of happiness. Nothing can injure the soul of a person who knows the good and does it. On the other hand, those who lack knowledge of the good will inevitably choose the bad over the good and will therefore be miserable. See Norman Gulley, *The Philosophy of Socrates* (New York: St. Martin's, 1968), p. 75–200.

44. Although Hobbes sometimes entertains the idea of a divine law, he basically means by "the laws of nature or natural law . . . the laws of self-preservation and power." See Frederick Copleston, *A History of Philosophy*, Book II, Vol. 4 (New York: Doubleday Image, 1985), pp. 44–46.

45. Spinoza, *Ethics*, vol. 4 prop. 24, p. 198.

46. Ayn Rand, *The Virtue of Selfishness* (New York: Signet Books, 1964), p. 23.

47. Friedrich Nietzsche, *Twilight of the Idols and the Anti-Christ*, trans. R. J. Hollingdale (Harmondsworth, Middlesex: Penguin Books, 1972), p. 115.

48. Cited in Arnold Lunn and Garth Lean, *The New Morality* (London: Blandford, 1964), p. 80.
49. William McGuire, ed., *The Freud/Jung Letters*, trans. Ralph Manheim and R. F. C. Hull (Princeton, N.J.: Princeton University Press, 1979), p. 294.
50. Ibid., p. 293.
51. See Rousas J. Rushdoony, *The Politics of Pornography* (New Rochelle, N.Y.: Arlington House, 1974).
52. See Giuseppe Prezzolini, *Machiavelli* (New York: Farrar, Straus & Giroux, 1967), pp. 61–66, 133–34.
53. Cf. Plato: "In our eyes God will be the measure of all things, in the highest degree— a degree much higher than is any 'man' they talk of." Plato, *Laws*, trans. R. G. Bury (Cambridge: Harvard University Press, 1961), 4: p. 295.
54. Kant, *Metaphysical Foundation of Morals*, p. 156.
55. Spinoza, *The Ethics of Spinoza*, ed. Dagobert D. Runes (Secaucus, N.J.: Citadel Press, 1976), p. 89.
56. Alfred Rosenberg, *Race and Race History and Other Essays*, ed. Robert Pois (New York: Harper Torchbooks, 1974), p. 112.
57. Calvin, *Institutes of the Christian Religion*, 3, 7, 1, p. 690.
58. Søren Kierkegaard, *Søren Kierkegaard's Journals and Papers*, ed. and trans. Howard V. Hong and Edna H. Hong (Bloomington: Indiana University Press, 1967), 1, A–E: p. 428.
59. Quoted in Rodney Clapp, "Faith Healing: A Look at What's Happening," *Christianity Today* 27, no. 19 (Dec. 16, 1983): p. 17.
60. Nygren, *Agape and Eros.*
61. One Buddhist scholar comments, "If Christian love might be described as sponta- neously and intensely personal in spirit, practical and direct in its expression, his- torically and socially minded in viewpoint, Buddhist loving-kindness must be de- scribed as systematic and calculated, indirect and impersonal, and atomistically individualistic." Winston King, *Buddhism and Christianity* (Philadelphia: Westminster, 1962), p. 91. King points out that in the Buddhist conception of love (*mettā*), the closer one gets to Nirvana, the less active one will be in the world. The "holy man" will exude *mettā* but will be ever less involved in active works of mercy.
62. Quoted in R. C. Zaehner, *Mysticism: Sacred and Profane* (New York: Oxford University Press, 1961), p. 170.
63. See C. S. Lewis, *The Four Loves* (New York: Harcourt, Brace & World, 1960).
64. *The Dialogues of Plato*, trans. B. Jowett (New York: Random House, 1937), vol. 1, p. 127. One should note that these are the words of Socrates and may not completely coincide with Plato's own position. Copleston maintains that Plato also taught that "no one does evil knowingly and willingly." Copleston, *A History of Philosophy*, Book I, Vol. 1 (New York: Doubleday Image, 1985), p. 219.
65. Epicurus declared, "We call pleasure the alpha and omega of a blessed life. Pleasure is our first and kindred good. It is the starting point of every choice and of every aversion." Yet he held that the suffering of pain may be encouraged in the short run if it results in a greater pleasure in the long run. See Jason L. Sanders, ed., *Greek and Roman Philosophy After Aristotle* (New York: Free Press, 1966), p. 51.
66. Herbert Marcuse, *Eros and Civilization* (London: Sphere Books, 1969), p. 187.
67. Herbert Spencer, *Social Statics* (New York: D. Appleton & Co., 1910), p. 8.
68. Bertrand Russell, *New Hopes for a Changing World* (New York: Simon & Schuster, 1951), p. 10.
69. According to one ethicist: "The Greek word *eudaimonia* means happiness, but the eudaemonistic theory of ethics is not hedonistic or utilitarian. The moral principle for the eudaemonist is not happiness or pleasure, but the preservation of life, vir- tuous activity, welfare, development, progress and perfection. Self-realization is the end sought." A. D. Mattson, *Christian Ethics* (Rock Island, Ill.: Augustana, 1938), p. 38.
70. Some ethicists—for example, Philip Wheelwright—place Stoicism in the category of

ethical rationalism rather than humanism because of its emphasis on the rule of reason rather than the fulfillment of human potentialities (as in Plato and Aristotle). Yet it cannot be denied that Stoicism formed an important part of the classical humanistic heritage by its concern for human dignity, its acknowledgement of the intrinsic worth of moral personality, and its advocacy of self-mastery for the sake of a more humane world.

71. Cicero, *Tusculanarum Disputationum*, Bk. 5, Ch. 28, Sec. 80. Cited in Burton Stevenson, *The Home Book of Quotations*, 8th ed. (New York: Dodd, Mead & Co., 1956), p. 2092.

72. *The Confessions of Augustine* trans. John K. Ryan (New York: Doubleday Image Books, 1960), p. 248.

73. Karl Holl, *Gesammelte Aufsätze zur Kirchengeschichte* (Tübingen: Mohr, 1928), 3: p. 85.

74. Leslie Dewart, *The Future of Belief* (New York: Herder & Herder, 1966), p. 32. See Thomas Aquinas, *Summa Theologica* trans. Fathers of the English Dominican Province (London: Burns Oates & Washbourne, 1914) Vol. 6, II–I, p. 84.

75. Blaise Pascal, *Aflame With Love*, ed. Robert E. Coleman (Wilmore, Ky.: Christian Outreach, 1978), p. 54.

76. Alburey Castell, *An Introduction to Modern Philosophy* (New York: Macmillan Co., 1946), p. 296.

77. According to the Buddhist scholar Winston King, "the general quality of equanimity is clear: it is emotionally neutral, detached and disinterested." *Buddhism and Christianity*, p. 79.

78. Quoted in Marie E. Richard, *Philip Jacob Spener and His Work* (Philadelphia: Lutheran Publication Society, 1897), p. 46.

79. Clyde S. Kilby, ed., *A Mind Awake: An Anthology of C. S. Lewis* (New York: Harcourt Brace Jovanovich, 1980), p. 129.

80. Helmut Gollwitzer, *An Introduction to Protestant Theology*, trans. David Cairns (Philadelphia: Westminster, 1982), p. 175.

81. William Barclay, *The Gospel of Matthew*, rev. ed. (Philadelphia: Westminster Press, 1975), 1: p. 89.

82. Francis Wright Beare, *The Gospel According to Matthew* (San Francisco: Harper & Row, 1981), p. 127.

83. *Luther's Works* 21: p. 17.

84. *Works of Martin Luther*, intro. Henry Eyster Jacobs (Philadelphia: A. J. Holman Co., 1915), 1: p. 193.

85. For Wang Yang-ming, the neo-Confucian sage, the mind (*hsia*) is the source of the good, the standard for moral cultivation and moral action. See Arthur F. Wright, ed., *Studies in Chinese Thought* (Chicago: University of Chicago Press, 1953), pp. 112–22.

86. Craufurd Tait Ramage, *Great Thoughts from Classic Authors* (New York: John B. Allen, 1891), p. 445.

87. Johann G. Fichte, *Reden an die deutsche Nation*, in *Sämmtliche Werke* Siebenter Band, Dritte Abteilung (Berlin: Verlag von Veit und Comp., 1846), p. 349.

88. Cited in Peter Caws, "Reconsideration: Alfred North Whitehead," *The New Republic* 167, no. 5 (Aug. 5 and 12, 1972): p. 34.

89. *The Essays of Michel de Montaigne*, trans. Charles Cotton and W. C. Hazlitt (New York: A. L. Burt, 1892), 1: p. 76.

90. See John Connell, *W. E. Henley* (London: Constable Publishers, 1949), p. 4.

91. See Martin Luther, *The Bondage of the Will*, trans. J. I. Packer and O. R. Johnston (Old Tappan, N.J.: Fleming H. Revell Co., 1957).

92. P. T. Forsyth, *The Principle of Authority*, 2d ed. (London: Independent Press, 1952), p. 389.

93. King, *Buddhism and Christianity*, p. 212.

94. Our persevering in the struggle is not in the strict sense a virtue because it is made possible only by the power of divine grace (cf. Rom. 9:16; Phil. 1:6; 2:12, 13; Eph. 2:9, 10).

95. See Max L. Stackhouse, *Creeds, Society and Human Rights: A Study in Three Cultures* (Grand Rapids: Eerdmans, 1984), p. 59.

96. Blaise Pascal, *Pensées and the Provincial Letters* (New York: Modern Library, 1941), p. 170.

97. Quoted in *Johann Arndt: True Christianity*, trans. Peter Erb, preface by Heiko A. Oberman (New York: Paulist, 1979), p. 95.

CHAPTER 4

Principles in Ethics

Behind the letter of the written code there stands a higher law which must never be broken—the demand of faith and love.

ROBERT BRINSMEAD

The growing hostility in contemporary statements of Christian ethics to keeping the commandments is profoundly in error.

CARL HENRY

If confession or church discipline is lost, then the commandment of God in preaching will be understood as no more than a proclamation of general moral principles which in themselves are devoid of any concrete claim.

DIETRICH BONHOEFFER

Love, if it stands for truth, may require us to do what appears unloving if we are to treat the other with respect.

STANLEY HAUERWAS

The Contemporary Debate

The debate today in the academic religious community revolves around whether ethical norms must be tailored to fit the existential and cultural situation in which people find themselves or whether these norms have abiding authority irrespective of the situation. The former position is embraced by those favoring a kind of situation ethics, the latter is upheld by those on the side of general principles in ethics. This polarity is not the very same as that delineated in the preceding chapter, though what was called theological ethics has more affinity with the situational type than might at first appear. When I discuss the position of Barth and Brunner in this connection, a certain coalescence of existential and theological ethics will become apparent. My own position will be made clear towards the end of the chapter.

Situation ethics and general principle ethics both go under many different names and include a great variety of emphases. The first is also referred to as contextualist ethics (Lehmann), the ethics of decision

(Forell), existentialist ethics, an ethics of freedom, and gospel ethics. In J. A. T. Robinson it takes the form of a morality of involvement and discovery (which he contrasts with a morality of obedience). Principle ethics has been described as an ethics of law, an ethics of casuistry, and a morality of obedience. More recently it has been known as *deontological ethics*, or an ethics of duty; its opposite is called *teleological ethics*, in which the ethical decision is based on the consequences and goals of an action.

Those who defend situational or existentialist ethics say that people come before principles. The other side argues that unchanging principles are necessary to give people a dependable basis for making moral decisions. Without moral absolutes a society might well fall into chaos.

Both of these ethical orientations have their own built-in perils. Traditionalist or principle ethics is always troubled by legalism or moralism, in which fidelity to the moral code is made the condition for moral worthiness. An ethics of freedom is confronted with the twin perils of relativism and antinomianism (living without the law).

Several decades ago Joseph Fletcher, then an Episcopal clergyman, wrote a provocative book entitled *Situation Ethics* in which he tried to present a viable alternative to traditionalist morality; the latter, he held, stifled human creativity and filled people with feelings of guilt that had no basis in reality.[1] Fletcher's alternative is not the only one in this first category of situationalist or existentialist ethics, but it is indubitably the one that has aroused the most controversy.

Fletcher maintains that "the ruling norm of Christian decision is love: nothing else." Love is defined as good will at work in partnership with reason, or reason calculating how love may best be served in any given situation. Ethical decision is dependent on a rational calculation of consequences. The criterion is not the "right" or the "good" but what is "fitting," what is contextually appropriate. The only intrinsic evil is malice, the only intrinsic good is love. Fletcher allows for principles but understood as maxims, not as laws or precepts that are binding in all circumstances. Principles can always be set aside in the name of love. Although he is open to a casuistry obedient to love, casuistry as well as legalism bears the brunt of his attack because of its lamentable dependence on a universal or absolute standard. Fletcher believes that one can discard rules with a good conscience, so long as it can be shown that the welfare or happiness of the greater number of people is served. The ethics he proposes is relativistic, utilitarian, empirical, and existential.

In this perspective, guilt has no place in ethical decision. We may be led to do some things universally deemed reprehensible, but with sorrow, not guilt, with regret, not remorse. If we reasoned wrongly concerning the outcome of a decision, it should be regarded as a mistake, not a sin.

In neo-Lutheranism, too, we find a search for a new kind of ethics that liberates us from the shackles of legalism and moralism. Joseph Sittler upholds absolute loyalty to Christ over absolute principles. William Lazareth concludes that "Christians do not have . . . 'principles to apply,' or 'ideals to realize,' or 'rules to obey.' "[2] Instead of law, neo-Lutheran theologians prefer to speak of paradigms of love to guide us in ethical decision.

At first glance, Karl Barth appears to stand for situational ethics, but actually he advances quite another view. At the same time, because he too rejects absolute principles in ethics, he is often considered closer to the new morality than to the old.

For Barth, our foundational criterion is the commandment of the living God, which is always direct and specific as opposed to general principles, which are abstract and universal. The divine commandment is an event, not a principle. Thus the task of evangelical ethics is to sound not unconditional imperatives but conditional imperatives addressed to concrete situations. "The commands of God in the Bible," he argues, "are not general moral doctrines and instructions but absolutely specific directions which concern each time the behaviour, deeds and omissions of one or more or many definite men in this historical context."[3] He is emphatic that "the Church never thinks, speaks, or acts 'on principle.' Rather it judges spiritually and by individual cases. . . . It preserves the freedom to judge each new event afresh. If yesterday it travelled along one path, it is not bound to keep to the same path today."[4]

Barth's position diverges from situational ethics much more than it converges. His theological contextualism proves to be quite different from Fletcher's empirical situationalism. According to Barth, we must wait upon God's Word anew in every situation, whereas Fletcher seeks to determine beforehand through rational calculation what God's will really is. Barth locates the norm for ethics in the living Christ who speaks to us through Holy Scripture rather than in an abstract principle like love, which lends itself to a myriad of interpretations. His ethics is Christological, rooted in the gospel. While Fletcher relies on human judgments, Barth appeals to the divine imperative. Fletcher's position is thoroughly empirical and data-centered, Barth's is characterized by loyalty to the Word of hope and promise that we hear in Scripture.

Barth holds to "criteria" over principles. Whereas principles are fixed and unbending, criteria are approximations. The Ten Commandments and the Beatitudes are *indications* of God's will, but they are not principles that can be directly applied to every situation. The absolute norm is the word of the living God, which is both command and promise. It is not love but the Christ who loves. And we discover how Christ loves by acquainting ourselves with the testimony in Holy Scripture. In contrast to Fletcher, Barth believes that some actions—for example, abortion—are absolutely wrong. Yet he allows for the possibility that the demands of faith and love in a particular situation might override the absolute.[5]

Barth has been accused of both intuitionism and subjectivism. One can see merit in these charges, considering Barth's description of the genuinely ethical decision as "a leap in the dark."[6] Yet he makes clear that this decision must be made in the context of the Christian community and in the light of the overall biblical witness. Gustafson is not too far wrong when he calls Barth's position an "informed and focused intuitionism."[7] Yet Barth would object to this way of describing his position, because he is emphatic that our norm is not subjective understanding but God's objective disclosure in Holy Scripture and church tradition.[8] To be sure, we can only know this by the eyes of faith, but faith must be in accord with, not in conflict with, the clear testimony of Scripture.

Like Fletcher, Barth attacks casuistry, the attempt to apply absolute norms to concrete cases, because it limits God's freedom. The casuistic method ties God down to a principle, whereas God may create a new principle that supersedes those that have come down to us by tradition (cf. Isa. 48:6,7).

Notably influenced by Barth, Paul Lehmann also states the case for an ethics of freedom that liberates us from the restrictions of the moral codes of the past.[9] He calls his position a contextual or *koinonia* ethics. Whereas Fletcher's contextualism implies that Christian action should be tailored to fit objective circumstances, Lehmann presupposes that Christian action should be carried out in the *koinonia* (fellowship of love) and in the context of faith. For Lehmann the goal in ethics is maturity rather than morality. Like Barth, he draws a sharp distinction between theological and philosophical ethics. Gustafson is probably right in saying that for Lehmann humanization functions as a persistent norm.

Emil Brunner, too, upholds an ethic that is existential and contextual. The basis for Christian ethics is the divine imperative, which is both gift and command.[10] The content of this imperative is existence-in-love. Brunner objects to casuistry because it turns the divine command into a law. While everyone perceives the law, only the faithful hear the divine command. Love abolishes the law because love is not calculating. In Brunner's view, the Decalogue is subethical, historically speaking, but when it is seen in the context of Christ's victory over sin and death it takes on a normative and binding character for the Christian. Brunner supplements his ethics of love with a concept of orders of creation (such as marriage and the family) that show us how to serve in love in the complex world in which we find ourselves.

Still another theologian who presents a cogent argument for an ethics of freedom over law is Dietrich Bonhoeffer. Like Barth, he makes a sharp distinction between "commandments" and "principles." "Unlike the ethical, the commandment of God is not a summary of all ethical propositions in the most general terms. It is not the universally valid and timeless in contrast to the historical and temporal. It is not principle, as distinct from the application of principle."[11] Indeed "the will of God is not a system of rules which is established from the outset; it is something new and different in each different situation in life, and for this reason a man must ever anew examine what the will of God may be."[12] Bonhoeffer also speaks of universal "mandates," including labor, marriage, and government, which guide us in our decisions in society, but they are not to be confused with the divine commandment.

For Bonhoeffer, the commandments are permissions to live as human beings before God. They differ from all human laws in that they command freedom.[13] The Decalogue reveals the limits of Christian action. It is expressed negatively. "Positive forms are brought out by living history, and are limited and judged by the Decalogue."[14]

Principles have a rightful place as guidelines for action, Bonhoeffer admits, but only as "tools in God's hand, soon to be thrown away as unserviceable."[15] We are called to walk by faith, not by the light of rational calculation of goals and consequences of an action. He can even say: "To follow in his steps is something which is void of all content. It gives us no intelligible programme for a way of life, no goal or ideal to strive after."[16]

Jacques Ellul would very likely agree. The eminent French Reformed lay theologian also espouses an ethics of freedom, but with the distinctive flavor of a philosophical actualism, which makes the contrast between his position and principle ethics even more striking. With characteristic bluntness he reminds us that "there are no Christian principles because nowhere does scripture tell us that God became a principle. It tells us that he became a man. Nowhere are we presented with ideas, with principles, but with God acting in reality."[17] Ellul, too, declares his opposition to casuistry: "If one holds to scripture, ethics cannot regulate cases, nor give just decisions."[18] Yet he is not to be placed in the same camp with Fletcher. Ellul realizes that love by itself cannot be a regulatory norm. When the Word of God is left out, love becomes partisan, selective, and capricious.

Thus far, I have examined those who espouse a new kind of morality that stands in tension, if not in conflict, with traditionalist ethics. But the latter also has its defenders.

United Church of Christ theologian Robert Fitch is very emphatic that principles are necessary for meaningful ethical discourse. Fitch takes to task existentialist ethics for making the will of God depend on intuition. In my opinion, his criticisms cannot with validity be applied to Barth or Lehmann, since they make the will of God rest on a decision within the context of Christian community and in the light of Scripture. Fitch's special concern is the area of sexual ethics, where the discarding of rules leads to sexual anarchy.[19] As he puts it, "Principle without compassion may be cruel, but compassion without principle corrupts."[20]

With a similar conviction that principles are needed in ethics, Paul Ramsey draws a contrast between "rule-agapism" and "act-agapism"[21] Rules can embody love, though we should start with persons, not with rules. Indeed, Ramsey arrives at rules on the basis of the requirements of love. Against Fletcher he argues that there are some things that people should never do, "things that might succeed better but would be *intrinsically* wrong" (italics mine).[22]

Despite his association with existentialist theology, Reinhold Niebuhr more properly belongs in the area of rule ethics.[23] He appeals to such universal norms as the ideal of love, freedom, and equality. Whereas "mutual love" is a norm that can be realized in history, the highest norm—"the mind of Christ," the "law of love," or "suffering love"—transcends history. It can be anticipated in moments of encounter with the living Christ, but it can never be a strategy directly applicable to the social arena. He calls love an "impossible possibility," which cannot be realized through human effort but can be experienced in the surrender of faith. In wrestling with social issues Niebuhr appeals not to the transcendent norm of love but to the natural or universal norm of justice.

Carl Henry typifies the uneasiness of traditionalist evangelicals with the new theology and morality. For Henry the commandments of God

revealed in the Bible are absolutely binding on all people. Love is not
a norm that stands in juxtaposition or tension with the commandments, but it is the way we apply the commandments to the situation
in which we live. Henry is adamant that we must uphold moral standards as well as the gospel of love. In his view, "The growing hostility
in contemporary statements of Christian ethics to keeping the commandments is profoundly in error."[24] He insists that "the doctrine of
redemption does not relax the believer's obligation to the Divine commandments, nor weaken his motives to observe them."[25] "Christian
ethics is not left to chart its course of divinely approved conduct by
self-reflection alone, or by an immediate spiritual impression traced to
'encounter.' "[26] It is "through an objective Divine outline alone that
[one] can discriminate between right and wrong directions of love in
action. The biblically revealed ethic of principles, commandments, examples, and applications provides such a content."[27] Henry is here referring primarily to the Sermon on the Mount, but he would also readily include the Decalogue. Henry would take issue with Brunner that
the Decalogue is subethical. On the contrary, it is divine revelation and
therefore universally binding.

Henry can be criticized for leaping from the absolute to the relative
without any mediating principles. He applies the absolute directly to
our social and historically conditioned environment. This makes sense
in the area of person-to-person relationships, but not in the area of
social conflict. Norman Geisler has chided Henry for neglecting con-
flict-situations in his ethical reflection.[28]

Finally, we should consider Lewis Smedes's retort to existentialist
ethics. Smedes is profoundly critical of an ethics of personal command.
He insists that the commandments that constitute the Decalogue "simply cannot speak to the normal conscience at all if they do not speak
as abiding laws."[29] In his view, basic biblical morality is common knowledge, and therefore he affirms the intention behind the classic doctrine
of natural law. For Smedes, there is a morality intended for everyone.
He definitely perceives a continuum between the morality of common
sense and the morality of the Bible. Though badly wounded, "our
moral sensibilities were not destroyed in the Fall."[30] He seeks to ground
justice in human rights, which have their source in our creation in the
image of God. Smedes has a positive view of the rational benevolence
espoused by Kant and Fromm, though he acknowledges that it is not
identical with agape. Rational norms can be helpful as we endeavor to
apply the imperatives of love. Not surprisingly, Smedes is highly critical of Anders Nygren's treatment of the differences between agape

and eros. Smedes sees eros fulfilled in agape, just as he sees the common morality fulfilled in the biblical revelation and human justice fulfilled in the righteousness of God and the peace of God (*shalōm*).[31]

Both Smedes and Henry reflect the distrust of latter-day Calvinistic evangelicalism for the dialectical theology represented by Barth and Brunner. When a disjunction is made between the commandment of God and the moral codes of Christian tradition, they understandably fear that we could be headed in the direction of relativism and subjectivism. The Common Sense philosophy of Thomas Reid and the Scottish Enlightenment with its trust in the reliability of the senses is noticeable in Smedes, though not so much in Henry, who is closer to the Enlightenment in its earlier phases, which emphasized deduction over induction, logic over experience. For both Henry and Smedes, cultural wisdom is not overthrown by the biblical revelation but instead amplified, purified, and fulfilled.

Need for a Prophetic Casuistry

In contradistinction to absolutist ethics on the one hand and existentialist ethics on the other, I propose the alternative of casuistic ethics. I am advocating, however, not a legalistic casuistry, which is condemned by Barth and Fletcher alike, but a prophetic casuistry in which the Word of God takes on concreteness and specificity through faithful hearing.

Casuistry can be defined as the attempt to apply absolute norms to concrete cases. It deals with mediating principles that carry the force of divine authority. These principles cannot be universalized, but they also cannot be reduced to maxims or guidelines, which are not really binding.

Neo-orthodox theologians have for the most part regarded with profound reservations any appeal to principles to guide practical conduct. In their view, "there can be no demarcation of the type of actions that love requires save the guidance perceived in the immediate situation of faith."[32] I am challenging this ethical stance on the grounds that it often leaves believers bewildered as they face the agonizing decisions of life. People rightly look to the church to give concrete guidance on moral issues, and simply to hold up the ideal of love is not sufficient.

Evangelical casuistry is the attempt to discern the will of God for a specific situation. We do not begin with abstract norms but with God's self-revelation in Jesus Christ. We see the norms and principles of both the Old and New Testaments exemplified and embodied in the life, death, and resurrection of Jesus Christ.

Casuistry deals with principles and rules of conduct. Evangelical casuistry focuses on directives given by the Spirit of God to the church that enable us to act both faithfully and intelligently in the situation in which we find ourselves. The commandment of God is applied to the way we live in the world of our time.

At first glance, my proposal might seem similar to the concept of "middle axioms" associated with J. H. Oldham, John Bennett, Paul Ramsey, and others.[33] For these theologians, middle axioms are concrete norms that mediate between the ethical ideal, sacrificial love, and the existential and cultural situation. Yet, in my opinion, there are significant differences. First, I agree with Fletcher that "middle axioms" is an infelicitous phrase, for an axiom is a self-validating, nonderivative proposition and cannot stand in the middle of anything.[34] Second, the way one arrives at middle axioms is through an empirical analysis of the cultural situation in light of the demands of love. The divine commandment, by contrast, is not the outcome of rational deliberation but the act by which people who are drifting in the wrong direction are confronted by the Word of God and are thereby forced to revise their presuppositions and conclusions.

Finally, middle axioms or middle principles as conceived by the ethicists in question might easily become ideological constructs that justify the special interests of a class or party within society. Feminists and black activists who clamor for affirmative action, as well as new religious rightists who press for prayer in the public schools and tax credits for parents with children in parochial schools, are not necessarily being obedient to the divine commandment. Instead they may actually be devising middle principles that can best advance the social agenda of their constituencies.

A middle principle in evangelical casuistry should be seen as a prophetic interpretation of the command of God for a specific situation. The norm is not the greater good of society rationally discerned or the happiness of the greatest number (as Fletcher saw it) but how God's kingdom can best be served.

Evangelical casuistry is based on the view that God's Spirit gives new illumination to the church in every age. The Spirit speaks through the Bible to the church, applying the scriptural commands to concrete issues as they arise. This is by no means a subjective criterion but the Word being illumined by the Spirit and then applied to the culture. This is the living Word of God, not to be confused with the prescriptions of a past era. It is the law enlightened by the Spirit, not the law dictated by the church tradition. The moral law, including that which we find in the Bible, is nothing more than a dead letter or an outmoded moral code unless it is acted upon by the Spirit.

God spoke through the prophets in biblical times, but he also speaks through the prophets in every age, including our own. The Puritan theologian John Robinson rightly declared that there is yet more light to break forth from God's holy Word. This light, one must hasten to add in this permissive era, does not contradict the light given in the past but amplifies and illumines it for the situation in which we find ourselves. Abortion, for example, is not dealt with in the Bible, but an increasing number of sensitive souls wrestling with Scripture are hearing a divine commandment against the abortion traffic, which casts a cloud over current Western civilization. The sixth commandment, "You shall not kill," is being given specificity when it is translated into the prophetic admonition, "You shall not abort unborn children!"

Casuistry is out of favor among most ethicists today because of its association with groups known for either excessive legalism or ethical chicanery. The Pharisees made middle axioms into a rigid legalistic code that excluded every action not specifically allowed. The Jesuits used middle axioms as a means of moral evasion. Jesuit casuistry took the form of probabilism, allowing every action not specifically condemned.

In the view presented here, mediating principles are not simply practical guides for behavior but prescriptions for behavior. They express the commandment of God for a particular situation. They are not simply human constructs but prophetic admonitions inspired by the Spirit. They are not human judgments so much as the very Word of God. They are not maxims or guidelines that only illustrate the situation (as in Fletcher) but directives given by the Spirit of God to the church so that the people of God might receive concrete moral guidance.

We are not to absolutize these mediating principles in the sense that they can be extended to all times and places. They are conditional, not unconditional, imperatives. They are not eternal truths but concrete divine commands that carry the force of absolute authority. They are not absolute prohibitions that hold true for all times and places. Otherwise, they become "principles" in the idealistic sense, abstract truths standing outside of human history and culture. We are not to tie down the freedom of God to an eternal principle; on the other hand, we must allow for God in his freedom to make use of principles or injunctions in every particular situation. These mediating principles or prophetic imperatives have a real but relative authority. They express the authoritative word of God for some, but not all, situations.[35]

Middle principles may, of course, function only as practical guides, but they may also take the form of divine commands. In the first case, these principles are only general indications or approximations of the divine will. In the last case, they should be seen as embodiments of God's will.

When the prophetic injunction is not given *in* faith and *to* faith, it then remains just a moral principle, a legalistic rule. When it is given in the context of faith—in obedience to the Word of God—then it becomes the very Word of God for our situation (in the sense not of an identity but of a unity with God's Word).

The prophetic declaration of the church is not in and of itself the divine commandment, but it is in this declaration that we hear the divine commandment. God does not speak the exact words uttered by the church, even the faithful church, but God speaks in, under, and through the witness of its prophets and apostles. When the cultural situation changes or when the church receives new light from God's holy Word, principles that the church espoused in one time and place may be sacrificed for more ultimate considerations.

A relevant example in Scripture of a conditional imperative is Paul's command to the women in the church of Corinth to be silent in public worship (1 Cor. 14:34, 35). It can be shown that the worship services of the church in Corinth were being interrupted by over-enthusiastic glossolalists, and the probability is that most of these were women prophets. Yet Paul did not intend to issue a universal command prohibiting women in all times and places from ever speaking publicly in the church. This is evidenced by the fact that on other occasions Paul permits and even encourages women to assume positions of spiritual leadership, including giving public testimony in the church.[36]

Prophetic counsel, as opposed to idealistic preaching, is concrete and specific. But for that very reason it often calls people into a situation entailing a compromise with ethical ideals. Sometimes we have to give up the values we cherish in order to follow Christ into the darkness. Our mandate is to incarnate the gospel imperatives in the cultural situation, but the more specific our directives become, the more likely they are to involve us in compromise and moral ambiguity.

Yet compromise can take one of two forms. It can be a "creative compromise" in which we willingly forego ethical purity in order to be faithful to our mission of being witnesses and ambassadors of Jesus Christ.[37] Or it can be a destructive compromise, which entails the sacrifice of what is essential in the gospel in order to gain a hearing from the world. It can be "the faithful compromise of obedience seeking to be relevant to the world" or "the fruitless disobedience of compromise with the world."[38] The first is motivated out of love and concern for the will of God; the second is dictated by opportunism or by cowardice (or sometimes both).

A creative compromise involves following Christ into the dereliction and turpitude of the world and thereby losing our innocence but possibly gaining in moral stature. Many of the Christians in Nazi-occupied Europe were confronted with the dilemma of telling the truth to their Nazi interrogators or hiding the Jews. A great number of pastors urged their congregations to tell a lie for the sake of preventing the murder of the Jews. A moral principle was thus sacrificed out of faithfulness to the divine imperative.[39]

Middle principles or prophetic admonitions point to and convey the general will of God in a particular cultural context. Yet the concrete will of God for a person's life must be discerned by everyone individually. Sometimes this will conflict with the prophetic affirmations of the church. It may also involve us in an ever greater degree of moral ambiguity. The higher the degree of relevance, the greater the probability for compromise. An absolute right sometimes entails relative wrongs. An ethical decision may not be humanly justified, but it may nevertheless be divinely commanded.

Abraham's sacrifice of his son Isaac involved what Kierkegaard called "the teleological suspension of the ethical," but such an example can never be made into a guiding principle by the church, since it would appear to countenance a practice that contradicts the accumulated wisdom of the church through the ages. Yet this does not mean that this story has no continuing theological relevance or significance. On the contrary, it can be used by the church for instructional purposes once it is seen in the light of the whole counsel of God, revealed most fully in the life, death, and resurrection of Jesus Christ.[40]

In evangelical theology, we are justified not by human wisdom, not even by laudable motivations, but only by the blood of Christ. Edward Leroy Long rightly observes: "Casuistic choice is between ethical grays, compromises, and ambiguous alternatives. God accepts choices made within this pattern as the reasonable sacrifice of faith. His redemptive power, not the virtue and cleverness of human works, heals the breach between human effort and divine demands."[41] Yet how singularly unpalatable this sounds to generations nurtured on possibility thinking and the do-it-yourself syndrome.

Because of the need for specificity and cultural relevance, the law of God must be expressed in mediating principles or what might be better called prophetic imperatives. It was so in the past, and it must be in our time. We need prophetic interpretations that are in accord with the basic intent of the commandments of God and the Sermon on the Mount. These prophetic affirmations cannot be universalized or absolutized, but they still indicate or express the will of God for a particular people in a given cultural context. They should be seen as God's Word to his church in a given time and place, not just as God's Word to a particular individual. Those who hear the Word of God and act upon it comprise the remnant of true believers, which is not identical with but which resides within the institutional church. They are bona fide servants of God and not simply instruments of his providential will.

The ethics of casuistry I uphold can be described as an ethics of responsibility, or still better as an ethics of obedience. Such an ethics is quite different from an ethics of prudential calculation. It is not our clever assessment of motives and consequences that determines the rightness of an action but fidelity to the divine commandment (cf. Prov. 3:1–2, 5–6).

Reinhold Niebuhr's ethics, which is set against the older casuistry, has also been called an ethics of responsibility. Yet despite his criticisms of casuistry, Niebuhr does acknowledge the right of the church to construct approximate or concrete norms. Unlike Niebuhr and John Bennett, I propose norms derived not from the universal wisdom of the race but from a wrestling with Scripture and the wisdom of church tradition. Bennett appeals to such general criteria as justice, freedom, openness to truth, and concern for human welfare, as well as to middle axioms.[42] I believe that in the last analysis our ethical decision must be based not on political expedience or sociological wisdom but only on the divine commandment, the unity of the gospel and the law, which we discern in Holy Scripture. Sociology can be a tool but never a guide or norm in determining how the ethical issue is to be understood and resolved. We can draw upon sociological wisdom, but we must never let it be a criterion for ethics or religion.

Casuistry in the evangelical sense is not trying to arrive at a Christian consensus but trying to discover the will of God for a particular situation. It involves striving to hear the Word of God to the church in our day. Some hear and some close their ears. My position, it seems to me, is still in basic accord with Barth's. Though critical of legalistic casuistry, he nonetheless acknowledged: "There is a practical casuistry, an active casuistry, the casuistry of the prophetic *ethos*. It consists in the unavoidable venture . . . of understanding God's concrete specific command here and now."[43] Barth did not develop this theme, but he opened the door to the kind of delineation presented in this chapter.

An ethics of casuistry deals with relativities as well as absolutes. The final norm cannot be grasped except when it is expressed in relative terms. We must never confuse the relative formulation with the absolute imperative, but at the same time we must never appeal to the absolute directly as though relative articulations had no relevance or authority.

Evangelical casuistry calls the Christian into involvement in the conflicts of the world, and as a result our hands may well become stained. Some well-meaning Christians have therefore advocated withdrawal from the cultural arena into citadels of righteousness where a high standard of morality can be maintained without undue cultural contamination.[44] Despite its obvious attractions, such a strategy constitutes a lost opportunity. While culture is the arena where compromise with the ultimate ideal is inevitable, it is also the medium in which Christian values can be manifested. It is the battleground where the claims and imperatives of faith need to be fought for and carried forward. The Christian ethic calls us to make our stand not outside human culture but precisely in its midst, for Jesus Christ is Lord of every area of life, and his will is that all should bow down before him and acknowledge him as Lord and Savior of the nations (Ps. 86:9; Isa. 66:18, 19; Phil. 2:10, 11; Eph. 1:9, 10).

Because the divine commandment can never be identified with or reduced to any mediating principle that is at the disposal of human reason, we can speak of an ethics beyond casuistry, one that directs us to the living God himself and not to an ethical calculus (as we see in Fletcher). We must also uphold a faith beyond ethics, for the ethical command is not the last word of faith. The last word is "Behold, I make all things new" (Rev. 21:5). Ethics concerns the penultimate realm, the issues of land, peace, and bread (Lenin), but faith points us toward the ultimate—the last judgment, salvation, the new heaven, and the new earth. Ethics is fulfilled in faith, just as faith is manifested and demonstrated in a life of costly discipleship.

Toward an Ethics of the Law and Gospel

In forging a new theological ethic, we need to steer clear of moral relativism on the one hand and legalism and rigorism on the other.

Jesus cautioned his hearers against the leaven of the Pharisees and Sadducees (Matt. 16:6), but he also announced his intention to fulfill the law, not to abolish it (Matt. 5:17). He criticized the Pharisees not for zealously upholding the law but for putting their own teachings in the place of God's commandment (Mark 7:7-9). They lacked the spirit of love.

In accord with the biblical witness, I contend that love should be united with law. Law is still a criterion, but it is law illumined by the gospel and then applied to the situation. The cultural situation is the field of moral action, but the norm is derived not from the situation but from the Spirit in union with the Word. Moral values are based not on human needs (as in Harvey Cox) but on the revelation of God as attested in Holy Scripture. It is in the light of revelation that we know what our real needs are.

Fletcher seems to hold that love is a norm readily available, at least to people of faith. Yet Proverbs reminds us that what may appear to be the loving or right action may very well end as "the way to death" (14:12 NEB). Fletcher equates agape with the will of God. I believe (with Harmon Smith) that it should be seen more concretely as obedience to the will of God in the service of our neighbor. Contrary to what Fletcher says, love is not self-contained or self-explanatory. It gains its direction and content from the commandments of God.

Fletcher argues that adherence to principles conflicts with loyalty to the gospel. This may be true in some cases, but may not principles be employed in the service of the gospel? May not rules serve as well as impede the gospel? Fletcher says that we are to bring to the situation the spirit of love working in partnership with reason, which then enables us to assess the consequences and goals of any given act.

In situation ethics, people are always free to choose the loving act that will contribute to the happiness of their neighbor. In evangelical ethics, on the contrary, people are frequently faced only with possibilities tainted by sin, and no matter what they do, they fall short of the ideal of love. The *best* act open to people in a given situation is not necessarily a *loving* act. To kill someone, for example, is hardly ever a loving act, but in self-defense or in the defense of our innocent neighbor, it may be necessary.

Such an act, from my perspective, can never be a source of satisfaction. Qualms will always linger. Fletcher, however, believes that we can discard even time-honored principles with a good conscience. Guilt has no place in his ethical system. But Scripture tells us that in every ethical decision we fall short of the perfect will of God, and therefore, we should have guilt as well as sorrow. This means that our dependence must be on the free mercy and grace of God. We must never take pride in human ingenuity for resolving the discords and antinomies of life. In seeking to know the will of God for a given situation, our primary recourse is prayer, an element not suprisingly missing in Fletcher.

I hold that Christ in Scripture, not love, is the infallible norm for ethical action. It is Christ who interprets the law. He shows us what true love is and also which means are the best available for applying the claims of love to the concrete situation. Love is not the criterion but the method. The regulatory criterion is God's self-revelation in Jesus Christ attested in Holy Scripture and elucidated in church tradition.

I heartily concur with Hauerwas's trenchant criticism of situation ethics: "To appeal to love is but to blur the pain and the glory of living morally in this life. The credibility of Christians is hurt not by their failure of good will, but by their refusal to face the reality that even good will cannot act without hurting. The greatest enemy of the Christian life is not self-interest, but sentimentality."[45]

Our choice today is clear. On the one hand, we have moral pluralism and relativism, in which, as one proponent puts it, "it is up to modern man to choose a morality for himself" that "is at once more moral than any single morality, and more inclusive than any one system. This means that modern man must be something of an eclectic and a syncretist, willing to recognize the validity of many diverse approaches to morality."[46] On the other hand, we have a biblical morality based on the law and gospel, which utterly rejects such a smorgasbord mentality.

There is no revealed morality, but there is a divine commandment that is revealed. Morality is a human response to the commandment of God. Therefore morality as such is always ambiguous, but its ground and goal are culturally transcendent.

The law of God as we find this in Scripture is not overthrown by faith, but on the contrary upheld and confirmed (Rom. 3:31). At the same time, we uphold the law imperfectly (Rom. 7), and this is why even our well-meaning actions need to be justified by the grace of God.

Where laws conflict, one must act in the service of Christ with fear and trembling. We cannot act with a clear conscience, as Fletcher claims, for sometimes we have to choose the bad over the worse. So at best we will have a guilty or uneasy conscience even when we are trying to be faithful to the imperatives of the gospel. We always fall short of the highest to which God calls us, even though we follow what we believe to be his will in a specific situation. The perfectly good or loving act is not always possible for us. Paul Ricoeur has referred to an "ethics of distress" in which no conventional ethical norms can be applied. I would rather say that norms are utilized but sometimes transcended out of fidelity to the gospel. Christ does not direct us to the pathway of evil, but he guides us through evil to greater good.

Principles versus Commandments

Such a dynamic relationship with our Lord cannot be subsumed under the category of "principles." For this, among other reasons, evangelical theology in the Reformation tradition places the accent on commandments rather than on principles. Yet the role of principles is reinterpreted in such a way that it is not totally negated but relegated to a subsidiary place.

Principles are related to the divine essence, commandments to the sovereign will of God. In scholastic thought the essence of a thing is its nature considered independently of its existence. This means that it would then be possible to appeal to eternal ideas or abstract truths independent of the will of the living God (which has happened in idealistic philosophy).[47] Principles are eternal truths capable of being discovered by the mind. Commandments are existential truths revealed by God to the whole person.

A *principle*, according to standard definitions, has three main meanings: a basic truth or assumption, a rule or standard for behavior, and a fixed or predetermined policy or mode of action.[48] Where the reference is to ethics, evangelical theology could accept the second definition without reservations but would have some difficulty with the first and much with the third. It views with suspicion any claim to an absolute or universal moral truth, especially when this claim is rooted in human knowledge or reason. In evangelical theology, principles must always be seen as directives given by God or by the church, not as universal truths inherent in the mind or capable of being discovered by the mind. With regard to the third definition, evangelical theology of the kind I uphold opposes any fixed or predetermined policy or unalterable formula on the grounds that these limit the freedom of God and subvert the biblical command to wait on God constantly for his guidance and direction.

Casuistic ethics in the evangelical sense begins not with eternal principles or abiding values but with God's word. It then seeks to relate this to concrete cases rather than vice versa. Our decision can be tested by its fruits, but it cannot be based on its possible fruits. Here we have principles in the context of prophetic casuistry as opposed to rationalistic ethics.

Against philosophical actualism, I maintain that the conception of the good in the mind of divinity is prior to the event of the good in human history.[49] Yet against rationalistic idealism, I deny that there is an idea of the good independent of the will of God.[50] The source of the good lies not in an idea in the mind of God but in the living God himself who embodies and personifies the good. He wills the good because his nature is good, not because his thoughts conform to the idea of the good. He thinks good thoughts because he is God; he is not God because he thinks good thoughts. Just as his will is in accord with his nature, so his nature in turn reflects his will.[51]

While God's will is surely congruous with his hidden wisdom, God is nevertheless not reducible to what he thinks (as in Aristotle), for his essence is in the unity of his will and thought. The God of the Bible is not a static good but active and dynamic will. Yet God wills what he essentially is, and this means that his will is at the same time the fount of all wisdom. To speak of the will and the wisdom of God are two ways of describing the same reality.[52] God eternally wills the good, and this is why the good is ultimately rooted in his will or in his being as will suffused by wisdom. He eternally wills to be, just as he eternally wills to love. He is being in becoming, not a static, immobile being. He is always God in action, not God as an eternal principle or transcendent ideal.

God's commandment is rooted in the constitution of God's nature as love and holiness. It is a word that always includes the promise of redemption, just as his word of promise encompasses his command. This word from God signifies the unity of his will and wisdom, his commanding and his truth. It is ever the same and yet always new. It necessarily reflects God's unalterable will and purpose for humanity, yet always addresses a concrete moral situation.

There is both universality and particularity in the divine commandment. Codified moral law in the Judeo-Christian tradition is based on the divine commandment, but there is always something of the relative in moral law, whereas the divine commandment is absolute. Nonresistance to evil, for example, is not a universal principle that holds true for all situations, but it is an ethical ideal that pertains to some, but not all, situations. It can be shown to have its origin in a divine commandment given in the context of the preaching of Jesus to his disciples concerning the new life in the kingdom of God (Matt. 5:38–42). That it is not a general principle, however, is made clear by the fact that

Jesus took up a whip and drove the money changers out of the temple (John 2:15). The law of nonresistance is a criterion that enables us to understand the divine commandment, that prepares us to hear this commandment in the situation in which we find ourselves.

Our indefeasible criterion in ethics is not the law understood as the ordinances of God objectified in the precepts of the tradition but rather "the law of the Spirit of life in Christ Jesus" (Rom. 8:2). The ground for ethical action is the living Word of God, addressed to us through the Bible and through church tradition but whose directives always contain something new, disturbing, sometimes even shocking. Those who absolutize the principles of the past are really looking for a security blanket to shelter them from the hard decisions of life. By this means they avoid taking up the cross in lowly discipleship and following Christ wherever he might lead us.

Hidebound traditionalists do not have to go through the agony of ethical decision making. They glibly believe that there are "clear and distinct" answers to all ethical problems. No ethical issue defies a rational resolution. People of faith, on the other hand, recognize that in many cases no moral principle is directly applicable, that one must nevertheless heed the call of Christ and go forward confident in the knowledge that our feeble efforts to obey are covered by the blood of Christ and that the validity of our obedience will be made clear by the fruits of the Spirit of Christ in our lives.

Notes

1. Joseph Fletcher, *Situation Ethics: The New Morality* (Philadelphia: Westminster, 1966).
2. William Lazareth, *The Bulletin: Moravian Theological Seminary* (Fall 1968), p. 8.
3. Barth, *Church Dogmatics*, III, 4, p. 12.
4. Karl Barth, *Against the Stream*, trans. Stanley Godman and E. M. Delacour (London: SCM Press, 1954), p. 114.
5. Barth, *Church Dogmatics* III, 4, pp. 420, 421.
6. Ibid., p. 16.
7. Lecture to the Karl Barth Society, Elmhurst College, Elmhurst, Ill., Oct. 13, 1978. See also James M. Gustafson, *Protestant and Roman Catholic Ethics* (Chicago: University of Chicago Press, 1978), pp. 41–42.
8. For a further discussion of Barth's method in theological ethics, see chap. 7, pp. 117–21.
9. Paul Lehmann, *Ethics in a Christian Context* (New York: Harper & Row, 1963).
10. Emil Brunner, *The Divine Imperative*, trans. Olive Wyon (Philadelphia: Westminster, 1947).
11. Bonhoeffer, *Ethics*, p. 277.
12. Ibid., p. 38.
13. Ibid., p. 281.
14. Dietrich Bonhoeffer, *Gesammelte Schriften* I (Munich: Kaiser Verlag, 1958), p. 358.
15. Bonhoeffer, *Ethics*, p. 69.
16. Dietrich Bonhoeffer, *The Cost of Discipleship*, trans. R. H. Fuller (London: SCM Press, 1959), p. 49.

17. Ellul, *To Will & to Do*, p. 302.
18. Ibid., p. 209.
19. See Robert Fitch, *The Decline and Fall of Sex* (New York: Harcourt Brace, 1957).
20. Robert Fitch, *Of Love and of Suffering* (Philadelphia: Westminster, 1970), pp. 33, 34.
21. See Paul Ramsey, *Deeds and Rules in Christian Ethics* (New York: Charles Scribner's Sons, 1967).
22. Paul Ramsey, *Fabricated Man* (New Haven: Yale University Press, 1970), p. 30.
23. James Gustafson also places Niebuhr in this category. See Gustafson, "Context versus Principles," *Harvard Theological Review* 58, no. 2 (April 1965): pp. 186–88.
24. Carl F. H. Henry, *Christian Personal Ethics* (Grand Rapids: Eerdmans, 1957), p. 357.
25. Ibid., p. 375.
26. Ibid., p. 301.
27. Ibid.
28. Norman Geisler, *Options in Contemporary Christian Ethics* (Grand Rapids: Baker, 1981), p. 67.
29. Lewis B. Smedes, *Mere Morality* (Grand Rapids: Eerdmans, 1983), p. 10.
30. Ibid., p. 12.
31. The elements of ecstasy and spontaneity in agape love are underplayed by Smedes, whereas the rationality of love is highlighted.
32. Edward Leroy Long, *Conscience and Compromise* (Philadelphia: Westminster, 1954), p. 34. Long's criticisms pertain mainly to the existentialist side of neo-orthodoxy. When Barth embarked on his *Church Dogmatics*, he moved away from existentialism, assigning the Scriptures a more important role in determining spiritual and ethical norms.
33. My position also approaches that of Edward Leroy Long, who defends the principle of a Protestant casuistry and the validity of middle principles. Yet Long is not Christocentric enough in my estimation. His norm is the principle of love or the law of love, not God's self-revelation in Jesus Christ, which makes clear that the living God of the Bible is not only love but also majesty and holiness.
34. Fletcher, *Situation Ethics*, p. 32.
35. We are here confronted with the paradox that the truly prophetic declaration, which mediates and embodies God's commandment, is both absolute and relative. It is absolute in the sense that it is absolutely binding on all for whom it is intended. But it is relative in that it pertains to a particular situation and does not necessarily hold true for all times and places.
36. See Donald G. Bloesch, *Is the Bible Sexist?* (Westchester, Ill.: Crossway Books, 1982), pp. 43–46.
37. On Troeltsch's understanding of the "creative compromise" see Ernst Troeltsch, *Christian Thought: Its History and Application* (New York: Meridian Books, 1957), pp. 89–91, 130–31. See also Benjamin A. Reist, *Toward a Theology of Involvement* (Philadelphia: Westminster, 1966), pp. 156–68. Troeltsch anticipated a similar emphasis in Reinhold Niebuhr.
38. Long, *Conscience and Compromise*, p. 163.
39. Augustine and Kant regarded the command against lying as absolutely binding and pertaining to all cases. For a lucid discussion of their positions see Norman Geisler, *Options in Contemporary Christian Ethics*, pp. 44–51. Ethical rigorists often appeal to Ecclesiasticus 7:13: "Refuse ever to tell a lie; it is a habit from which no good comes" (NEB) cf. Lev. 19:11; Ps. 101:7; Prov. 6:17; 12:19; 17:20).
40. See chap. 11, note 25.
41. Long, *Conscience and Compromise*, p. 161.
42. See John Bennett et al, *Storm over Ethics* (Philadelphia: United Church Press, 1967), pp. 15–18.
43. Barth, *Church Dogmatics* III, 4, p. 9.
44. This is the traditional strategy of monasticism, both Christian and non-Christian, though many monastics felt called to return to the world after having been fortified by a period of conventual enclosure.

45. Stanley Hauerwas, *Vision and Virtue* (Notre Dame, Ind.: University of Notre Dame Press, 1981), p. 119.
46. Brooks R. Walker, *The New Immorality* (New York: Doubleday, 1968), p. 220.
47. Horace Bushnell, who was greatly influenced by philosophical idealism, could even portray God as being under the principle or law of vicarious love. God does not impose this principle upon us, but "it is with him as an eternal, necessary, immutable law, existing in logical order before his will, and commanding, in the right of its own excellence, his will and life." *The Vicarious Sacrifice* (New York: Charles Scribner, 1866), p. 308.
48. *The American Heritage Dictionary*, 2d college ed. (Boston: Houghton Mifflin Co., 1982).
49. By actualism or activism (I am using these terms synonymously) I mean any theory that holds to the metaphysical priority of act over being, of event over idea. For example, Karl Barth in his dialectical phase could describe God as the "coming" rather than the "existing" deity.

   In recent times a metaphysics of action has been associated with such thinkers as Maurice Blondel; Rudolf Eucken; Giovanni Gentile, the philosopher of Italian fascism; M. de Unamuno and J. Ortega y Gasset, Spanish existentialists; D. Rudolf Bultmann; and the early Karl Barth. See John Macquarrie, *Twentieth-Century Religious Thought* (New York: Harper & Row, 1963), pp. 60, 130, 169, 173–4, 199–202; Dagobert D. Runes, ed., *Dictionary of Philosophy* (Totowa, N.J.: Littlefield, Adams & Co., 1962), pp. 4, 5, 100; Michele Federico Sciacca, *Philosophical Trends in the Contemporary World*, trans. Attilio Salerno (Notre Dame, Ind.: University of Notre Dame Press, 1964), pp. 36–62; 116–22; and Hans Urs von Balthasar, *The Theology of Karl Barth*, trans. John Drury (New York: Holt, Rinehart & Winston, 1971), pp. 171–74. For a perceptive critique of both the actualism of the theology of crisis and the ontologism (theorizing that revolves about being in itself) of traditional Catholic thought, see Dietrich Bonhoeffer, *Act and Being*, trans. Bernard Noble (New York: Octagon Books, 1983). Bonhoeffer makes a valiant attempt to overcome the polarity between a metaphysics of act and one of being.

   Closely related to actualism is voluntarism, which holds that the primary stuff of the universe is blind, arbitrary (sometimes purposive) will or infinite creative activity. We find this orientation in Fichte, who contended that being is not the cause of doing but being is brought forth for the sake of doing. See Wilhelm Windelband, *A History of Philosophy*, trans. James H. Tufts (New York: Harper & Row, 1958), p. 594. It is also present in Schelling, who postulated a dark infinite striving at the heart of reality; in Schopenhauer, who depicted the ultimately real as a blind will to live; and in Nietzsche, who viewed the will to power as the all-embracing principle in nature and society. Both Fichte and Nietzsche had a discernible influence on the activist Ortega, who maintained that life, the core of reality, is action in the world—not being but doing.

   Both actualism and voluntarism are often categorized as types of idealism, since the primary reality is not matter but spirit, life, or activity. Yet because of their emphasis on will and action over intellect, they signify an important qualification of the idealistic tradition.

   My position is not to be confused with either actualism or voluntarism, for the ultimately real in biblical perspective is neither act nor will but the living God, who encompasses act and will within himself. God cannot be explained in terms of the concept of omnipotent will, but both will and omnipotence need to be reinterpreted in the light of God's self-revelation in Jesus Christ by which we come to know God as unbounded love.

50. For this reason, it is theologically more astute to speak of the affirmation of the good in the triune being of God than of an idea of the good in the mind of God (which smacks of the older idealism). The good is what God wills, not simply what God thinks.

51. One can even say that God's nature is his will to love, though this must be understood as a holy love as well as a love informed by wisdom. Because the true God

is a Trinity, it can be said that his will to love belongs to his eternal being. He coexists as a fellowship of love.

52. If we uphold the orthodox doctrine of the simplicity of God, in which God is understood to be free from any and all composition, we must then affirm the unity of his will and essence, his action and his intellect. Therefore, the mind of God is not to be seen as prior to his will, but these two symbolic concepts are simply different ways of describing the one, indivisible God, who acts with a single-minded purpose.

CHAPTER 5

Two Kinds of Righteousness

For I tell you, unless your righteousness exceeds that of the scribes and Pharisees, you will never enter the kingdom of heaven.

MATTHEW 5:20

I used to think that being nice to people and feeling nice was loving people. But it isn't. Love is the most immense unselfishness, and it is so big I've never touched it.

FLORENCE ALLSHORN

In obedience man adheres to the decalogue, and in freedom man creates new decalogues.

MARTIN LUTHER

Sacrificial love is . . . a form of love which transcends the limits of love. It is a form of love which cannot be embodied in any moral code.

REINHOLD NIEBUHR

The good that you do, no matter how ideal, is nothing but the good of the earth, in no way commensurate with the requirement of God, with that which he calls good.

JACQUES ELLUL

Two Moralities

One of the ongoing debates in contemporary theology is whether the Christian can affirm only one morality or two. In the latter case, the demands of faith are considered qualitatively different from the codes of morality of even religiously oriented cultures.

The climate today is receptive to the idea of one morality, which pertains to both church and world. In this perspective, love and justice, salvation and liberation, are practically the same. Not only liberal Protestants but also avant-garde Catholics have come to deny that there is a distinctively Christian morality beyond "generally valid natural morality."[1] For them, "human morality" and "Christian morality" are "materially identical." Natural law or natural justice is seen as the foundation of morality, and the biblical directives are regarded as simply the amplification and clarification of what is already given in nature or history.

I contend that a faith informed by the total biblical witness would have to affirm two moralities: natural goodness and kingdom righteousness. The first has a validity in its own right, but before God (*coram Deo*) it is woefully deficient. The second has its basis not in human possibilities but in the breaking into human life of a new reality. Philosophy at its best has some perception of natural goodness, whereas theology focuses on the spiritual righteousness of the kingdom of God.

Jesus made it very clear that there is a qualitative gulf between the legal righteousness of Judaic tradition and the higher righteousness of the kingdom of God. Without denying the rightful place of the first, he contended that those who take up the cross in costly discipleship are summoned to a style of life that radically transcends the righteousness of the scribes and Pharisees (Matt. 5:17–20). The lesser righteousness is not to commit adultery by union of our bodies; the greater is not to commit adultery in the heart. The lesser righteousness is not to steal; the greater is to renounce the right to reparation for wrongs suffered. The lesser is to forgive when amendment of life is evident; the greater is to forgive unconditionally. The lesser is to love those who can be expected to reciprocate in love; the greater is to love our enemies, to do good and lend, expecting nothing in return (Luke 6:35).

Jesus insisted that he had come not to overthrow the righteousness of law but instead to fulfill the law and the prophets (Matt. 5:17). He urged his followers to aspire to the higher righteousness without neglecting the duties associated with the righteousness of law (Luke 11:42; Matt. 23:23). The latter is an obstacle to spiritual growth only when we trust in it for our salvation, when we take pride in it (cf. Mark 7:8; Luke 18:9).

For the apostle Paul, the righteousness of law must always be clearly differentiated from the righteousness of faith (cf. Rom. 3:21; 9:30–33). The law is holy, righteous, and good (Rom. 7:12), yet it is incapable of making people right in the sight of God because of human sin, which corrupts our moral sensibilities. The righteousness that redeems is the righteousness of Christ, whereby, despite our sins, we are accepted in the favor of God on the basis of God's atoning work on the cross. This righteousness needs only to be received by faith, but once it is received it produces fruits of repentance in our lives, fruits that do not earn salvation but testify to a salvation already enacted on our behalf. The fruits of faith, moreover, signify a new power working within us that moves us to acts of self-sacrifice beyond the requirements of the law (cf. Rom. 12:14–21). For Paul the evangelical righteousness of the gospel does not simply fulfill the legal righteousness of Judaic tradition but overthrows it as a condition for salvation.

The basic polarity in the theology of Augustine was that between civic virtue and true virtue.[2] Civic virtue, he explained in *The City of God*, is something good in its own right, but not a sufficient ground for eternal salvation because its chief motivation is the desire for respectability and glory. True virtue, by contrast, wills everything out of love for God. This true *pietas* is the foundation for genuine order in society. Augustine nevertheless saw civic virtue as the authentic shadow and anticipation of true virtue.

Augustine perceived the radical difference between natural and supernatural morality without condemning the first. "The righteousness of the scribes and Pharisees," he said, "is that they should not kill; the righteousness of those who will enter the kingdom of God is that they should not be angry without cause."[3] Augustine recognized that the divine command sometimes challenges the moral precepts that hold society together. "When God commands something contrary to the customs or laws of a people, it must be done, even if it has never been done before."[4]

Thomas Aquinas was also emphatic that there are two moralities, though he never lost sight of the continuity between the two, as enthusiasts sometimes did. Thomas distinguished between acquired justice, which is a purely human justice, and true justice. The first is a justice that is understood and respected by the world. The second is the justice that makes us righteous in the sight of God. It is none other than the divine justification infused in us by grace.

Thomas also made a distinction between the moral and theological virtues. The first are temperance, courage, fortitude, and justice (the classical virtues of Hellenistic culture), and these have both a natural and a supernatural side. The theological virtues—faith, hope, and love—are not human possibilities at all but must be created within us by the Spirit of God.

In the sixteenth century, Martin Luther sharpened the lines between the two moralities by contending that the spiritual righteousness of the kingdom of God calls into radical question all natural wisdom, morality, and religion. It is incomprehensible to reason but available to simple faith.[5] At the same time, he saw the necessary place for a civil righteousness that is accessible to the "natural man" and that is conducive not to salvation but to the preservation of society.

Luther discovered that the righteousness of God received only by faith is qualitatively different from the righteousness of law. It is deeper and wider than all retributive justice. It is the gracious gift of God to the undeserving. He likened it to a white garment that covers our sinfulness and thereby renders us acceptable in the sight of God. It is an extrinsic righteousness imputed to us because of the merits of Jesus Christ and is to be sharply contrasted with the intrinsic righteousness that people can acquire on their own, even with the aid of grace.

Standing in the Lutheran tradition, Dietrich Bonhoeffer drew a vivid distinction between the immanent righteousness of history, which rewards and punishes people's deeds, and the eternal righteousness of God, which tries and judges their hearts.[6] The immanent righteousness of history is that people reap what they sow (Gal. 6:7–10). The eternal righteousness of God is that Christ reaps what we have sown (Col. 2:13, 14). It challenges natural wisdom by heralding a righteousness that transcends the laws of justice. According to Bonhoeffer, the "Christian message stands beyond good and evil", for otherwise the grace of God is made dependent on the measure in which humanity is able to perceive good or evil; the basis is then "laid for a claim of man upon God, and in this way God's sole power and glory would be assailed."[7]

In Bonhoeffer's view, the basis for natural morality lies in a moral awareness or moral sense, which is possessed by all people, Christians and non-Christians alike.[8] The basis for discipleship under the cross lies in the gift of grace, which comes to us through the sacrificial life and death of Jesus Christ. "The passion of Christ is the victory of divine love over the powers of evil, and therefore it is the only supportable basis for Christian obedience."[9]

Natural morality is self-defeating because it either encourages people to trust in themselves or imposes a set of rules that bind or cripple the human spirit. Bonhoeffer rejected the idea of imposing a morality from without and sought a new morality having its source in the renewal of the mind from within.[10]

This Lutheran motif reappears in Reinhold Niebuhr, but in a new way. For him, the principal polarity is between personal and group morality, love and justice. The sacrificial love of the cross is a possibility in person-to-person relationships, but justice is the norm in the area of social conflict. According to Niebuhr, collective morality never escapes moral ambiguity, and this is why he could speak of "moral man" in an "immoral society."[11] Yet personal morality is not exempt from the taint of self-interest, and only rarely can one reach the heights of self-sacrifice and forgiveness. On such occasions moral achievement must be seen paradoxically as a gift of grace, which introduces into the situation new possibilities that could not have been predicted or determined.

In the Russian Orthodox theologian Nicolas Berdyaev, we again find a keen perception of two moralities. Berdyaev described the Christian ethic as "the morality beyond morality," for it opens to people a horizon beyond the prescriptions of law.[12] In his perspective, grace makes one not merely good but also creative—compassionately creative. The "man of faith" is not so much law-abiding as "creatively free."[13] Moral action in the Christian sense is focused not on the "abstract good" but on the "concrete living person."[14] The kingdom of God cannot be reduced to a movement of social reform or a humanitarian program; instead, it should be seen as "both social and cosmic transfiguration."[15]

The Reformed theologian Jacques Ellul also approaches the moral problem in the light of the criterion of faith. His principal distinction is between the requirement of the Spirit of God and common morality. The latter is associated with maintaining social order and therefore has a relative validity. The morality the world upholds refers to penultimate things, whereas the morality God requires has to do with the last things—"the end of the ages." Because the morality of the world has as its aim the preservation of social order, it can be accepted by the Christian with qualifications.

In contrast to one side of Barth's theology, Ellul denies that Christian ethics have a universal validity.[16] Non-Christians, he says, cannot be expected to live as Christians. Jesus Christ, to be sure, is Lord of the world as well as the church, but it must not be forgotten that this is a world in revolt. The key to a new social order lies in the creation of a "new kind of man." Human justice makes use of the sword, whereas divine righteousness is the way of the cross. "All that human justice can do is to limit the evil inflicted by men on their fellowmen by coercive means."[17] Those who have been made free to embrace divine righteousness constitute the believing remnant who bear witness to a kingdom not of this world, one that contradicts the expectations and hopes of this world.

Finally, we need to consider Karl Barth's approach to this question. It is incontestable that Barth envisaged two moralities, two kinds of righteousness. In his earlier years, when he was aligned with the theology of crisis or dialectical theology, he saw human righteousness mainly in negative terms: "Human righteousness is . . . in itself an illusion: there is in this world no observable righteousness. There may, however, be a righteousness before God, a righteousness that comes from Him."[18] On other occasions he was willing to acknowledge the reality of a natural goodness that the world can perceive, but he saw it fraught with dangers: "This all-too-human goodness of ours is our sin, and it is worse and more dangerous than what we label as wicked in ourselves and others."[19]

Barth as a dialectical theologian posited an infinite qualitative difference between natural morality and the righteousness of God. Indeed, the "Kingdom of God has its beginning on the other side of the Cross, beyond all that is called 'religion' and 'life,' beyond conservatism and radicalism."[20] Consequently, the claims of the kingdom lie beyond both morality and amorality. The peace of God is wholly different from peace as the world understands it. "There is suffering and sinking, a being lost and a being rent asunder, in the peace of God."[21]

As his theology developed, however, Barth began to see the rightful place for human righteousness, though he continued to posit a qualitative disjunction between it and divine righteousness, which is pure love and mercy. Yet they cannot be divorced, for human righteousness must be informed by divine righteousness. We can only seek and pray for the righteousness of the kingdom, but we can actually contribute to human righteousness by our deeds of mercy and social action. Our human righteousness can at best correspond to divine righteousness, but it cannot advance it or extend it. It can be a witness and parable of divine righteousness, which has already been established in Jesus Christ but is yet to be revealed to the whole of creation at his second advent. Human righteousness is done out of loving solidarity with the oppressed. By the power that comes to us through an encounter with Jesus Christ, who personifies and exemplifies divine righteousness, we can join the struggle against human unrighteousness and disorder, the city of the devil. Yet because Christians still move in the sphere of human unrighteousness, they "are well advised not to make extravagant gestures nor to make too big a song about what they do."[22] At the same time, in their striving for human justice "they are in all humility righteous people—sinners, but righteous sinners."[23]

In summary, on the basis of the witness of the prophets and apostles as well as the fathers of the church, one can say that there are two kinds of morality, both having a claim to validity but neither of which should be confused. The morality of preservation or civil righteousness concerns order in society. The morality of redemption or spiritual righteousness has to do with love of God and neighbor. Whereas force pertains to the morality of preservation, the violence of love characterizes the morality of redemption. Force is rationally defensible in some situations, but it is never morally redemptive.

Civic law, it should be remembered, does not always reflect moral law. The common morality must be resisted when it becomes a cloak for immorality. Civil righteousness can only be properly understood in the light of spiritual righteousness. The criterion for human justice is the love of God revealed in Jesus Christ. This is why, as Augustine so wisely observed, only Christian states can make real progress toward a truly just social order.

The Basis for Natural Goodness

Just as human evil is a mystery, so also is human goodness. There is no doubt that some of the great philosophers have led exemplary lives. Many of these men and women have demonstrated the classical virtues of temperance, fortitude, wisdom, and justice. Confucius resonates with a major body of Western philosophical tradition when he contends that perfect virtue is comprised of courtesy, magnanimity, earnestness, sincerity, and kindness.[24] The Christian theme of vicarious identification with the oppressed appears in the American Socialist Eugene Debs:

> So long as there is a lower class, I am in it;
> While there is a criminal element, I am of it;
> While there is a soul in jail, I am not free.[25]

Yet while natural goodness wins the general approval of humankind, it is found to be woefully lacking when measured against the perfect holiness of the living God. The prophet says, "A man's whole conduct may be pure in his own eyes, but the Lord fixes a standard for the spirit of man" (Prov. 16:2 NEB). Paul reaffirms the vision of the Psalmist: "There is no one righteous, not even one; there is no one who understands, no one who seeks God" (Rom. 3:10, 11 NIV; cf. Ps. 14:1–3). Even when Christians do good works, they must be ever conscious that their goodness falls short of the perfection God demands and that their works as well as their inner being need the justification of God. This is why Barth could say, "A good work is always a work of penitence, a work that is done in that repentance and distress and with that cry for mercy."[26]

Despite the fall into sin, Scripture nevertheless makes clear that human beings continue to reflect the goodness of God. Even in our total depravity—which signifies that every part of our being is infected by sin—the glory of our origin still shines through. The *imago Dei* has not been eradicated but only defaced by sin. We are still related at the very core of our being to the God who is perfect love and perfect holiness, a God who will not let us go even in our rebellion.

In addition to our indissoluble relationship to God, which is expressed by the symbol "image of God," there is the undeniable reality of common grace, the general work of the Holy Spirit in which he preserves and upholds a lost and despairing humanity. God has not left himself without a witness among the nations (Acts 14:17), and this tells us that the work of his Spirit is not restricted to the church, though redemption is only possible through personal faith in Jesus Christ.

The insights and moral truths that philosophers stumble upon in their searchings more often than not stand in tension, if not conflict, with the basic thrust of their systems. Kant, for example, had a glimpse of the reality of radical evil within man, but he could not reconcile this insight with his Enlightenment presuppositions and was compelled finally to qualify it so that its offense was removed.[27] Nonetheless, because secular philosophers are in touch with the reality of the God whom they deny or misunderstand, they can arrive at some notions of natural justice in harmony with the biblical revelation.

Moses realized that the moral uprightness of the people of Israel would be recognized as such by pagan nations. His counsel was to keep the commandments and do them, "for that will be your wisdom and your understanding in the sight of the peoples, who, when they hear all these statutes, will say, 'Surely this great nation is a wise and understanding people' " (Deut. 4:6).

Jesus acknowledged the reality of natural goodness, though he made clear that it merited no salvific reward. Even the Gentiles, he said, loved and supported their friends and relatives (Matt. 5:46–48). Even evil people know how to give good gifts to their children (Luke 11:13). God's grace reaches outside the parameters of the elect community. Even pagans are beneficiaries of the grace of God: "He causes his sun to rise on the evil and the good, and sends rain on the righteous and the unrighteous" (Matt. 5:45 NIV; cf. Prov. 29:13).

The apostle Paul was likewise aware of the reality of a natural goodness. He declared that when Gentiles who are without the law do by nature what the law requires, they are a law unto themselves (Rom. 2:14).[28] He recognized that the rulers set over us by God "hold no terror for those who do right, but for those who do wrong" (Rom. 13:3 NIV). If we wish to be free from the fear of those in authority, then we are urged to "do what is right." Paul is very probably here thinking of a natural morality, not of the higher righteousness of the kingdom, which often sets one in conflict with governmental authority.

There are several New Testament texts in which *righteous* is practically equivalent to respectable, virtuous, honest, as these are understood in the surrounding Hellenistic culture (cf. Matt. 27:19, 24; Phil. 1:7; 4:8; Luke 12:57; 1 Pet. 2:12). Yet in these passages as in many others the tendency is for this "respectability" to be constituted "before God." This is especially evident in Acts 4:19, 2 Thessalonians 1:6, and Ephesians 6:1.

In his innovative and stimulating *Christian Commitment*, Edward John Carnell argues that we can come to a knowledge of God by virtue of our moral and spiritual environment, apart from special revelation.[29] The fact that all people have a sense of moral justice makes it possible to lead them to the higher law of consideration and then finally to the law of love. In his view, the higher laws include rather than annul the lower. Carnell's position patently conflicts with that of the Protestant Reformation, which held that because of human sin, any natural knowledge we have of God and his moral law is sufficient only to condemn us (cf. Rom. 1:20, 21). Natural goodness does not lead to redemptive righteousness because of sin in the human heart, which obfuscates our moral sensibilities and bends our will in the direction of evil. Natural goodness does not prepare the way for redemption, but it is a reminder of the reality of a holy God who has acted to redeem us in Jesus Christ.

Beyond the Prescriptions of the Law

The higher righteousness goes beyond the prescriptions of the law, even though at the same time it fulfills the spirit of the law. It contradicts code morality by its patent disregard of rules and obligations in the act of answering the cry of human anguish. It often contravenes moral convention by its generosity of spirit and its sensitivity to human need. "At certain crucial points," Barth observes, "the Bible amazes us by its remarkable indifference to our conception of good and evil."[30]

The parable of the laborers in the vineyard illustrates how the righteousness of the kingdom appears to contradict moral consensus (Matt. 20:1–16). All receive the same wages, even though some arrive late, which seems unjust. Even those who worked only one hour are still paid the same. The others complain to the householder that they have not been treated fairly. But Jesus replies to one of them: "Friend, I am doing you no wrong; did you not agree with me for a denarius? Take what belongs to you, and go; I choose to give to this last as I give to you" (vv. 13, 14).

Agape signifies the breaking in of a new reality in human life that cannot be harmonized with moral codes or legal taboos. Agape is the golden extreme that challenges moral decorum and subservience to tradition. This is why the great saints of the church have almost unanimously been condemned as moral transgressors.

Just as agape is not congruous with the spirit of moral justice, so it cannot be reconciled with paternalistic altruism. Altruism is a regard for the interests of the other. Agape is the sacrifice of one's own interests for the sake of the other. Altruism tries to raise deprived people to a higher level. Agape descends to the level of the rejected.

Natural goodness is not to be deprecated, but it is not the same as Christian obedience. It is the difference between doing one's duty and serving selflessly, abiding by the law and walking in the light, adherence to a moral code and costly discipleship under the cross. Whereas moral convention stresses the need to fulfill an obligation, Christian obedience is characterized by sacrificial love; it may even entail breaking an obligation in the name of love.

The higher righteousness means to forgive the inexcusable, not merely to forgive what can be excused. It is not only to desist from killing but to refrain from lethal words and actions. It involves not only renouncing adultery but also expunging all adulterous thoughts. Those who take up the cross and follow Christ are not content simply to be their brother's keeper, but they also seek to be their brother's brother and sister. They bless those who persecute them (Matt. 5:44; Rom. 12:14) and willingly go two miles with those who demand one mile (Matt. 5:41). To those who would rob them of their coat, they also give their cloak (Matt. 5:40; Luke 6:29). The law of Judaic tradition that demanded an eye for an eye and a tooth for a tooth is now superseded by the law of nonresistance (Matt. 5:38, 39; Luke 6:29), or the law of nonretaliation (1 Pet. 2:23).

To overcome evil with good, to bless rather than to curse one's enemies, points to the radical character of Christian love. For Confucius goodness should be repaid with goodness, but wrong must be repaid with justice. He expressly rejected love of enemies as unfair and demeaning. In Judaism hating one's enemies was more or less permissible and sometimes even expressly sanctioned. The monks of the Qumram community were told to hate "the outsiders, the sons of darkness."[31]

Natural goodness, while meriting praise in the eyes of society, is not acceptable to God because it is mixed with selfish motivations and marred by an ignorance having its roots in hardness of heart. One may have good intentions but lack the wisdom and insight that come through a deep sensitivity to human need. As the old adage says, the road to hell is paved with good intentions. God looks into the human heart and sees the evil therein (cf. Gen. 6:5; 8:21; Jer. 17:9, 10). The prophet Isaiah humbly confessed: "All our righteous acts are like filthy rags" in the sight of God (Isa. 64:6 NIV).

Those who defend the semi-Pelagian position—that people on their own can take the first steps toward the righteousness of God—often point to Acts 10, the story of Cornelius, the Roman centurion who was baptized by Peter. It was said of Cornelius that he feared God and gave alms generously. On first meeting Cornelius, Peter declares, "I perceive that God shows no partiality, but in every nation any one who fears him and does what is right is acceptable to him" (Acts 10:34, 35). Those of a semi-Pelagian bent contend that Peter was sent to Cornelius to bring him faith as a reward for his good works. A more careful reading of this story reveals that Cornelius was a God-fearer, a Gentile who had some acquaintance with the Hebrew Scriptures. He could not have been a God-fearer apart from the quickening work of the Holy Spirit that moved him to seek for the salvation promised by Jesus Christ. Cornelius was able to come to Christ because he was elected for salvation by the grace of God that goes out to undeserving sinners. He was accepted by virtue of his election in Christ, not on the basis of his own righteousness. It should be remembered, too, that Cornelius before his conversion, when he was only a seeker of salvation, had not yet obtained the forgiveness of sins, which is conditional on faith (Acts 10:43). The Holy Spirit fell on him when he heard the gospel message expounded by Peter, and he was then baptized into the body of Christ.

The motivations of even God-fearing Christians are not acceptable to God, since sin coexists with the best of intentions. This is why we are saved not by good works but only by grace. Those who have done all they are commanded to do must still confess, "We are unworthy servants; we have only done what was our duty" (Luke 17:10; cf. Matt. 20:1–16). Justice goes out to the deserving, but it is the undeserving who receive the love and grace of God.

The Christian is accepted because of the righteousness of Jesus Christ, which is imputed to all those who have faith. This righteousness is the ground and goal of the Christian life. It is an alien righteousness (Luther) that is not infused into us but covers our sinfulness. We can make contact with it by the Holy Spirit, but it always remains something outside us.[32] We can bear witness to it by the kind of lives we lead, but the righteousness of life, which is always imperfect, must never be confused with the righteousness of faith, which alone justifies the sinner.

In the power of the grace that comes to us, we can make progress toward the righteousness of Jesus Christ, but we always fall short of this goal. We can act in faith and love, but we never fulfill the demands of faith and love. We can keep the commandments, but we cannot fulfill the law. The righteousness of the kingdom can be reflected in our lives but not perfected.

The Christian life consists not so much in beneficence as in blessedness. It is more than being helpful; it is being passionately concerned. It entails more than being courteous and magnanimous; it means being compassionate. When Calvin drew upon his meager resources to provide medical care and burial expenses for the plague-stricken nephew of his friend Farel, even to the extent of selling part of his cherished library, this was an act of love far exceeding magnanimity and moral decorousness.[33] After his conversion, Francis of Assisi dedicated himself to serving the lepers whom he had hitherto scorned. On one occasion he gave a leper on the side of the road all the money he had and bent over and kissed the man on his hand, which was full of sores, thereby giving poignant testimony to the Christian's solidarity with the oppressed.[34] This surely goes beyond what justice requires.

Christian obedience is characterized not by exhibiting virtue but by radiating love. It is not do-goodism but generosity of spirit. It is compassionate daring on the basis of being loved by God. It is well doing on the basis of being well received by God. Our good works should be seen as the evidence of being blessed by God. What constitutes the Christian life is not morality (as the world understands this) but faith and its fruits.

Divine righteousness is the source and mainstay of the Christian life. It is not striving for an ethical ideal but cleaving to this righteousness that enables us to persevere and triumph over adversity. Divine righteousness is not a distributive or retributive justice but a "substitutive justice" (Ellul). It signifies the substitution of grace for nature.

Sin and Virtue

Between evangelical and legalistic religion, there is an ineradicable gulf. The first is grounded in the gospel of redeeming love (*agape*); the second is oriented about law (*nomos*). The disparity between the two becomes apparent when we examine the way in which they understand sin. In legalistic religion, sin is a violation of a moral taboo, or the breaking of a moral code. In evangelical religion, on the other hand, sin means wounding the heart of God. It is not so much a trangression of law as a violation of trust. It is an offense not so much against moral precepts as against love. The core of sin is not falling short of the moral ideal but the isolating and aggrandizing of the self, which the Bible calls "hardness of heart." In the biblical view, sin is a corporate state of alienation from God, not just an act of wrongdoing. The opposite of sin in legalistic religion is virtue; in evangelical religion, it is faith.

On the subject of virtue, we can also discern some notable differences. Virtue in Hellenistic religion and philosophy signifies a meritorious quality that contributes to wholeness and uprightness in character. It is a habitual form of conduct that enables one to realize one's better or nobler self. It is strength of character that leads to courageous deeds. It is conformity in disposition or conduct to the standard of the right.

Evangelical Christianity does not denigrate the life of virtue, but it insists that virtue is not enough. Virtue and knowledge are to be fulfilled in love (2 Pet. 1:5–7), and love (agape) is something that happens to us before it is exercised by us. When Christians love God, Barth says, "the work of the Spirit is being done, because this love happens without and against them and only so for them and really and properly to them. So it becomes their own love, poured out in their hearts, the love of their own hearts, that is why it can subsequently be said that no one and nothing can separate them from it."[35]

As Christians we are called not simply to a life of virtue but to a life that transcends virtue. A virtuous life is a possibility for the "natural man" but Christian obedience is life in the Spirit, that which transcends and defies the humanly possible. It is no accident that evangelical Christianity speaks more of the fruits or graces of the Spirit than of human virtues. When Catherine of Genoa kissed the lips of a victim of the plague in the hospital where she ministered, she was not acting virtuously but out of the folly of love, willingly jeopardizing her life and ministry by exposing herself to a contagious and virtually fatal disease.

It is possible to speak of Christian virtue but always as something incomplete and deficient. The hope of the Christian lies not in the cultivation of virtue but in the gracious condescension of the living God to the level of sin. Our hope is anchored in the ground and source of all virtue—Jesus Christ.

Stoicism was noted for its marked emphasis on the life of virtue, which supposedly enabled people to endure in a time when the foundations of civilization were being shaken and even shattered. It gave the reflective spirits of the world the courage to face and to overcome adversity. Barth ably shows the disparity between this kind of virtue and the grace that fortifies the Christian: "Stoic detachment from life with people in the world has most decidedly never been the kind of blessing demanded of a Christian. He can only bless if he counters his persecution by particularly living with the people in the world, rejoicing with them, weeping with them, being human with them."[36]

Biblical Christianity is adamant that the striving for holiness manifested in the lives of the saints in biblical and catholic tradition cannot be meshed with the life of virtue acclaimed by the great philosophers through the ages. Saints, unlike sages, place their trust not in reason or virtue but in the blood of Christ, which exposes our virtues as "splendid vices" (Augustine) and justifies us even while we still remain in sin. Christians are given a new horizon of freedom and meaning that places them at odds with the values the world holds dear. "Who stands his ground?," asks Bonhoeffer. "Only the man whose ultimate criterion is not in his reason, his principles, his conscience, his freedom or his virtue, but who is ready to sacrifice all these things when he is called to obedient and responsible action in faith and exclusive allegiance to God."[37]

The suffering of the saint is not the same as that of the public hero, who is admired and applauded by the world for feats of courage and acts of self-sacrifice. Bonhoeffer, has these pertinent words of wisdom: "It is infinitely easier to suffer as public heroes than to suffer apart and in ignominy. It is infinitely easier to suffer physical death than to endure spiritual suffering. Christ suffered as a free man alone, apart and in ignominy, in body and in spirit, and since that day many Christians have suffered with him."[38]

Social Justice and Kingdom Righteousness

One of the running debates in contemporary theology has to do with the relation of social justice to the higher righteousness of the kingdom of God. There is an integral relationship, but there must be no confusion between the two. Social justice is doing one's duty in the social realm; kingdom righteousness is going beyond the call of duty. The first is concerned with safeguarding the rights of all, especially the poor; the second calls people to walk in the light of the gospel of redemption. The first advocates freedom and equality in the economic and political areas of life; the second heralds the liberty of the children of God. In a society ruled by the norms of justice, we treat one another as equals. But in the kingdom of God we embrace one another as brothers and sisters in Christ. The Christian faith commends not mere service but service united with spiritual care. It upholds not simply a helping hand but a sacrificial spirit. Agape is not paternalistic altruism but identification with the plight of our fellow human beings in suffering love.

Social justice should be regarded as a sign and witness of kingdom righteousness. It may also be a stepping-stone to this higher righteousness. That is to say, it may create a thirst in people for the holiness and goodness of God.

Jesus fed the hungry, but it appears that his main purpose was to focus the attention of his hearers on God's great generosity to sinners (John 6). He healed the sick primarily for the same reason, hoping to stir up faith in the living God. The sight of the man born blind was restored by Jesus as a sign of the dawning of the new age (John 9). This was also the case with the healing of the ten lepers, though only one was awakened to faith in the Redeemer (Luke 17:11–19).

Both humanitarian works of mercy and works of social reform are at best approximations of kingdom righteousness. If the church identified itself with the cause of social justice, this might indeed make people more receptive to the kingdom message. Social justice is a partial fulfillment of the law of God; the eschatological kingdom is the perfect fulfillment of the teachings of the law. Social justice is related to the law of God; the righteousness of the kingdom is related to the gospel. Social justice is conducive to human happiness; Christian obedience brings blessedness—contagious, radiant joy.

A just society will give people the freedom and time to be attentive to spiritual values. But it may also open the door to false values. Seven more demons can enter the soul of a nation after the demon of poverty is exorcised (cf. Matt. 12:43–45).

Social justice is to be seen as a fruit and consequence of the righteousness of the kingdom which already grips the faithful and impels them to action. The kingdom is already in our midst, for the risen Christ dwells among us (cf. Luke 17:21); it is up to us to recognize this fact and then dedicate ourselves to the service of the needy and forsaken as a token of our gratitude for God's immeasurable gift of redemption.

Our Lord made abundantly clear that the kingdom of God is both a gift and a task, but the former has priority. The kingdom is likened to a treasure already present, though hidden in a field (Matt. 13:44), to a costly pearl waiting for its buyer (Matt. 13:45–46), to a net already cast (Matt. 13:47–48), to seed already sown (Matt. 13:3–8, 18–23). We cannot bring in the kingdom, but we can lay hold of its reality by renouncing all earthly attachments and dedicating ourselves wholly to its service (Luke 9:60–62; 14:26–33; Matt. 10:37–38). We cannot create the treasure or the costly pearl, but we can tell others where they may be found.

Social justice is a fruit of faith and love and a means to faith and love. It is a necessary fruit, though not a necessary means, since people in poverty can find the grace of God just as readily (and sometimes more so) as people in comfortable circumstances. At the same time, the cares that cripple people in poverty prove to be obstacles to the right hearing of the message of the kingdom. It is not only riches but also poverty that can be an impediment to the service of the kingdom of God.

Progress toward social justice must never be confused with the coming of the kingdom. The kingdom of God is present only where people enter into the higher righteousness, the fellowship of sacrificial love (the *koinonia*).

In fulfilling the great commission of our Lord, we should avoid both the spiritualization of the gospel (reducing it to spiritual values or moral principles) and its politicalization (confusing it with a program for social change). As the church confronts the burning social and moral issues of the day, it must strive to preach the whole counsel of God, and therefore a gospel that will have political relevance. But the message itself should be centered on God's gracious act of reconciliation in Jesus Christ, whereby the sin and guilt of the world are taken away for all those who repent and believe.

Notes

1. See Richard A. McCormick, "Notes on Moral Theology," *Theological Studies* 32, no. 1 (March 1971): pp. 71–78; and Leonardo Boff, *Jesus Christ Liberator* (Maryknoll, N.Y.: Orbis, 1978), pp. 82–83.
2. Augustine's typology is similar to the distinction that Jonathan Edwards draws between natural virtue and true virtue. For Edwards the "truly virtuous mind, being as it were under the sovereign dominion of love to God, above all things, seeks the glory of God." *The Nature of True Virtue* (Ann Arbor, Mich.: University of Michigan Press, 1960), p. 25. Like Augustine, Edwards believed that the natural virtues were basically forms of illegitimate self-love.
3. *The Preaching of Augustine*, ed. Jaroslav Pelikan (Philadelphia: Fortress, 1973), p. 23.

4. *The Confessions of St. Augustine*, trans. John Ryan (New York: Doubleday, 1960), p. 87.
5. Cf. "All the works of God are unsearchable and unspeakable, no human sense can find them out; faith only takes hold of them without human power or aid." *The Table Talk of Martin Luther*, ed. Thomas S. Kepler (New York: World Publishing Co., 1952), p. 39.
6. Dietrich Bonhoeffer, *Prisoner for God*, ed. Eberhard Bethge, trans. Reginald Fuller (New York: Macmillan Co., 1954), p. 21.
7. Dietrich Bonhoeffer, *No Rusty Swords*, trans. Edwin H. Robertson and John Bowden (New York: Harper & Row, 1965), p. 41.
8. Robin Lovin maintains with some cogency that Bonhoeffer struck a position between Barth and Brunner, preserving the distinction between moral righteousness and Christian obedience (stressed by Barth) but with Brunner "giving moral righteousness a foundation in reality and a theological significance." *Christian Faith and Public Choices*, p. 152.
9. Dietrich Bonhoeffer, *The Cost of Discipleship*, p. 130.
10. See Dietrich Bonhoeffer, *Christ the Center*, trans. John Bowden, intro. Edwin H. Robertson (New York: Harper & Row, 1966), p. 14.
11. See Reinhold Niebuhr, *Moral Man and Immoral Society* (New York: Charles Scribner's Sons, 1932).
12. For Berdyaev, "the morality of the Gospel is paradoxical and contrary to the morality of our world even at its highest. . . . The Gospel morality is not a norm or a law because it is the morality of paradise and is beyond our good and evil, beyond our legalistic distinctions between good and evil." Nicolas Berdyaev, *The Destiny of Man*, 3rd ed., trans. Natalie Duddington (London: Geoffrey Bles, 1948), p. 123.
13. Nicolas Berdyaev, *Truth and Revelation*, trans. R. M. French (New York: Collier, 1962), p. 155.
14. Berdyaev, *Destiny of Man*, p. 106.
15. Berdyaev, *Truth and Revelation*, p. 128.
16. See Ellul, *To Will & to Do*.
17. Jacques Ellul, *The Theological Foundation of Law*, trans. Marguerite Wieser (New York: Seabury, 1960), p. 133. He is here quoting approvingly from Suzanne de Diétrich's "*Le fondement biblique du Droit*," in *Le Sémeur* (May 1945).
18. Karl Barth, *The Epistle to the Romans*, trans. (from sixth ed.) Edwyn C. Hoskyns (1933; reprint, New York: Oxford University Press, 1975), p. 75.
19. Karl Barth, *Ethics*, ed. Dietrich Braun, trans. G. W. Bromiley (New York: Seabury, 1981), p. 339.
20. Barth, *Epistle to the Romans*, p. 159.
21. Quoted in Malcolm Boyd, "A Personal Half-Century," *Christian Century* 91, no. 22 (June 5, 1974): p. 611.
22. Karl Barth, *The Christian Life*, trans. G. W. Bromiley (Grand Rapids: Eerdmans, 1981), p. 267.
23. Ibid.
24. *The Analects or the Conversations of Confucius with His Disciples*, trans. William Edward Soothill (London: Oxford University Press, 1937), 17, 6: p. 190.
25. Cited in Daniel Day Williams, *The Spirit and the Forms of Love* (New York: Harper & Row, 1968), p. 261. Though profoundly influenced by Christianity, Debs was a philosophical deist. It should be noted that he identified with the down-and-outs but not with the up-and-outs. See Harold W. Currie, *Eugene V. Debs* (Boston: Twayne Publishers, 1976), pp. 95–128.
26. Barth, *Ethics*, p. 109.
27. Despite his shrewd insight into the innate propensity to evil within humankind, Kant nevertheless concluded, "For man, therefore, who despite a corrupted heart yet possesses a good will, there remains hope of a return to the good from which he has strayed." *Religion within the Limits of Reason Alone*, 2d ed., trans. Theodore M. Greene and Hoyt H. Hudson (LaSalle, Ill.: Open Court Publishing Co., 1960), p. 39.

28. For Paul this is more of a theoretical possibility than a practical actuality because of sin that corrupts the human heart and subjugates the human will. He may also here be thinking of Gentile Christians (as Augustine, Markus Barth, and Ellul seem to hold).

29. Edward John Carnell, *Christian Commitment: An Apologetic* (New York: Macmillan Co., 1957). Carnell makes clear that only by grace can one come to a saving knowledge of God. On our own we can come to a conscious awareness of the existence of God, but we will lack personal acquaintance with God as Lord and Savior.

30. Karl Barth, *The Word of God and the Word of Man*, trans. Douglas Horton (Boston: Pilgrim, 1928), p. 38.

31. See Hans Küng, *On Being a Christian*, trans. Edward Quinn (New York: Doubleday, 1976), p. 259.

32. Paradoxically, even when Christ dwells within us by his Spirit, he nonetheless remains distinct from us. He is the source of our new life in the Spirit, but we are never absorbed into his being.

33. Thea B. Van Halsema, *This Was John Calvin* (Grand Rapids: Zondervan, 1959), pp. 84, 85.

34. See René Fülöp-Miller, *The Saints that Moved the World*, trans. Alexander Gode and Erika Fülöp-Miller (Salem, N.H.: Ayer Co., 1984), pp. 171, 172.

35. Karl Barth, *A Shorter Commentary on Romans* 2d ed. (London: SCM Press, 1963), p. 105.

36. Ibid., p. 155.

37. Dietrich Bonhoeffer, *Letters and Papers from Prison*, ed. Eberhard Bethge, trans. Reginald Fuller (New York: Macmillan Co., 1962), p. 19.

38. Ibid., p. 31.

CHAPTER 6

Love and Justice

But let justice roll down like waters, and righteousness like an ever-flowing stream.

AMOS 5:24

Because people do not fortify justice, they justify force.

BLAISE PASCAL

Love without justice is a Christian impossibility, and can only be practiced by those who have divorced religion from life, who dismiss a concern for justice as "politics" and who fear social change much more than they fear God.

ALAN PATON

The ship of the law cannot change the heart, but it can restrain the heartless until they change their mind and heart.

REINHOLD NIEBUHR

The Current Discussion

If we are to hold kingdom service and social action in biblical perspective, we need to understand the polarity between love and justice, to become aware of their inseparability and also their signal discontinuity.

The tendency today in the circles of academic theology is to identify love and justice. Love becomes the more inclusive category. Justice is defined as social love or as love expanded. In liberation theology justice is love in action. According to Paul Ricoeur, "Justice is the efficacious, institutional, and social realization of love."[1] For Fletcher it is "Christian love using its head, calculating its duties, obligations, opportunities, resources."[2]

This monistic orientation stands in marked contrast to the prevailing attitude during the heyday of neo-orthodoxy several decades ago. For Reinhold Niebuhr love is transcendent, heedless, and sacrificial; justice, on the other hand, is historical and discriminating, concerned with balancing interests and claims. According to Brunner, love is concrete, personal, and nondeliberate, whereas justice is "lawful, deliberate, impersonal and objective, abstract and rational."[3] Tillich contends that love of power structures is not possible, but love of persons is. We therefore have a different ethical situation when the focus is on adjudicating social claims. Indeed, in Nygren, it seems, love and justice are opposed, the first being associated with disinterestedness, the second with self-interest. Ellul, too, stresses the gulf rather than the continuity between love and justice.[4]

This dualistic tendency is noticeable in other theological streams currently under attack. In the older Catholic thought, love was seen as a supernatural virtue and justice as a natural virtue. In the dispensational theology of Herman Hoyt, justice, which characterizes the old dispensation, is superseded by love, the New Testament ideal.[5]

Today, it seems, love is generally regarded as an immediate possibility. While Niebuhr conceived of love as a transcendent ideal that critiques and corrects human justice, John Howard Yoder regards love as the means to actualize justice.[6] The accent is on the implementation of love, not compromise with the ideal of love. Triumphal love rather than suffering love (as in Niebuhr) is the new emphasis.[7] Some theologians (Hall Peebles and Tyler Thompson) absorb justice into love and thereby deny the theological validity of retributive justice. But if love and justice are equated, does not this eradicate the sense of moral outrage at a heinous evil?

In my view, we should oppose both those who make love a substitute for justice (political conservatives) and those who strive to bring in the kingdom of love by a revolution in consciousness or even one of violence (the radicals). We should also stand firm against the neoliberals who hold up the utopian vision of a full-fledged welfare state or classless society. The principal question is then not so much whether people get what they deserve but whether they receive what they need.[8]

Definitions

Against Ellul, I contend that justice does have a universal content, though its meaning is deepened and clarified in the light of the biblical revelation. For Plato and Aristotle it meant giving people their due, but this way of stating it is also found in the Old Testament (cf. Ps. 28:4; Lam. 3:35 NKJV). The law of justice is also affirmed by our Lord: "Whatever measure you deal out to others will be dealt back to you" (Matt. 7:2 NEB; cf. Gal. 6:7). To be sure, once we spurn the voice of conscience, we begin to lose sight of the norms of justice. This is why the prophet could say, "Evil men do not understand justice, but those who seek the Lord understand it fully" (Prov. 28:5 NIV).

Justice basically means fair treatment. It involves an equitable apportionment of goods and power. It entails freedom from harassment and exploitation. Niebuhr is not far from the truth when he conceives of it as a compound of equality and liberty, and these two are often hard to mesh.

In classical ethical theory, justice has various aspects. Distributive justice means giving every person his or her due; communative justice is establishing a collective order of freedom and mutuality. Retributive justice is restoring balance and order, paying the good what they deserve and the evil what they deserve. Justice in this sense is merited requital.

In the Old Testament, justice has meanings more comprehensive than the Hellenistic understanding. Justice in Old Testament thought involves bringing people into a right relationship with one another, not simply giving people their due reward. These meanings are not mutually exclusive, but the Hebraic vision is deeper. When people have a right relationship with one another, their claims are recognized, their rights are guaranteed. In both the Old Testament and rational philosophy justice is associated with equity as well as with freedom. In the Hebraic view, God's final purpose for us is *shalōm*, a just peace with joy in God's creation. *Shalōm* combines justice, peace, and love.

The idea of human rights in Western political thought is often traced to Stoicism. The Old Testament does not seem to have a theory of universal human rights, but it does speak of the need to safeguard the rights of the poor. Whereas in rational philosophy human justice is generally associated with the idea of the Good, in the Old Testament it is related to the will of the living God.

Love (agape) means having an infinite preference for our neighbor's welfare. It consists in a sacrificial giving to others as opposed to a self-regarding quest for the possession of the supreme good (eros). It is preferring God's glory and the good of one's neighbor over one's own welfare and interests. It is living not according to the golden rule but beyond it. Agape is self-giving, outgoing love, the love that does not seek its own (1 Cor. 10:24; 13:5). It is the suffering love that bears affliction rather than returns affliction (Matt. 5:39–42). It is gratuitous love, going out to the undeserving. Justice, on the other hand, always goes out to the deserving. Its rule is "to each according to his desert or works." According to Brunner, agape is the bestower of worth; justice is the appraiser of worth.

Lewis Smedes rightly says: "Love does not cancel anyone's rights. But agapic love moves one freely to *forgo one's claim* on what one has a right to have."[9] Love may well entail the surrender of rights if this results in meeting the agonizing needs and hurts of our neighbor in distress.

Justice, on the other hand, is intent on safeguarding our natural rights, on ensuring that each person receives a fair share of the goods. It seeks tolerance and mutual respect among peoples. But love goes beyond tolerance. It is not content with coexistence. It aims for fellowship at the deepest level. It wishes the other person to be not simply a friend but a brother or sister in Christ.

Nygren makes a fairly good case that in rabbinic Judaism love is exclusive and particularistic, directed toward one's neighbor in the original and restricted sense of a person who lives in one's immediate vicinity and therefore participates in the same cultural and moral ethos.[10] According to Nygren, the New Testament idea of the universal and unconditional character of love radically transcends the Old Testament view. The emphasis in Judaism is on *nomos* (law), not agape.[11] My position is that there are hints and even glimpses of the universal character of God's love and grace in the Old Testament. The Old Testament anticipates the New Testament vision, even though it drastically falls short of it. For Nygren, agape tends to exclude both eros and *nomos*. As I see it, Christian love encompasses a concern for justice but goes beyond it.

Ultimate and Penultimate Ideals

Justice may be regarded as the penultimate ideal and love as the ultimate. Holiness, too, should be seen as an ultimate ideal, representing the unity of love and justice, gospel and law. Holiness is living in intimate communion with the true God and serving him in loving obedience.

Justice is a rational ideal; love is an ideal or goal of faith. Justice is dependent on politics, which has aptly been defined as the "art of the possible." Love, on the other hand, is an "impossible possibility" (Reinhold Niebuhr), dependent on the work of grace within the believing subject.

While justice is equivalent to fairness, love is closer to foolhardiness. Justice is giving one's neighbor a fair deal, ensuring the proper distribution of goods. Love involves sacrificing the self for the good of others. Paul enjoined, "Let no one seek his own good, but the good of his neighbor" (1 Cor. 10:24).

If justice is directly related to law, so law is integrally related to the gospel. If the gospel fulfills and transcends the law, so love fulfills and transcends the norms of justice.

Justice involves calculating rights and setting limits on each person's interest to prevent people from taking advantage of others. Love contains an element of disinterestedness, placing the other's interest above one's own. While justice calls for "a balance of competing wills and interests" (Reinhold Niebuhr), love entails the subordination and sacrifice of one's interests to the interests of another.

Whereas justice is conditional on right action and right response, love is unconditional, not dependent on the worth or fitness of the object of love. Justice means cooperation in the democratic process, pressing one's claims in the public arena. One can fight for justice, but one can only surrender to love.

Niebuhr has rightly pointed out that justice always entails coercion; the love of the cross, by contrast, signifies nonresistance, not even nonviolent resistance. Pure love contains an element of heedlessness. It means to be oblivious to one's own safety or reputation. As Niebuhr (and Ellul as well) reminds us, love is an eschatological ideal. It can be anticipated in purely personal encounters, but it is not a practical possibility in group confrontations. Pure love cannot be a weapon in temporal conflicts. It is not at our disposal. We cannot rely on love alone to bend power structures or resolve social conflicts.

Yet the paradox is that love is the source and goal of justice. It is also the measuring stick by which we are guided in our striving for justice. The ideal of love suggests possibilities for transcending the present achievements of justice. Love makes justice creative and equitable by exposing the gap between every particular stride toward justice and the perfection of the cross. Thus love negates as well as fulfills the claims of justice. Love does not allow us to rest content with what has been achieved thus far. Love as self-sacrifice motivates us to give up inordinate self-seeking and thereby to become more just.

The search for justice invariably involves a compromise with the ideal of love. Justice is the application of love to concrete moral situations in society. It is then no longer pure love but reciprocal or mutual love. God sometimes calls us into situations where compromise is required in order to be relevant and responsible.

Love in the New Testament sense includes a concern for justice. While justice should be informed by love, love will not cancel out justice. Kyle Haselden has shrewdly observed that many Christians prefer "cheap love" to "costly justice."[12] According to Niebuhr, "Love without power simply surrenders the world to power without love."[13] Love will enable us to use power for the ends of justice.

At the same time, we should keep in mind that love goes beyond the obligations of justice. Jesus said, "Love your enemies and pray for those who persecute you" (Matt. 5:44). The law of love is not "an eye for an eye and a tooth for a tooth" but turning the other cheek (Matt. 5:38–42). Those who champion a rigorous norm of justice maintain that the punishment must fit the crime. Love, by contrast, means to bless those who persecute us, to refuse to retaliate in kind. The love of the cross signifies forgiveness, not fairness. To be sure, the demands of the law of God were satisfied by the sacrifice of Christ, but his sacrifice goes far beyond what law requires. Moreover, God's decision to forgive us led to the sacrifice on Calvary. It was not the condition for this sacrifice, though the sacrifice was necessary for his forgiving love to reach us.

To take up the cross and follow Christ does not mean to acquiesce in the face of evil but to overcome evil with good. Nonresistance as the New Testament presents it means that love replaces hatred, not that love replaces justice.

Just as temporal power can check and restrain the forces of evil in the old aeon, so the power of suffering love is the power of the kingdom of God itself. Only this kind of power is redemptive; worldly power is preservative. Love is the power that is displayed in weakness, exemplified in the death of Christ on the cross (1 Cor. 1:27, 28; 2 Cor. 12:9). Love changes the spirit of a person, but it is not an instrument in social conflict. Bands of disciples can make this kind of witness, but not nations. Nations can possibly be moved to contrition and repentance through the preaching of the law of God, but nations cannot love other nations as God in Christ loved sinners. If this were so, then the nation would itself be the kingdom of God. There are no regenerate nations, but there are regenerate persons within nations seeking to awaken their people to the demands of justice.

Temporal power can prepare the way for the kingdom of God only indirectly, that is, by ensuring the conditions for the freedom of the Word of God. Some Christians are called by God into politics and responsible positions in society. Others, like John the Baptist and Jesus himself, are called to be signs of the new aeon and eschew politics. The first kind of Christian will use temporal power whereas the second will generally rely on the power of love alone. Neither way is higher than the other; both fulfill the obligations of the church to society in their own way. The Old Testament prophets urged the kings of their time to exercise power and correct inequities. So it should be with the prophets of the church today.

Pope John XXIII wisely said, "Let love be the motive and justice be the method of our social action." The problem of social ethics is to relate the heedlessness and spontaneity of love with the calculation and coercion of justice. As Niebuhr put it, "Justice may be the servant of love, and power may be the servant of justice."[14]

Social justice is not the same as the righteousness of the kingdom where love is the sole motivation and the basic method. A just society is only an approximation of the perfect brotherhood of love foretold by the prophets. This perfect brotherhood is an eschatological reality. It takes place beyond history, but it also impinges on history. It can even be realized in part within history, as Niebuhr also recognized, though this was not always apparent in the way he presented his arguments. In history it takes the form of fellowships of mutual love rather than the perfection of agape—sacrificial love. The brotherhood of mutual love is the ideal and perfection of justice.

Social justice is a sign of the spiritual righteousness of the kingdom. It is also a means by which we advance toward the perfect righteousness embodied in Jesus Christ. Yet it is only an indirect and primarily negative means, serving to restrain the powers of the old aeon. It can, however, create the political climate that allows the church the freedom to proclaim the Word in the public arena.

Yet natural justice is not the same as redemptive righteousness. A regenerated Christian will not only have a sense of justice but will be "filled with the fruits of righteousness" (Phil. 1:11). A just society can nonetheless serve the cause of kingdom righteousness. It can make sure that everyone has the possibility of understanding the scriptural words, since literacy is necessary if people are to receive the Word of God in written form. At the same time, all orders and kingdoms in this world will disappear when God creates his world anew (Bonhoeffer).

Justice can be legislated, but not love. One of the apostles speaks of the judges, kings, and prophets "enforcing justice" (Heb. 11:33). Pascal declared, "Because men do not fortify justice, they justify force."[15] I do not agree with Russell Kirk that "society is held together by love and common interests, not by force or fraud."[16] Because of sin in the human heart, people will not respond to social change apart from the power of the sword, even though the sword by itself is insufficient to effect lasting social change.

Trying to bring together biblical and Hellenistic motifs, Paul Tillich contends that the Christian goal in society should be "creative justice" rather than proportional justice. Creative justice "is expressed in the divine grace which forgives in order to reunite. . . . Creative justice is the form of reuniting love. . . . Love reunites; justice preserves what is to be united."[17] Tillich here draws a very close correlation between love and justice. Because "creative justice" is so dependent on the work of divine grace, it is questionable whether it could ever be a human strategy for altering social relationships by civil law. The truth in Tillich's typology is that justice is not fulfilling until love acts upon it and within it. Yet by conceiving of love as "the drive towards the unity of the separated," he is not able to see the tension between the self-giving love of the cross (agape) and the claims of justice.[18]

The quest for justice is occasioned by the reality of exploitation and oppression, which have their source in human sin. Justice is therefore something temporal. It belongs to the old aeon, as do civil laws. It concerns this fallen world of sin and strife. Love, on the other hand, is a fruit of faith. It pertains to both this world and the world to come. Even the Christian must be restrained by law as well as challenged by love. Laws with teeth are necessary because of sin. Faith and love are necessary for salvation.

How Christians respond to evil will be somewhat different depending on their role in society. When the evil is directed to the Christian as an individual, then he or she should respond not by force but with the kind of love that disarms the enemy (cf. Rom 12:20, 21). When the Christian as a citizen of the state confronts evil directed at society as a whole, then political pressure, even coercion, will be required. It is in this light that we can understand Luther's paradoxical statement: "A Christian should not resist any evil; but within the limits of his office, a secular person should oppose *every* evil" (italics mine).[19]

Nonresistance to evil as Jesus taught is not to be confused with appeasement of evil.[20] Nonresistance means no retaliation in kind, but it does involve a creative response to evil. The witness of the cross serves to expose evil in the light of truth. In the secular order, evil is restrained by the power of the sword. In the kingdom of God, evil is overcome by the power of suffering love.

The people of God are called to engage in social action for the sake of just laws. Niebuhr rightly reminds us that the true end of politics is "proximate solutions and limited objectives." Our goal in this world is not a utopian society (as in Marxism) but simply a more tolerable and equitable social order. We should strive not for the highest but for what is rationally feasible under the given conditions. At its best, politics utilizes power in the service of justice with the motivation of love.

Politics is the art of compromise. It is always geared to immediate results. It relies heavily on manipulative technique. Unless it is ultimately informed by a spiritual perspective, however, it will lose sight of its final goal and become fanatical and ideological.

In contrast to social action, evangelism focuses upon salvation and kingdom righteousness. It sees itself in the service not of justice and peace but of faith and love. Evangelism always has a certain priority in the life of the Christian, but social service and social action are its necessary fruits and consequences.

Kyle Haselden has wisely said that the goal of Christian action is "neither justice nor mercy but a community which includes and goes beyond both." Distributive justice is only a means, not the final end of Christian action. Our means, moreover, should be consonant with the end—a just community.[21]

Some radical activists cry for justice, not charity. It is true that charity can take the form of paternalism, but justice can take the form of repressive egalitarianism. Charity understood as agape is necessary if we are ever to reach true brotherhood and sisterhood. People are to be pitied unless they are gripped by the vision of a higher righteousness that transcends and corrects the partial justice that can be achieved by political means.

Over a decade ago we were confronted by the hippie slogan, "Make love, not war." We were told that our reliance should be only on love, not on politics. Yet love in the sense of agape is something that can only be received by faith. We don't "make love," but we can experience love through faith in Jesus Christ.

We should remember that there is a violence of love and a struggle in love. To be loving persons in obedience to the great commandment means to crucify the old nature. There is also a wisdom in love that recognizes that the mere willing of love on the part of individuals is not sufficient. Our goal is a holy community where God's law is respected and the rights of the weak and poor are protected. This holy community is not the kingdom of God, but it can be a sign and parable of the kingdom.[22]

Love calls for social involvement, an involvement that will necessarily entail coercion. Mutual love means to utilize power in the service of both agape and justice.

God's Love and Holiness

There is a polarity even more basic than that between love and justice: that between the divine love and holiness as transcendent realities on the one hand and social justice as a rational ideal on the other. Liberal theology is prone to define God's nature exclusively in terms of love, blithely obscuring the biblical truth that God is sovereign power and majestic holiness as well. There is a qualitative gulf between the divine holiness and social justice as there is between the divine love and social justice.

At the same time, we need to ascertain the integral relationship between human love and justice on the one hand and the divine love and holiness on the other. Just as love contains a concern for justice, so holiness contains a disposition toward mercy. Yet social justice as a rational ideal is only an imperfect reflection of God's holiness. Mutual love as a human possibility is only a broken anticipation of the agape of God.

God's love and holiness exist in tension. Yet they are organically related. God's love is a holy love concerned about wrongdoing and injustice and demanding social holiness and righteousness. God's holiness is a loving holiness, which forgives and forbears. His holiness is perfected in love just as his love is infused by holiness.

It is helpful to reexamine the Reformation position on this subject. For Luther, God's righteousness is not conceived in terms of distributive justice but is identified with the grace by which he justifies the ungodly.[23] The essence of God's being is love, not justice. For Calvin, on the other hand, God's love is subordinated to his holiness. A. H. Strong, who was heavily influenced by Calvin, maintained that justice is "a principle of God's nature, not only independent of love, but superior to love."[24] W. G. T. Shedd held that justice inheres in God's nature, but mercy is God's disposition.

My position is that the two are equally important and that the atonement of Christ can only be understood in the light of the effort of God to reconcile the demands of his holiness with his boundless compassion. Love does not cancel out holiness but satisfies the claims of holiness. Likewise in the realm of human history, love does not annul but instead fulfills the claims of justice. In both cases law is upheld by love even while it is transcended by love. A community under the Lordship of Christ should be governed by love but characterized by obedience and justice.

Love without justice degenerates into anarchy. Justice without love becomes tyranny (as in Marxist regimes). Love and justice must be united in the divine holiness, the ultimate criterion for moral and social endeavor.

Justice must be related not only to love but also to piety, which is the sense of God's holiness. We should therefore be equally alert to the polarity between piety and justice. Reflecting on Augustine's *City of God*, Paul Lehmann has declared, "Without justice there can be no society, and without piety there can be no justice."[25] Augustine defined justice after the manner of Cicero as giving to people what is due to them. Cicero as a good Stoic argued that this law of justice is planted in the human mind by divine creation. The basic content of human reason is the law of justice. Piety, on the other hand, is an elemental sense of reverence before the divine. For Augustine, piety is the genuine worship of the true God, not the worship of the many demons or false gods. Cicero was unable to believe in God or the gods in a realistic sense, though he did believe in justice. Cicero rejected the divine foreknowledge of future things, basing his case on the freedom of the will. In wishing to make people free, he made them sacrilegious. Augustine, by contrast, perceived that people become free only through the fear of God, the author and bestower of perfect freedom.

The Christian Hope

The Christian hope is the perfect realization of love, the perfected fellowship of believers, the eschatological city of God. It should be seen not as the fulfillment of worldly hopes but as a new creation. It is not simply the restoration of Paradise but a new and more glorious Paradise.

In this hope we can strive for justice in human history. Indeed, Niebuhr has rightly observed that "justice cannot be approximated if the hope of its perfect realization does not generate a sublime madness in the soul."[26] In his words, "The kingdom of God is not of this world; yet its light illuminates our tasks in this world and its hope saves us from despair."

As Christians, we must be willing to "bury the hopes of today and the morrow," for temporal hopes are deceptive.[27] We need a faith that can endure tribulation and disillusionment. At the same time, faith needs to be nurtured by the hope that Jesus Christ is Victor (Johann Christoph Blumhardt). His victory has already been realized in his cross and resurrection triumph. It will be consummated and revealed to the whole creation at his second coming, in the eschaton.

The theology of liberation calls for a utopian faith, one in which the promises of God can be fulfilled now in earthly history. Heaven becomes secularized into a this-worldly utopia, a classless society as this is conceived of in messianic socialism. Salvation becomes liberation from oppression. It is an agenda doomed to failure, for violence begets violence. The old repressive order is likely to be displaced by a new tyranny. Authoritarian regimes may well be supplanted by totalitarian ones that demand submission to the dictates of the state in every area of life.

Evangelical theology calls for a robust faith as opposed to a utopian faith. This is a faith that will seek for justice in the spirit of love. At the same time, it will be acutely conscious that the only justice realizable in this world is a proximate one. It acknowledges that this world is a "vale of tears," that the Christian life is a life under the cross. It perceives that sometimes Christians are compelled to choose the lesser evil in the area of social conflict, and therefore even the works of the Christian need the cleansing blood of Christ.

Evangelical theology is a theology of the cross, but it makes a modest place for a theology of glory as well. The glory that is to come can be anticipated now in moments of faith and surrender to God. Paul declares that God "has put his seal upon us and given us his Spirit in our hearts as a guarantee" (2 Cor. 1:22; cf. Eph. 1:13, 14). The Good News Bible describes the gift of the Spirit as "the guarantee of all that he has in store for us" (2 Cor. 1:22). We now have the first fruits of the glory that is to come (Rom. 8:23). Meanwhile, we "groan inwardly as we wait for adoption as sons, the redemption of our bodies" (Rom. 8:23).

On the basis of the biblical promises, Christians have the confidence that the perfect fellowship of love will be realized beyond this world. It will come in God's own time and in his own way. Yet even now we can set up signs and parables of the coming of the kingdom. Because the biblical promises include the millennial hope, we can look forward to the realization of some of these promises in earthly history. Yet even these are only tokens of the glory to come—the new heaven and the new earth that signify both the crown of creation and the apex of redemption.

Appendix on Reinhold Niebuhr

Since Reinhold Niebuhr is my principal mentor in this discussion, a closer examination of our agreements and differences is in order. For Niebuhr, it should be remembered, love and justice are polarities, not dichotomies. The opposite of love is not justice but ill will.

On the other hand, Niebuhr contends that love is qualitatively different from justice. Love is heedless, sacrificial, and self-negating, whereas justice is discriminating, partial, and self-preserving. This accounts for his tendency at times to bifurcate love and justice: "The religious ideal in its purest form has nothing to do with the problem of social justice."[28] Niebuhr confessed: "I am unable to construct an adequate social ethic out of a pure love ethic. I cannot abandon the pure love ideal because anything which falls short of it is less than the ideal. But I cannot use it fully if I want to assume a responsible attitude toward the problems of society."[29] To be sure, he came more and more to insist that love must be related to justice in a dialectic of fulfillment and negation if it is to make an impact on the social situation.

Niebuhr follows Luther over Calvin in viewing love as the essence of God.[30] It is not surprising, given the context of his Lutheran tradition, that Niebuhr conceives of love as unmotivated and spontaneous rather than deliberate and purposive. Niebuhr could never speak of a strategy of love, but he could speak of a strategy for justice.

By portraying love as powerlessness and suffering passivity, he shows he does not fully appreciate the fact that love also makes demands.[31] His stress is on the passivity, the trust, and the surrender in love but not on the binding imperatives of love. He is emphatic that while love can be present in justice, justice is not present in love. "There is only one standard that has any business being read into the heart of God and that is the ultimate standard of love."[32]

Niebuhr modifies his position slightly when he discusses mutual love, which is already a step away from pure agape love. Mutual love does make a place for deliberation and conscious action, and this is the highest possibility for human beings within history. The pure sacrificial love of the cross is an "impossible possibility." It stands at the edge of history rather than becomes incarnate within history. It impinges on history but does not take root in history. Niebuhr declares: "The perfect love of Christ comes into the world, but it does not maintain itself there. The cross stands at the edge of history and not squarely in history; it reveals what history ought to be but not what history is, or can be."[33]

At times it seems that for Niebuhr love is outside of human history.[34] Here we see an affinity with Plato, who made a sharp distinction between the Idea of the Good and temporal reality. Is Niebuhr's law of love equivalent to Plato's Idea of the Good? For both, it appears, the pursuit of the good directs us beyond history to eternity.

Niebuhr's emphasis is on love as a gift rather than a task. Thus love is not a moral achievement that we can take pride in but a fruit of faith that wells up spontaneously within us by the power of God's grace. Christian obedience consists in the search for justice, but it must be informed by the experience of love. Justice is something we help to create; love is something that happens to us irrespective of human preparation or deliberation.

Niebuhr defines the will of God so completely in terms of the law of love that he sometimes loses sight of the truth that the biblical God is also one of holiness and justice who uses power to accomplish his will.[35] God is not only love, but he is also light, absolute moral holiness; and this means that sin must be expiated, judged, and punished.[36] Niebuhr views the cross of Christ primarily as an incomparable revelation of the inscrutable riches of God's mercy rather than an expiatory sacrifice designed to satisfy the claims of divine justice (Anselm). Yet Niebuhr acknowledges the valid concern of this older theory, which came to dominate Protestant orthodoxy.

As he matured in thought, Niebuhr endeavored to make a place for the judgment of God on sin as well as God's mercy toward the sinner. He contended that God not only shows his love for us in Christ but also takes upon himself the consequences of our sin by suffering with us and for us.[37] Niebuhr had considerable difficulty with substitutionary theories of the atonement,[38] but he sought to preserve the truth in such theories—namely, that God condescends to share the pain of our sin, thus showing that his law cannot be abrogated as well as opening the way of salvation to us. The cross reveals the suffering love of God, which awakens people to the gravity of their sin and thereby induces them to repent. Christ's sacrifice signifies not so much that the debt of sin has been paid as that the power of love is available to overcome sin. It does not so much effect our salvation as make our salvation possible by exposing us to the reality of suffering love.[39]

Niebuhr came to see that the highest justice is the holiness of God's love, which overcomes by vicarious suffering. Yet does not God also overcome by the might and power of law, which restrains and subdues the forces of evil in this aeon? Niebuhr clearly recognized this aspect of God's activity but refused to assign it any redemptive power. (I would argue that it might prepare the way for redemption.) He had much to say about the tragic fall of nations but attributed their demise to their own pride, which irremediably clouded their vision. While he was reluctant to speak of a divine intervention in history in the form of wrath and judgment, he nevertheless sought to relate the hubris of the nations to the divine nemesis. Yet it seems that the wrath of God is but a symbol for the essential structure of the world as it reacts against the sinful corruptions of that structure.[40]

Niebuhr was fond of emphasizing the unconditional and disinterested character of love, but this is to overlook the many biblical passages that allude to the partiality in love. Does love simply forbear and forgive, or does not love also lead directly to acts of justice on behalf of the oppressed?[41] Niebuhr would hold that taking up the sword may be an act of justice but never of love.[42]

Finally, Niebuhr sees justice rooted in the "common experience of mankind."[43] The norms of justice are "generated in the customs and mores of communities." I regard the judicial sentiment in humankind as being grounded in our creation in the image of God and in our contact with the common grace of the Spirit of God. Niebuhr would acknowledge the transcendent source of the norms of justice, but in presenting his case for the universality of these norms he appeals to the collective experience of the race. But it is precisely here that I have trouble with Niebuhr, since an impartial investigation of the mores of various cultures yields a greater diversity in morality than his typology can admit. Like him, I hold that there are norms of justice that have a universal import, but I believe that only in the light of the biblical revelation do we have an adequate understanding of the nature of these norms.

Niebuhr is to be congratulated for maintaining the moral dualism of the New Testament and the Protestant Reformation in his incisive delineation of the paradoxical relation between love and justice. He is also to be applauded for stressing their indissoluble relationship, especially in his later writings. He is critical of both Nygren and Brunner for separating love and justice, though there are times when Niebuhr himself tends to make an overly sharp demarcation. Yet he is on solid biblical ground in his contention that grace makes one not simply "good" in the sense of living up to the requirements of moral law but instead compassionately creative in the sense of love that goes beyond the law. Niebuhr's theology is a welcome corrective to all legalism and moralism, but it needs to be balanced by a concern for the life of holiness, emphasized by the Catholic mystics, Calvin, and Wesley. We need to recognize that justice must be informed not only by love but also by piety—the fear of the living God, based on the experience of his holiness and majesty.[44]

Notes

1. Quoted in José Miguez Bonino, *Doing Theology in a Revolutionary Situation* (Philadelphia: Fortress, 1975), p. 114.
2. Fletcher, *Situation Ethics*, p. 95.
3. Brunner, *The Divine Imperative*, p. 450.
4. Jacques Ellul writes: "To say that the establishment of terrestrial justice is a concrete way of expressing love and that power is a way to achieve it seems to me historically and politically untrue. Some fine approximations to terrestrial justice may be found which are the opposite of love, e.g., the admirable Roman system." *The Ethics of Freedom*, ed. and trans. Geoffrey W. Bromiley (Grand Rapids: Eerdmans, 1976), p. 369. See also Gene Outka, "Discontinuity in the Ethics of Jacques Ellul," in *Jacques Ellul: Interpretive Essays*, ed. Clifford G. Christians and Jay M. Van Hook (Urbana: University of Illinois Press, 1981), pp. 177–228.
5. See Robert G. Clouse, ed., *War: Four Christian Views* (Downers Grove, Ill.: InterVarsity, 1981), pp. 29–57.
6. See John Howard Yoder, *The Politics of Jesus* (Grand Rapids: Eerdmans, 1972).
7. Yoder, for example, sees love as a political strategy rather than a transcendental ideal. While still making a place for suffering love, he sees this not as passive submission to persecution or intimidation but as nonviolent resistance to entrenched evil.
8. It was Karl Marx who declared, "From each according to his abilities, to each according to his needs!" "The Criticism of the Gotha Program," in *Capital, The Communist Manifesto and Other Writings by Karl Marx*, ed. Max Eastman (New York: Modern Library, 1932), p. 7.
9. Lewis B. Smedes, *Love within Limits: A Realist's View of I Corinthians 13* (Grand Rapids: Eerdmans, 1978), p. 38.
10. Nygren, *Agape and Eros*, pp. 247–60.
11. Nygren's stance is supported even by Deuteronomy 6:4 where the love of God is expressly commanded. Love is nonetheless portrayed as a new law rather than the new reality of grace that transcends law.
12. Kyle Haselden, *Mandate for White Christians* (Richmond, Va.: John Knox, 1966).
13. Quoted in *Presbyterian Life* 20, no. 21 (Nov. 1, 1967): p. 22.
14. Reinhold Niebuhr, "Is There Another Way?" in *Love and Justice*, ed. D. B. Robertson (Philadelphia: Westminster, 1957), [pp. 299–301], p. 300.
15. Quoted in Haselden, *Mandate for White Christians*, p. 94.
16. Russell Kirk, "What's This Word 'Conservatism'?" *Telegraph Herald*, Dec. 16, 1969, p. 4.
17. Paul Tillich, *Love, Power, and Justice* (New York: Oxford University Press, 1954), pp. 66, 71.
18. Tillich tries to make a place for agape as a quality of love, but basically it is in the service of eros. It perfects eros by purifying and deepening it. See ibid., pp. 24–34, 115–25.
19. *Luther's Works*, ed. Jaroslav Pelikan (St. Louis: Concordia Publishing House, 1956), 21: p. 113.
20. Voltaire fondly hoped that the way to pacify belligerent parties was by inviting them to dinners. But despite his well-meaning efforts to reconcile warring factions in Geneva, it soon became evident that bitterness and estrangement cannot be overcome in this way. See Voltaire, *Romans et Contes* (Paris: Garnier, 1958), pp. 334, 335; and

Gustave Desnoiresterres, *Voltaire et la société au XVIIIe siècle* (Paris: Didier, 1869–1876), 7: pp. 8–10.

21. Haselden, *Mandate for White Christians*, pp. 108, 110.
22. The holy community will take a different form today than it did with Calvin and the Puritans. We should strive no longer for a theocratic commonwealth but instead for a just society that will take into consideration the pluralism of modern times. Yet we dare not ever forget that true justice cannot exist without piety, the fear of the living God.
23. See Philip S. Watson, *Let God be God!* (London: Epworth, 1948), pp. 33–70; and Gordon Rupp, *The Righteousness of God* (London: Hodder & Stoughton, 1963), pp. 81–256.
24. Quoted in George Barker Stevens, *The Christian Doctrine of Salvation* (New York: Charles Scribner's Sons, 1911), p. 178.
25. Paul Lehmann, (Niebuhr Lectures, Elmhurst College, Elmhurst, Ill., March, 1975).
26. Niebuhr, *Moral Man and Immoral Society*, p. 277.
27. See the German-American Pietist hymn, "One Thing Needful, Greatest Blessing," *A Book of Chorales*, ed. Frederick R. Daries (St. Louis: Eden Publishing House, 1957), no. 74.
28. Niebuhr, *Moral Man and Immoral Society*, p. 263.
29. Reinhold Niebuhr, "Must We Do Nothing?" *The Christian Century* 49, no. 13 (March 30, 1932): p. 417.
30. A case could be made that Luther, much more than Niebuhr, envisioned the activity of God in terms of both love and power. Luther contended that God rules with his left hand by the force of law and with his right hand by the gospel of grace. Elements of this dualism are also present in Niebuhr to a degree, for he can occasionally speak of "an Assyrian rod" in the hand of God and of the majesty of God which is "able to subdue all false majesties" *Discerning the Signs of the Times* (New York: Charles Scribner's Sons, 1946), p. 63. Niebuhr was convinced that God finally conquers by the power of the powerlessness of love, which drives sinners to repentance. Luther would say that God finally triumphs by the power of both his justice (which creates hell) and his love (which creates heaven).
31. He writes: "This way of complete non-resistance is rightly understood by Christianity as standing on the edge of history and eternity and not in history. The Christ who reveals the character of God to us is completely powerless." Reinhold Niebuhr, "Politics and the Christian Ethic," *Christianity and Society* 5, no. 2 (Spring 1940): p. 26.
32. Reinhold Niebuhr et al. *Education Adequate for Modern Times* (New York: Association Press, 1931), p. 65.
33. Quoted in James M. Wall, "Facing the 'Perfectionism' Backlash," *The Christian Century* 94, no. 30 (Sept. 28, 1977): p. 835.
34. Niebuhr has stated, "There can be nothing absolute in history, no matter how frequently God may intervene in it." "Must We Do Nothing?" *The Christian Century* 49, no. 13 (March 30, 1932): p. 417. Cf. Reinhold Niebuhr, *The Self and the Dramas of History* (New York: Charles Scribner's Sons, 1955), p. 60. Yet this would seem to deny not only the realization of the perfection of love in history but also the incarnation of God in Jesus Christ. It is debatable whether Niebuhr ever succeeded in uniting the Jesus of history and the Christ of faith.
35. Cf. Niebuhr: "It is the central insight of the Christian religion that God is not an omnipotent God, whatever the theologians have said, but a suffering God, and whatever omnipotence he possesses is the omnipotence of love." Niebuhr et al, *Education Adequate for Modern Times*, p. 51. Cf. Niebuhr, *Interpretation of Christian Ethics*, pp. 23, 31.

As Niebuhr developed his theology, however, he more and more made a place for the sovereignty of God and for the dimensions of justice and power in God as well as love. (Here we can discern the influence of Paul and Augustine, as well as the Reformers.) Yet for Niebuhr God's sovereignty remains basically one of love. The triumphant return of Christ expresses "the final supremacy of love over all the forces of self-love which defy, for the moment, the inclusive harmony of all things under the will of God." Reinhold Niebuhr, *The Nature and Destiny of Man* (New York: Charles Scribner's Sons, 1951), 2: p. 290. The resolution of the conflicts in history is seen in terms of the divine mercy and the forgiveness of sins, though not before there is a final judgment on sin.

It is interesting to note that H. Richard Niebuhr was sharply critical of his brother for interpreting Jesus' ethic exclusively in terms of the perfection of love. See H. Richard Niebuhr, *Christ and Culture* (New York: Harper, 1951), pp. 15–17. See also H. Richard Niebuhr, "A Communication: The Only Way Into the Kingdom of God," *The Christian Century* 49, no. 14 (April 6, 1932): p. 447. On H. Richard Niebuhr's influence on his brother see Richard Fox, *Reinhold Niebuhr: A Biography* (New York: Pantheon Books, 1985), pp. 144–48, 183–92.

36. This other side of divinity is often overlooked or downplayed in liberal theology (which includes the early Niebuhr). God condescends to our level as suffering servant, but he is also majestic Lord and holy Father. The unity between the avenging power of his holiness and the powerlessness of his love can be grasped only by faith. It is certainly not rationally obvious. God's love is a suffering love, indicating his willingness to undergo affliction for the sins of his people. But God is also holiness, and this means that he must act decisively and unalterably against sin. He can act against sin because he is holy as well as loving. He can bear the penalty for sin because he is loving as well as holy.

Niebuhr remained convinced that God is essentially love, but he came to see this love in dialectical relation to God's power and justice. These are both fulfilled and contradicted by the majesty of his love. The paradox of God's majestic power and the powerlessness of his love is skillfully depicted by Niebuhr in his sermon, "The Power and Weakness of God," in *Discerning the Signs of the Times*, pp. 132–51.

37. Niebuhr, *The Nature and Destiny of Man* 2: pp. 55, 56.

38. He could even say that such theories "outrage the moral sense." Reinhold Niebuhr, *Beyond Tragedy* (New York: Charles Scribner's Sons, 1937), p. 18. In Niebuhr's theology, Jesus is not the scapegoat for human sin but the one who powerfully reveals that God, who is infinite love, swallows up evil within himself and thereby destroys it (p. 168).

39. Niebuhr says that it is in the experience of "contrition and in this appropriation of divine mercy and forgiveness that the human situation is fully understood and overcome." *The Nature and Destiny of Man* 2: p. 57.

40. Ibid., pp. 56, 211. Cf. Niebuhr, *Faith and History* (New York: Charles Scribner's Sons, 1949), pp. 105, 109, 122, 123, 132.

41. Niebuhr does not wish to exclude the spirit of justice from the realm of love, but he nevertheless sees the highest form of love as standing in contradiction to the demands of justice even while fulfilling these demands. See his insightful essay, "Love and Law in Protestantism and Catholicism," in *Christian Realism and Political Problems* (New York: Charles Scribner's Sons, 1953), pp. 147–73.

42. It is well to note that Scripture portrays Jesus Christ (who is both holiness and love) coming again as triumphant king and with his holy ones overthrowing the entrenched powers of wickedness by force. Cf. 1 Cor. 15:23–27; 2 Thess. 2:8; Rev. 14–20; Isa. 24–27; Dan. 7:9–14; Zech. 12–14; and Joel 3:1–16. Christ conquers, however, not with carnal weapons but by "the breath of His mouth" and "the brightness of His coming" (2 Thess. 2:8 NKJV; cf. Isa. 11:4; Rev. 19:15).

43. Niebuhr, *Christian Realism and Political Problems*, p. 148.

44. For a further discussion of Niebuhr's ethics, see chap 10, pp. 183–86.

CHAPTER 7

Law and Gospel in Historical Perspective

If the Spirit of grace is absent, the law is present only to accuse and kill us.

AUGUSTINE

Before, I was free, and walked in the dark without a lantern: now, possessing the law, I have a conscience, and I take a lantern when I walk in the dark. God's law does nothing for me, but to awaken my bad conscience.

MARTIN LUTHER

Let us therefore learn to maintain inviolable this sacred tie between the law and the Gospel, which many improperly attempt to break.

JOHN CALVIN

Every command in holy writ is only a covered promise. . . . God hath engaged to give whatsoever he commands.

JOHN WESLEY

For *love* is the only meaning of the law: therefore *obedience* to the law can only be an *echo or response to God's love*.

G. C. BERKOUWER

One of the perennial issues within classical Protestantism is the enigmatic relationship of the law and the gospel. Besides the sacraments, this is perhaps the principal dividing mark between Reformed and Lutheran traditions. It remains a subject of lively debate today.

Roman Catholicism

In Roman Catholicism the law and the gospel are generally understood as aspects of the whole counsel of God, and occasionally there is some overlapping. The gospel is often equated with the teachings of Jesus as well as with the proclamation and teachings of Paul. Sometimes it is depicted as a higher law—the law of love. It is seen as both the fulfillment and transcendence of the Mosaic law. Thomas Aquinas said the new law is the Spirit enabling us to obey the moral law and even write new laws.

When Catholic theologians in the Thomistic tradition speak of law, they generally mean an ordination of reason for the common good made by one who is responsible for the welfare of society. The purpose of law is to achieve an orderly community and the proper distribution of goods. The eternal law refers to the directives of the divine mind for creation and its unfolding. The manifestation of the eternal law in nature is the natural law. Positive human law is the natural law particularized. The revealed law is what is given in Holy Scripture and is to be seen as a supplement to natural law. It is also a corrective to natural law, for natural law is invariably obscured by sin.[1]

The Christian life is characterized by obedience to the law, which basically means keeping the commandments. But it is also marked by striving to live up to the law of love, which is the highest commandment. It is not faith alone but faith perfected by love that is the hallmark of life in the Spirit.

While all Christians are said to be under the commandments of God, those who receive the call to live exclusively for Christ are under the counsels of perfection—poverty, celibacy, and obedience. These counsels are associated with the gospel just as the commandments are associated with law; this explains why they are called the evangelical counsels. Because those who embrace the so-called religious life are given greater grace, it is assumed that they can live up to the perfect law of love.

In a significant strand in Catholic tradition, the law is accepted as a means of salvation, even apart from the gospel.[2] A person who lives up to the law written on conscience (the natural law), it is held, can merit the grace that leads to justification. Against Pelagianism and semi-Pelagianism, Thomistic theology teaches that one can realize one's innate possibilities for good only with the aid of prevenient grace.

In recent years, Catholic theologians have endeavored to restate the relationship between law and gospel in the light of the ecumenical discussion. Walter Kasper defines law as the disclosure of God's will in both conscience and the word of revelation in salvation history.[3] The gospel, on the other hand, is not primarily a doctrine to be believed or a new law but the proclamation of God's free pardon to sinners. The gospel does not annul God's will but calls the believer into a new obedience—to the demands of faith and love. Catholic theologians, in contrast to their Lutheran counterparts, are inclined to emphasize the positive relationship between law and gospel. Augustine's aphorism is often cited: "The law was given so that grace might be sought; grace was given so that the law might be fulfilled."[4] According to Avery Dulles, the gospel liberates us from the power of sin and death, but it also binds us to the demands of Jesus Christ, who will reward us on the last day on the basis of our faithfulness and diligence.[5]

Luther

Few theologians have drawn a sharper distinction between the law and gospel than Martin Luther. Both are necessary for the unfolding of salvation, but whereas the law proceeds from the holiness of God, the gospel proceeds from his grace.

Luther sees the law of God exemplified in the Decalogue, although the law is in the New Testament too, just as the gospel is in the Old Testament. In addition, the law is written on the hearts of human beings everywhere. The law is immediately present with all people, whereas the gospel is mediatively present.

Law in this theology is a general norm, but not an indefeasible criterion for Christian life. The law signifies the command of God, while the gospel refers to the promise of God. The law can be discovered by reason, though only imperfectly, while the gospel must be given by revelation. For Luther the Decalogue, the Old Testament summation of law, is not so much a code of morals as a code of prohibitions. It has the negative effect of restraining human rapacity and bridling the flesh, but it cannot make us good because original sin still exerts a paralyzing influence in human life.

Both the law and the gospel comprise the Word of God, but this unity is not rationally discernible. It can only be accepted by faith. In Luther's understanding, the one and the same word in the Bible can strike the hearer as either law or gospel, depending on whether it is received as promise or command.

The gospel, being the message of free grace, sets one free from the restraints and burdens of the law. It is not rigorous conformity to precepts but liberty in the Spirit that characterizes the Christian life. Luther could even say, "In obedience man adheres to the decalogue and in freedom man creates new decalogues."[6]

In contrast to Catholic tradition, Luther posits an antithesis between the law and the gospel. "It is impossible that the gospel and the law should dwell together in one heart, for of necessity either Christ must yield and give place to the law, or the law to Christ."[7] He could appeal to such verses as John 1:17: "For the law was given through Moses; grace and truth came through Jesus Christ." Or to Galatians 3:25, 26, where Paul declares we are "no longer under a custodian" but are now all "sons of God, through faith." Or to Romans 6:14, where Paul assures his hearers that they are no longer "under law but under grace."

Luther basically saw the law as the "hammer of judgment" that convicts us of sin and thereby prepares us to hear the good news of God's mercy. The chief purpose of the law is to condemn us and to drive us to despair. The law also has a supplementary purpose for Christians of reminding them of their sin. It is a "gauze in the wound," but there is no healing in the wound. Because Christians are still sinners, they constantly need to be directed by the law back to Christ.

While the law condemns, the gospel saves. The law accuses, the gospel heals. Luther would be inclined to say that the law *always* accuses. The law is for secure sinners; the gospel is for alarmed sinners. He would be loath to say, as did later Reformed theologians, that the second face of the law is the gospel and the second face of the gospel is the law. Luther sees the law as both a tyrant and a schoolmaster. These are both part of its spiritual use. A favorite verse of his was Romans 5:20: "Law came in, to increase the trespass." What the law brings us is an uneasy conscience, which Luther likened to a lantern that accompanies one as one walks in the dark. God's law does nothing except to awaken one's bad conscience.

In Luther's theology evangelical repentance is worked by the law and the gospel together. In this process the law precedes the gospel, but he allowed for the fact that repentance can also come from the gospel alone.[8]

Besides its spiritual use, where the law is the hammer of judgment and the mirror of conscience, Luther also spoke of a civil or political use of the law, which he called its first use. Here its function is to restrain our rapacity and protect us in the structures of the common life. The law makes us insecure with respect to our own righteousness (its spiritual use) and secure within the structures of life in the world (its political use). But even in this so-called first use of the law, the law still accuses us, since it shows us that we need redemption.

A continual subject of debate in scholarly circles is whether Luther held to a third function of the law—providing a pattern for the Christian life. It is indisputable that Luther himself never used the expression "the third use of the law," though Melanchthon appears to have used it after 1535. Such scholars as Werner Elert, Gerhard Ebeling, and

Ragnar Bring hold that Luther knew nothing of a third function of the law. Helmut Thielicke and Paul Althaus, on the other hand, contend that the idea of the law as pattern and guide for Christian life is definitely present in Luther. Luther himself declared, "The law is to be retained by the believers so that they might have a pattern for doing good works."[9] In seeking to do justice to this neglected dimension in Luther's theology, Althaus distinguishes between the "divine command" and the "law."[10] With the coming of the gospel the law is abolished, but the command is restored with qualifications. The law is a limited, temporary form of the divine command, a form which the gospel, in Christ, has superseded and abolished.

According to Thielicke, Luther for the most part spoke of a twofold use of the law of God—its civil use and its spiritual or theological use. Yet he did not adhere to this typology exclusively, for on occasion he also saw the law as a guide for the Christian life.[11] Wingren holds that Luther spoke only of the two uses of the law, but he nevertheless did preach Christ as example.

Many Lutherans who accept the third use of the law are inclined to view the law only negatively, denying it any positive function. According to one scholar: "Inasmuch as the regenerate believer is still a sinner and retains his old nature, he still needs the accusatory function of the law. But this is actually only the second use of the law extended into the lives of Christian believers.[12] The Formula of Concord related the third use of the law to the regenerate, not insofar as they are righteous but insofar as they are sick and frail.[13] The Formula of Concord also propounded that the gospel may turn into a condemning law when it meets with unbelief.

Luther held that God rules people by the law as their Creator and Judge. By the gospel he rules as their Redeemer and Sanctifier. People experience God as wrath in the first and as sheer grace and mercy in the second.

A growing number of modern interpreters of Luther hold that the law and the gospel must be related eschatologically, referring to the two aeons.[14] Since the old aeon continues to exist, the law is still necessary even for the Christian. For these scholars, the law is not the form of the gospel (as in Barth) but the form of this age.

Luther perceived the Christian life in terms of freedom in the Spirit. This means freedom from the law and freedom for service in discipleship. The Spirit sets us free to follow Christ as Lord and Example. He was fond of citing Paul in 1 Corinthians 10:23: " 'All things are lawful, but not all things are helpful.' " (cf. 1 Cor. 6:12). Yet he was adamant that Christians are still sinners: we are always righteous and always sinners at the same time. Therefore we still need the law as a taskmaster to direct us ever again to Christ.

We also find in Luther the distinction between the station or office and the person. Our responsibilities to God and our neighbor are different in our personal relationships and in our station in life where we are obliged to fulfill our civic obligations. As Christians, he said, we should not resist any evil, but as citizens holding public office we should oppose every evil.[15]

Luther tried to make a place for keeping the commandments of God, but this was definitely subordinated to the demands of love, which sometimes contradict the letter of the commandment. "When the law impels one against love, it ceases and should *no longer be a law;* but where no obstacle is in the way, the keeping of the law is a proof of love, which lies hidden in the heart. Therefore you have need of the law, that love may be manifested; but if it cannot be kept without injury to the neighbor, God wants us to suspend and ignore the law."[16]

Calvin

Wilhelm Pauck has hailed Calvin as one of Luther's keenest and most faithful students. Yet in the area of law and gospel, their paths definitely diverge. For Calvin, the law of God is essentially the Decalogue, the revealed law of God, though it also includes the Sermon on the Mount as well as the precepts of conscience.[17] It can be said that for Calvin there is one moral law written on the consciences of all people and revealed in Scripture. He stressed the continuity between the natural law, the Decalogue, and the moral teachings of Jesus.

The gospel is not a law but the announcement of God's incomparable grace revealed in Jesus Christ. While the law restrains us, the gospel liberates us for service in freedom. There is nonetheless a recognizable unity between the law and the gospel, and Calvin begins with this unity. Despite an obvious antithesis between the letter of the law and the Spirit or the gospel, he perceived a unity of substance between them. The gospel ratifies and confirms what had been promised in the law: Christ "declares, that his doctrine is so far from being at variance with *the law,* that it agrees perfectly with *the law and the prophets,* and not only so, but brings the complete fulfillment of them."[18] There is thus a real "agreement between the law and the gospel."

Unlike Anabaptists, Calvin claimed that Jesus was "the best interpreter of the "old law," not the giver of a new law. He sometimes referred to Christ as "the soul of the law." In contrast to Lutherans, Calvin posited not two covenants (works and grace), but one—that of grace, which is present in both the Old and New Testaments. This is why he could preach a series of sermons on the gospel according to Isaiah. For him, the church begins not at Pentecost but with Abraham; its fulfillment is at Pentecost.

Calvin insisted that law and gospel belong together. "Let us therefore learn to maintain inviolable this sacred tie between the law and the Gospel, which many improperly attempt to break. For it contributes not a little to confirm the authority of the Gospel, when we learn, that it is nothing else than a fulfillment of the law; so that both, with one consent, declare God to be their Author."[19] The gospel can be distinguished from the law only quantitatively, not qualitatively. For the one is only "a literal doctrine," the other is "a spiritual doctrine." The first is only "engraven on tables of stone," the second is "inscribed on the heart."[20] The gospel does not transcend good and evil but is instead a higher or evangelical righteousness.

Calvin saw three uses for the law: to bring us to humility and repentance, to restrain our rapacity, and to serve as a practical guide for conduct—the last being, in his view, its principal use. He argued that the Decalogue is designed to form us and prepare us for every good work.

The law, then, is basically something holy and good. Its terrorizing work is the consequence of sin and is therefore accidental. We are saved by the gospel, but we are instructed by the law. The law does not produce sin but finds sin in us. Calvin was convinced that Christ is our example as well as our Savior. Although he affirmed the priority of justification over regeneration, he devoted the main part of his *Institutes* to delineating the life of regeneration.

In Calvin's theology, the preparation for the gospel is not the law by itself but the Holy Spirit working through both law and gospel. His emphasis was neither the law *before* the gospel (as in Luther) nor the law *after* the gospel (as in Barth) but the law *with* the gospel.[21] The law is included in the gospel and vice versa.

For Calvin, it is by the law that we come to humility, which is "a true preparation for seeking Christ." Yet this is what believers or those destined to believe learn from the law. Calvin recognized that there is a repentance of the law that is incomplete or deficient, but true repentance is gospel repentance where not only the sting of sin is felt but also God's mercy arouses trust.[22] It is our misery that drives us to

Christ, but no one would flee to him without first being assured of God's mercy and loving kindness. Calvin could say of repentance that it "proceeds from an earnest fear of God" and then assert that "the beginning of repentance is a sense of God's mercy." The same could be said of faith itself.

The Christian life is not freedom *from* the law but freedom *for* the law. Christian liberty does not annul the demands of the law but enables us to obey them. The one who has been touched by the grace of God does not flee from the law but lovingly embraces the law. Calvin sees the Christian as free from the rigid requirements and consequent burden of the law but not from its abiding intention.[23] He reminds us that our Lord did not come to abolish the law but to fulfill it (Matt. 5:17). What Christ abolished is not the law but the "obscurity" of the law.[24] The law upholding the Sabbath, he says, enjoins people "to abstain from their own works, not from the works of God."

For Calvin, the state, too, is under the law, but a law enlightened by the gospel. This means that the church has a positive duty to guide the state regarding the content and implications of the law of God for its time. His vision was a holy community in which church and state would exist in harmonious interaction under the law of God, with the church proclaiming the law and the state implementing it in daily life.

The danger in Calvinism is legalism, in which keeping the law becomes a condition for being in the favor of God. The danger in Lutheranism, on the other hand, is antinomianism, where all restraints of the law are discarded in a celebration of Christian freedom. The sixteenth-century Lutheran theologian John Agricola denied the third use of the law and became a champion of the Antinomian party in the church. The Formula of Concord (1577) sought to counter the errors of the Antinomians by pointing to the need for the law after conversion.

Anabaptists and Pietists

Among the Anabaptists, representative of the left-wing Reformation, the person of Christ and his teachings became a "new law." This "new law" was in discontinuity with the old law. What to Thomas were "counsels of perfection" were now seen as binding on all Christians. Poverty and celibacy, however, did not have the same significance, though evangelical obedience was regarded very highly. While eschewing perfectionism, the Anabaptists called their people "to obey the commands of God and lead lives of holiness."[25] The baptism of the Spirit became a baptism into the fire of persecution by the world.[26] Not

surprisingly, legalism was a constantly recurring temptation in Anabaptist circles, but this was countered by their staunch adherence to
the gospel as the forgiveness of sins and to "grace alone" as belonging
to the heart of the Christian message.

Anabaptists who tended toward spiritualism were inclined to dismiss the written law completely for the perfected Christian and to make
the love of God alone the criterion for action. "Every commandment,"
said Hans Denck, "all morals and law, in so far as they are composed
and written in the Old and New Testaments, are abrogated for a true
disciple of Christ, for he has a law written in his heart that he love
God alone, according to which he can direct all his actions, though he
has nothing in writing."[27] Such a position tends to make Scripture su-
perfluous; yet Denck contended that only to the degree that one is
transformed by the light of Christ is the written law done away with.
To the degree that one lacks the light given by the Spirit, one is still
subject to the law.

No less committed to obedience and discipleship under the cross
were the Pietists in the continental Reformed and Lutheran churches.
While generally holding to the third use of the law as a guide in the
Christian life, they also emphasized its condemning function, which
leads to faith in the gospel. Philip Spener argued that the law alone,
however, cannot effect a right repentance; in addition to the condemning word of the law one must be acquainted with the treasures
of salvation offered by Christ in his gospel. Spener distinguished between legal and evangelical repentance. Whereas the former is born
out of one's own struggle to overcome despair, the latter is derived
from faith and the power of the Spirit.[28]

Spener did not hesitate to uphold Christian perfection as a valid
goal, though he cautioned that in daily life we could attain it only to
a degree. Drawing a distinction between "having sin" and "doing sin,"
he contended that only those who commit sin consciously are guilty
of "doing sin." Despite the fact that it is Christ alone who fulfills the
law, Christians as disciples of Christ are given the grace to keep the
law.

John Wesley

Another theologian passionately concerned with obedience to
Christ was John Wesley, whose evangelical theology was molded by
Moravian Pietism and English Puritanism. For Wesley, the law not only
reveals to us our true nature, thereby moving us to seek for Christ,

but it also serves to draw those who are justified into a deeper relationship with Christ.[29] It functions both as a schoolmaster that leads us to Christ and as a guide and norm for Christian life. God's law is not made void through faith; on the contrary, faith is the means by which God's law is established.[30] The law is not the basis of salvation but a guidepost that helps us to remain on the way to salvation. It is not a means of justification, though it plays an important role in our sanctification by keeping us aware of the sin that lingers within and of the ideal of perfection toward which we must strive.

Wesley believed that there can be a preparation for faith in Christ, since all people are heirs of prevenient grace that enables them to seek for faith. In his view, repentance and conviction of sin precede faith, though the fullness of repentance follows faith. Works of the law can awaken within us a desire for faith, but they do not justify us. The fruits of faith, on the other hand, give evidence of the genuineness of our justification. In contrast to Luther, Wesley did not see an antithesis between James and Paul but instead a complementarity. They were referring to both a different kind of faith and a different kind of works. Paul was condemning the works of the law while James was upholding works that proceed from faith. Paul was affirming the power and efficacy of saving faith in Jesus Christ, while James was lamenting the powerlessness of a purely intellectual faith in Christ.

Experience as well as the study of Scripture had convinced Wesley of the integral relationship between law and gospel. He had learned

that there is no contrariety at all between the law and the gospel; that there is no need for the law to pass away, in order to the establishing the gospel. Indeed neither of them supersedes the other, but they agree perfectly well together. Yea, the very same words, considered in different respects are parts both of the law and of the gospel: if they are considered as commandments, they are parts of the law; if as promises of the gospel.[31]

We can take heart from the fact that "every command in holy writ is only a covered promise. . . . God hath engaged to give whatsoever He commands. Does He command us then to 'pray without ceasing,' to 'rejoice evermore,' to be 'holy as He is holy'? It is enough: He will work in us this very thing: it shall be unto us according to His word."[32]

Wesley nevertheless came to draw a distinction between "the law of works," from which Christians are emancipated, and "the law of faith," in which the commands of God are fulfilled by faith working through love. While we are dead to the law of works, "God has established another law in its place, even the law of faith: and we are all under this law to God and to Christ: both our Creator and our Redeemer require us to observe it."[33] As in his perception of God's promises hidden in God's commands, Wesley here anticipates a similar emphasis in Karl Barth.

Wesley went beyond the Pietists in his belief that Christians can be perfected in love through a second work of grace, which like the first needs only to be received by faith. He was convinced that through the gift of perfect love Christians could live in victory over sin. Nevertheless, even in the state of entire sanctification, we are still guilty of involuntary transgressions. We will always be troubled by infirmities and temptations, but we need not and should not be sinners. Wesley defined sin as a conscious transgression of a known law of God. This clearly stands at variance with the prevailing Reformation understanding of sin as an inherent inclination to evil that is never eradicated entirely in this life, even by sanctifying grace.

The dangers in both Pietism and Methodism are legalism and perfectionism. Obedience to the law becomes the condition for remaining in the salvation provided by Christ, and holiness in heart and life is seen as an achievement as well as a gift.

Niebuhr and Bonhoeffer

A formidable opponent of all moralism and perfectionism was Reinhold Niebuhr. As one standing in the tradition of Lutheranism, Niebuhr upheld Christianity as a religion of grace rather than law.[34] In his view, the grace of God calls us to take responsibility in the life of the community even though such action may violate the ideal of love.[35] But we can be confident that in our social involvement our sins are covered by the grace of God if we but cling to Christ in his mercy and forgiveness.

For Niebuhr the law of love is a higher standard of righteousness than law. It both fulfills and negates the demands of the law. At the same time, the Christian religion cannot be reduced even to the law of love, since grace is assured us through faith even though we fall short of this law in our daily lives.

If we are to function as responsible citizens of the state, however, we must supplement the law of love with general principles of justice, such as equality and freedom, which are drawn from the wisdom of the race. In a sense, then, the law of justice (or the moral law) precedes the promises of the gospel, since it directs us to these promises, and it also follows the gospel by giving guidance to our decisions in the civic or social spheres of life.

In Niebuhr's' apologetic endeavor, which is especially evident in his sermons, we see at work the Lutheran principle that law prepares the way for redemption by reminding us of our guilt and sin. This consciousness of guilt may lead to a creative despair that induces faith.[36] Only when we despair of ourselves and perceive the limits of our goodness and wisdom are we ready to hear the good news of God's unmerited forgiveness. The gospel is the answer to the knowledge of the human predicament provided by the law.

Dietrich Bonhoeffer, too, reflects the Lutheran heritage by acknowledging the tension between law and gospel. Yet he also provides a corrective to Lutheranism by emphasizing the integral relation of the two and the decisive role of obedience in the Christian life. The commandment of God, which is the norm for ethics, "transcends the difference between the law and the gospel. Christ calls, the disciple follows; that is grace and commandment in one."[37] Obedience to the call of Christ precedes even the gift of faith, though it remains a dead work of the law until it is fulfilled in faith. After faith our obedience must be deepened and expanded or else we will fail to perceive the significance of the claims of God upon us. When we allow our lives to fall prey to disorder and indiscipline, it becomes exceedingly difficult for us to hear God's commandment and to grasp the meaning of his judgment and mercy.[38]

Bonhoeffer was intent on combating the heresy of cheap grace, which he saw in the established state-supported churches of Europe. It was manifested in baptism without church discipline, absolution without personal confession, forgiveness without repentance, grace without discipleship. While insistent that our justification has its source only in God's free mercy, he was equally adamant that it must give rise to works of repentance and obedience if it is genuine. This is why he could assert, "The only man who has the right to say that he is justified by grace alone is the man who has left all to follow Christ."[39]

Karl Barth

Barth upholds not the antithesis between law and gospel (as in Luther) but instead their underlying harmony (as in Calvin). With the Reformed fathers he seeks to ground ethics not in love as such but in "obeying the commandments as *God's* commandments. The Law keeps its place beside the Gospel as another, a second, reality, equally true and commanding and necessary because the one God stands behind both, because the one Holy Spirit imparts both to men."[40]

Whereas Luther grounded the law in the holiness of God, Barth sees its source as the love of God. "The law should not be so unequivocally grouped with the *devil*, *sin*, and *reason*, as it sometimes is in Luther, nor should it be understood in a relation to God's *wrath* that is so clearly taken for granted."[41] On the contrary, it does not stand over against the gospel as something that accuses and destroys us but rather is a preparation for the gospel. The law like the gospel is a product of the grace of God and is given for the sake of our redemption.

In contradistinction to classical Reformed Protestantism, Barth entertains basically two uses for the law: to prepare the way for the gospel and to guide our response to the gospel. He rejects the political use of the law, for he does not acknowledge any positive relationship between God's law and human laws. The law cannot be made into a legislative or ethical standard which can determine or preserve conduct. Although God's commandment is heard by all people, it is invariably misunderstood because of sin. The law is fully or rightly known only as it appears with the gospel. Barth seeks to derive norms for the state not from the Old Testament law but from the person and work of Jesus Christ.

Barth heartily concurs with the Reformed tradition that the second face of the law is the gospel and the second face of the gospel is the law. The law, he argues, is the form of the gospel, and the gospel is the content of the law. The law is the grace of God in veiled form and the gospel the grace of God in unveiled form. It is not only the gospel that sets us free but also the law, since it leads directly into the gospel.[42] The law is not found alongside the gospel but in the gospel. The law, rightly understood, can never be reduced to a set of ethical standards but is to be seen as the law of freedom capable of being grasped only by faith.

Going further than Calvin, Barth maintains that the gospel has priority over the law, even in the area of knowledge. We first hear the gospel and then are able to understand the law. Whereas Calvin's emphasis was on the law with the gospel and Luther's on the law before the gospel, so Barth's is on the gospel before the law. The law is basically a response to the gospel. Barth reminds us that even the Decalogue begins with the announcement of inconceivable grace. The evangelical indicative is prior to the moral imperative.[43] It is the misused or misinterpreted law that comes before the gospel.[44]

In Barth's theology, when the commandments of God are viewed in the light of the gospel, they become permissions rather than simply prohibitions. "You shall not" becomes "You need not." The imperatives are transposed into indicatives, the demands into promises. The law is a permission because it both orders human beings to live in response to the gospel and gives them the freedom to do it. In commanding, God provides the power to obey. The law is to be seen as an opportunity for service, and therefore it becomes a privilege. We are invited, not ordered, to care for our neighbor in love. "You shall not kill" becomes "You may live." The No is made to serve the Yes.

On the basis of Barth's theology, it is possible to offer a Christological interpretation of the commandments that constitute the Decalogue, a venture in which Barth himself sometimes engaged. The first commandment now becomes an invitation to fellowship with the one Lord, Jesus Christ (cf. Matt. 22:1–14; Luke 14:15–24). The sixth commandment is transposed into a permission to embrace Christ, the giver and fount of life. "You shall not kill" may now be translated "You need not deny life (Christ)."

The divine commandment always directs us to Christ, for he is the supreme and definitive manifestation of God's grace.[45] We are called to pattern our lives after his example. This does not mean that we must copy the historical details of his lifestyle, but it does mean that we are to look to his life and death in determining our response to ethical issues in the present.

Barth acknowledges that the law always critiques us, but it does not necessarily condemn us. Because it critiques us, it can function as a guide or corrective. But the so-called ethical use is not the finishing point. It leads immediately into its spiritual use—to prepare the way for and reveal the gospel of free grace.

According to Barth, the law of God is a guide and norm for all peoples, not just Christians. Here he appears to be in tension with one side of Calvin's theology.[46] The "natural man" will also hear the divine commandment but will misunderstand it as a law of works. If we hear it as a law of grace, then we hear it as the law of the spirit of life in Christ Jesus. It then becomes the law of grace and liberty.

It should be recognized that the differences between law and gospel are overcome in Barth's theology. For example, the command of Jesus to the paralyzed man, "Rise up and walk," follows immediately upon his declaration of assurance, "Your sins are forgiven" (Luke 5:23). Because this command is really an extension of the word of forgiveness, it could be interpreted as both law and gospel (Arthur C. Cochrane).[47]

The divine commandment and the divine promise are two sides of the same coin.

The law by itself separated from the gospel becomes a misunderstood or misused law. "Where there is only Law, only an armour of virtue and duty, however strong and brilliant, what place is there for the Gospel," asks Barth, "and how can the Law really be fulfilled?"[48]

Our motivation for obedience to the law is gratitude for the love of God revealed in the gospel and clarified by the law. Because Jesus Christ is the content of both law and gospel, the Christian life is to be seen as a glad response to God's incomparable grace in the freedom that comes to us through both law and gospel.

Just as the law of God is reinterpreted as the law of freedom in Barth's theology, so sin is also given a new meaning. No longer the transgression of an external moral code, as in legalistic religion, it is now viewed as the breaking of a personal relationship. It is the refusal to let the Spirit have his way in our lives.

Not surprisingly, Barth's original and creative exposition of the relationship of law and gospel has come under attack, especially from Lutherans.[49] Wingren accuses Barth of minimizing human guilt. He interprets Barth as saying that the gospel is primarily a "clarification" of the law rather than an act in which human guilt is removed. He also complains that Barth makes the gospel legalistic. Barth does affirm that the gospel includes an imperative even while it is basically an indicative. In his theology, the judgment of the law is not separated from the love revealed in Jesus Christ but now becomes a form of this grace and love.

At first glance, Barth's position seems close to that of Ritschl, a pillar of liberal theology in the later nineteenth century, but their differences are far more significant.[50] Ritschl anticipated Barth by holding to the priority of gospel over law. He contended that it is only within the community of faith and love that we can gain true knowledge of our sin. From the perspective of faith, the law becomes a law of love, the moral imperative of the kingdom of God. Ritschl envisions the kingdom of God as the moral unification of the human race brought about by the action of love. He here shows the influence of Kant who conceived of the kingdom as an ethical commonwealth existing under the laws of virtue, which are entirely internal and noncoercive. In Ritschl's theology, God is exclusively love, and references to the wrath and punitive judgments of God in the Bible are dismissed as products of a limited horizon.[51]

While sharing Ritschl's concern for ethics and community, Barth

sharply challenges this theology.[52] First of all, he understands the kingdom of God not as a cultural or even a religious possibility but as an
eschatological reality that breaks into our world from the beyond. Barth
also vigorously affirms the dimensions of wrath and judgment in the
activity of God, though he sees them as subordinate to God's love,
indeed as forms of God's love. For Ritschl sin is defined as ignorance
with respect to its origin and as selfishness in its content. Barth can
also speak of sin in terms of human ignorance of God, but this, he
insists, is a guilty ignorance: as sinners we wilfully suppress the knowledge of ourselves given in our humanity, which reflects the *imago Dei*
even in the state of sin.[53] Sin cannot erase but certainly obscures the
indissoluble relationship between God the Creator and man the creature. For Barth, our ignorance is not excusable and by that fact forgiv-
able (as with Ritschl) but is a sign of unbelief and rebellion that can
only be atoned for and expiated. Whereas Ritschl understands sin primarily in terms of deeds, Barth with the Reformers conceives of sin as
a state of enmity with a holy God.[54] While Ritschl sees the law as the
universal imperative of love, Barth views the law as a particular divine
commandment that kills in order to make alive, that judges in order
to bring us to a renewed trust in God's mercy and forgiveness.

Dispensationalism

Presenting a radically different understanding of law and gospel is
dispensational fundamentalism, a strand of theology that has had a
considerable impact on the American scene. Associated with such
names as John Nelson Darby, James H. Brookes, James M. Gray, C. I.
Scofield, Lewis Sperry Chafer, and Charles C. Ryrie, it represents a
creative restatement of the gospel.[55]

The Christian life is depicted as the separated life—separated from
the sin of the world and unto godliness and holiness. The "man of
faith" is no longer under the Jewish law, which belongs to an older
dispensation, but is now under the gospel. The people of God are
called out of the apostate church as well as the world as we enter now
into the last days.

In this perspective, the law and the gospel are severed, for they
signify two contrasting dispensations. The gospel is not found in the
Old Testament nor does the church have its genesis in Israelite history
(as Calvin alleged). Law and grace are mutually exclusive. To Scofield,
"It is . . . of the most vital moment to observe that Scripture never, in
any dispensation, *mingles* these two principles. Law always has a place

and work distinct and wholly diverse from that of grace."[56] Hal Lindsey believes that "to mix these principles robs the law of its bona fide terror and grace of its creative freeness."[57] When one is under grace, one is no longer under the Mosaic Law. The gospel signifies freedom from the law, though sometimes in this kind of theology the gospel is unwittingly transposed into a new law.

A distinction is also made between the church age and the kingdom age, which is entirely in the future. The first represents the present dispensation between the resurrection of Christ and his second coming. The second will begin when Christ ushers in his millennial reign at his Parousia. In this scenario, the epistles of Paul pertain to the church age and the Gospels to the age of the kingdom. The teachings of Jesus form part of the law of the old dispensation, but they are also to be applied in the millennial kingdom. They are beneficial to the Christian in this present age but are not of primary significance.

Dispensationalists have been accused of both a new legalism and antinomianism. By championing freedom from the Mosaic law, they seem to leave the Christian without any guidelines except love. On the other hand, by emphasizing the binding character of the Pauline commands (such as women keeping silent in the churches), they sometimes lapse into a legalistic orientation.

Some critics of dispensationalism have detected similarities to Marcionism. The radical dispensationalists, like the Marcionites, elevate the Pauline epistles and call into question the Christian significance of the Old Testament. They also tend to deemphasize the historical Jesus.

There is, of course, no one theology that has universal authority among all who identify themselves as dispensationalists. Whereas some would see the mission of the church exclusively in terms of the heralding of the gospel of free grace to a lost and dying world, others would make an attempt to unite evangelism with discipleship, the proclamation of the New Testament church with the teachings of Jesus.

What I appreciate in the witness of such groups as the Plymouth Brethren, the original propagators of dispensationalism, is their emphasis on the free grace of God as the only source of salvation, their acknowledgement of the radically new character of the gospel, and their understanding of the Christian life as one of Christian liberty. They also have New Testament warrant for their contention that when a church becomes apostate it is then the obligation of Bible-believing Christians to sever ties and organize new fellowships. While mainline denominations have reduced the gospel to a set of ethical principles, dispensationalists have, for the most part, remained true to the New

Testament and Reformation teaching that the gospel is basically the proclamation of God's reconciling action in Jesus Christ to save sinners from sin, death, and hell.

Where I take issue with dispensationalists is in their elevating to the level of dogma such marginal doctrines as the millennium, the rapture of the saints, and the great tribulation, as well as such questionable doctrines as the restoration of glory to Israel as a political entity. At times, these themes become the primary content of their sermons on Christ and his kingdom. I also take exception to their tendency to separate the two Testaments, thereby losing sight of Calvin's insight into the one covenant of grace with two manifestations. Again, the call to separation is often sounded too early so that churches that need renewal from within are left to wither on the vine.

We need to recover Luther's understanding that the church is not a gathered fellowship of true believers separated from the world by virtue of a divine infusion of holiness but instead a hospital for sick souls, a church that recognizes itself as a company of sinners always in need of divine grace and mercy. We should, of course, seek for a regenerate church membership but at the same time bear in mind that it is not our task to separate the wheat from the tares. This will be done by our Lord himself at the time of his second coming (Matt. 13:24–30; Mark 4:26–29).

Notes

1. See Ernst Troeltsch, *The Social Teaching of the Christian Churches*, trans. Olive Wyon (London: George Allen & Unwin, 1931), pp. 257–343.
2. See Heiko Oberman, *The Harvest of Medieval Theology: Gabriel Biel and Late Medieval Nominalism* (Grand Rapids: Eerdmans, 1967).
3. Walter Kasper, "Law and Gospel," in *Encyclopaedia of Theology: The Concise "Sacramentum Mundi,"* ed. Karl Rahner (New York: Seabury, 1975) [pp. 834–36], p. 835.
4. Avery Dulles, "Justification in Contemporary Catholic Theology," in *Justification by Faith: Lutherans and Catholics in Dialogue* ed. H. George Anderson, T. Austin Murphy, and Joseph A. Burgess (Minneapolis: Augsburg Publishing House, 1985), vol. 7, [pp. 256–77], p. 277. See Augustine, *De Spiritu et Littera* 19, 34.
5. Dulles, "Justification in Contemporary Catholic Theology," p. 276.
6. Quoted in Bonhoeffer, *Ethics*, p. 253.
7. *The Table-Talk of Martin Luther*, trans. William Hazlitt (Philadelphia: Lutheran Publication Society, n.d.), p. 125.
8. Paul Althaus, *The Theology of Martin Luther*, 2d printing, trans. Robert C. Schultz (Philadelphia: Fortress, 1970), pp. 261, 262.
9. Luther, *Werke* (Weimar Ausgabe) 39: 274. Quoted in Althaus, *Theology of Martin Luther*, p. 272.
10. See Paul Althaus, *The Divine Command*, trans. Franklin Sherman (Philadelphia: Fortress, 1966).
11. Thielicke, *Theological Ethics* 1: pp. 133–35.
12. Robert D. Brinsmead, "Verdict," 2, no. 6 (Special Issue 1980): p. 28.

13. *The Formula of Concord*, in *The Book of Concord*, trans. and ed. Theodore G. Tappert (Philadelphia: Fortress, 1959), pp. 563–68.

14. See William Lazareth, " 'Just War' in a Nuclear Age?" *The Bulletin: Moravian Theological Seminary* (Fall 1968): pp. 1–17; and Gerhard O. Forde, "Forensic Justification and Law in Lutheran Theology," in *Justification by Faith 7*: p. 302.

15. *Luther's Works*, ed. Jaroslav Pelikan (St. Louis: Concordia Publishing House, 1956), 21: p. 113.

16. Martin Luther, "The Church Postil," in *Works*, ed. J. N. Lenker (Luther House, 1905), 5: p. 175.

17. *John Calvin's Sermons on the Ten Commandments*, ed. and trans. Benjamin W. Farley, foreword by Ford Lewis Battles (Grand Rapids: Baker Book House, 1980), pp. 23–25.

18. John Calvin, *Commentary on a Harmony of the Evangelists, Matthew, Mark and Luke*, trans. William Pringle (Grand Rapids: Eerdmans, 1949), 1: p. 275.

19. Ibid., p. 278.

20. John Calvin, *Institutes of the Christian Religion*, rev. ed., trans. John Allen, vol. I (Philadelphia: Presbyterian Board of Christian Education, 1936) II, 11, 7, p. 496.

21. It should be noted that this is a matter of emphasis only, for both Luther and Barth also held that law and gospel belong together. For a helpful study on Calvin's conception of the law, see I. John Hesselink, *Calvin's Concept and Use of the Law* (Ph.D. diss., Basel University, 1961). Also see I. John Hesselink, "Luther and Calvin on Law and Gospel In Their Galatians Commentaries," *Reformed Review* 37, no. 2 (Winter 1984): pp. 69–82.

22. John Calvin, *Institutes of the Christian Religion*, Vol. I ed. John T. McNeill trans. Ford Lewis Battles (Philadelphia: Westminster, 1960), III, 3, 4, pp. 596–97. In contrast to Bucer, Calvin held that only gospel or evangelical repentance is properly designated as repentance. At the same time, he acknowledged that there can be remorse over sin and fear of God's wrath that lead not to Christ but to deeper condemnation.

23. Cf. Calvin: "The authority of our law must not be deprecated, for it contains the truth of God which abides forever, which never varies, and which does not perish." *Calvin's Sermons on the Ten Commandments*, p. 48.

24. Ibid., p. 98.

25. Harold J. Grimm, *The Reformation Era: 1500–1650* (New York: Macmillan Co., 1965), p. 267.

26. See George Huntston Williams, *The Radical Reformation* (Philadelphia: Westminster Press, 1962), pp. 304–9; Robert Friedmann, *The Theology of Anabaptism* (Scottdale, Pa.: Herald, 1973), pp. 134–38; and Jaroslav Pelikan, *Reformation of Church and Dogma (1300–1700)* (Chicago: University of Chicago Press, 1984), pp. 314–22.

27. Quoted in Henning Graf Reventlow, *The Authority of the Bible and the Rise of the Modern World*, trans. John Bowden (Philadelphia: Fortress, 1985), p. 57.

28. See Dale Brown, *Understanding Pietism* (Grand Rapids: Eerdmans, 1978), p. 90–92.

29. See Harald Lindström, *Wesley and Sanctification* (Wilmore, Kentucky: Francis Asbury Press, 1980), pp. 75–82.

30. John Wesley, "The Character of a Methodist," in *The Works of the Reverend John Wesley* (New York: T. Mason & G. Lane, 1839), vol. 5, p. 241.

31. *John Wesley's Forty-Four Sermons*, (London: Epworth, 1975), p. 255.

32. Ibid., pp. 255–56.

33. John Wesley, *A Plain Account of Christian Perfection* (London: Epworth, 1952), pp. 70, 71.

34. Niebuhr's position reflects his original affiliation with the Pietistic, Lutheran-oriented Evangelical Synod of North America, which later merged with the German Reformed Church to become the Evangelical and Reformed Church (now a part of the United Church of Christ). See chap. 2, note 9.

35. See Reinhold Niebuhr, "Why the Christian Church is Not Pacifist," in *Christianity and Power Politics* (New York: Charles Scribner's Sons, 1940), pp. 1–32.

36. Reinhold Niebuhr, *The Nature and Destiny of Man* (New York: Charles Scribner's Sons,

1951), 2: pp. 56–57, 117, 206–7; idem, *Faith and History*, (New York: Charles Scribner's Sons, 1949), pp. 160–65.

37. Bonhoeffer, *The Cost of Discipleship*, p. 49.
38. Bonhoeffer, *Ethics*, p. 136.
39. Bonhoeffer, *The Cost of Discipleship*, p. 43.
40. Karl Barth, *The Word of God and the Word of Man* trans. Douglas Horton (Boston: Pilgrim Press, 1928), p. 264.
41. Barth, *Ethics*, p. 90.
42. For an insightful, though not altogether balanced, critique of Barth's position see Helmut Thielicke, *Theological Ethics* 1: pp. 98–117.
43. Isaiah 6 tends to support Barth's view, for the commandment follows rather than precedes the announcement of the forgiveness of sins. The knowledge of sin, moreover, is derived not from the universal awareness of moral law but from a personal encounter with the living God. Cf. Isa. 12:6; 35:1–4.
44. On Barth's conception of the misused law see Gerhard O. Forde, *The Law-Gospel Debate* (Minneapolis: Augsburg, 1969), pp. 142–47, 172–74.
45. Barth, *Church Dogmatics*, II, 2, pp. 566–83.
46. See Calvin, *Institutes*, ed. John T. McNeill trans. Ford Lewis Battles, 4, 20, 16, pp. 1504–1505.
47. Theological conversation with Arthur Cochrane, March 9, 1982. University of Dubuque Theological Seminary.
48. Barth, *Church Dogmatics*, III, 4, p. 71.
49. Lutheran theologians who tend to agree with Barth include Helmut Gollwitzer, Eberhard Jüngel, Hermann Diem, and Gerhard Heintze. For Barth's comments on his Lutheran critics see *Church Dogmatics*, IV, 3, 1, pp. 370, 371.
50. For Ritschl's position on law and gospel see Forde, *The Law-Gospel Debate*, pp. 96–119.
51. Albrecht Ritschl, *The Christian Doctrine of Justification and Reconciliation*, trans. H. R. Mackintosh and A. B. Macaulay (Clifton, N.J.: Reference Book Publishers, 1966), pp. 255–84, 350–67.
52. See Barth, *Church Dogmatics*, IV, 1, pp. 381–83, 490; and idem, *Protestant Theology in the Nineteenth Century* (Valley Forge, Pa.: Judson Press, 1973), pp. 654–61.
53. Barth, *Christian Life*, pp. 115–53; and idem, *Community, State and Church*, ed. Will Herberg (New York: Doubleday Anchor Books, 1960), pp. 87, 88.
54. Barth, *Church Dogmatics* IV, 1, p. 382.
55. See Norman C. Kraus, *Dispensationalism in America* (Richmond, Va.: John Knox, 1958); Charles C. Ryrie, *Dispensationalism Today* (Chicago: Moody, 1965); John F. Walvoord, *The Blessed Hope and the Tribulation* (Grand Rapids: Zondervan, 1976); and Daniel P. Fuller, *Gospel and Law* (Grand Rapids: Eerdmans, 1980).
56. C. I. Scofield, *Rightly Dividing the Word of Truth* (1896; reprint, Neptune, N.J: Loizeaux Brothers), p. 34.
57. Hal Lindsey with C. C. Carlson, *Satan Is Alive and Well on Planet Earth* (Grand Rapids: Zondervan, 1972), p. 179.

CHAPTER 8

An Ethics of the Law and Gospel

It is for freedom that Christ has set us free. Stand firm, then, and do
not let yourselves be burdened again by a yoke of slavery.

GALATIANS 5:1 NIV

Make neither of your own righteousness a safe-conduct to heaven, nor
of God's mercy a safe-conduct to sin.

AUGUSTINE

Preach the law to the proud, the gospel to the broken-hearted.

MARTIN LUTHER

The congregation acknowledges and bears witness to God's love for
the world in Jesus Christ as law and gospel. The two can never be
separated; nor can they ever be identified.

DIETRICH BONHOEFFER

God's Word can indeed say many things to us. It not only can comfort
us, heal us, vivify us, it not only can instruct and enlighten us, it can
also judge us, punish us, kill us, and it actually does all of these.

KARL BARTH

A Biblical Alternative

In contradistinction to both legalism and situational ethics, I propose an ethics of the law and gospel. This position can be shown to
be solidly grounded in the biblical and apostolic faith. It should also
be seen as an alternative to a kingdom-of-God ethics (Rauschenbush,
Ritschl, Segundo, Moltmann, the early Braaten), which verges on utopianism and triumphalism.

By the law I am thinking of the moral law but also and above all
of the divine or revealed law, which deepens and expands the meaning
of the moral law. I do not have in mind the ceremonial law of the Old
Testament nor the ecclesiastical law nor the civil law. This moral law
(or what is better described as a moral order) is written into the con-

stitution of the universe and therefore can also be called the natural law. Yet its directives are not universally trustworthy because they are obscured by sinful reason. At the same time, we know enough to render us inexcusable (Rom. 1:20, 21). The moral law is revealed and amplified in the biblical revelation which makes explicit what is implicit in nature and conscience.

In this discussion, the gospel refers to the apostolic message of reconciliation and redemption through the suffering, death, and resurrection of our Lord Jesus Christ. We are justified by the gospel despite our transgression of the law. The gospel contradicts all ceremonialism, ritualism, legalism, and moralism. What the gospel does away with is the old externalism, but not the demands of the law.

The gospel signifies both the fulfillment and negation of the moral law of God. Jesus said that he had come not to abolish the law and the prophets but to fulfill them (Matt. 5:17; cf. Rom. 13:10). But he also declared, "You have heard that it was said to those of old. . . . But I say to you . . ." (Matt. 5:21, 22, 27, 28, 33, 34, 38, 39, 43, 44 NKJV). The imperatives of the gospel deepen and radicalize rather than relax the demands of the law.

In the light of the gospel, the law is heightened rather than lessened. It is now seen in its true perspective—as the demands not of a moral code but of faith and love. The law that promoted sin and death because of human incapacity and unwillingness to obey the dictates of God is superseded by the law of grace, in which promise and command are united. Paul contended that we are no longer under "the law of sin and death" but now under "the law of the Spirit of life in Christ Jesus" (Rom. 8:2; cf. Rom. 7:9). We are no longer under the taboos of Judaic tradition but now "under the law of Christ" (1 Cor. 9:21).

Our new status does not invite us to relax our diligence. Jesus told his disciples that our righteousness must exceed the righteousness of the scribes and Pharisees (Matt. 5:20). He warned the Pharisees that they ought to seek the higher righteousness without neglecting the duties of rabbinic law (Luke 11:42). Whereas rabbinic law required tithing, the higher righteousness demands that one give up everything for the sake of the kingdom (Matt. 13:44, 45). The rich man who came to Jesus and asked what he must do to inherit eternal life was told, "Go, sell everything you have and give to the poor, and you will have treasure in heaven. Then come, follow me" (Mark 10:21 NIV). This is to be understood not as a general moral principle (as utopian communalists would have it) nor as a counsel of perfection that pertains to those who would embark on the religious life (as in traditional Roman Catholic spirituality); instead, it is a divine commandment intended for that particular man whose riches constituted an obstacle to the kingdom. At the same time, it is a commandment that throws much light on the nature of Christian discipleship under the cross.

Nowhere in the Bible is the law portrayed as a tyrant or a curse. The prophet declared, "It pleased the Lord for the sake of his righteousness to make his law great and glorious" (Isa. 42:21 NIV). Paul called the law "holy . . . just and good" (Rom. 7:12). Yet it has the effect of being a tyrant or a curse when we disobey it. Sin deceives, but not the law (Rom. 7:11). "The sting of death is sin," said Paul, "and the power of sin is the law" (1 Cor. 15:56). When we defy the law we must suffer the consequences of our sin—the condemnation of the law.

The Lutheran scholar Ragnar Bring detects a signal difference between Luther and Paul on this subject.[1] Paul, unlike Luther, did not see the law as primarily a curse or tyrant, as a power allied with sin and death. For Paul we do not overthrow the law but by our faith uphold the law (Rom. 3:31). Faith reaches out and fulfills the righteousness that the law demands. Bring pays tribute to Luther for his creative interpretation of law and gospel but cautions that this must not be confused with Paul's position. He nonetheless acknowledges that Luther grasped the essential core of Paul's message—that our righteousness does not come from the law but from God.

Certainly biblical faith teaches that the law is a preparation for the gospel, but this is the law illumined by grace, the law united with the Spirit. The law by itself can prick our consciences. It can condemn, but in and of itself it cannot save. The law is a stepping-stone to Christ only when we realize that it is basically a blind alley as far as salvation is concerned. Paul confessed, "If it had not been for the law, I should not have known sin" (Rom. 7:7). The law functions first of all as a mirror to show what we really are apart from Christ.

In addition, the law is a guideline for Christian conduct, an objective standard that shows us the way to live. It is a regulative norm for Christian life, however, only when united with the gospel, only when seen in the light of the gospel. The believing sinner can regard the law as "a friendly guide" (Berkouwer). Helmut Thielicke acknowledges this third use of the law and sees Calvin and Luther as very close on this point.[2]

The orthodox Lutheran dictum that the law always accuses is not valid. It can be a lamp that lightens our pathway (Ps. 119:105; Prov. 6:23), a lodestar that keeps us on the road to life. Though it may well be an occasion for despair for the one who persists in sin, it can be a source of consolation and strength for the one who appeals to the mercy of Christ.

The law is given to afflict the comfortable but also to guide the afflicted. In addition, it serves to restrain the sinner. Here we see its three uses in classical Protestantism: a mirror, a restraint, and a guide.

In contradistinction to both Lutherans and Calvinists, I contend that the principal use of the law varies according to the existential situation in which people find themselves. When the church or world is arrogant and self-satisfied, it needs to hear the law as the word of judgment and condemnation. When sinners are in agony because of their sin, they need to hear the promise of mercy given in the gospel, which sends them back to the law as a guide for righteous living. When people are tempted to take the law into their own hands, they need to hear the threat of the higher law that holds them accountable before God.

The Decalogue is a codified form of the law of God, as is also the Sermon on the Mount. Taken by themselves, they represent moral truths that clearly partake of the relativity of culture and history. When illumined by the love of Christ and united with the mind of Christ, however, they become absolute criteria. They are transmuted from general moral truths into divine commandments for our time that carry the authority of the voice of the living God.

I agree with Jan Milič Lochman that the validity of the Decalogue for Christians "is not the validity of an abstract law." The commandments

are valid in the living context in which they were set and given to us by God himself. . . . Within this life-giving context we must seek the concrete meaning of the Ten Commandments for the actual situation of our churches and congregations. This meaning is not something we already have or will ever have "at our finger tips," firmly in our possession. God's commandment is never valid as a dead and deadening "letter" but only as an imperative venture of freedom and love, the precise content of which must always be sought and practised in the given circumstances in which we find ourselves.[3]

The Decalogue in and of itself represents prohibitions designed to preserve moral order and advance justice in society. When seen in the light of the gospel, the Ten Commandments become positive guidelines for action. Barth's observation is helpful: "This God and the Bible, His commanding and its commanding, are not to be separated."[4] For this reason the Decalogue "is the foundation statute of the divine covenant of grace and valid for all ages" and for "all the situations of our lives."[5]

When united with the norm of the gospel, the deepest intention of the law is fulfilled. We should not go to a criterion outside the law but to one within the law. The law is the form of the gospel and the gospel is the content of the law (Barth); the two are distinct and yet inseparable. The true meaning of the law cannot be apprehended apart from the gospel. But conversely, the full intent of the gospel cannot be understood apart from the demands of the law.

There will always be a tension between the infinite requirement and the finite commandment (Paul Ricoeur). Yet we hear the voice of the living God only in and through the finite commandment, the word of interpretation pronounced by the prophets and priests of the church. We hear the living word of God only in conjunction with the written word and the proclaimed word.

The love of the Lord Jesus Christ gives us the power and motivation to fulfill the law (at least partially). It makes it possible for us to keep the commandments. Jesus said, "If you love me, you will keep my commandments" (John 14:15). The evidence of our love for Christ is our willingness to abide by his directives (cf. John 15:10; 1 Cor. 7:19; 1 John 2:4; 3:24; 5:2, 3; 2 John 6; Rev. 12:17; 14:12). Paul contended that by our works of faith and love we do not overthrow the law but uphold it (Rom. 3:31). He was here thinking of the whole Torah and not simply of the Decalogue.

Love transcends the law, but it does not cancel the law. It supersedes the letter of the law but is in accord with the spirit of the law. How do we know what love is? The apostle declares that "love is the fulfilling of the law" (Rom. 13:10; Gal. 5:14).

The norm for Christian ethics is not derived from the existential and cultural situation but instead applied to it. Yet the situation will partly determine the way it is applied. Moral values are based not on human need (as Harvey Cox says) but on the revelation of God in Jesus Christ.

Some situationists, such as Fletcher, have depicted love as absolute, but this is understood as a rational norm—the law of love—rather than the breaking in of the new reality of grace, which transcends the human imagination and turns around the human will. Situationists are disposed to think of love as a simple human possibility and therefore invariably confuse agape with brotherly or mutual love.[6] William Hamilton, for example, does not hesitate to equate Christian love with natural human love instead of with agape, the transforming grace of God.[7]

The norm for Christian conduct is not love as such but Jesus Christ, who unites love and truth, who calls us to obedience. He commands us to love and shows us how to love. Our appeal is both to the Christ who loves and the Christ who commands. Because his command is given to us in Scripture, the unity of the Spirit and the Word becomes our final criterion for ethical action.

We are called not to renounce the law but to embrace and love the law (Ps. 119:97, 165). The Psalmist declares, "I delight to do thy will, O my God; thy law is within my heart" (Ps. 40:8). Paul wrote, "The law is holy, and the commandment is holy and just and good" (Rom. 7:12). Upholding the law also involves embracing the Lawgiver, the holy God revealed in Jesus Christ. It means being conformed to the spirit of the law which comes from God.

We are justified only by the gospel, not by the law (Gal. 2:16). Yet we are justified for the law, for holiness. We are justified by faith, but for works (cf. Ps. 105:45; Eph. 2:10). Because the law is not a means to our justification, in one sense it can be said that the law is superseded and annulled.[8] It was in this context that Paul declared, "Christ is the end of the law, that every one who has faith may be justified" (Rom. 10:4; Gal. 3:25, 26). Yet the fruits of justification are realized only in obedience to the law, and this means obedience to the Lawgiver, the living God. The law is not a means to salvation, but it is a means to righteous living. We do good works not in order to be saved but because we are already saved and are impelled to witness to this by our love.

The gospel frees us from the burden of the law and from its penalty but not from obedience to the law. The gospel sets us free to obey, even to fulfill the law. We are paradoxically at the same time free *from* the law and *for* the law. We are freed from the burden of the law in order to live by the spirit of the law. In fact, as Paul points out, "the love of Christ leaves us no choice. . . . His purpose in dying for all was that men, while still in life, should cease to live for themselves" (2 Cor. 5:14, 15 NEB). Our Lord put it succinctly, "He who has my commandments and keeps them, he it is who loves me" (John 14:21; cf. John 14:15; 1 John 2:5). To love means to live in obedience to God's commands (2 John 6).[9]

The purpose of regeneration is spiritual and ethical obedience. This note is already found in Ezekiel: "And I will give them one heart, and put a new spirit within them; I will take the stony heart out of their flesh and give them a heart of flesh, that they may walk in my statutes and keep my ordinances and obey them; and they shall be my people, and I will be their God" (Ezek. 11:19, 20). Barth summed it up nicely: "Our return to obedience is indeed the aim of free grace. It is for this that it makes us free."[10]

Unity of the Law and Gospel

The gospel and law form an indissoluble but at the same time paradoxical unity. It is indissoluble because they both have their source in divine revelation. It is paradoxical because they appear to stand in tension, even in conflict, and yet this tension is resolved through faith in Jesus Christ as both Lord and Savior. Even Luther acknowledged this unity but contended that it was not obvious even to an illumined reason and could be grasped only by faith.

I agree with the theme of classical Reformed theology: "The second face of the Law is the Gospel, and the second face of the Gospel is the Law." This means that every promise of the gospel contains an imperative and every imperative of the law contains a promise. The law, to be sure, is basically a command, just as the gospel is primarily a promise, but they are not these things exclusively.

Both law and gospel can be a means of grace, but only when related to the other. The Lutheran theologian Edmund Schlink put it well: "As the law cannot be preached without Christ, so Christ's work cannot be preached without the law."[11]

The gospel apart from the law becomes cheap grace. It then promotes not the righteousness of God but antinomianism. The law apart from the gospel issues in works-righteousness or legalism. It also subverts the righteousness of faith that alone saves from sin. Apart from the gospel the law is merely ethical. Apart from the law the gospel becomes exclusively spiritual, removed from life in this world.

As the law drives us to the gospel, so the gospel points us ever again to the law. According to the Puritan divine Samuel Bolton, "The law sends us to the gospel that we may be justified; and the Gospel sends us to the law again to inquire what is our duty as those who are justified."[12]

The grace of God confirms the divine origin of the law, but it is not given primarily to serve law. It is given for the full salvation of humanity and therefore also for the greater glory of God. The church father Irenaeus declared, "The glory of God is man fully alive." God is glorified not when his people are brought to despair but when they are elevated to fellowship with him.

Dispensationalism tends to sever the unity of law and gospel, and this is also true of Lutheranism. The Reformed tradition, on the other hand, has accentuated this unity, though sometimes at the price of losing sight of the continuing tension between the two.

In Jesus Christ we see the unity of law and gospel. He is both the Lawgiver and the fulfillment of the law. He is also the embodiment of the gospel. Jesus Christ radicalized and internalized the law, and this is why his actions often seemed to go counter to the letter of the law.

The gospel does not oppose the demands of the law, but it does contradict the misunderstanding of the law as this had developed in legalistic Judaism. At the same time, it is in basic harmony with the original intention of the law.

Although law and gospel are complementary, they are not equal. Unity connotes interdependence but not equality. The law was given through the mediation of angels (cf. Acts 7:53; Gal. 3:19 NIV), while the gospel was given directly by God in the person of Jesus Christ. Grace is prior to the commandment, and this means that evangelism has priority over social service. At the same time, the law also plays a role in evangelism just as the gospel does in social service.

Against much traditional Calvinism, I contend that the gospel is distinguished from the law qualitatively as well as quantitatively. It is both the fulfillment and the negation of the demands of the law. The law separated from the message of salvation in Christ differs qualitatively from the gospel. It then exists as a law of works and condemnation.[13] It is still the law of God, but it is a misunderstood law.[14] When it is united with the gospel in faith, however, it then becomes the form of the gospel, and the qualitative distinction is overcome. Only when the law becomes at one with the claims of the gospel is it an effectual preparation for the gospel as well as a dependable guide for Christian living. This is because promise and command are now united in the one Word of God.

The gospel is not simply a means to the law as a higher end, but the law is now taken up in the gospel. We demonstrate our allegiance to the gospel by living in the spirit of the law. Our obedience to the law is a witness to the truth and integrity of the gospel.

The fundamental criterion in theological ethics is neither the law nor the gospel but the gospel-law. This is the law redefined by the gospel and the gospel supplemented by the law. The law is now transformed into the divine commandment, which is grace and command in one (Bonhoeffer). It is still to be distinguished from the gospel, which is basically the divine promise.

True freedom is freedom for obedience. It is not independence from the claims of the moral law but absolute dependence on the God who enables us to obey and fulfill this law. True freedom is not seeking to be master of one's fate and captain of one's soul (William Henley) but finding one's true master in service to the oppressed and despised of the world.

Does the law prepare the way for grace? While the law brings knowledge of sin (Rom. 3:20; 7:7), the person under sin seeks to suppress this knowledge. Consequently, apart from the light of Christ, the law yields a misunderstanding rather than a true perception of the human condition. The law by itself can arouse feelings of unworthiness, but it cannot lead us to confess we are sinners. It can remind us of our guilt, but only the law united with the gospel can convict us of our sin.[15]

It is the Spirit of God who awakens us to the real gravity of our condition, to our dire need for God's grace and mercy. "Without the Holy Spirit," Thielicke points out, "our distress would not have taught us to pray; it would have led us to curse. Without the Holy Spirit, the Law would not have been a custodian or schoolmaster to lead us to Christ; it would have been the pedagogue of death."[16]

In articulating Luther's position, Regin Prenter maintains that only in its spiritual use does the law drive sinners to the fount of God's mercy.[17] But this is not the law as such, as a universal principle of life. It is the law that is preached in conjunction with the gospel. It is the law that is illumined by the light of the Holy Spirit, who makes it "a servant for the task of preparing man for Christ."[18] Prenter argues that for Luther "the spiritual use of the law and the gospel is one saving word of God, the tempted and conquering, the crucified and the risen Christ, *one* living Lord."[19]

Not until we know Jesus Christ are we really confronted with the full significance of the law.[20] Then we also come to know the gravity of our sin and the depth of the judgment of God upon sin. Once we grasp the horrendous fact that it is our sins that sent Jesus to the cross, we are then moved to repentance and faith.

As Calvin perceived, the knowledge of God's love and forgiveness comes prior to our repentance. It is our misery that drives us to seek Christ, but none of us would flee to him without first being assured of God's goodness toward us.[21]

Can the law in its third (or ethical) use prepare the way for the gospel? The law as an ethical guide concerns the penultimate more than the ultimate. It has to do with our obligations to our fellow human beings in the world in which we live. At the same time, the motivation for our works of love is grounded in gratitude for what God has done for us in Christ. The goal of the Christian life is to let the light of the gospel shine through our good works so that people will give glory to the Father in heaven (Matt. 5:16). In our Christian activity, moreover, we are always acutely aware that these works will be judged on the last day. Therefore ultimate concerns impinge on and shape our penultimate tasks.

The law of God by itself cannot save and therefore cannot provide the solution to the human predicament. Its function is to point us to the gospel by reminding us of our sin and even more of God's grace that pardons sin. When united with the gospel, the law can be an instrument in our conversion, moving us by the Spirit to trust in God's love and mercy. It is in this light that we can appreciate the words of the Psalmist: "The law of the Lord is perfect, converting the soul" (Ps. 19:7 NKJV).

Lutheran Ethics

The Lutheran tradition has given fresh insight on the law in its spiritual use—as a taskmaster leading us to the gospel. It is to be commended for preserving the Pauline emphasis on grace alone and faith alone in the appropriation of salvation. In Lutheran Pietism there was also a salutary emphasis on the holy life.[22] The Pietists rightly saw that the whole counsel of God involves the divine commandment as well as the word of salvation, that we are called not only to faith in Jesus Christ but also to right conduct.

Even so, there has been a continuing tendency in Lutheranism to downplay the law of God in the living of the Christian life. A gospel ethic or love ethic is often contrasted with an ethics of law. A gospel reductionism has prevented many from appreciating the role of the commandments of God in Christian discipleship. This tendency is especially pronounced in neo-Lutheranism, though it is also present in Lutheran orthodoxy. When Bultmann describes Christian freedom as freedom from "all claims from within the world" or from "*all . . . norms of value,*" it creates the perhaps misleading impression that the codified law of God is no longer normative for the community of faith.[23] Eric Gritsch makes this astounding statement: "My freedom to care for my neighbor is nourished by the promise that before God morality does not matter at all."[24] Roy Harrisville totally rejects the third use of the law. Commenting on Romans 12:1–2 he contends that such terms as "summons," "demand," and "imperative" do not apply to the Christian life.[25] The only concepts he allows are "responsibility," "opportunity," and "possibility."

One can detect in neo-Lutheran theology a deemphasis on sanctification, indeed a complete subordination of sanctification to justification. It is said that we move forward in the Christian life but not upward.[26] But is not grace a power in us as well as divine favor toward us? Is not Barth on more solid ground when he depicts justification and sanctification as two sides of reconciliation? We are justified by faith, but we are sanctified by love. Both are decisive for divine election to find its goal in our lives.

Too often Lutherans portray the law as an obstacle to Christian liberty rather than a catalyst that gives form and content to the life liberated by grace. But the loving embrace of the law of God is how Christian freedom manifests itself. The Psalmist declared, "I will live in perfect freedom, because I try to obey your teachings" (Ps. 119:45 GNB).

The Lutheran emphasis on the law before the gospel also needs to be reexamined. Is not the fuller biblical picture that the grace of God is prior to the law? Adam and Eve were given life before they were told not to eat from the tree of knowledge. The Exodus from Egypt, the act by which God delivered his people from slavery, preceded the giving of the law on Mount Sinai. The prophet Ezekiel speaks of the outpouring of the Spirit as the prerequisite for the observance of the ordinances of God (Ezek. 36:26–32). Paul points out that the promise given to Abraham antedated the giving of the law, which came 430 years afterward. "For if the inheritance is by the law, it is no longer by promise; but God gave it to Abraham by a promise" (Gal. 3:18).

The law only drives us to grace when grace enables us to apprehend the law. Calvin realized that true repentance does not result from a fear of God's wrath but from an awareness of God's forgiveness: "The beginning of repentance is a sense of God's mercy."[27] The law therefore presupposes grace.

It is commonly said in neo-Lutheran circles that Jesus did not introduce a new law but only paradigms of love. Yet it is obvious that both Jesus and Paul gave specific commands. These commandments give content to the law of love. Salvation includes both promise and mandate, both deliverance and command, both faith and obedience.

While Luther was right that the law in its spiritual use drives us to repentance, is not there also a constructive use of the law that can guide the Christian in daily living? Although it is true that the law was originally given not for the just but for the lawless and disobedient (1 Tim.

1:9), is it not to show the lawless the meaning of true righteousness, which can be realized by faith working through love? Luther saw that the Christian insofar as he or she is a sinner is still under the law, but he also acknowledged that the Christian as one sanctified by Christ is called to follow Christ as example (here we see a possible convergence with Calvin).

Lutherans are correct that the law leads to the gospel, but does not the gospel also lead us to the law? If we love God, we will also strive to keep his commandments. Indeed, we shall know those who love Christ by their willingness to keep his commandments (John 14:21).

For neo-Lutherans the law is not the form of the gospel (as in Barth) but the form of this age. William Lazareth considers the church "primarily the agency of the gospel in the new age of Christ" and the state "primarily the agency of the law in the old age of Adam."[28] From my perspective, the law in its spiritual use is better described as the form of God's moral outrage against sin (Lutherans, I think, could subscribe to this). But in addition, I regard the law as a stepping-stone to the gospel and as the norm for Christian life together with the gospel.

Lutherans are fond of describing the gospel as the balm of God's grace and the law as the rod of God's anger. But is not the gospel, too, a sword that slays? (Calvin seemed to think so.)[29] The gospel, too, confronts us with the majesty of a holy God. It is an aroma of life to those who are being saved but an aroma of death to those who reject its claims (2 Cor. 2:16 NKJV).

Hendrikus Berkhof criticizes the Lutheran bifurcation between law and gospel, which is also found in Emil Brunner: "In our judgment this separation on the one hand overemphasizes man's understanding of his own existence . . . while on the other hand the gospel is robbed of its dimension of judgment and turned into pure grace."[30]

Lutherans tend to appeal to Paul's words in 1 Corinthians 10:23 that " 'all things are lawful,' but not all things are helpful." But as the Revised Standard Version correctly notes, the former is a quotation and does not wholly represent Paul's position. It was the slogan of the libertines. Bultmann comments that Paul accepted this slogan but then went on to place it in a proper context.[31] For Paul, our freedom is limited in two ways: when it is injurious to our neighbor and when it becomes an occasion for slavery to sin (cf. 1 Pet. 2:16).

Although the neo-Lutherans' attack on the theology of "decisionism" has some validity, I do not find their alternative satisfactory. "Decisionism" is an appellation given to modern revivalism in which it is implied that salvation is contingent on a personal act of commitment of faith to Jesus Christ. In Reformation theology, our commitment of faith is a result of grace rather than the condition for receiving grace. It is unfortunately true that an incipient Pelagianism is common in much of modern evangelicalism. At the same time, we must ask these questions: Are we saved apart from the decision of faith? Is not the decision of faith a necessary act by which God's grace becomes concrete in our lives? Lutherans often depict faith as wholly passive, but while it is true that we can only receive when grace first comes to us, we must not neglect the other side of the paradox: faith is also the act by which we lay hold of grace. We must oppose both monergism (in which God does it all) and synergism (in which God and man work together to realize salvation). The paradox is that God does it all but in and through human response and decision. The downplaying of the necessity for a personal conversion and decision has led many Lutherans to a kind of sacramentalism in which grace is believed to be dispensed automatically through the right performance of sacramental acts. It goes without saying that this is to fall into the heresy of cheap grace.

The Lutheran tendency to derive norms from sources other than biblical revelation (such as the orders of creation) is also suspect. This opens the door to natural theology and presupposes that the Christian does not need to appeal exclusively to Jesus Christ for guidance and direction. I acknowledge that once we have faith in Christ, our eyes are opened to the moral order present in nature and conscience. But it is only in his light that we see light (Ps. 36:9), and this means that nature and conscience can only be derivative, never foundational authorities for the life of faith.

With Luther and against neo-Lutheranism I see the primary dualism as between faith and unbelief, sin and grace, the kingdom of God and the kingdom of darkness. When neo-Lutherans explicate the two kingdoms, it seems they are thinking mainly of church and state, the spiritual and temporal realms, or gospel and law. Paul Althaus has convincingly shown that behind the dualism of church and state is the deeper dualism of God and the devil, and these two kingdoms intrude into both church and state.[32] The moral dualism of both Luther and Calvin cannot be recaptured until we regain a realistic belief in the presence of a demonic adversary to both God and humanity.

The Holiness Corrective

While Lutheranism and Anglicanism were drawn to sacramentalism and the Reformed churches to a rigid predestinarianism, Pietism and

Methodism sounded the call to personal regeneration. Yet by the nineteenth century the fervor in the awakening movements had begun to wane. It is not surprising, therefore, that in this same century the Holiness movement arose to rekindle the passion of original Wesleyanism for personal holiness and piety.[33] This is a concern I fully share, but I wish to ground it in a theological understanding that is in basic continuity with the total biblical witness and the faith of the Reformation.

The Holiness movement represents that strand of evangelicalism tracing its spiritual roots to John Wesley, who urged his followers to seek a blessing beyond conversion that would bring entire sanctification or perfect love. This second work of grace would effect complete cleansing of sin, though even the sanctified Christian must continue to struggle against temptation and infirmity. The Holiness movement went beyond Wesley in calling this second experience "the baptism of the Holy Spirit." Theologians and spiritual writers associated with this movement of renewal include Phoebe Palmer, Samuel Brengle, Hannah Whitall Smith, Joseph H. Smith, Charles Finney, Andrew Murray, Daniel S. Warner, Oswald Chambers, A. W. Tozer, J. Sidlow Baxter, and Theodore Hegre.

Holiness theology, like Pietism in general, does not constitute a monolithic system, but it does contain certain salient emphases common to all of its advocates. Holiness thought on the whole denies the spiritual use of the law for sanctified Christians. The law is no longer a word of admonition reminding us of our sin, even less a hammer of judgment bringing us to despair, for sanctified Christians, it is said, have attained victory over sin. They are no longer under law but under love. Against this rosy picture, I contend that even the best of Christians sin against love as well as law and therefore stand in constant need of God's forgiveness and mercy. Paul confessed that the sin that he would not, he did, and the good he would do, he left undone (Rom. 7).[34]

Instead of a perpetual striving for perfection, Holiness theology prefers to speak of a breakthrough to victorious living. But does not holiness in the biblical sense consist in an active struggle against sin and death rather than a state of being purified from sin, in the unceasing mortification of our sinful nature rather than sinlessness? Some (not all) Holiness luminaries have referred to the state of higher grace as one of sinless perfection or entire sanctification.

Works-righteousness is also an ever present danger in Holiness theology. Some writers, such as John Morgan, regarded the attainment of a certain degree of holiness as a necessary condition for justification.

Others—for example, C. W. Ruth—considered some progress in holiness necessary to retain the grace of justification. Charles Finney believed that conversion is the sinner's own act, and that the Spirit merely induces one to change.

In Holiness theology, it seems, grace is no longer the act by which God receives sinners into his favor but a God-given quality that adorns the human soul. This is clearly a reversion to the Catholic conception of grace. At their best, the Holiness writers have tried to hold both of these conceptions of grace in tension.

The strength of the Holiness movement is that it has sounded the call to holiness in a time of moral decay and thereby challenged the easy believism and cheap grace that have particularly marred Reformed and Lutheran Protestantism. It has reminded us that there are more blessings in store for us after conversion. The priority it assigns to mission, its demonstration of the fellowship of love, and its commitment to social reform and the priesthood of all believers (including the ministry of women) are also to be greatly appreciated.

Barth's Contribution

While I have freely drawn from the insights of both the Pietist and Holiness traditions, it should be obvious by now that Barth's theological ethics has played a major role in the development of my own understanding in this area. His enduring contribution is his reinterpretation of the law of God as indissolubly united and coordinate with rather than antithetical to the gospel. He acknowledges that the law apart from the gospel is one of sin and death, which is how the law is perceived by the "natural man." But in the context of Christian faith, the law is transformed by grace to become a directive of love. The law that drives us to the cross as well as the law that keeps us on the way of the cross is a transformed law, one of grace and liberty.

At the same time, Barth, in my opinion, is overeager to ascertain the unity of the law and the gospel and therefore underestimates the tension between them. Calvin also emphasized their unity but still believed that the law never ceases to be law, that it always remains the commandment of God. Barth sometimes gives the impression that the imperative is transposed into an indicative to the point of practically becoming a dimension of the gospel. Barth is right that the divine commandment includes grace, the promise and power to obey. But we must insist that it remains a commandment even while it may also be heard as a permission.

Barth sees one covenant history, though he acknowledges that the covenant has two sides—law and gospel. Yet in emphasizing their indivisible unity, he sometimes fails to do justice to the radical newness of the work of redemption in Jesus Christ. He does recognize that creation as the external basis of the covenant is complete in itself and that redemption signifies a wholly new work of grace made possible by creation but not necessitated by creation as such. He would nevertheless be reluctant to say that the law of the Old Testament is annulled by Christ. Instead, this law is now illumined as the prefiguration of the gospel. Yet in speaking of the new covenant, the Epistle to the Hebrews declares that the Lord "treats the first as obsolete. And what is becoming obsolete and growing old is ready to vanish away" (Heb. 8:13). Barth would probably argue that what is made obsolete are the sacrifices and ceremonies associated with the old covenant, such sacrifices being merely types or anticipations of the perfect sacrifice that was yet to come.[35] In addition, he might contend that what is overturned is the legalistic perversion of the law of God into a covenant of works, which we see in rabbinic Judaism.[36]

Both Barth and Calvin are surely right that even for the prophets of the Old Testament salvation is not obtained by observing the law; then, as now, it was secured by grace. Where the new covenant in Christ differs is that it is based on a much better sacrifice by which our sins are not simply covered but actually cleansed (Heb. 9:25, 26).[37] Because Barth sees the hidden Christ in Old Testament history, he is able to affirm the unity of the two testaments in the one covenant of grace exemplified and fulfilled in the incarnation and atonement of Jesus Christ.[38]

Lutherans have accused Barth of removing the threatening and condemnatory dimensions of the law by viewing it as a word of grace for the sinner and not essentially as a word of judgment on sin. The threatening power of the law then becomes an illusion, for human beings are already justified and sanctified in Jesus Christ and need only to realize the significance of this fact for their lives. Barth might reply that while there is a law that comes prior to the gospel—that of sin and death—this is the misunderstood law. When we see it rightly in the light of the gospel, we come to understand that its threat of condemnation has been removed by the cross of Christ. We also come to realize that the wrath of God, though real, is simply a form of God's love, that his anger over sin is the anger of love that will not desist until the sinner is turned to the way of life and salvation.

The principal dualism in Barth is not between faith and unbelief or law and gospel but between the "nothingness" (the chaos or darkness) and the living God. The distinction between elect and reprobate is relativized, since even the reprobate are secretly elect and even the elect are prone to be reprobate. Jesus Christ alone is both elect and reprobate. In him the whole human race is elected to salvation, and because of him the threat of reprobation has been permanently removed. Christ takes upon himself the guilt, sin, and reprobation that we deserve to suffer so that we might become the elect people of God.[39]

For Barth even the essential distinction between God's holiness and love is overcome, since he saw God's holiness and righteousness as "perfections of the divine loving." In this theology, love alone is the essence of God and his holiness is simply a form of his love. Bernard Ramm rightly asks whether Barth has lapsed into a monism of love.[40]

Barth has also been criticized for not seeing the Decalogue as the supreme standard for states and their laws.[41] He proposes a Christological ethic by which we deduce norms for the state from the cross and resurrection of Jesus Christ. It is questionable, however, whether the norms of social righteousness can be made to rest on a highly subjective interpretation of the redemptive work of Christ rather than on the objective prohibitions and affirmations that constitute the Decalogue and the Sermon on the Mount.

My principal difficulty with Barth is his downplaying of faith in the realization of salvation. He refuses to say that our salvation is realized in faith because this supposedly takes away from the objectivity and all-sufficiency of the one sacrifice on the cross. The subjective pole of salvation is simply our coming to appreciate the significance of this event for our lives through the illumination of the Holy Spirit. But does not Scripture claim that we are lost in sin until we are awakened by the Spirit to a living faith in Christ?[42] Has Barth fully grasped the paradox of salvation—that it is both an objective act of God for us in past history and a subjective act of trust and surrender in our present history?[43] Barth should nevertheless be commended for trying to recover the objectivity of both salvation and revelation in opposition to the subjectivism and experientialism that characterized the neo-Protestant theologies of Schleiermacher and Troeltsch and the existentialist theologies of Bultmann and Tillich.

Two Governments

Following both Luther and Calvin, I see two governments, those of church and state, as well as two kingdoms, those of light and darkness.

The secular government is under the law of God even if it does not yet know this, and the spiritual government under the gospel or the higher law of love. The law in its second use (according to Reformed understanding) is a norm for the secular state, functioning as a restraint on lawless conduct. It can be known brokenly in conscience and nature. But it is truly known only in the light of the person and work of Jesus Christ. This why only Christian states (as Augustine realized) have any possibility of being firmly anchored in moral order, for only Christians have been granted the illumination that gives them an abiding insight into the will and purpose of God for the world as well as for the church. Regrettably, very few states claiming to be Christian have been paragons of civic virtue, the result being that time and again Christianity has been brought into disrepute.

The church has the right to remind the state of the higher law of love, the higher righteousness of the kingdom. The justice that it is possible to achieve in the secular realm must be measured by the standard of perfect righteousness that we see in Jesus Christ. This means that civil law is subordinate to moral law, just as moral law is subordinate to the claims and promises of the gospel.

What I am advocating is not an equal obedience to two different authorities, but an absolute obedience to spiritual authority (the living God) and a relative obedience to temporal authority. When Jesus said, "Give to Caesar what is Caesar's, and to God what is God's" (Matt. 22:15–22 NIV), he was not implying that Caesar has an equal claim with God to one part of our existence.[44] On the contrary, he was intending to convey that the little that allegedly belongs to Caesar (his face was inscribed on the coin in question) must be returned to him, but only as a sign of our respect for the order in society that exists by virtue of the permission and sanction of God. What we owe to God as our Creator and Redeemer is our unremitting devotion, and this is something that can never be given to any worldly authority.

Conservatives often appeal to Romans 13 in support of the view that Christians owe obedience to the authorities placed over them by God. Radicals sometimes appeal to Revelation 13 to show that Christians may have to defy the state out of loyalty to Christ. As I see it, Christians are under an obligation to support political authorities in their role of maintaining order in society. The ruling authorities in society in this sense become the ministers of God's judgment, executing his wrath on wrongdoers. But Revelation 13 reminds us that a state may also sometimes become demonic, that it may try to arrogate to itself power that belongs only to God. The ruling authorities are still servants of God, but now they become rebellious servants. The primary loyalty of the Christian is to the living God who rules the world by his left hand through the sword of the state and by his right hand through the mercy and love of the gospel. When our absolute loyalty to God conflicts with our relative loyalty to the state, we "must obey God rather than men" (Acts 5:29). But even in civil disobedience Christians are to show respect for the state by patiently accepting the retribution meted out to offenders and transgressors of its laws.

The Whole Counsel of God

Willingness to make a witness of this sort is grounded in our responsibility as Christians to be the salt and light of the world (Matt. 5:13, 14). The church is not to withdraw from the fray but is called to proclaim both law and gospel to the wider society in which it finds itself. It should not simply point to parables of the kingdom or paradigms of love but preach the divine commandment, even though this will invariably be misunderstood by those without faith. Such people must nevertheless be exposed to the truth, for only in this way can they be held accountable for their actions.

The church of Jesus Christ has both a prophetic and a kerygmatic ministry. It is called to preach the gospel as the hope of the world and the law as the divine judgment on the world. It should uphold the law of God as both a guide for Christian life and as the divine commandment that convicts us of our sin. In both roles the law directs us to the gospel. As the hammer of God's judgment, it prepares the way for repentance. As a guide for discipleship under the cross, it prepares the way for holiness.[45]

The church also has the obligation to remind the state that the law of God is normative for social and political life. In its preaching and teaching, it should uphold the law as the standard of the righteousness that God demands. In this way the church plays an indirect role in promoting justice and order in society.

We are motivated to obey the law both out of the repentance that the law induces and out of gratefulness for the gospel that the law exhibits and reveals. In each case, the law directs us to Jesus Christ, who is both its end and its fulfillment. The law of sin and death belongs to the present age that is passing away, but the law of the spirit of life is eternal, for it belongs with the gospel as the infallible standard for faith and practice in the kingdom that shall have no end.

An ethics of the law and gospel is an evangelical alternative to the many other ethical options available today, which for the most part are grounded in the wisdom of culture and human experience.[46] It can be shown to be more biblically true as well as more faithful to the seminal insights of the Reformation than its rivals, even in the area of social concern. Against an ethics of natural law, it appeals not to universal principles, allegedly discovered in nature and conscience, but to God's self-revelation in Jesus Christ attested in Holy Scripture. Against an ethics of love, it contends that in dealing with complex social issues the norms of love must be united with the quest for justice if real progress is to be made in securing justice and liberty for all. Love apart from law becomes sentimental, just as law apart from love becomes legalistic and rigoristic. Against a kingdom-of-God ethics, as we find in liberation theology, it makes a convincing case that the vision of utopia conflicts with the biblical promises of the millennium and the new heaven and the new earth. It is the difference between salvation through the free grace of God and salvation through human ingenuity and diligence. Against an ethics of eudaemonism it upholds the biblical paradox that only through surrender to the love of God and dedication to the glory of God by the honor of his law and gospel does true happiness come to us as a by-product of a more lofty goal.

Appendix on the Order of Law and Gospel

Because of the chronological precedence of the Old Testament law to the advent of Jesus Christ, I think it wise to retain the traditional order of law and gospel. At the same time, this is not a law divorced from the gospel or independent of the gospel but one that anticipates and bears witness to the gospel. To be sure, this positive relationship between law and gospel can only be ascertained in the light of the gospel. This is why I could also speak as does Barth of gospel and law. With Barth I believe that what is implicit in the law and the prophets becomes explicit in the life, death, and resurrection of Jesus Christ.

Perhaps it is better to conceive of one reality—the law together with the gospel (or vice versa), since only in this way are we able to preserve the paradoxical unity of promise and command. Nevertheless, the two dimensions of this one reality cannot be absorbed into one another but remain distinct even in their unity.

It is interesting to note that even though his preference was for the order gospel-law, Barth could still affirm the legitimate place of the classical formulation.[47] Just as resurrection follows death, so the gospel follows law. But it follows the misunderstood law that works sin and death. The misunderstood law is not a propaedeutic to the gospel, but it sets the stage for the redemption that the gospel offers. For Barth law-gospel is not so much an intelligible order as an event in which the sinner encounters the grace of God.

It could be argued that in another sense the law precedes the gospel as its anticipatory form or prefiguration. By expressing the will of God, the law directs us to Jesus Christ, who fully embodies this will. Of course, one's inward eyes must have been opened by the Spirit to appreciate this function of the law. Only the Spirit enables us to know the law as it really is—the manifest will of God, which calls for honor and respect, rather than a word that inspires dread or terror.

Does the Spirit also work through the misunderstood law in preparing sinners for the light of the gospel? I agree with Barth that the misunderstood law by itself leads to death, but it does not produce the death that leads to life. Only the Holy Spirit does this, and when the Spirit works through the preaching of the gospel the misused law is then converted into the divine command, which carries with it the note of promise.[48] "You ought," which indicates a weakening of the law by fallible human reason, is transposed into "You shall be," which indicates power to persevere and conquer.[49] Like the law that works judgment and wrath, the divine command warns people of sin, but it is always recognized as the word of the One who saves people from sin and therefore the One who is the friend rather than the enemy of sinners.

The law directs us to Christ both by reminding us of our sin and by encouraging us to live the kind of life that is pleasing to God. But in each case, this is the law that is preached in conjunction with the gospel. It is the law that is used by the Spirit to bring hope and guidance to sinners who have been saved only by God's grace. It is the law that slays, but only in order to make alive. It is the law that proceeds from the gospel, but only in order to lead us back to the gospel.[50]

Notes

1. Ragnar Bring, *How God Speaks to Us* (Philadelphia: Muhlenberg, 1962), pp. 86–100.
2. Helmut Thielicke, *Theological Ethics* 1, pp. 133–35. Thielicke does acknowledge that the main strand in Luther supposes only two uses of the law (p. 55).
3. Jan Milič Lochman, *Signposts to Freedom,* trans. David Lewis (Minneapolis: Augsburg, 1982), pp. 85–86.
4. Barth, *Church Dogmatics,* II, 2, p. 706.
5. Ibid., pp. 685, 708.
6. While Joseph Fletcher rightly grasps the differences between *agape* and *philia,* he nevertheless includes self-love within agape. He also qualifies the radical principle of love for one's enemies. *Situation Ethics,* pp. 110–15.

7. See Thomas J. J. Altizer and William Hamilton, *Radical Theology and the Death of God* (Indianapolis: Bobbs-Merrill Co., 1966), pp. 49, 50, 87, 169.

8. Although the commandment was given for our salvation (Ps. 71:3 NKJV), it does not accomplish its objective because of sin (Rom. 3:19, 20). At the same time, it still plays a role in our salvation by preparing us for the gospel (Gal. 3:19–25).

9. Cf. Calvin: "All who love God are solely concerned with being obedient to his law and with keeping his commandments." *Calvin's Sermons on the Ten Commandments*, p. 77.

10. Barth, *Church Dogmatics*, II, 2, p. 30.

11. Edmund Schlink, *Theology of the Lutheran Confessions* (Philadelphia: Muhlenberg, 1961), p. 86.

12. Samuel Bolton, *The True Bounds of Christian Freedom* (1645; reprint, Edinburgh: The Banner of Truth Trust, 1978), p. 71.

13. The Judaizers are the most striking example of Christians in the New Testament who sought to subordinate gospel to law and thereby distorted the true meaning of the law. Ragnar Bring has these perceptive comments on the misunderstanding of the law in rabbinic Judaism, which also came to prevail among the Judaizers: "While the Jews trusted in their physical descent from Abraham, they rejected the spiritual relationship with Abraham which was constitutive for God's covenant with him. They became instead like Ishmael, who was physically a descendant from Abraham but had no promise. Ishmael became a symbol of a covenant different from that made with Abraham. He, the son of the expelled slave, became a symbol of the Israel which received the law at Sinai but did not submit to it in expectation of the coming righteousness, and thus like him was driven out and cursed. . . . The Judaizers understood the law in the false Jewish sense as a condition and means of righteousness. But Paul makes known to the Galatians through a typological exegesis of a well-known narrative from a book of the Law that they had taken Hagar and Ishmael as prototypes instead of Sarah and Isaac, and that spiritually they belonged with Hagar and Ishmael." Ragnar Bring, *Commentary on Galatians*, trans. Eric Wahlstrom (Philadelphia: Muhlenberg, 1961), pp. 220, 221.

14. Calvin comes close to this position when he declares, "The law has been obscured and has had a veil over it, preventing the fathers from having known God in such a way and as intimately as we know [him] today." *Calvin's Sermons on the Ten Commandments*, p. 52. Calvin is firm that Christ is the end of both the ceremonial and the moral law. As the fulfiller of the moral law, however, Christ at the same time confirms and establishes its validity. See the discussion by Benjamin Farley in the above book, p. 25.

15. It can be argued with some cogency that Paul did not know himself as a sinner until his conversion. Previously, he had thought of himself as a self-righteous Pharisee (cf. Acts 26:5; Gal. 1:13, 14).

16. Thielicke, *Theological Ethics* 1: p. 256.

17. Regin Prenter, *Spiritus Creator*, trans. John M. Jensen (Philadelphia: Fortress, 1953), pp. 218–24.

18. Ibid., p. 218.

19. Ibid., p. 221. Where Prenter (and Luther) differ from Barth is that they see the law as a revelation of the *Deus nudus* rather than a revelation of God's grace in the form of judgment. Yet in drawing such a close correlation between law and gospel, Prenter approaches Barth's position.

20. It is well to note that Luther could also make statements to this effect. Gerhard Heintze argues quite convincingly that in Luther's sermons, as opposed to his formal theological works, law and gospel are dynamically interrelated so that the knowledge of sin has its ground not in the law as such but in the passion of Christ. An existential, as opposed to a purely intellectual, knowledge of sin is given only through the gospel or the law illumined by the gospel. Gerhard Heintze, *Luthers Predigt von Gesetz und Evangelium* (Munich: Chr. Kaiser Verlag, 1958). Not surprisingly, Barth heartily endorses Heintze's important study in *Church Dogmatics* IV, 3, 1, p. 371.

21. Cf. Calvin on Romans 6:21: "The light of the Lord alone can open our eyes to behold the foulness which lies concealed in our flesh." John Calvin, *The Epistles of Paul the Apostle to the Romans and to the Thessalonians*, ed. David W. Torrance and Thomas F. Torrance, trans. Ross Mackenzie (Grand Rapids: Eerdmans, 1960), p. 135.

22. See Peter C. Erb, ed., *Pietists: Selected Writings* (New York: Paulist Press, 1983).

23. Rudolf Bultmann, *Theology of the New Testament*, trans. Kendrick Grobel (New York: Charles Scribner's Sons, 1951), 1: pp. 342, 343. Bultmann does maintain that the Christian is still under the demand of love, the spirit of the law. But he does not tell us in what sense the Christian is bound to the specific demands that comprise the Decalogue. He says that we are free from all claims that the world might address to us, but do we not sometimes hear God's command in the cries of those who are bedeviled by poverty and oppression?

24. Eric W. Gritsch, *Born Againism* (Philadelphia: Fortress, 1982), p. 100.

25. Roy A. Harrisville, *Romans* (Minneapolis: Augsburg, 1980), p. 190.

26. Cf. Prenter, *Spiritus Creator*, pp. 79, 80, 87, 97.

27. John Calvin, "Commentary on Hosea 6:1," in *Commentaries on the Twelve Minor Prophets*, trans. John Owen (Edinburgh: Calvin Translation Society, 1846), p. 215.

28. William Lazareth, " 'Just War' in a Nuclear Age?" *The Bulletin: Moravian Theological Seminary*, (Fall 1968), p. 5.

29. *Calvin's Sermons on the Ten Commandments*, p. 257.

30. Hendrikus Berkhof, *Christian Faith*, trans. Sierd Woudstra (Grand Rapids: Eerdmans, 1979), p. 195.

31. Bultmann, *Theology of the New Testament*, pp. 341, 342.

32. Paul Althaus, *The Ethics of Martin Luther*, trans. Robert C. Schultz (Philadelphia: Fortress, 1972), pp. 43–82.

33. See Melvin E. Dieter, *The Holiness Revival of the Nineteenth Century* (Metuchen, N.J.: Scarecrow, 1980); Vinson Synan, *The Holiness-Pentecostal Movement* (Grand Rapids: Eerdmans, 1971); Delbert R. Rose, *A Theology of Christian Experience* (Minneapolis: Bethany Fellowship, 1965); Charles Edward White, *The Beauty of Holiness* (Grand Rapids: Zondervan, 1986); and *The Devotional Writings of Phoebe Palmer*, Donald W. Dayton, ed. (New York: Garland, 1985).

34. Wesleyans argue that Paul in Romans 7 was referring to his pre-Christian experience. Luther, Calvin, and Barth, on the contrary, held that Paul was describing the paradoxical state of the Christian as being both in sin and grace. Everett Harrison suggests that Paul is depicting a hypothetical situation in which a Christian tries to resolve the problem of sin and temptation on his own apart from the grace of Christ and the power of the Spirit. Another possibility is that Paul is referring to the very real dark periods in a Christian's life when God withholds his grace in order to test his children or to chastise them for persistent sin. My position is similar to the Reformers': Paul had in mind the actual state of the Christian who, though sanctified in Christ, intermittently falls from his sanctification. This fall into sin may be occasioned by God's withdrawal of his grace or by an inexplicable failure to lay hold of the grace available in Christ. For an engaging discussion of possible interpretations of Romans 7 see Everett F. Harrison, "Romans" in *The Expositor's Bible Commentary*, ed. Frank E. Gaebelein (Grand Rapids: Zondervan, 1978), 10: pp. 83–85. Interestingly, Harrison does not consider the possibility of God withholding his grace.

35. It is surprising that there is no exposition of Hebrews 8:13 in Barth's *Church Dogmatics* despite its relevance to the law-gospel debate. There is a discussion of relevant passages in Hebrews in *Church Dogmatics* IV, 1, pp. 273–283.

36. Unlike Barth, Philip Hughes maintains that the Old Testament dispensation is rightly understood as a covenant of works designed to prepare the way for the covenant of grace inaugurated by Jesus Christ. See Philip Edgcumbe Hughes, *A Commentary on the Epistle to the Hebrews* (Grand Rapids: Eerdmans, 1977), pp. 295–302.

37. See the helpful explanatory comment in *Harper Study Bible*, ed. Harold Lindsell (Grand Rapids: Zondervan, 1977), p. 1813.

38. For Barth's penetrating criticism of the neo-Reformed theology that affirms two covenants—works and grace—see *Church Dogmatics* IV, 1, pp. 53–66.

39. One must not, however, ignore another strand in Barth that fully admits the dreaded reality of a final reprobation for those who deliberately reject and deny the grace offered in Christ. In one of his earlier writings, Barth declares: "Predestination is a truth of the eschaton. Therefore we cannot say that there are now the elect and the reprobate, but we can and must certainly believe that there will be such. . . . We dare not say that damnation is cancelled out by universal grace. Holy Scripture speaks of both election and reprobation." Karl Barth, *Gottes Gnadenwahl* (Munich: Chr. Kaiser Verlag, 1936), pp. 48, 51. Barth goes on to say that reprobation is not the last word from God but the next to the last word (pp. 51, 52).

In his *Church Dogmatics* final damnation is pictured as a grim possibility that hangs over the godless but as something that has not yet taken place. It seems that Barth does make a place for a final judgment in which believers will be separated from hardened unbelievers, but this separation is relativized by the fact that God's grace continues to pursue and rule over even those who wilfully reject their election in Christ. Even those who make their bed in hell are claimed by and confronted by the grace of a God whose mercy is greater than his judgments. Barth's universalism is one of hope for all humankind because of the sovereignty and universality of divine grace, but he does not explicitly affirm the final return of all to God (*apokatastasis*); in fact, he emphatically rejects this doctrine. God's grace and love become destructive for those who deliberately and obstinately reject his gift of salvation in Jesus Christ. Yet Barth leaves open the question of whether the self-condemned sinner can forever hold out against God's inexorable love.

40. Bernard Ramm, *The Evangelical Heritage* (Waco, Tex.: Word Books, 1973), p. 119.

41. See Jean Lasserre, *War and the Gospel*, trans. Oliver Coburn (Scottdale, Pa.: Herald Press, 1962), p. 155.

42. In his later writings, Barth endeavors to correct this objectivistic slant. "As the event of salvation it thus takes place, not just primarily there and then in Him, but also secondarily and no less really in the knowledge of salvation created by Him. It is thus the case that the one who participates in this knowledge participates in the event of salvation itself." *Church Dogmatics*, IV, 3, 1, p. 217.

43. See Donald G. Bloesch, *Jesus Is Victor!: Karl Barth's Doctrine of Salvation* (Nashville: Abingdon Press, 1976).

44. For a probing and incisive analysis of the text in question see Jean Lasserre, *War and the Gospel*, pp. 86–95.

45. Cf. Calvin: "The Law inculcates a conformity of life, not only to external probity, but also to internal and spiritual righteousness." *Institutes of the Christian Religion*, rev. ed., trans. John Allen, vol. I, (Philadelphia: Presbyterian Board of Christian Education, 1936), 2, 8, 6: p. 401.

46. For an in-depth discussion of these various options see chap. 10.

47. See Karl Barth, "Gospel and Law," in *Community, State and Church* [pp. 71–100], pp. 95–97.

48. Conversely, when the divine command is no longer heard as the voice of the Redeemer, it is transposed into a law of sin and death, a moral code that stifles rather than revives, an external standard that enslaves rather than liberates.

49. For Barth's discussion of the eschatological dimension of the divine command see "Gospel and Law," pp. 81–87. Also see Forde, *The Law-Gospel Debate*, pp. 147–149.

50. Interestingly, in an examination of the political use of the law in Lutheran symbolic writings, Bonhoeffer concludes: "Both sequences are, therefore, theologically justified and necessary: gospel and law as well as law and gospel. In the symbolic writings the second sequence predominates. But in both sequences the gospel is the 'actual' kingdom of God." *Ethics*, p. 314.

CHAPTER 9

Christian Caring

Bread for myself is a material problem: bread for other people is a
spiritual problem.

NICOLAS BERDYAEV

The soul of the care of the poor is the care of the poor soul.

TERESA OF AVILA

Man is not just a belly in search of bread. He's a soul in search of God.

CLARENCE JORDAN

There is no use talking about love if it does not relate to the stuff of
life in the area of material possessions and needs. If it does not mean
a sharing of our material things for our brothers in Christ close at home
and abroad, it means little or nothing.

FRANCIS SCHAEFFER

Its Christological Basis

Not all service to the needs of our neighbor is Christian caring. The
latter is distinguished from mere humanitarian service by its enduring
Christological basis. Christian caring is first of all anchored in the self-
giving love of God in Jesus Christ. As God's love, it proceeds from
fulness to poverty and is to be contrasted with the spiritual forms of
natural love that proceed from poverty to fulness. The first connotes
the paradoxically glorious descent of God to humanity in Jesus Christ,
the second the deceptively glorious ascent of humanity to God. God's
love is a suffering love, involving his vicarious identification with the
travails and shame of a despairing humanity. It is also an atoning love,
one that makes reparation for sin. It signifies the substitution of
Christ's righteousness for our sin so that we can be accounted righteous
before a holy God.

Christian caring is also based on the self-giving love of Jesus to his
fellow human beings. As Matthew testifies, "The Son of man came not
to be served but to serve, and to give his life as a ransom for many"
(Matt. 20:28). Jesus realized his vocation as Lord by laying down his

life for his people, even for his enemies. He demonstrated his unique style of life by washing his disciples' feet (John 13:1–20). His headship was realized in the role of a servant. He was exalted in his humiliation (Barth). He overcame by "revolutionary subordination" (John Howard Yoder).

We should keep in mind that Jesus Christ is not only our Savior but also our Lord. He commands as well as redeems. He not only invites us to faith but also demands from us obedience to the imperatives of love. He is our Savior, our Pattern, our Master, our Teacher. To emphasize only his saving work is to magnify the gospel apart from the law. To dwell only on the example he gave us and the precepts he taught us means to substitute the law for the gospel.

The Christian motivations for mission and service have both a theocentric and a Christocentric focus. First, there is the desire to glorify God, which should permeate every aspect of our existence (cf. Ps. 86:12; Matt. 5:16; Rom. 15:5, 6). We glorify God, moreover, by upholding Jesus Christ, his promise and his claims, before the world— in our words and in our acts (2 Cor. 9:13, 14).

We are also motivated to acts of Christian caring out of gratefulness for what God has done for us in Christ (Phil. 4:6; Col. 4:2; Eph. 5:1, 2, 4; 1 John 4:11). We cannot earn or merit the salvation that Christ purchased for us through his own blood, but we can show how thankful we are for his act of incomparable love by serving others as Christ has served us. This particular note is given special emphasis in the Heidelberg Catechism. We must do good works, we are told, because "just as Christ has redeemed us with his blood he also renews us through his Holy Spirit according to his own image, so that with our whole life we may show ourselves *grateful* to God for his goodness and that he may be glorified through us . . ." (italics mine).[1]

Again, admiration for Christ's life of perfect love leads us to follow his example. His demonstration of selfless service arouses within us a desire to pattern our lives after his (cf. 1 Pet. 2:21–24; Rom. 11:14; Heb. 12:3–4; 2 Thess. 1:10 NKJV). We are reminded here of the moral influence theory of the atonement, but this theory is only heretical when it is made a primary or exclusive emphasis. Christ as Pattern is indeed a motif of apostolic Christianity, but the Christ who is embraced as Pattern must also be upheld as Savior and Lord.

Holy fear is another legitimate motivation for Christian service (cf. Isa. 8:12, 13; Job. 28:28; Prov. 9:10; Sirach 34:13, 14; Matt. 10:28; Heb. 10:31). Jesus is not only lowly servant but also sovereign king and Lord. Our salvation is imperiled and our growth in faith is blocked if we fail to demonstrate our faith in a life of obedience (cf. Pss. 2:11, 12; 34:11; 111:10; Prov. 1:7; Luke 12:4, 5; 2 Cor. 7:1). While acknowledging thankfulness as a superior incentive to action, Lutheran theologian Adolf Köberle insists that holy fear is also necessary if the Christian is to go forward toward holiness in life and thought.[2]

Liberal theology tends to downplay the motivation of fear as unworthy of the Christian. But we should remember that the God whom we worship is not only our heavenly Father but also our Lord and King; he is not only love and mercy but also majesty and holiness. He not only creates light but also brings about darkness (Isa. 45:7). He not only saves from judgment but also executes judgment. He not only raises up but also casts down and destroys. Jesus cautioned his hearers to be watchful and vigilant lest they be found wanting when our Lord appears on the day of reckoning (Matt. 25:1–13). Luther held that it is not necessary for Christians to be "altogether without fear. For nature always remains within us, which is weak, and cannot stand without fear of death and Christ's judgment."[3] Yet he was also profoundly aware of the paradox that when we throw ourselves on God's mercy, we find that we are upheld by his grace. Our dread of his judgment, which is occasioned by our sin, is then transmuted into a holy fear born out of love.

In evangelical and fundamentalist circles, we frequently are told to fear hell, whereas holy fear is directed to God. Jesus explicitly urged his disciples to place their fear in the One who has power to cast into hell (Matt. 10:28–31), but hell itself should not be the focus of our fear if we are in fact Christians (cf. Rom. 8:1). Indeed, hell together with sin and death is precisely what has been overcome by Jesus Christ (cf. Matt. 16:18, 19; John 12:31, 16:11, 33; Acts 2:27, 31; 1 Cor. 15:24–28; Col. 2:15; Rev. 1:18, 17:14). When we place our fear in God, we are then able to live with our fear, for we sense that our God is a present help and refuge even in our sin. The fear of God is not the servile fear of a slave toward a cruel master (as is the fear of hell) but a filial fear that contains elements of awe and respect for the holiness and majesty of God. It is the kind of fear that Rudolf Otto elucidates in his magnificent *Idea of the Holy* where the one who encounters the holy God is filled with both irresistible fascination and awe-inspiring dread.[4]

The basis of our holy fear, however, is not simply the personal encounter with God but also the scriptural warnings concerning the judgments that God metes out to sinners (cf. Matt. 5:29, 30; 22:1–14; 25:31–46; 2 Cor. 5:10–11; Heb. 9:27; 12:25; Jude 15; 2 Pet. 3:7).[5] When we proceed to place our fear in the just and holy God, the threat of his judgments is then rightly seen as the unremitting concern of a loving Father who wishes to keep his children on the straight and narrow way for their benefit and salvation (Matt. 10:29–31).[6]

Again, Christians are drawn to a life of service in the hope of winning others for Christ (cf. 1 Cor. 9:19–27). If we let the gospel shine in our lives, those around us may see our good works and give glory to the Father who is in heaven (Matt. 5:16). Paul told the Corinthians that they themselves were a letter of recommendation. They show by their deeds that they "are a letter from Christ delivered by us, written not with ink but with the Spirit of the living God, not on tablets of stone but on tablets of human hearts" (2 Cor. 3:1–3). The Heidelberg Catechism urges us to live an exemplary life "so that we ourselves may be assured of our faith by its fruits and by our reverent behavior may win our neighbors to Christ."[7]

Finally, Christians are motivated by love—love for God, for Jesus, and for our fellow human beings. Paul made it clear that it is the love of God that impels us (2 Cor. 5:14; cf. John 13:35; 15:12–17; Rom. 5:5; 1 Thess. 3:12; Eph. 5:2; Heb. 10:24). Love is the crown of the fruits of the Spirit (Gal. 5:14, 22). It is the gift that shall remain after prophecy and knowledge pass away (1 Cor. 13:8). Faith is the foundation, but love is the apex and goal of the Christian life. It is that peculiar ingredient that sharply differentiates Christian caring from all other kinds of service and mission.

The Church's Twofold Mission

God's act of love for the world in Jesus Christ gives the church its reason for being. As the people called out by God for a particular service, the church is a sign of the dawning of the new age. It is motivated by a spiritual mission but one with two dimensions. They are both critical for the life of the church, but they are not equal in importance. This is made clear in Acts 6:1–4, where the twelve apostles summon the wider body of disciples and declare: "It is not right that we should give up preaching the word of God to serve tables. Therefore, brethren, pick out from among you seven men of good repute, full of the Spirit and of wisdom, whom we may appoint to this duty. But we will devote ourselves to prayer and to the ministry of the word." Preaching (*kerygma*) and teaching (*didache*) take precedence over social service (*diakonia*), but the last is by no means relegated to insignificance. Indeed, it is seen as the cardinal sign and evidence of our fidelity to the great commission (Matt. 7:16–23; 1 John 4:21; 5:2).

The primary mission of the church is to share the good news of what God has done for us and for the whole world in Jesus Christ (Matt. 28:19, 20; Mark 16:15, 16; Luke 24:47, 48; Acts 1:8). It is our expectation and goal that in and through this proclamation people will be delivered from their sins and brought into a right relationship with the living God.

Although the gospel story is communicated primarily through the kerygmatic proclamation, God also deigns to use other means—Bible reading, lives of self-giving service, intercessory prayer, worship done in spirit and truth, and the celebration of the sacraments. It is not only the proclaimed Word (the sermon) but also the written Word (the Bible), the demonstrated Word (the Christian life), the celebrated Word (worship) and the visible Word (the sacraments) that carry the message of salvation through the free grace of God to a lost and sinful world. Yet it is the word of proclamation that is the heart of worship, the central focus of Scripture, the guide for Christian living, and the source of meaning in the sacraments. The gospel must be proclaimed in word and deed, but the word gives direction to the deed just as the deed gives substance to the word.

Evangelism is the privilege God gives to all Christians—sharing the story of God's love with our neighbor for whom Christ died. It is the peculiar responsibility of those who are called to the public ministry of the Word—pastors, teachers, and elders. Not all sermons will be exclusively evangelistic, but the evangel or saving message of the cross should be at the heart of every sermon. I fully share these sentiments of Nels Ferré: "Evangelism as the ardent and the authentic witness of what God has done in history and for us is the heartbeat of faith."[8]

The highest service the church can give to the world is the conversion of souls (1 Cor. 9:19; Jude 23; James 5:19, 20). Our task, Gregory of Nyssa realized, is to bring souls to "health," thereby saving them from the "disease" of sin "that ends in death."[9] As Maximus the Confessor put it, "Love is made manifest not only in the sharing of money but much more in sharing the word of God."[10] William Booth, the founding general of the Salvation Army, had his priorities right when he declared, "Go for souls—and go for the worst." Zinzendorf echoed the sentiment that inspired the great Moravian missions: "My joy until I die: to win souls for the Lamb!"

Jesus performed his signs and wonders partly in order to draw people's attention to his messianic identity and mission. He fed the five thousand with loaves and fishes out of compassion, to be sure, but he was frankly disappointed that they failed to see the sign in this miraculous meal (John 6:26). When his hearers asked what they must do to be doing the works of God, he replied: "This is the work of God, that you believe in him whom he has sent" (John 6:29). On another occasion he declared, "If I am not doing the works of my Father, then do not believe me; but if I do them even though you do not believe me, believe the works, that you may know and understand that the Father is in me and I am in the Father" (John 10:37–38). The signs and wonders that followed the preaching of the gospel failed to convince scoffers of the truth of Jesus' message, but they did play a part in confirming the faith of those who believed on the basis of his resurrection from the dead (Mark 16:20; Acts 14:3; Rom. 15:18, 19; 2 Cor. 12:12; Heb. 2:4).

Growth and nurture in the faith are important for the health of the body of Christ, but even more crucial is the decision of faith whereby one becomes engrafted into this body. Baptism in and of itself is insufficient to save people from sin, but it can plant the seed that makes them receptive to the gospel. Pope John Paul I voiced the concern of many Roman Catholic leaders of our time: "The priority of the church ought to be to evangelize those who have already been baptized."[11]

A second dimension of the mission of the church is Good Samaritan service. This essentially constitutes the cultural mandate of the church, though it does not necessarily exhaust it. The church of Jesus Christ is to be not only a prophetic church that proclaims the promise and the commandment of God but also a priestly church that ministers to the spiritual and material needs of its members and of the world around it. Yet even in its priestly function, its overall aim is still to bring people to God. The motivation is love, but the goal is evangelism. Evangelism, of course, is not to be confused with proselytism or spiritual conquest, for we by ourselves cannot gain souls for the kingdom. Despite all our diligence and ingenuity, the conversion of souls is still to be understood as the surprising work of the Spirit of God in and through and sometimes over and against our broken witness. Our task is to share the good news so that people might be brought to a saving knowledge of Christ, but we are only the servants and instruments of grace; Christ alone is the bestower of grace and therefore the sole Savior.

Christian service differs from humanitarian work by virtue of its motivation and goal. The Christian is motivated by the love that descends into the depths of human depravity; the humanitarian is motivated by the hope of reclaiming people for a meaningful role in society. The Christian is intent above all on bringing people into a right relationship with God; the humanitarian seeks to instill a sense of self-worth and social grace. Christian service is not simply social service but spiritual care. The care of souls means much more than feeding the hungry and clothing the naked; it involves introducing people to the living Christ who alone saves from sin, death, and hell. The ultimate aim in our service to the poor and needy is to make them aware of their absolute dependence on God. Teresa of Avila summed it up in one memorable sentence: "The soul of the care of the poor is the care of the poor soul."

The work of Mother Teresa, founder of the Missionary Sisters of Charity, has often been mistaken for humanitarian endeavor. But she has made it abundantly clear that she regards spiritual destitution as the gravest problem afflicting the homeless and diseased on the streets of Calcutta and other cities of India where her order has built homes for the dying. What these people most need, she says repeatedly, is to be made aware that they are loved by Jesus, the incarnate Son of the living God.[12]

William Adams Brown has put it well: "The deepest of all the needs of man is not physical comfort or relief from suffering, but faith in some abiding reality which justifies sacrifice and lends meaning and dignity to life."[13] The humanitarian is aware of the agonizing psychic and physical needs of humankind, but the Christian knows that there is a still more urgent need—to come to know the almighty God who alone can satisfy the yearnings and desires of the heart (Ps. 37:4). Augustine rightly said, "Our hearts are restless till they find rest in Thee."[14] Only the gospel satisfies this spiritual hunger, but this does not mean that the other needs are merely peripheral and therefore of scant interest to the ambassadors of Christ.

Faith is the foundation of our social service, but faith works through love (Gal. 5:6). Faith finds its goal in love; love has its basis in faith. The apostle makes it crystal clear that we cannot love the children of God unless we revere God and keep his commandments (1 John 5:2–5). Faith in God provides the motivation and power to love the children of God just as God loves us in Jesus Christ.

Political action is not an integral element in the mission of the church but grows out of it. It is an invariable by-product of both the spiritual and cultural mandates of the church, and this means that the gospel has political implications. Indeed, in Carl Braaten's graphic words, "The simple fact of preaching the gospel is like putting sticks of dynamite into the social structure."[15] General William Booth recognized that attention should be given to the person whose "circum-

stances are sick, out of order, in danger of carrying him to utter destitution, or to prison."[16] A sick society will intensify the sin and lostness
of humanity; the church must therefore address social as well as personal sin in its message.

The church is called to renounce power for itself, but it should uphold the right use of power for the sake of justice. John Calvin gives
voice to this political responsibility of the Christian: "Let us also remember not only to refrain from every form of injurious activity and
wrong, but at the same time, insofar as we can, let us not permit anyone to be wronged or injured."[17] The church should focus its attention
not only on faith seeking love but also on love seeking justice (William
Lazareth).

The evangelical proclamation will have far-reaching political and
cultural ramifications. The ministers of the gospel should denounce
social evils as well as personal sin. Reinhold Niebuhr has observed that
no one takes offense at the mere preaching against sin, but when we
become specific in our denunciations, then we begin to disturb people,
then the gospel becomes the sword that slays.

The church gains evangelical power by the preaching of the gospel
and social relevance by the preaching of the law. It behooves Christians
in their secular vocations to implement the law, but the church qua
church should give guidance in this area. Its role is not to offer specific
solutions to social problems (though on rare occasions it may have to
do this), but it should point directions. The church must not aspire to
be a power structure in society that in effect becomes a rival state. This
is the temptation of clericalism, which invariably accompanies theocratic experiments. The church's proper function is to be the moral
monitor of society. It should aspire to be neither master nor servant of
the state but its conscience (Martin Luther King). Christians should
seek for the grace to season society, not for the power to control it (cf.
Matt. 5:13; 13:33).

Bonhoeffer makes a helpful distinction between penultimate and
ultimate concerns. The penultimate refers to the concerns of this present age—land, peace, bread. The ultimate refers to the last things—
eternal life, the resurrection of the dead, the final judgment. Just as
the gospel focuses on the ultimate, so the law pertains to the penultimate. Sometimes the church must address the penultimate in order
to prepare the way for the ultimate, sometimes social service will have
chronological priority over evangelism. "To provide the hungry man
with bread," Bonhoeffer says, "is to prepare the way for the coming
of grace."[18] William Booth had as his motto "soup, soap, and salva-

tion." He, too, perceived that we often need to minister to the material needs of our hearers before they are able or willing to listen to our gospel.

Misunderstandings of the Christian Mission

The mission of the church can be subverted from both the right and the left. Because of the pressures of ideology, the church needs especially to be alert to the misunderstandings of its mission in our day.

First of all, the mission of the church can be spiritualized. Its message is then concerned solely with the salvation of the individual soul. Salvation itself, moreover, is wrongly understood as deliverance out of this world into a higher or spiritual realm. This is the ancient Gnostic heresy, but it is also found in that strand of Christian mysticism influenced by Neoplatonism as well as in radical Pietism. In this perspective, Christianity becomes an attempt to ascend from the material to the purely spiritual. The Christian life is interpreted in terms of a world-denying asceticism. Faith becomes an interior experience. The emphasis is not on the journey into the world's afflictions (the biblical view) but on the journey to the center of the soul. Endeavoring to counter a false otherworldliness, Teresa of Avila reminded those in her charge: "Though we do not have our Lord with us in bodily presence, we have our neighbor, who, for the ends of love and loving service, is as good as our Lord himself."[19] The Quaker divine William Penn shared a similar vision: "True godliness doesn't turn men out of the world, but enables them to live better in it and excites their endeavors to mend it."[20]

Again, the Christian mission can be psychologized. In this case, salvation is equated with happiness, peace of mind, internal stability. Sin becomes sickness or negative thinking. The remedy is therapy, which is designed to bring about catharsis or enlightenment. Faith becomes an inner attitude—toward both God and the self. Salvation is mentalized, faith is privatized. Today we hear much talk of holistic salvation, and more often than not this betrays a psychologizing of salvation and ipso facto an accommodation to bourgeois values. The goal in life is held to be eudaemonia—personal well-being or self-realization. This perversion of faith is found from one end to the other of the theological spectrum—in the older liberalism, existentialism, the positive thinking movement, and the electronic church.

Finally, the Christian mission can be ethicized or politicized. Here we see the equation of the spiritual with the secular so that the service of our fellow humans becomes by that very fact the service of God. Worship and prayer are reduced to political reflection and action. Sin is redefined as a false consciousness or acquiescence to exploitation and oppression. The vertical dimension of the Christian life is absorbed into the horizontal. This is the temptation in secular or liberation theology, which currently dominates the great conciliar bodies (such as the World Council of Churches).[21] But it is also present in the new religious right, which confuses the message of the kingdom of God with a particular political agenda.

Martin Luther King sagaciously observed that political action can never be a solution to the human problem but at best a necessary palliative or stopgap measure. He was painfully aware that laws with teeth are necessary to protect the helpless and innocent from potential oppressors, but laws can never make people love one another. Something more is needed—the transformation of the human heart through the moving of the Spirit of God. "Desegregation will break down the legal barriers and bring men together physically, but something must touch the heart and souls of men so that they will come together spiritually."[22]

Christians are often tempted to rely on the force of law to accomplish their objectives rather than on the power of love. In Calvin's theocratic experiment in Geneva compulsory Sunday worship was written into the civil law. Carl Henry is wiser in such matters: "Christians are not to rely on legal implementation to fulfill divine imperatives that they themselves are to communicate to the nonbelieving world through preaching and persuasion."[23] At the same time, Christians should not be encouraged to withdraw from the secular arena into private enclaves of righteousness. Henry makes clear that the people of God must be in the vanguard to ensure protection for the weak and equity for the poor. "As citizens of two worlds Christians know that the penalty for withholding exemplary guidance and involvement for the social common good is to surrender the political arena by default to non-Christian alternatives. Far worse, lack of public engagement in the world is tantamount to defection from the Redeemer's army of occupation and liberation."[24]

The two basic temptations confronting the church today are spiritualization and secularization. (The latter encompasses both the psychologizing and politicizing deformations of the gospel.) Against world-denying mysticism and radical pietism, the Christian faith calls for active involvement in the great social issues and problems of the world. Against humanitarianism or ethicism, the Christian faith upholds not mere service but the cure of souls, offers not simply a helping hand but a sacrificial spirit.[25] Christian service, moreover, entails ministering to those in need in the *name* of Christ (Mark 9:41). One cannot be saved from sin unless one knows the *name* by which God has acted to deliver us (John 3:18; Acts 3:16; 4:12).

The Christian is acutely aware that "man does not live on bread alone but on every word that comes from the mouth of the Lord" (Deut. 8:3 NIV: cf. Matt. 4:4). Whitehouse reminds us that the early church, "while resisting the gnostics' radical mistrust of physical actuality, vehemently contested all tendencies to assume that material principles are ultimate."[26] Our goal is not health, wealth, and prosperity on earth but life with God in eternity. Our earthly endeavors and achievements are to be seen not as ends in themselves but as means to our final destination—the eschatological vision of God and fellowship with the saints in glory.

In its evangelistic task the church must resist those voices from the left that reinterpret evangelism as the altering of social horizons and substitute the self-development of peoples for the conversion of souls. With equal vigor it must disengage itself from those on the right who divest evangelism of its prophetic dimension, thereby separating the preaching of the gospel from the preaching of the law. Biblical faith upholds a prophetic evangelism: in announcing the good news we should also denounce those things that impede or contradict the good news.

Virtually all current misunderstandings of the church's role in society are associated with the impact of ideology on the church's faith and mission. When the church becomes united with a particular ideology, its commitment to its divine purpose is invariably compromised. An ideology is here understood as a vision of a new social order that proves to be a rationalization for special interests in society. In an ideology, ideas become tools in social restructuring, weapons in the class struggle. Much more will be said on this in chapter 13.

Today we need a restatement of the Christian mission that gives priority to the gospel proclamation but unites it with the cruciality of social service. Our task is to perceive the social and political implications of the gospel without converting the gospel into a political program. We would do well to recognize that there is a Christian center (the gospel) and a Christian periphery (cultural application).[27] There can be no center without a periphery. The center always takes precedence over the periphery, but the center will dissolve without a periphery.

We should not delude ourselves into thinking that we can bring in the kingdom of God by social engineering. At the same time, we should not retreat into political quietism, abandoning society to the powers of darkness. We can set up signs and parables of the kingdom and by so doing hasten its coming (2 Peter 3:12). We cannot convert social structures, but by the grace of God we can convert people who are in a position to humanize social structures. We should work for a society where all people receive their due reward or a fair share of the goods but also where Christians are free to follow the imperatives of the gospel. We should work for a society where the powers of evil are restrained, where the weak are protected against the strong. And how can we escape the conclusion that the most helpless and weak today, the poorest of the poor, are the unborn children whose lives are needlessly aborted on the grounds of either personal inconvenience to the mother or their alleged inability to make a useful contribution to society?

Christians today in their deeds and words are called to hold up the ideal of crucified love, nonresistance to evil, as the law of the kingdom of God.[28] In addition, we should give more attention to the strategy of nonviolent resistance as a means of political coercion and as an approximation of the transcendent ideal of the kingdom. While, as Bonhoeffer pointed out, the law of the kingdom of God can never be a law for the secular order, it can be treated as a transcendent criterion by which the secular order can move toward a higher degree of justice.

Changing Emphases

It is sad but true that the church often tailors its message to reflect the spirit of the times (the Zeitgeist), showing itself less a prophet to the times than a product of the times. The cultural emphasis in the sixties was on social protest. Civil rights marches were held, and boycotts against discriminating firms were organized. It was fashionable to identify with oppressed minorities. The gospel was converted into a program for social change. The heroes of young people were such charismatic figures as Martin Luther King, Jr., César Chavez, Malcolm X, James Reeb, Jerry Rubin, Abbie Hoffman, Herbert Marcuse, Angela Davis, Saul Alinsky, Camilo Torres, and Daniel Berrigan. The theological scene was dominated by the theology of revolution, secular theology, and the death-of-God theology.

In the late sixties and through the seventies the emphasis turned inward. Now the rage was exploring the inner recesses of the self. Group guidance and sensitivity training were in vogue, and experimentation in psychedelic drugs was common. This was the age of narcissism, with the flower children and the Jesus people as self-appointed prophets. Community life held a powerful and sometimes baleful attraction for many idealistic young people. They congregated around celebrated gurus such as Alan Watts, Timothy Leary, the Maharishi Yogi, Morton Kelsey, Alan Ginsberg, David (Moses) Berg, Bob Dylan, and Sun Myung Moon. In his prescient book *The Greening of America*, Charles Reich labeled this inward revolution the rise of "Consciousness III."[29]

If ethics was the salient theme in the sixties, spirituality became the fashion in the seventies. While the sixties lamented the death of God, the seventies reconceived God as a creative power or force within nature and history. The early seventies were characterized by a search for transcendence, though it was a transcendence within immanence. In the later seventies and early eighties this took the form of an interest in spiritual formation. The transition from the sixties to the seventies signaled a movement from the Age of Revolution to the Age of Aquarius.

In the eighties, the emphasis on spirituality has been increasingly united with the themes of peace, justice, and liberation. Revolution is again in fashion, though this time spiritual as well as social revolution.[30] The spirituality being celebrated is still for the most part secular or this-worldly. Naturalistic mysticism reigns supreme, as attested in the attention given to Teilhard de Chardin, Nikos Kazantzakis, Carl Jung, Fritjof Capra, Sri Aurobindo, and Theodore Roszak. Instead of a flight from technology, there is a rush to embrace technology as the catalyst of a cultural and spiritual revolution.[31]

The danger today is that spirituality will be divorced from a transcendent revelation. The gospel is being dehistoricized and ethicized. The Eternal Now or the Christ Spirit figures more prominently than the Jesus Christ of biblical history.

In an age adrift in a sea of pluralism, hazy mysticism, and latitudinarianism, it is imperative to recover the integrity of the gospel, to reclaim the divine authority and primacy of Scripture. Only then will we come to appreciate the real meaning and importance of evangelism, social service, and worship done in spirit and truth.

It is time to get our priorities straight. Against the technological society, with its emphasis on productivity, creativity, and efficiency, the church should stress the priority of being over action, faith over works (cf. Col. 1:9, 10; 2:6–7; Eph. 2:8–10; 2 Pet. 1:3–8). I reject Norman Pittenger's contention that "all 'being' is found only in 'doing.'"[32] I am equally uncomfortable with liberation theology's elevation of praxis over dogma. Evangelical Christianity insists that the knowledge of God comes before the service of God. Orthodoxy, orthodoxa (right praise), and orthopraxis are all crucial, and they are all inseparable. There can be no worship done in spirit and in truth apart from right dogma, but right dogma is arrived at through the practice of Christian love as well as the unceasing struggle of faith to lay hold of God's blessings. Before both meaningful worship and a fruitful life can be attained, there needs to be an outpouring of the Holy Spirit, which instills in us a living faith as well as a confident hope in the promises of God. The gift of faith takes precedence over right theology as well as right worship. Pope John XXIII and Karl Barth were united in believing that the key to spiritual renewal in our times lies in a new Pentecost.

As Christians we must wrestle against both the technological illusion and the political illusion. The first assumes that every problem, even of a moral and spiritual kind, is capable of being remedied by right technique. The second presupposes that every problem has a political solution.[33] Alvin Toffler, the philosopher of the new technological liberalism, maintains that the fault lies not in people but in the socioeconomic system. What needs to be changed is the system, and people can bring this about if they are properly motivated and informed.[34] Here we see a striking convergence of conservative (capitalist) and socialist ideology.

The technological society determines the validity of performance on the basis of whether it produces the desired results. John Howard Yoder rightly urges the church to resist this mentality: "The key to the obedience of God's people is not their effectiveness but their patience. . . . The triumph of the right, although it is assured, is sure because of the power of the resurrection and not because of any calculation of causes and effects."[35]

Present-day Temptations

In an age when people are pinning their hopes on both politics and technology, it is important that the church resist the temptations of both quietism and utopian activism. George Hunsinger, supposedly following Barth, advocates uniting a biblically informed or conservative theology with a progressive politics.[36] The Confessing Church in Nazi Germany tried to maintain a biblical theology but was tempted to ally it with conservative politics. The churches in Holland, Norway, and Britain, on the other hand, were open to a progressive or socialist politics but tried to base this on a liberal theology with the result that Christ was superseded by social concerns. My position is that the people of God may in one situation throw their support behind conservative politics (with its emphasis on family solidarity and moral values in the school system) and in another support progressive politics (with its stress on equality and human rights). There may even be occasions when church people find that it is God's will for them to be apolitical. The church must always resist alliances with any type of politics or ideology, for only in this way will it be enabled to speak the Word of God with credibility and power.

We should oppose the false pietism (to be distinguished from original Pietism) that glibly holds that individual conversion is the answer to the social problem. It is certainly the beginning of an answer, but conversion needs to be supplemented by growth and nurture in the faith, and this includes gaining an awareness of the presence of corporate sin as well as of personal sin. Conversion, moreover, must continue throughout life, and if we rest content on the laurels of a past experience, we may well be blocking the Spirit's sanctifying work in our lives.

Some of the luminaries of classical Pietism can help us to counter the cultural religiosity of our time. Johann Christoph Blumhardt's warning has a contemporary ring:

> When I look at the conversions of today, I see so much lacking that I am afraid they will be a detriment unless people stop making the conversion experience the main thing. The Lord will give nothing, will reveal nothing of that for which we hope, unless the *change of heart* remains the first and last thing. . . . The outcome of one's own repentance is to produce further repentance—which thought also belongs to the gospel. But whatever does not come out of one's own repentance is about as effective as soap bubbles against fortress walls.[37]

Christoph Blumhardt, who inherited his father's mantle as an evangelist and healer and was active for a time in the religious socialist movement, also gives a timely rebuke to latter-day evangelicalism:

> What is the purpose of our existence? The main thing is not to make sure that we are speedily saved. Anyone who thinks that is making a big mistake. The most important thing is to be fighters and to bring the world under God's feet. The main thing is that we should be the voice of justice on earth, and no longer tolerate the rule of sin and Satan. Then we are allied with God.[38]

Eberhard Arnold, charismatic founder of the Society of Brothers, combined both Pietist and Anabaptist motifs. He remained unconvinced "that the social question is solved by conversion; for this a long path of healing is needed, and at the same time intervention by God himself."[39] He has caustic words for the kind of piety that is too introspective, too conscious of itself as a religious exercise:

The reality of repentance and of our smallness is effective only if one takes the smallness for granted. As long as that which moves us is not God and His kingdom but instead "my" heart, "my" inadequacy, "my" remorse and "my" repentance, the whole thing is and remains a completely heathen idolatry.[40]

Personal transformation is at the heart of social reformation, but the former by itself will not suffice. We need to go on to Christian perfection, to grow "in the grace and knowledge of our Lord and Savior Jesus Christ" (2 Pet. 3:18), to the extent that we are given both practical wisdom and spiritual insight concerning the role of the church in a society that is surely becoming ever more aggressively pagan. As we fortify ourselves daily in the battle with the principalities and powers that continue to beguile the world, we should be buoyed up by the certain knowledge that Jesus Christ is already the victor and that this victory will be speedily unfolded as history draws toward a close.

Notes

1. Allen O. Miller and M. Eugene Osterhaven, eds. and trans., *The Heidelberg Catechism with Commentary* (Philadelphia: United Church Press, 1963), question 86, pp. 147–48.
2. Adolf Köberle, *The Quest for Holiness*, trans. John C. Mattes (Minneapolis: Augsburg, 1938), p. 168.
3. Cited in Wilhelm Herrmann, *The Communion of the Christian with God*, ed. Robert T. Voelkel (Philadelphia: Fortress, 1971), p. 253. Luther, *Sämmtliche Werke*, (Erlangen, 1826–57), x. 77.
4. Rudolf Otto, *The Idea of the Holy*, trans. John W. Harvey (New York: Oxford University Press, 1958).
5. Köberle maintains with some cogency that besides the " 'numinous trembling' before the incomprehensible, unspeakable depths of divine mysteries," the fear of God also includes "a conscious, ethical seriousness in viewing a judgment according to works to which even the disciple, who is in a state of faith, must submit." *Quest for Holiness,* p. 165.
6. Cf. Augustine: "If you fear God, cast yourself into His arms, and then His hands cannot strike you." *Sermons.* Cited in David Manning White, ed., *The Search for God* (New York: Macmillan Co., 1983), p. 148.
7. Heidelberg Catechism, question 86, p. 148.
8. Nels Ferré, *The Christian Understanding of God* (New York: Harper, 1951), p. 9.
9. George A. Maloney, ed., *Pilgrimage of the Heart: A Treasury of Eastern Christian Spirituality* (New York: Harper & Row, 1983), pp. 196, 197.
10. *Maximus Confessor: Selected Writings* trans. George C. Berthold, intro. Jaroslav Pelikan (New York: Paulist Press, 1985), p. 38.
11. Quoted in *Christianity Today* 23, no. 21 (Sept. 7, 1979): p. 52.
12. See Malcolm Muggeridge, *Something Beautiful for God: Mother Teresa of Calcutta* (New York: Harper & Row, 1971).

13. William Adams Brown, *Church and State in Contemporary America* (New York: Charles Scribner's Sons, 1936), p. 299.
14. *Basic Writings of Saint Augustine*, ed. Whitney J. Oates (New York: Random House, 1948), 1: p. 3.
15. Carl E. Braaten, *The Future of God* (New York: Harper & Row, 1969), p. 143.
16. William Booth, *In Darkest England and the Way Out* (New York: Funk & Wagnalls, 1890), p. 221.
17. *Calvin's Sermons on the Ten Commandments*, p. 200.
18. Bonhoeffer, *Ethics*, p. 137.
19. Cited in *Decision* 10, no. 10 (Oct., 1969): p. 13.
20. *The Witness of William Penn*, ed. Frederick B. Tolles and E. Gordon Alderfer (New York: Macmillan Co., 1957), p. 48.
21. An editorial in *Christianity Today* expresses the reservations of evangelicals concerning the growing politicalization of the World Council of Churches: "The goal of the World Council is not primarily freedom and justice, but change in the social, and especially the economic, structure of society." *Christianity Today* 26, no. 5 (March 5, 1982): p. 17.
22. Martin Luther King, Jr., *Strength to Love* (New York: Harper & Row, 1963), p. 23.
23. Carl F. H. Henry, "Church and State: Why the Marriage Must be Saved," in *The Christian as Citizen*, ed. Kenneth Kantzer (Carol Stream, Ill.: Christianity Today Institute, 1985), p. 10.
24. Ibid., p. 13.
25. Already in precarious health, Pascal invited a destitute family into his home and then discovered one of the children had smallpox. He graciously decided that it was he and not the child who should leave. Happily, he was able to find a place to stay with his brother-in-law. Such sacrificial service and generosity of spirit qualitatively transcend the expectations of humanitarianism. Humanitarians advocate a reasonable service to those less fortunate but not anything involving the crucifixion of the human will or the sacrifice of health, reputation, or even life itself. See Charles E. Hummel, *The Galileo Connection* (Downers Grove, Ill.: InterVarsity, 1986), p. 275.
26. W. A. Whitehouse, *Creation, Science, and Theology* (Grand Rapids: Eerdmans, 1981), p. 209.
27. See the discussion in George Hunsinger, "Barth, Barmen and the Confessing Church Today," *Katallagete* 9, no. 2 (Summer 1985): pp. 25, 26.
28. Nonresistance is not a universal principle that can be directly applied to each and every situation but a goal that can be approximated through grace as the Christian seeks to follow in the footsteps of the Master.
29. Charles A. Reich, *The Greening of America* (New York: Bantam Books, 1971).
30. The votaries of the New Age speak of the need for a spiritual revolution, which will alter consciousness, in addition to a social revolution, which will change society. See, for example, Theodore Roszak, *Person/Planet: The Creative Disintegration of Industrial Society* (New York: Doubleday, 1978).
31. Despite his warnings against the misuse of technology and burgeoning technocracy, Theodore Roszak can find hope in the technological revolution: "What technology has brought us is the superior means of shared experience and, under the threat of thermonuclear annihilation, the necessity of universal caring. It has brought the apparatus that enables us, and the crisis that forces us to turn the old vision into an historical project." *Where the Wasteland Ends* (New York: Doubleday, 1972), p. 20.
32. Norman Pittenger, *After Death—Life in God* (New York: Seabury, 1980), p. 38.
33. See Jacques Ellul, *The Political Illusion*, trans. Konrad Kellen (New York: Alfred A. Knopf, 1967).
34. See Alvin Toffler, *The Third Wave* (New York: Bantam Books, 1981).
35. Yoder, *The Politics of Jesus*, p. 238.
36. Hunsinger, "Barth, Barmen and the Confessing Church Today," pp. 26–27.
37. Vernard Eller, ed., *Thy Kingdom Come: A Blumhardt Reader*, (Grand Rapids: Eerdmans, 1980), p. 30.

38. Cited in Emmy Arnold, ed., *Inner Words for Every Day of the Year* (Rifton, N.Y.: Plough Publishing House, 1975), p. 39.
39. Ibid., pp. 57, 58.
40. Ibid., p. 50.

CHAPTER 10

Alternatives in Ethics Today

> Beloved, do not believe every spirit, but test the spirits to see whether they are of God; for many false prophets have gone out into the world.
>
> 1 JOHN 4:1

> They determine what can be God's word, not by starting from God who speaks it, but starting from man who receives it, and then they still claim it is God's word.
>
> MARTIN LUTHER

> One of the limits of socialism is that thus far even in its most powerful and fruitful manifestations . . . it has not been able to do more than oppose to one egoism, that of the middle-class, another egoism, that of labor.
>
> KARL BARTH

> I would not judge a man by the presuppositions of his life but by the fruits of his life.
>
> REINHOLD NIEBUHR

Having delineated my position to a considerable extent in previous chapters, I now wish to explore in some detail the wider range of ethical options today. Although this typology is not intended to be exhaustive, it does purport to introduce the reader to the leading contenders.[1] In the concluding section, I present a further statement of my own position over against these rival approaches to the ethical question.

Situationalism

Situation ethics is usually associated with Joseph Fletcher, but there are other scholars who identify themselves as situationalists. John Giles Milhaven champions the new morality in *Toward a New Catholic Morality,* in which he contends, like Fletcher, that the only absolute is love.[2] J. A. T. Robinson's position is remarkably similar. Juan Luis Segundo accepts the label "situation ethics" as a fair description of his position, though certain emphases of his would place him more in the camp of liberation ethics. Because situationalists do not agree on all points, I am focusing on Fletcher as representative of this approach.[3]

The situationalist contends that the only criterion is love, but this is love divorced from the teaching of the law and united with reason. Love is defined as goodwill at work in partnership with reason. We employ reason to decide what action best serves love. Love is not a transcendent ideal but an intrinsic norm. Perfect love is held to be a real possibility even in this sinful world. Love is closely related to justice; indeed, justice is defined as love expanded.

The method in situationalist ethics is a rational calculation of ends and consequences. Love determines which actions redound to the greatest good for the greatest number of people. This type of ethics is utilitarian, pragmatic, and teleological. It is also relativistic, since the demands of love vary according to the situation.

Situation ethics is a kind of humanitarianism united with relativism and pragmatism. It is an ethics of human advancement. Sin is linked with ignorance. Nothing is deemed intrinsically evil except ill will. There is no real place for prayer in this kind of rationalism. Our alleged sins are really the products of mistaken judgments. We should have sorrow over bad judgments but not guilt.

Are situationalists such as Fletcher right that no act can be considered intrinsically evil? Surely, Christian faith condemns torture as an unequivocal evil, even if the end is to help humanity. The wanton killing of innocents, even in warfare, is also a palpable evil, however lofty the motivations. Idolatry is always an evil, though one might deem it expedient in certain situations to remain silent rather than make a public outcry against it. Daniel did not openly protest against the royal decree to worship no other god than the king but quietly remained steadfast in his own faith, not even offering resistance when he was subsequently arrested and led away to what appeared to be certain death (Dan. 6; cf. Dan. 3).

By reducing love to a rational calculation of what is best for us and our neighbor, Fletcher and other situationalists lose sight of the transcendent and ecstatic dimensions of love. They fail to see that love in the sense of agape challenges the goals and hopes of a rational humanity. Such love is a product of faith more than the outcome of rational determination.

Stanley Hauerwas claims with some perspicuity that "the ethics of love is often but a cover for what is fundamentally an assertion of ethical relativism. It is an attempt to respond to the breakdown of moral consensus by substituting the language of love for the language of good and right as the primary determinate for the moral."[4] In effect, the appeal to love blurs "the pain and the glory of living morally in this life."[5]

Love needs an anchor in law, but the situationalists recognize no abiding moral principles, no authoritative moral tradition. Love is sometimes likened to the gold that is extracted from the ore of the Decalogue; what is left can be discarded.[6] The only absolute, the only criterion, is love. But does not the law give content and direction to the practice of love? Love goes beyond the law, but law is surely not discarded when we dedicate ourselves to love. I contend that the gold (love) is never our permanent possession, and therefore we need to extract it continually from the ore (the historical and cultural matrix that determines how love is understood and appropriated). Neither love nor the good is self-explanatory, but both gain meaning and direction from the commandments given in Holy Scripture.

I have argued elsewhere that the ultimate criterion is neither love nor law but the living Christ who shows us how to love and illumines the meaning of law so that it serves love. Christ, moreover, is not love as such but the Holy One who loves. The love of Christ forgives the sinner but does not tolerate the sin. Fletcher's permissive love contrasts with the biblical depiction of love as searing and holy, a love that includes the dimension of wrath and judgment as well as grace and mercy.[7]

Historical-Relational Ethics

The Catholic theologian Charles Curran endeavors to plot a middle way between situational and traditional ethics. He claims that "the concept of natural law as a deductive methodology based on eternal and immutable essences and resulting in specific absolute norms is no longer acceptable to the majority of Catholic moral theologians writing today."[8] Whereas the classical approach emphasizes "the eternal, the universal, and the unchanging, and often employs a deductive methodology," the "historically conscious approach" stresses "the particular, the individual, the contingent, and the historical, and often employs a more inductive methodology."[9] Curran's position might be called an inductive relationalism or, even better, a historical relationalism. This approach embraces both the connotations of relativity through historical consciousness and continuity with the historical tradition of the church. It might also be called an empirical relationalism or a responsibility relationalism.

Curran takes pains to differentiate his position from several other alternatives. The natural law approach minimizes the power of sin in human relationships, which blurs and distorts our perceptions of the universal law of God. Natural law theory affirms that "certain actions are right or wrong no matter what the consequences,"[10] but this fails to consider the concrete effects or implications of our acts. On the other hand, if we focus exclusively on consequences (the thrust of situationalism), we then ignore other important dimensions of morality such as intention, motivation, personal growth, and so on. What should guide us in our deliberations, he says, is whether authentically human values are increased or diminished.

Curran sees the individual in multiple relationships with others and regards moral goods as interrelated. There may even be a conflict between moral goods. Conscience is appealed to above external authorities. Yet he acknowledges that conscience may be wrong if it summarily disregards the guidance and experience of the church. Conscience should listen to the church as a moral teacher, but it must finally be true to its own light. "The ultimate criterion of the truth of conscience is not conformity to the truth existing out there but . . . the self-transcendence of the human subject striving for authentic development."[11]

The primary biblical paradigm behind this model is covenant rather than law. Sin is redefined as breaking with love in our dealings with God and humanity rather than transgressing against a moral code. What makes sin mortal is not that it is an act against the law of God but rather that it breaks "our relationship of love with God, neighbor, world and self."[12] Considering his approach more universal than historical Christianity, Curran denies "that there is an exclusive Christian content to morality in terms of either the concrete decisions made by Christians or the proximate attitudes, goals, and dispositions they propose as normative for human existence. Non-Christians can and do share these same values, norms, goals, attitudes, dispositions, and acts."[13]

Curran can justly be accused of relegating the Bible to the status of a mere aid in understanding rather than a ruling norm. Scripture is used to illustrate what is basically a subjective or even a natural norm. It is the inner light (conscience) in union with church tradition rather than the Word of God that is the final norm. Relevance is prized over obedience, authenticity over fidelity to the divine commandment. His reliance is on flashes of insight that lead us to will the good rather than on an authoritative Word from the beyond which we hear in Holy Scripture. The historical analysis of the situation rather than God's self-revelation in Jesus Christ is determinative for ethical decision.

Natural Law Ethics

Like Curran, most ethicists today are skeptical of reliance on natural law. Yet natural law ethics is not without its defenders, among them University of Notre Dame professor Ralph McInerny, who tries to show the relevance of Thomas Aquinas's thought for the modern day.[14] McInerny, following Thomas, posits a universal moral consciousness that yields certain prescriptions for conduct. This universal moral sense is clarified and illumined by the revealed law in the Bible, but it is nonetheless binding on both Christians and non-Christians. Natural law is defined as "the view that there are true directives of human action which arise from the very structure of human agency and which anyone can easily formulate for himself."[15]

With Thomas, McInerny holds to moral absolutes that admit of no exceptions whatsoever. Against Fletcher, he recognizes that there are absolutely wrong actions. One such example is lying. Yet he says that not all intentional deception falls under the rubric of lying. Similarly, even though all murder is wrong, not all killing can be classified as murder. While insisting on the universal and binding character of natural law precepts, McInerny acknowledges relative moral principles that are generally but not always binding.[16]

As a good Thomist, McInerny holds to an inequality of basic human values and a hierarchy among them. Yet to accept an objective hierarchy of values does not imply that one may act directly against any basic value with impunity.[17]

McInerny attacks consequentialism on the grounds that "wrong actions are in themselves evil and can never become good in any time or place or other circumstances."[18] He admits that the consequences of an action are not irrelevant, for they often form a part of our intention in action. Yet "no consideration of putative good consequences which might flow from it can justify the doing of an action bad in kind."[19]

The only reliable guide is "a well-formed" conscience. Conscience is defined as "the purely cognitive appraisal of the particular in the light of general principles."[20]

McInerny is of the firm conviction that we cannot achieve perfect happiness, union with God, apart from the aid of divine grace. This is why natural theology "is best carried on within the ambience of the faith."[21] Grace enables us to attain both our natural and our supernatural ends. Natural happiness is the gateway to supernatural bliss, just as natural law is the preamble to revealed law.

John Macquarrie also espouses a natural law ethics but combines it with an existentialist theology.[22] For Macquarrie natural law ethics should be severed from its traditional essentialistic framework and reconceived in dynamic terms. Natural law should no longer be restricted to the natural order of things but expanded to encompass the whole range of human insights and experience. In Macquarrie's theology, it seems, natural law has no clearly defined content. Once we define it, it then becomes a positive law, which is historically and culturally conditioned.

The problem with any natural law theory is that it does not sufficiently take into consideration the noetic effects of sin. It is said that people are more seriously wounded by sin in the moral order than in the intellectual order. Yet every attempt to spell out the intellectual content of natural law can be shown to be historically and culturally conditioned. While all people seem to have a moral sense, when they begin articulating what this means, their own cultural and religious background proves to be determinative in their judgments. We need to take seriously this telling criticism of Erik von Kuehnelt-Leddihn: "Is there such a thing as a natural law in the sense that we all 'naturally' reject murder, lies, deceit, wanton cruelty, adultery, theft, or contempt of parents? As a world traveler and student of ethnology I deny this in the face of a certain Christian theological tradition."[23]

Eudaemonism

Even more incompatible with biblical or evangelical ethics is eudaemonism, the position of classical humanism (Socrates, Plato, Aristotle). In this view, the aim or goal of the ethical life is eudaemonia, happiness or well-being. It is to be differentiated from the pleasure of the hedonists in that it connotes the development or perfection of human capabilities. It is not the pleasureful life but the integrated life or the fulfilled life that is considered worthy of our commitment.[24]

Eudaemonism can be found in both Augustine and Aquinas, who sought a biblical-classical synthesis in which the highest values of Hellenistic civilization were incorporated into a Christian life- and worldview.[25] For these theologians, it is not happiness per se but the higher happiness that is the end of ethical endeavor. It is not the comforts of life, as in hedonism, but integration and fulfillment in the vision of God that is the aim of the spiritual quest. The perfection of the self is realized in union with the living God, the ground and goal of the self.[26] Regrettably, in my judgment, the self-regarding love of eros takes precedence over the self-giving love of agape in both of these scholars.

Erich Fromm is a noteworthy example of classical humanism in our day. Fromm opposes both naturalism, which reduces the human being to instinctual drives, and nihilism, which considers the quest for meaning in life futile. He upholds the dignity and uniqueness of humanity. His position is reflected in the words of his co-worker Ruth Nanda Anshen: "Mankind can finally place its trust not in a proletarian authoritarianism, not in a secularized humanism, both of which have betrayed the spiritual property right of history, but in a sacramental brotherhood and in the unity of knowledge."[27]

Like the classical humanists, Fromm sees the goal of the ethical life as happiness or well-being. He is poignantly aware that "happiness in its present meaning usually implies a superficial, contented state of satiation."[28] What he means by happiness is the full realization of our creative potential, the unfolding of our capacity to love and to relate to our fellow human beings. At times he sees happiness as a concomitant of the productive realization of our potentialities; at other times he identifies the two.[29] He quotes approvingly from his mentor Spinoza: "Happiness is not the reward of virtue, but is virtue itself; nor do we delight in happiness because we restrain our lusts; but, on the contrary, because we delight in it, therefore are we able to restrain them."[30] The opposite of happiness is not sorrow or pain but depression resulting from "inner sterility and unproductiveness."[31] Norms are to be derived not from an authoritative divine revelation but from a rational analysis of their capacity to promote "the optimum of growth and well-being and the minimum of ill-being."[32] Fromm acknowledges his indebtedness to Aristotle, Plato, and Spinoza, but he also draws from the Old Testament prophets, Jesus, Lao-tze, and Gautama Buddha.[33]

Fromm valiantly upholds eros, the resolute affirmation of life, over thanatos, the love of death. Eros is a unitive love that strives to bring things together into a higher synthesis. In affirming ourselves we affirm our solidarity with humanity. In loving both ourselves and others we fulfill the yearning within us for unity and wholeness. He declares, "In the act of loving, of giving myself, in the act of penetrating the other person, I find myself, I discover myself . . . I discover man."[34] Love is "the overcoming of human separateness . . . the fulfillment of the longing for union."[35] When we fuse ourselves with another person, we transcend the prison of our separateness. "In the act of loving I am one with All, and yet I am myself, a unique, separate, limited, mortal human being. Indeed out of the very polarity between separateness and union, love is born and reborn."[36]

Love is not the sacrifice of the self for the welfare of others (as in agape) but instead an appreciation of the genuinely human qualities in ourselves and in others. It is an affirmation of life in its fulness, and this includes affirming our fellow human beings as well as ourselves. Love does not proceed simply out of need and weakness (as in the classical eros) but out of strength—the desire to share our knowledge and talents with others who are less fortunate.

In Fromm's ethics, we can detect at least a partly conscious effort to unite the eros ideal of classical philosophy with the ideal of rational benevolence associated with the Enlightenment of the later seventeenth and eighteenth centuries. The quest for our own self-realization is held in tension with a rational altruism in which the needs of our fellow human beings are respected and affirmed. Yet the eros ideal is the dominant one. Brotherly or humanitarian love is subordinated to the mystical love of oneness with reality. We lend a helping hand to others in order to be healed of our separateness and alienation, in order to be made whole. Self-love is the basis and goal of neighbor love. Love is the creative power within us by which we relate ourselves to the world and make it truly ours.[37]

It was Immanuel Kant, the eminent philosopher of the late Enlightenment, who challenged the classical ethics of eudaemonism, maintaining that the goal of the exemplary life is not happiness but virtue. As he put it, "Morality is not properly the doctrine how we should *make* ourselves happy, but how we should become *worthy* of happiness."[38] Kant saw love in terms of the law of love, obedience to the categorical imperative within us. Morality is fulfilling our duty rather than gaining happiness. The motive that stimulates a person to obey the law is reverence for the law itself. Kant recognized that civilization progresses only at the cost of human happiness. Yet he believed that happiness would be the probable fruit of a life of virtue, and he regarded the union of virtue and happiness as the highest good. Our goal is a virtuous life, a life in accordance with the dictates of conscience, but our hope is that happiness might crown such a life in the end.

Love in the later Enlightenment came to be interpreted in terms of *nomos* (law) rather than agape or eros. To love was to act in accord with the moral law, to treat people as ends in themselves, not as means only. In the Kantian perspective, love for oneself, striving for one's own happiness, can never be a virtue. We find the purpose of our existence in fulfilling our obligations to our fellow human beings.

Fromm rejects Kant's thesis that love of ourselves is not worthy of a virtuous people.[39] Whereas Kant opposes self-love, Fromm sees it as the basis and goal of all other love. While Kant envisages love as a law, Fromm regards it as an art or achievement. For Kant the highest virtue is obedience to the moral imperative within; for Fromm it is self-realization. Nevertheless, in Fromm's philosophy, too, we find the ideal of rational altruism—giving to others without asking for anything in return.[40]

Yet it can be shown that the gift love of benevolence still flows out of need—to gain moral integrity (Kant) or to realize our full potential for happiness (Fromm). In evangelical Christianity, on the other hand, perfect love or agape is not based on need, for the need for salvation and eternal happiness has already been filled by faith. Instead, it rises spontaneously out of the human soul as a token of our joy and gratefulness for what has already been done for us in Jesus Christ. Spinoza defined benevolence as "the desire of benefiting one whom we pity."[41] Christianity views love as the act of identifying ourselves with the sufferings of others. It is more than a feeling of sympathy: it is a declaration of solidarity. We do not wish simply to help those in need in order to raise them up to our level, but we willingly descend to their level so that we can find God together in the midst of tribulation and affliction.

The ethical goal in the evangelical perspective is neither happiness (Fromm) nor a virtuous life that merits happiness (Kant) but the letting go of our dreams, hopes, and aspirations in order to serve the world for which Christ died. In losing ourselves for the sake of others, we find ourselves in the end. Self-realization is the paradoxical by-product of the surrender and loss of the self for the happiness and gain of our neighbor in need.

Enlightened Egoism

Risking all in this way is more than the rationalistic mind can countenance. Reckless disregard for self is patently imprudent. Far more palatable is the ideal of enlightened self-interest, which, like the ideal of rational benevolence, we owe to the Enlightenment. Already Spinoza concluded that "the more each person strives and is able to seek his own profit, that is to say, to preserve his being, the more virtue does he possess."[42] This attitude was cultivated laboriously by the Physiocrats and brought to fruition in the works of Adam Smith. For Smith the situation was simple: "Not from benevolence do we expect bread from the baker but from his self-love."[43] Smith believed that each person pursuing his or her own enlightened self-interest would produce a "natural harmony" and "inevitable progress." The perfectly virtuous man will strive to advance his own welfare, but always conscious of how this relates to the good of the whole.[44]

Adam Smith's position is not an unqualified egoism, even though the egoistic motive is present throughout his philosophy. He seeks to hold together prudence, justice, and benevolence. By prudence he has in mind the care we should exert for our own interests and that of our families. By justice he means the observance of legal rules that protect us from unlawful coercion. Benevolence signifies a spirit of magnanimity and generosity that should characterize our actions toward others, especially toward those less fortunate. Benevolence is an "ornament which embellishes, not the foundation which supports the building."[45] By benevolence we are able to win the affection of others, so even in the so-called highest virtue an egoistic impulse remains.[46] "Humanity does not desire to be great but to be beloved."[47] In his remarks on love, self-love is virtually always at the fore: "As to love our neighbor as we love ourselves is the great law of Christianity, so it is the great precept of nature to love ourselves only as we love our neighbour, or, what comes to the same thing, as our neighbour is capable of loving us."[48]

Smith was convinced that the more wealth increases, the more people are enabled to liberate and fulfill themselves. The pursuit of the wealth of nations provides the necessary dynamic conditions for personal happiness and well-being. Wealth signifies not simply the expression of natural power but the realization of human personality. Smith acknowledged imperfections in the fabric of capitalism, but these could be overcome through proper education.

Irving Kristol in our day concurs with Smith "that human behavior can in large measure be explained as the rational pursuit of self-interest."[49] Kristol sees "bourgeois acquisitiveness" as "both natural and good, arising not from the desire to gain at someone else's loss but from 'the desire of bettering our condition'—a desire that is universal—and in fact contributing to the improvement of *everyone's* condition."[50] The pursuit of happiness should be "organically related to the instinct to better one's condition by diligent application."[51] Each person pursuing his or her own enlightened self-interest will produce a society characterized by harmony and progress.

A more blatant ethical egoism is to be found in Ayn Rand, who would nevertheless hasten to describe her position as "enlightened," since it is supposedly based on reason, which in this context means rigorously consistent thinking united with empirically verifiable experience. "Every man . . . is an end in himself, he exists for his own sake, and the achievement of his own happiness is his highest moral purpose."[52] Selfishness is considered the highest virtue and rational selfishness the ground for ethical decision. "Only a rationally selfish man, a man of *self-esteem* is capable of love—because he is the only man capable of holding firm, consistent, uncompromising, unbetrayed values."[53] Because reason is our basic means of survival, only "that which is proper to the life of a rational being is . . . good; that which negates, opposes or destroys it is . . . evil."[54] Big business, in her view, is the most oppressed minority, since it is unfairly made a scapegoat for the problems of a society where private initiative is being increasingly stifled by government bureaucracy.

Enlightened egoism is the ethics of self-preservation. To advance the self means to contribute indirectly to the good of the whole. This ethical philosophy emphasizes liberty over justice, economic productivity over equality. Freedom is interpreted mainly in terms of opportunity for growth and development, unhampered by governmental and social restraint. Natural rights are espoused, but the right of property is deemed among the most valuable. Self-love is considered a virtue, not a sin. Individualism is prized over collectivism. The ideal is not the welfare state but the opportunity state, one in which each person is given the freedom to develop his or her talents and capabilities to the utmost.

Needless to say, this position stands in palpable tension if not outright conflict with the New Testament ideal of self-sacrificing love. It is not self-renunciation or self-denial for the sake of others but self-affirmation and self-fulfillment for the sake of ourselves that is celebrated as the highest of virtues. Despite such a patently non-Christian stance, various attempts are being made today to forge an alliance between evangelical Christianity and this kind of ethics, which provides the theoretical basis for free-enterprise capitalism.[55]

Liberationism

Diametrically opposed to an ethics of self-aggrandizement and laissez faire is liberationism, which seeks to replace greed and domination by a kingdom of freedom that answers the cries of the oppressed for justice and liberation. Among those who identify with liberation ethics are José Míguez Bonino, Juan Luis Segundo, Gustavo Gutiérrez, Leonardo and Clodovis Boff, Rosemary Ruether, Rubem Alves, José Miranda, Hugo Assmann, Frederick Herzog, and Robert McAfee Brown. Clodovis Boff expresses the guiding motif of this kind of theology and ethics: *"Liberation is the social emancipation of the oppressed. Our concrete task is to replace the capitalist system and move toward a new society—a society of a socialistic type."*[56]

Many liberation theologians appeal to Karl Barth who declared, "God always takes His stand unconditionally and passionately on this side and on this side alone: against the lofty and on behalf of the lowly."[57] In other words, God has a preference for the poor, and this theme is gladly embraced by all liberationist thinkers. Where Barth differs from the liberationists is that he sees the solution to the problem of the poor not in social revolution but in a universal awakening to the reconciliation already effected through Christ's atoning work on the cross, which needs to be appropriated in faith and repentance.

To the credit of liberation theologians, they generally try to amass biblical support for their position, but it is legitimate to ask whether they read the Bible in the light of the Marxist dialectic of history. Karl Marx perceived history in terms of the dialectic of the class struggle, one that leads from oppression to revolution, finally culminating in justice. The kingdom of God is identified with a kingdom of freedom, a classless society in which the old antagonisms and hatreds will at last be overcome. It seems that the Marxist dialectic is given a Christian veneer by at least some liberation theologians.

The otherworldly and eschatological dimensions of the kingdom of God are subordinated to this-worldly and utopian goals. Gutiérrez considers liberation from political and economic oppression "a salvific event . . . the historical realization of the Kingdom."[58] Rubem Alves champions a political humanism which he understands as a "new type of messianism, which believes that man can be free by the powers of man alone."[59] Sin is redefined as "the abandonment of responsibility," idolatry becomes "comfort without involvement" (José Míguez Bonino).[60] Our hope is in "the horizon of freedom" or the promise of history rather than the personal return of Jesus Christ. Juan Luis Segundo speaks of "this world becoming the new heaven of God."[61]

Predictably, the mission of the church is drastically revised in this theology. Our task is no longer to convert people to the Christian religion but to plant the seeds of liberation in the hearts and minds of the oppressed (Moltmann). Herzog urges us not to impose strange dogmas upon people who are not Christian but instead take "the radical risk of sharing corporate selfhood with the wretched of the earth."[62] The self-development of oppressed peoples of the third world supplants the call to evangelize the heathen.

The gospel itself is given a new meaning. No longer the good news of a substitutionary sacrifice by a God-Man, it now becomes a call to solidarity with the poor. Salvation is reinterpreted as deliverance from political oppression. Conversion is reconceived as "conscientization," the raising of our consciousness to the needs of the oppressed. Jesus' death on the cross is treated as a political event, a paradigm of revolutionary struggle.

The goal of the Christian life is envisaged as humanization as opposed to Christianization (Pietism), self-realization (classical humanism), or eternal happiness (the old Catholicism). The call to heroism supplants the call to personal sanctification. Prayer becomes reflection on and openness to what God is doing in history. A mysticism of fraternity takes the place of a mysticism of identity.

Despite its flagrant distortion of biblical faith, liberation theology and the ethics it spawns cannot be lightly dismissed. It has attracted some of the leading thinkers of our generation. It reminds us that the salvation that Christ came to bring applies to the whole person—mind, soul, and body. It reclaims the theological truth that right understanding is inseparable from Christian practice, that faith, love, and justice belong together. It bids us consider that if there is such a thing as a just war, there might also be a just revolution, one that could have the sanction of God in redressing social wrongs.

Yet liberation ethics can be faulted for politicizing the gospel, for confounding human justice and divine justification.[63] It entertains the dubious hope that the promise of the kingdom can be realized by social revolution. It fails to see that the way of the cross cannot ultimately be reconciled with the way of the sword. José Miranda uses the story of Jesus driving out the money changers from the temple to give religious sanction to the use of violence for just ends, but this betrays a grave misunderstanding of Jesus' role and mission.[64]

Both Thomas Aquinas and John Wesley distinguished between works of mercy and works of piety, attributing priority to the latter. In other words, our obligations to God himself come before our obligations to our neighbor. Liberationists contend that works of justice are of more importance than either works of piety or mercy. But this is to misread and distort the plain teachings of the Scriptures.

Many liberationists have uncritically accepted the Marxist prescription that the way to change the individual is to alter the social environment, and therefore they place their hope in social revolution and education. They would do well to ponder these words of the disillusioned Communist Milovan Djilas, who was imprisoned by Tito for pressing for reforms in a socialist society: "We now see that a revolution cannot change a nation. Revolution only changes the form of power and poverty, but not the nation itself."[65]

Liberationists rightly perceive that the growing disparity between rich and poor is a moral, even a spiritual, problem. They err, however, when they espouse social revolution as the way to overcome social inequities and when they distort the life and teachings of Jesus to lend moral justification to their social agenda. I agree with Tullio Vinay, founder of that radical venture in Christian discipleship, the Agape community in Italy,[66] that whereas it was once necessary to stress the need for a new world, a just society, on the basis of the gospel ethic, it is now important in the light of a resurgent secular humanism to contend that the beginning of a new world lies in personal commitment to Jesus Christ as Savior and Lord.[67] Social change and personal renewal belong together, but the latter must always have priority if we are to remain true to the biblical mandate.

Graded Absolutism

Whereas liberationist thinking emphasizes the role of historical consciousness in shaping values, Norman Geisler, Dallas Seminary professor, champions an ethic of universal principles based on God's revelation of his purposes in nature and Scripture.[68] He aptly calls his position "graded absolutism"; it might also be described as ethical hierarchicalism. Geisler's endeavor incorporates elements of both Thomism and dispensationalism.

According to Geisler, morality is discovered, not created by humans. Its fundamental principles are embedded in nature and conscience, but these principles are clarified and illumined in the light of special revelation (Holy Scripture).

Geisler holds to a hierarchy of values. There is no one absolute, for example, but many absolutes. He points to Jesus' words concerning the "weightier matters of the law" (Matt. 23:23) and the "greatest" and "least" commands (cf. Matt. 22:36–40).[69] God has many moral attributes, each of which is the basis of a different moral absolute. Where two absolutes appear to stand in tension, we should abide by the higher standard. Mercy has priority over justice, love has priority over truth. Geisler's appeal is not to an extrinsic end but to a higher intrinsic norm. So long as one chooses the higher moral value, one is without guilt.

Geisler contrasts his graded absolutism with both unqualified absolutism (which we see in Augustine, Kant, and John Murray) and conflicting absolutism (as in neo-orthodoxy). He rejects unqualified absolutism because its defenders are forced to introduce qualifications in order to do justice to the biblical texts and therefore become inconsistent. The Bible, for example, speaks highly of Rahab's deception of the king of Jericho (cf. Josh. 2:4–6; Heb. 11:31; James 2:25), but it is explained that God blessed her mercy, not her lie. Geisler repudiates conflicting absolutism because it means that people are compelled to break one of the commandments and therefore must be accounted guilty before God.

He upholds what he calls the-greater-good-over the-lesser-evil-view. This permits one to live above sin so long as one's position is based on the hierarchy of values. Conflicting absolutism, he argues, implies an amillennial view, for it seems that the kingdom of God can never be fully realized in this world. Graded absolutism is more in accord with the premillennial view, which holds that real victory over sin can be realized in earthly history.[70]

This more sanguine approach, he contends, could bring relief to many guilt-ridden people whose guilt has no factual basis. We often feel guilty because we think we are breaking a moral law, but if we can be persuaded that we have actually chosen a higher moral value, then guilt no longer has a hold on us. When we discover that God did not blame us for doing our best in conflict situations, then our "self-image and worth" will increase "measurably."[71]

In my opinion, Geisler's position is closer to the Enlightenment than to either medieval Catholicism or the Reformation. In his view, antinomies can be resolved in many instances not by changing our values but by changing our factual understanding of the situation. His appeal is not to the divine commandment but to a rational scale of values. Moral choices are determined, so it seems, primarily by rational calculation. Nothing is said of the need for prayer and confession of sin. When one is in a conflict situation, there is no need to fear and tremble before a holy God, as Isaiah and Luther did. It is only a matter of determining which absolute is highest on the scale of values.

Geisler's buoyant optimism concerning the moral potentiality of humanity contrasts sharply with the pessimistic view of the Reformation.

He really believes that a "full, guiltless participation in the social and political process is possible."[72] He also contends that so long as we live up to the light within us we will be given the added supernatural light necessary for salvation.[73] But this is the stance of semi-Pelagianism, which was roundly condemned by the Second Council of Orange in 529.

Geisler can also be accused of drawing a bifurcation within God. Lying, he says, may be justified on the basis of the nature of God as merciful, but not on the nature of God as true. But surely there must be a unity between God's attributes! Geisler sees such a unity only in a hierarchy of values.

Finally, his approach seems to presuppose that the criterion for the good lies in the nature of God, which reason is capable of penetrating. In the biblical view, on the other hand, the criterion for the good is the will of God, which is, of course, consonant with his nature but is not necessarily implied by his nature. The will of God, moreover, cannot be known except in God's free decision to make it known—and then only to the eyes and ears of faith. Geisler arrives at the good by a rational analysis of the nature of God, whereas in the kind of evangelical theology I uphold it is God who determines the good by revealing his will to those who seek for it in faith and repentance.

Christian Realism

In sharp contrast with this evangelical rationalism is Christian realism, associated most often with Reinhold Niebuhr. Other scholars who can be placed in this general category include John Bennett, John Courtney Murray, Paul Ramsey, Roger Shinn, and Dennis McCann.[74] Despite their conservative politics, Michael Novak and Richard Neuhaus also share an affinity with the realistic approach delineated by Niebuhr.[75] Because the emphases of all these men differ somewhat, I shall focus primarily on Niebuhr's position.

Christian realism maintains that the ethic of pure love needs to be united with the rational norm of justice in order to be relevant to the cultural situation. Whereas love is a transcendent ideal, justice is an immediate or historical goal. Nevertheless, a commitment to justice and love by itself cannot control institutionalized power, for large social groupings are guided only by interest and checked only by power. Yet, Niebuhr contends, power can be made to serve justice.

Christian realism is a teleological rather than deontological type of ethics. Its method is a rational determination of the consequences of any given action. What is feasible is permissible if the desired objective is gained. Because there is moral ambiguity in every ethical situation, especially where groups are involved, the proper attitude should be one of penitence. We should never take pride or satisfaction in our moral achievements, knowing that before God (*coram Deo*) our hands are not clean.

It should be kept in mind that Niebuhr uses *realism* and *idealism* in this context to denote political dispositions rather than metaphysical stances. *Realism* means "the disposition to take all factors in a social and political situation . . . into account, particularly the factors of self-interest and power." *Idealism* signifies "loyalty to moral norms and ideals, rather than to self-interest."[76] For Niebuhr, a realistic interpretation must include elements of idealism or else it quickly degenerates into power politics. He acknowledges that a realistic position may err in obscuring the residual capacity within mankind for justice and devotion to the larger good.

We can be grateful to Niebuhr for his astute warnings against utopianism. He rightly reminds us that the kingdom of God can never be identified with any social movement or human achievement. He gives due recognition to the tragic dimension of life, to the fact that even the highest of moral achievements are inevitably subverted by prideful self-assertion. This dark side of human existence is often obscured in liberation theology, which pictures eschatology primarily in terms of realization or fulfillment rather than of judgment (as in Christian realism).

Again, Niebuhr discerns the heart of the gospel—the justification of the ungodly. When the gospel is reduced to ethical maxims or experiences of spiritual renewal, then we are no longer in continuity with the apostolic witness concerning the person and work of Jesus Christ. In Niebuhr's eyes, even the righteous are only partly righteous and therefore remain in need of the forgiveness of sins throughout their earthly existence.

Finally, Niebuhr recognizes that the demands of love exceed the requirements of justice. He is to be commended for keeping us aware that the norms of the kingdom of God, self-sacrifice and forgiveness, go beyond the rational norms of equality and freedom. I think Niebuhr is right to conceive of pure love as an "impossible possibility," since the hope of its realization in human life is dependent on divine grace.

I have already shared some of my reservations on Niebuhr's ethics,[77] but I wish to elaborate on them here. First he tends to make the kingdom of God entirely otherworldly and futuristic. The kingdom is always coming, but it is never here. It remains for him a transcendent ideal that impinges on history but never really becomes incarnate in history. But is not the kingdom already realized in the community of faith?

Again, Niebuhr underplays the sanctifying work of the Holy Spirit. He acknowledges Christ *in us* as well as Christ *for us;* yet he can state that we are saved "in principle, not in fact." He does not allow for the fact that personal regeneration can be a decisive factor even in power politics. Jimmy Carter's diplomacy of personal piety in which he was able to reconcile Sadat and Begin and thereby defuse a potentially explosive conflict would probably not have taken place if he had relied on Niebuhr's counsel.

Although Niebuhr sees Christianity as a "gospel of grace" rather than a "law of love," he nonetheless accepts the latter as his criterion in ethics. But the law of love practically means the natural law, encompassing such norms as equality, freedom, and mutual love.[78] Niebuhr appeals much more to these universal natural norms than to the imperatives of the gospel or the divine commandment. In his earlier days, he made this candid confession: "A reasonable person adjusts his moral goal somewhere between Christ and Aristotle, between an ethic of love and an ethic of moderation. I hope there is more of Christ than of Aristotle in my position. But I would not be too sure of it."[79] Did Niebuhr's apologetic approach, in which he sought to commend the faith to its cultured despisers, lead him to compromise certain Christian distinctives?

With the advent of nuclear and chemical weapons, we are indeed facing an entirely new ethical situation. Niebuhr perceived that America would be confronted by moral destruction if it should use these weapons and by physical destruction if it should disarm unilaterally.[80] Describing the new weapons as "our ultimate insecurity and our immediate security,"[81] he refused to recognize that a new kind of pacifism may be the divine commandment for our time. He often claimed that Gandhi's pacifism would never have worked against Hitler. Yet both the Danes and Bulgarians successfully defied the Nazi command to round up and deport the Jews.[82] We should also note that the Polish labor union Solidarity has wrung some costly concessions from the Communist government in Poland, though it is uncertain whether Solidarity will continue to receive the full support of the Polish people. Niebuhr might retort: In view of the fact that we are still living in an unredeemed world, can pacifism ever be a consistent strategy for nations, even though it has on occasion been successfully employed by resistance movements within nations? Can the Christian ethic be directly applied to world conflicts?

Niebuhr sought a synthesis of Renaissance and Reformation insights, and this perhaps accounts for the ambiguities in his system of thought. While the Renaissance stressed the infinite possibilities of man, the Reformation placed the accent on human corruption and depravity. Niebuhr saw in Christ the perfect expression of "the infinite possibilities of love in human life,"[83] which challenges human lethargy and imagination. It sometimes seems that his position is based not on the regenerating power of the Holy Spirit but on human creativity that will inevitably result in tragedy unless tempered by the wisdom that comes from an awareness of human limitations. Yet he was insistent that human possibilities can be fulfilled only by divine grace.[84] Niebuhr perceived that human nature contains "both self-regarding and social impulses and that the former is stronger than the latter."[85] This indeed was the basis for his Christian realism.

The struggle in Niebuhr was between his pragmatism and his idealism, and this was never resolved. Both his quest for workable solutions to power conflicts and his loyalty to ideals that transcend moral conflict show the influence of the American culture that shaped his life and thought. His confidence in the divine grace that enables men and women to aspire to moral ideals as well as his poignant awareness of the sin that corrupts every moral achievement can be traced to his roots in the Reformation and in biblical Christianity.

Theocentric Naturalism

One of the most articulate and probing ethicists of our day is James Gustafson, professor at the University of Chicago Divinity School, who in his two-volume magnum opus presents the case for a radically theocentric ethics.[86] He readily acknowledges his indebtedness to H. Richard Niebuhr, his teacher at the Yale Divinity School, who tried to make a place in theology for God's majesty and power. He also shares Niebuhr's appreciation for Ernst Troeltsch, the theologian of historicism, who maintained that our religious beliefs and moral values are inextricably bound up in the web of history and culture. But while Niebuhr made a valiant effort to transcend relativism by a commitment to "the absolute faithfulness of God-in-Christ,"[87] it is an open question whether Gustafson can avert this peril.

Because he approaches ethics from a contextualist or historicist perspective, it follows that there are no absolute, timeless truths but only historically and culturally conditioned insights that need to be tested scientifically. Indeed, he claims that not only culture but also nature is a source of moral wisdom. This is why it is necessary to draw on both the natural and social sciences in any assessment of theological and ethical assertions.

Gustafson's approach is theocentric because he holds that human values and goals must be subordinated to trust and wonder in the God whom he defines as "the ultimate ordering power in the universe."[88] God does not exist for the sake of humanity, but humanity can serve this power who both bears down on us and sustains us.

At the same time, he is also admittedly naturalistic, for he sees God not as a transcendent personal being who intervenes in nature and history but instead as an impersonal power (or powers) that works through the processes and patterns of nature and history.[89] Gustafson's court of appeal, moreover, is not divine revelation but human experience that is tested by the scientific method. The credibility of theological assertions rests on their consistency with the evidence about the universe provided by the natural and behavioral sciences. Revelation is simply the awakening of religious sensibility to the mystery and wonder of nature; it definitely is not the communication of meaning by a living God who confronts people personally in a divine-human encounter.

Given this radical departure from biblical faith, it is not surprising to find Gustafson using "God" and "Nature" interchangeably, though he resists identifying the Orderer of nature with the works of nature. His position is remarkably akin to that of ancient Stoicism, which practically divinized nature.[90] It seems that Gustafson's God is the soul or spirit of the world rather than the Creator and Lord of the world. Like the Stoics, he calls for a courageous resignation to and cooperation with the powers at work in the cosmos. He speaks highly of natural piety, which is characterized by awe, reverence, and gratitude for what is. The physical orderliness of nature becomes the paradigm for the moral order of humanity.

In this scheme of things, biblical authority fades into insignificance. The Bible is a source of support for Gustafson only as a record of the religious experience of a particular people in history. We can learn from this record how people in another day responded to the awesome powers that shape the cosmos, but we cannot be bound to their myths, which are the product of a particular historical matrix and are now shown to be outdated, though not irrelevant. Gustafson almost completely ignores the Old Testament, though he does appreciate Jesus as exemplifying "theocentric piety and fidelity."[91] At the same time, he rejects the Jesus Christ of orthodoxy—the preexistent Son of God made flesh—as well as the resurrection of Jesus from the grave. He also denies any kind of life after death and is content to face the future with the courage to live and endure in a world of uncertainty.

The God that Gustafson upholds is inaccessibly remote, and this has led some of his critics to accuse him of deism. Yet his God is not detached from the universe but is actively at work within it, reshaping and remolding it. All we can know about this God, however, are "signs" and "signals" of the divine ordering in nature. We cannot even be assured that this God is one whose essence is love, for Gustafson points to the destructive as well as the beneficent powers at work in nature.

The goal of ethical action seems to be the common good, but the precise content of this good is arrived at through a partnership of religious tradition with the natural and behavioral sciences. Even then, it is a good that pertains only to our particular period in history, and it may well change when circumstances change.

What Gustafson has given us is a refurbished natural theology that makes a place for law, even for rules, but not for the gospel, which celebrates God's act of reconciliation and redemption in Jesus Christ. For Gustafson, the foundational criterion for ethical action is the Book of Nature as seen through the eyes of the empirical sciences.

While identifying with the Reformed tradition because of its emphasis on the sovereignty and glory of God, he admits to being very selective in what he chooses from it. He appreciates Calvin's perception of the inseparability of nature and God (though he misreads this),[92] but he rejects Calvin's Christology and high view of biblical authority.

Karl Barth is viewed more as a foil than as a positive support. In contradistinction to Barth, Gustafson tells us that his model is not "one of God personally relating to human beings as persons in the spheres of their moral activity" but rather "one of powers that are impersonally ordering the world of which human activity is a part."[93]

Gustafson can be commended for perceiving the importance of the historical and cultural context in ethical action, but he has gone too far by losing sight of the transcendent ground for Christian moral decision. In his view, there is no sharp distinction between the natural and moral order. Revelation is reduced to insight into the divine ordering of human experience; piety is reinterpreted as awe and wonder before the mystery of nature; theology is transmuted into an enterprise that ventures to say some things about God on the basis of an examination of our affective responses to the world; God is no longer transcendent Lord and Savior of the world but "the power and ordering of life in nature and history which sustains and limits human activity."[94] At the price of being relevant to the world of science and philosophy, Gustafson depersonalizes the God of Scripture and ends with a philosophical construct that may well arouse the curiosity of the world but certainly will not command its allegiance.

Evangelical Contextualism

Palpably removed from the preceding option and much more consciously biblical is evangelical contextualism, associated in our time with such luminaries as Karl Barth, Emil Brunner, Dietrich Bonhoeffer, Helmut Thielicke, and Jacques Ellul.[95] It has an unmistakable continuity with the Reformation, Pietism, and Puritanism. Because, like the others, this is an ideal type, it does not represent any of the aforementioned scholars completely. Since this is the type I identify with, my own position will be unfolded as I delineate its salient emphases.

This position is evangelical because it is based on the gospel and the law illumined by the gospel. It is biblical because the gospel and the law comprise the central content of Holy Scripture, the primary source of our knowledge of divine revelation. It is contextual because the ethical decision is made in the context of the fellowship of faith (*koinonia*), and it is related to the context of personal and social need. Its method is from the gospel through the church to the cultural situation.

The indefeasible criterion in this type of ethics is not the divine ordering in nature (as in Gustafson), nor the law of love (as in Reinhold Niebuhr), nor simply the spirit of love (as in the older liberalism), nor love united with reason (as in situationalism). Instead, it is the divine commandment, which unites love and truth. This commandment also signifies the union of law and gospel, the divine imperative and the divine promise.

Our ultimate appeal is not to general principles (as in natural law ethics) but to the personal address of God as we hear this in and through the gospel proclamation. Karl Barth put it well: "General moral truths . . . do *not* have . . . no matter what their derivation, the force of the true command, for in them the decisive choice between concrete possibilities is still according to what seems best to us."[96] Nevertheless, we acknowledge the normative role of the Decalogue and the Sermon on the Mount, which give us some indication of the will of God for our particular period in history.

Our norm is derived neither from the cultural and historical situation nor from common human experience but from the living Word of God, Jesus Christ.[97] It is therefore an extrinsic norm, one that transcends human subjectivity as well as cultural relativity. It is an absolute norm, but it is made available to us through the historical witness that constitutes Holy Scripture.

Although it is absolute in its origin, it is concrete and specific in its thrust. It is always related to the actual situation in which we find ourselves. Its focus is never on an abstract ideal but always on the concrete good.

For the evangelical contextualist, the way of the cross is most adequately represented by *agape* rather than by *eros* or *philia* (brotherly love). Agape involves the denial of the self for the good of the neighbor. It ipso facto excludes both self-aggrandizement (as in power ethics) and self-sanctification (as in mysticism). The emphasis is on sacrificial service rather than mutual support (as in fraternalism). The focus is on vicarious identification rather than paternalistic benevolence (as in humanitarianism). The religion of the cross is characterized not by the securing of the self from harm but by the forgetting of the self in love.[98]

The striking contrast between the ethics of the world and the way of the cross is brought home to us by George MacDonald: "The love of one's neighbor is the only door out of the dungeon of self. The man thinks his consciousness is himself; whereas his life consists of the inbreathing of God, and the consciousness of the universe of truth. To have himself, to know himself, to enjoy himself, he calls life; whereas, if he would forget himself, tenfold would be his life in God and his neighbors."[99]

This kind of ethics is best described as one of evangelical obedience and is to be sharply distinguished from both prudential calculation (as in an enlightened egoism) and self-realization (the ethics of eudaemonism). In this perspective, ethics is a response to the free grace of God revealed and fulfilled in Jesus Christ. It is by no means an attempt to earn grace or even to prepare ourselves for grace. It is rather a call to serve grace in the power of grace. Christian freedom is not freedom from the law but freedom for the law. But this is the law no longer misunderstood as a legal code but now rightly seen as the spirit of life in Christ Jesus.

Barth's position is sometimes construed as an ethical intuitionism, but this reflects a failure to understand his theological method.[100] Barth does not discount the necessity for taking into consideration the motivations and consequences of our actions, but he insists that these things cannot be finally determinative in our decision.[101] We must also search Holy Scripture for possible analogies to our situation. In addition, we should consult the witness of the fathers of the church, even though this witness in and of itself cannot be the last word. Finally, we should seek to discover the will of God in importunate prayer. None of these activities can procure the divine commandment, but they can enable us to recognize it when it is revealed.

For Barth and other evangelical contextualists, God himself must enlighten us concerning the meaning of his will and purpose for our lives, but this act of self-revelation is not a flash of light in a world of darkness; it is an illumination fully consonant with the road signs that keep us on the straight and narrow path (the Decalogue, the Sermon on the Mount, the lives of the saints). God's commandment is never a rational conclusion, but even less is it an arbitrary or irrational request incapable of being reconciled with the witness of the prophets and apostles and the wisdom of the church through the ages.

At the same time, evangelical contextualists are fully aware of the discontinuity between the revelational and the rational. They take with the utmost seriousness these words of Isaiah: "My thoughts are not your thoughts, neither are your ways my ways, says the Lord. For as the heavens are higher than the earth, so are my ways higher than your ways and my thoughts than your thoughts" (Isa. 55:8, 9). This is why, even as Christians, we should always allow for some discrepancy between our hopes and expectations and the commandment of the living God.

Evangelicals in this tradition speak more of graces than of virtues. Virtues indicate the unfolding of human potentialities, whereas graces are manifestations of the work of the Holy Spirit within us. It is not the fulfillment of human powers but the transformation of the human heart that is the emphasis in an authentically evangelical ethics.

The peace that Jesus came to bring "transcends all understanding" (Phil. 4:7 NIV; cf. John 14:27). It is qualitatively different from the peace that the world knows and seeks. It is not peace of mind but a divine discontent that moves us to seek reconciliation with our adversaries. It is not the absence of conflict but the presence of God in the midst of conflict, making all things new. It does not dull the sensibilities but rejuvenates the spirit even in the trial of bearing the cross.[102] Eberhard Arnold paints this graphic picture: "The peace of God is a force like a streaming flood, a reviving wind, an almighty power. It alone can bring all the mills of human work into action. It can be compared to a mighty torrent whose waters overflow, while the overwhelming power and movement of its depths perform the greatest task."[103]

Similarly, Christians who stand in the tradition of the Reformation find it difficult to harmonize the cultural understanding of happiness with the biblical grace of joy. Happiness signifies the satisfaction of human desire; joy indicates the surge of transforming power within us that enables us to delight in the presence of God and to serve our neighbor in self-giving love. Happiness is the fulfillment of our dreams and hopes; joy is the breaking in of a new horizon of meaning that relegates our dreams and hopes to insignificance. Happiness is temporal and fleeting (cf. Ps. 49:18, 19). Joy is eternal and abiding.

Obviously happiness in the sense of contentment and security in life is not in itself a bad thing, but it must never be made the primary concern. Bonhoeffer gives us this trenchant reminder of the priorities in the moral life: " 'Seek God, not happiness'—this is the fundamental rule of all meditation. If you seek God alone, you will gain happiness: that is its promise."[104]

The goal in evangelical contextualism is to glorify God in every area of life. We glorify God when we seek the welfare of our neighbor even above our own. We glorify God when we work out our salvation with fear and trembling (Phil. 2:12). We glorify God when we put off the old nature and put on the new (Eph. 4:22–24).

How utterly different is the ethics of the world! Here the aim in life is the perfection or well-being of the self (eudaemonism); or it is the attainment of the highest pleasure (Epicureanism); or it is the possession of the highest good (Eros spirituality); or it is the happiness of the greatest number (utilitarianism); or it is a proletarian utopia inaugurated by social revolution (Marxism). Our Lord gives us this counsel: Seek first the kingdom of God and his righteousness, and the necessities of life will then be yours as well (Matt. 6:33).

We should pray for mastery over self but only in order to be fit instruments in the service of our Lord. We should pray for greater faith but only so that we can manifest greater zeal for the honor of God and greater love for our neighbor. We should pray for our own salvation but only so that others might see the light within us and be led to give praise to their Father in heaven (Matt. 5:16).

Evangelical contextual ethics transcends the polarity between theocentricity and anthropocentricity. It recognizes with Irenaeus that "the glory of God is man fully alive," but it also perceives with Amandus Polanus[105] that "the glory of man is the living God." God's glory does not mean the reduction of humanity to nothingness but the raising up of humanity to fellowship with its Creator and Redeemer as well as with the whole company of the saints.

Notes

1. Other ethical options not covered in this chapter include existentialism (Bultmann, Tillich), anarchic or romantic pacifism (Tolstoy, Dorothy Day), and hedonism (Wilhelm Reich, D. H. Lawrence). Pacifism is dealt with in the last chapter. Tillich, it should be noted, represents a blend of existentialism and eudaemonism.
2. John Giles Milhaven, *Toward a New Catholic Morality* (New York: Doubleday, 1970).
3. Because Fletcher's position has already been discussed, though cursorily (see chap. 4, pp. 49–50), I shall try to give a brief recapitulation and some further amplification.
4. Stanley Hauerwas, *Vision and Virtue*, p. 124.
5. Ibid., p. 119.
6. Cf. Fletcher, *Situation Ethics*, p. 71.
7. Meister Eckhart quotes from the Song of Songs 8:6, "Love is as strong as death and harder than hell," to illustrate the nature of genuine Christian love. *Meister Eckhart,* trans. Raymond Bernard Blakney (New York: Harper & Bros., 1941), p. 124.
8. Charles E. Curran, "Catholic Moral Theology Today," in *New Perspectives in Moral Theology,* ed. Charles Curran (Notre Dame, Ind.: Fides, 1974), p. 6.
9. Charles E. Curran, *Moral Theology: A Continuing Journey* (Notre Dame, Ind.: University of Notre Dame Press, 1982), p. 184.
10. Ibid., p. 53.
11. Ibid., p. 56.
12. Ibid., p. 46.
13. Ibid., p. 83.
14. Ralph McInerny, *Ethica Thomistica: The Moral Philosophy of Thomas Aquinas* (Washington, D.C.: Catholic University of America Press, 1982).
15. Ibid., p. 40.
16. Ibid., pp. 59–62.
17. Ibid., pp. 58, 59.
18. Ibid., pp. 88, 89.
19. Ibid., p. 89.
20. Ibid., p. 111.
21. Ibid., p. 121.
22. John Macquarrie, *Three Issues in Ethics*, pp. 82–110.
23. Erik von Kuehnelt-Leddihn, "Jews, Christians, and Gentiles," *National Review* 35, no. 20 (Oct. 14, 1983): p. 1282.
24. For a current restatement of eudaemonism, see Richard Taylor, *Ethics, Faith, and Reason* (Englewood Cliffs, N.J.: Prentice-Hall, 1985). Like Aristotle, Taylor regards pride as a virtue, defining it as "the justified love for oneself" (p. 100).
25. Nygren gives ample documentation for this thesis in *Agape and Eros*.
26. This ethical tradition reappears in Paul Tillich, though it is filtered through the medium of modern idealistic philosophy. Like the classical humanists, Tillich sees the moral ideal in terms of the actualizing of man's created potentiality through participation in the divine. *Morality and Beyond* (New York: Harper & Row, 1963), pp. 17–30.
27. Ruth Nanda Anshen, from the Preface to Erich Fromm, *The Revolution of Hope* (New York: Harper & Row, 1968), p. xiii.
28. Ibid., p. 121.
29. Fromm occasionally defines the perfected life in terms of well-being rather than happiness. Both are acceptable translations of the Greek *eudaimonia*. "Well-being is the state of having arrived at the full development of reason. . . . Well-being means

to be fully related to man and nature affectively, to overcome separateness and alienation, to arrive at the experience of oneness with all that exists. . . . Well-being means to be fully born, to become what one potentially is." Erich Fromm, D. T. Suzuki, and Richard De Martino, *Zen Buddhism & Psychoanalysis* (New York: Harper & Row, 1960), p. 91.

30. Erich Fromm, *Man for Himself* (New York: Holt, Rinehart & Winston, 1947), p. 172.
31. Ibid., p. 190.
32. Fromm, *Revolution of Hope*, p. 91.
33. Fromm shows his appreciation for his Jewish heritage in *You Shall Be as gods: A Radical Interpretation of the Old Testament and its Tradition* (New York: Holt, Rinehart & Winston, 1966).
34. Erich Fromm, *The Art of Loving* (New York: Harper & Brothers, 1956), p. 31.
35. Ibid., p. 33.
36. Erich Fromm, *The Sane Society* (Greenwich, Conn.: Fawcett Publications, 1968), p. 37. The "All" refers to the cosmic reality that he sometimes calls God. Elsewhere he says that to love God means to "become one with God." *Art of Loving*, p. 81. It should be noted, however, that in his philosophy God is a symbol for the full actualization of human potentiality or for the perfect unfolding of human personality. God is not a personal being but creative being unfolded to the maximum degree.
37. Fromm writes, "Love is not a higher power which descends upon man nor a duty which is imposed upon him; it is his own power by which he relates himself to the world and makes it truly his." *Man for Himself*, p. 14.
38. *Kant's Critique of Practical Reason and Other Works on the Theory of Ethics*, 6th ed., trans. Thomas Kingsmill Abbott (London: Longmans, Green & Co., 1948), p. 227.
39. Fromm, *Man for Himself*, pp. 121–123.
40. It is interesting to note that Lewis Smedes regards both Fromm and Kant as espousing an ethics of rational benevolence. While there is some truth in his argument, his reference to the supposed affinity between the two is simplistic, since Fromm, unlike Kant, is a eudaemonist. See Smedes, *Mere Morality*, pp. 47–48.
41. Baruch Spinoza, *The Ethics of Spinoza*, ed. Dagobert D. Runes (Secaucus, N.J.: Citadel Press, 1976), p. 69.
42. Baruch Spinoza, *Ethics*, trans. W. Hale White, (London: Oxford University Press, 1927), vol. 4, prop. 20, p. 195.
43. Quoted in John Patrick Diggins, *The Lost Soul of American Politics* (New York: Basic Books, 1984), p. 337. Note that this text cites George Gilder's claim that Smith was wrong to assume that behind the "invisible hand" of the marketplace were the motives of "selfishness," "avarice," and "greed" (pp. 337–38).
44. Robert Brank Fulton, ed., *Adam Smith Speaks to Our Times* (Boston: Christopher Publishing House, 1963), pp. 57, 58, 76.
45. Adam Smith, *The Theory of Moral Sentiments*, intro. E. G. West (New Rochelle, N.Y.: Arlington House, 1969), p. 125.
46. See Glenn R. Morrow, *The Ethical and Economic Theories of Adam Smith* (Clifton, N.J.: Augustus M. Kelley, 1973), pp. 57–58. Smith sought to combine elements of egoism and altruism, but it seems the former was dominant.
47. Smith, *Theory of Moral Sentiments*, p. xix.
48. Ibid., pp. 27, 28.
49. Irving Kristol, *Reflections of a Neoconservative* (New York: Basic Books, 1983), p. 155.
50. Ibid., p. 165.
51. Ibid., p. 175.
52. Ayn Rand, *For the New Intellectual* (New York: Signet Books, 1963), p. 123.
53. Ayn Rand, *The Virtue of Selfishness* (New York: Signet Books, 1964), p. 32.
54. Ibid., p. 23.
55. See chap. 13, note 15.
56. Leonardo Boff and Clodovis Boff, *Salvation and Liberation*, trans. Robert R. Barr (Maryknoll, N.Y.: Orbis Books, 1984), p. 116.

57. Karl Barth, *Church Dogmatics* II, 1: p. 386.
58. Gustavo Gutiérrez, *A Theology of Liberation*, trans. Sister Caridad Inda and John Eagleson (Maryknoll, N.Y.: Orbis Books, 1973), p. 177.
59. Rubem A. Alves, *A Theology of Human Hope* (Washington, D.C.: Corpus Books, 1969), p. 17.
60. See José Míguez Bonino, *Room to be People*, trans. Vickie Leach (Philadelphia: Fortress, 1979).
61. See Frederick Herzog, *Justice Church* (Maryknoll, N.Y.: Orbis Books, 1980), p. 96.
62. Frederick Herzog, *Liberation Theology* (New York: Seabury, 1972), p. 147.
63. Those liberationists who count Karl Barth among their mentors would do well to emulate his wisdom in vehemently resisting both the politicizing of theology (as with the German Christians) and the theologizing of politics (as with the religious socialists).
64. José P. Miranda, *Communism in the Bible*, trans. Robert R. Barr (Maryknoll, N.Y.: Orbis Books, 1982), pp. 76–78.
65. "Djilas as Hero," *National Review* 20, no. 50 (Dec. 17, 1968): p. 1252.
66. See Donald G. Bloesch, *Centers of Christian Renewal* (Philadelphia: United Church Press, 1964), pp. 69–82.
67. Tullio Vinay, *News from Riesi* (Oct. 15–Nov. 30, 1968), p. 4.
68. Norman Geisler, *Options in Contemporary Christian Ethics* (Grand Rapids: Baker, 1981).
69. Ibid., p. 24.
70. Ibid., p. 105.
71. Ibid., p. 107.
72. Ibid., p. 106.
73. Ibid., p. 32.
74. For a cogent defense of Christian realism see Dennis P. McCann, *Christian Realism and Liberation Theology: Practical Theologies in Creative Conflict* (Maryknoll, N.Y.: Orbis Books, 1981).
75. For the conservative element in Niebuhr's political philosophy, see Ronald H. Stone, *Reinhold Niebuhr Prophet to Politicians* (Nashville: Abingdon, 1972), pp. 126–29. Stone contends that it is a misunderstanding to view Niebuhr as a political conservative.
76. Reinhold Niebuhr, *Christian Realism and Political Problems*, pp. 119, 120.
77. See chap. 6, pp. 100–102.
78. For Niebuhr the principles of natural law are "not so much fixed standards of reason as they are rational efforts to apply the moral obligation, implied in the love commandment, to the complexities of life and the fact of sin, that is to the situation created by the inclination of men to take advantage of each other." *Faith and History* (New York: Charles Scribner's Sons, 1949), pp. 188–89. A case could be made that Niebuhr incorporates the Stoic idea of relative natural law, which signifies the accommodation of the transcendent ideals implied in the law of love to the imperfect world in which we live.
79. Reinhold Niebuhr, *Leaves from the Notebook of a Tamed Cynic* (San Francisco: Harper & Row, 1980), p. 132.
80. See Robert F. Rizzo, "Nuclear War: The Moral Dilemma," *Cross Currents* 32, no. 1 (Spring 1982): p. 80.
81. Quoted in Richard Fox, *Reinhold Niebuhr: A Biography* (New York: Pantheon Books, 1985), p. 241.
82. See Ronald J. Sider and Richard K. Taylor, *Nuclear Holocaust and Christian Hope* (Downers Grove, Ill.: InterVarsity, 1982), pp. 241–46.
83. Reinhold Niebuhr, *Beyond Tragedy* (New York: Charles Scribner's Sons, 1937), p. 17.
84. Niebuhr writes, "In Christ we have a revelation of both the human possibilities which are to be fulfilled and the divine power which will fulfill them." Ibid., pp. 23, 24.

85. Reinhold Niebuhr, *Man's Nature and His Communities* (New York: Charles Scribner's Sons, 1965), p. 39.

86. James M. Gustafson, *Ethics from a Theocentric Perspective*, 2 vols. (Chicago: University of Chicago Press, 1981, 1984).

87. H. Richard Niebuhr, *Christ and Culture* (New York: Harper, 1951), p. 239.

88. Gustafson, *Ethics from a Theocentric Perspective* 2: p. 1.

89. Gustafson readily admits his commitment to theological naturalism. See William Schweiker, "Theocentric Ethics: 'God Will Be God,' " *The Christian Century* 103, no. 2 (Jan. 15, 1986): pp. 36–38.

90. Other critics of Gustafson who discern his affinity to Stoicism include Lisa Sowle Cahill, "Consent in Time of Affliction: the Ethics of a Circumspect Theist," *Journal of Religious Ethics* 13, no. 1 (Spring 1985): pp. 22–36; and Stephen Toulmin, "Nature and Nature's God," loc. cit., pp. 37–52.

91. Gustafson, *Ethics from a Theocentric Perspective* 1: p. 276.

92. Gustafson, *Ethics from a Theocentric Perspective* 2: p. 36.

93. Ibid., pp. 28–29.

94. Gustafson, *Ethics from a Theocentric Perspective* 1, p. 84.

95. John Howard Yoder approaches this position, but his appeal is not to the divine commandment, which is inclined to vary somewhat according to the situation, but to the universal principal of nonviolence. Like Yoder, both Bonhoeffer and Ellul were pacifists, and Karl Barth toward the end of his life became a virtual pacifist.

96. Barth, *Ethics*, p. 83.

97. In contrast to Gustafson, the approach I uphold begins not with the context in which we find ourselves but with God's self-revelation in biblical history, which is historically and culturally mediated, to be sure, but which transcends every particular historical and cultural matrix. It then seeks to relate this world-transforming event to our contextual place in history.

98. Self-forgetfulness can be understood in terms of either biblical prophetic religion or mystical religion. To forget the self in the biblical sense means to set aside personal cares and concerns in order to serve our neighbor for whom Christ died. To forget the self in the mystical sense means to abandon the self to God, thereby foregoing responsibility for the care of souls, including our own. (This is especially true of the mysticism that takes the form of quietism, but there is an element of this in all consistent mysticism.) In the first case, self-concern is subordinated to a passionate concern for those in dire need. In the second case, self-concern is replaced by holy indifference.

99. George MacDonald, *Unspoken Sermons*, cited in David Manning White, *The Affirmation of God* (New York: Macmillan, 1984), p. 72. MacDonald's theology represents a synthesis of Scottish Calvinism and German romanticism. The idealistic-mystical strand in his theology occasionally obscures its evangelical foundations. See Rolland N. Hein, *The Harmony Within: The Spiritual Vision of George MacDonald* (Grand Rapids: Eerdmans, 1982).

100. For a welcome defense of Barth against the charge of intuitionism see John Howard Yoder, *Karl Barth and the Problem of War* (Nashville: Abingdon, 1970), pp. 47–49.

101. Barth criticized Bonhoeffer and his friends for not carefully weighing the consequences in their decision to assassinate Hitler. *Karl Barth's Table Talk*, ed. John D. Godsey (Edinburgh: Oliver & Boyd, 1963), p. 76.

102. Cf. Luther: The peace of God is "a peace which is hidden under the persecution and warfare of the cross." *Luther's Works*, ed. H. C. Oswald, (St. Louis: Concordia, 1972), 25: p. 91. Also cf. the anonymous author of the *Theologia Germanica:* "What kind of peace does Christ mean? He means the inner peace that comes in the midst of hardship, distress, much anguish and misfortune, strain, misery, disgrace, and whatever setbacks there are." *The Theologia Germanica of Martin Luther*, ed. and trans. Bengt Hoffman (New York: Paulist Press, 1980), p. 75.

103. Emmy Arnold, ed., *Inner Words for Every Day of the Year* (Rifton, N.Y.: Plough Publishing House, Hutterian Society of Brothers, 1975), p. 145.

104. Dietrich Bonhoeffer, *Life Together*, trans. John W. Doberstein (New York: Harper & Brothers, 1954), p. 84.
105. See Donald K. McKim, "Amandus Polanus," in *Evangelical Dictionary of Theology*, ed. Walter A. Elwell (Grand Rapids: Baker Book House, 1984), p. 861.

CHAPTER 11

Discerning the Will of God

My prayer is that your love for each other may increase more and more and never stop improving your knowledge and deepening your perception so that you can always recognize what is best.

PHILIPPIANS 1:9–10 JB

You should not believe your conscience and your feelings more than the word which the Lord who receives sinners preaches to you.

MARTIN LUTHER

To venture and do not what is agreeable but what is right, not to hover in the realm of possibilities but boldly to grasp what is real, not in escaping into thought but alone in action is freedom.

DIETRICH BONHOEFFER

At certain crucial points the Bible amazes us by its remarkable indifference to our conception of good and evil.

KARL BARTH

The Agony of Ethical Decision

The meaning of the will of God is perhaps the most perplexing question in theological ethics. One might reply that it is the law of God, but even this cannot be the final answer. The will of God is the law beyond the law, the voice of the living God within the law. The will of God is the gospel or the law united with the gospel. It is not to be confused with a dead letter or killing law of works, for it is the spirit of the law. It is the "mind of Christ," (1 Cor. 2:16), the law of love (Rom. 13:8; 2 John 6; James 2:8), "the law of Christ" (1 Cor. 9:21; Gal. 6:2), "the law of the Spirit of life" (Rom. 8:2) or "the law of liberty" (James 1:25).[1] The will of God is the divine imperative (Emil Brunner) or the divine commandment in which promise and command are united (Barth, Bonhoeffer).

The will of God is the way of the cross. It is not just an ideal but a present course of action. It entails sharing the burden of Christ for the salvation of our neighbor. It means taking up the cross in faith and following Christ into the darkness.

It is the Holy Spirit working through the fellowship of the church who makes the will of God known. The will of God, in other words, is a gift of God that opens the eyes of those who are blind and the ears of those who are deaf. The prophet ruminates: "The Lord God has given me his words of wisdom so that I may know what I should say to all these weary ones. Morning by morning he wakens me and opens my understanding to his will" (Isa. 50:4 LB; cf. Ps. 4:6; 24:5, 6).

The will of God is not abstract and universal but particular and concrete. It is not a system of rules established from the outset but something new and different in each episode of life; consequently, we must examine ever again what the will of God may be.[2]

Much as we might like it, the will of God is never simply available to human reason. It is often hidden in concrete alternatives that confront us. The agony of ethical decision consists in choosing between them.[3] How can we know the will of God when the alternatives seem equal or when they are not sufficiently clear? First, we should bear in mind that our ultimate goal is the glory of God. We should do that which will redound to God's glory and not to our own advancement or security. Second, we should accept the fact that no matter how we choose we will be unable to avoid mixed motivations. We should nonetheless press forward in the knowledge that God will have mercy on our best endeavors. Third, we should go to God in prayer seeking to be open to his guidance. God's will can be discovered only by those who pray for it (Wisdom of Sol. 9:17; 8:21). We should also reflect on the Word of God and decide in the light that comes to us from Scripture.

In addition, we should seek the counsel of our fellow Christians, especially those who are fathers and mothers in the faith. Rehoboam sought advice, but he followed the wrong counselors (1 Kings 12:6–11). He spurned the fathers in the faith and listened to the young men, who were impetuous rather than wise. He lacked the gift of discernment and therefore came to disaster.

Teresa of Avila has suggested that we consult someone with a high degree of learning, for we can more likely expect from such a person a greater depth of understanding. She did not denigrate genuine piety, but if obliged to choose between a person who was both learned and pious and one who was only pious, her choice would be the former.[4]

We should decide within the Christian community, but finally we must decide for ourselves. No counselor can make the decision for us. Our conscience is finally normative but only when it is informed by the Word of God and the wisdom of the church.

It is well to remember that one must be living the will of God in order to know it. The Psalmist says, "A good understanding have all those who do His commandments" (Ps. 111:10 NKJV; cf. John 7:17; 1 John 2:4–6). According to the apostle Paul, a reorientation in both thought and life is necessary in order to apprehend the path God opens to us: "Do not model yourselves on the behavior of the world around you, but let your behavior change, modeled by your new mind. This is the only way to discover the will of God and know what is good, what it is that God wants, what is the perfect thing to do" (Rom. 12:2 JB; cf. Phil. 1:9). This is the hermeneutic of obedience in which the discernment of the will and purpose of God is inseparable from the practice of the Christian life. Bonhoeffer gives us this relevant word of warning: "For him whose life has become a prey to disorder and indiscipline, it will be difficult to hear the commandments of God in faith. It is hard for the sated and the mighty to grasp the meaning of God's judgment and God's mercy."[5]

A decision should never be made in panic or desperation. If the will of God remains clouded in obscurity, it is better to wait than to act hastily (cf. Pss. 27:14; 130:5; Isa. 30:18).[6] But waiting on the Lord must not be confused with procrastination. There are situations in which we may have to decide within a very short time. We must then pray to God for wisdom and act with boldness and firmness. The ingredients of an ethical decision are summed up by Bonhoeffer: "Observe, judge, weigh up, decide and act."[7]

We should recognize that there will be an inevitable tension or even conflict between the desires of the human heart and the will of God (cf. Isa. 55:8, 9). Luther, according to one interpreter, saw the word of God as always coming to us "as *adversarius noster,* our adversary. It does not simply confirm and strengthen us in what we think we are and as what we wish to be taken for. It negates our nature, which has fallen prey to illusion; but this is the way, the only way, in which the word draws us into concord and peace with God."[8]

The will of God will invariably conflict with the expectations of the wider community in which we live (cf. Luke 6:26; John 15:19). Those prophets who play to the fears and hopes of people will always outnumber those who remain faithful to God's commandment. Hananiah predicted that the temple treasures and captives from Jerusalem would be returned from Babylon within two years (Jer. 28). But Jeremiah insisted that the Jews would be in Babylon a long time and that the exile was occasioned by Judah's sin. He predicted the speedy death of Hananiah, which occurred in the seventh month of that same year.

As a general rule, we should not decide on the basis of chance. To be sure, the apostles chose Judas's successor by lots (Acts 1:24–26; cf. Prov. 18:18), but their reliance was nevertheless on prayer. Lots may be used when supported by prayer, but our trust should never be in chance or fortune nor in any technique or method.

The Bible also warns us not to place our trust in dreams and visions (Deut. 13:1–3; Jer. 14:14; 23:25–28; Zech. 10:2).[9] Wesley reiterated the warning against relying on "visions and dreams," on "sudden impressions or strong impulses of any kind." "Remember it is not by these you are to know what is the will of God on any particular occasion; but by applying the plain Scripture rule, with the help of experience and reason, and the ordinary assistance of the Spirit of God."[10]

Nor should we make our decisions on the basis of intuition or subconscious desire. The "quiet time" should be used not to get in touch with the subconscious or with the collective unconsciousness but to prepare ourselves to hear God's Word. This is why it is strongly advisable to include the reading of Scripture or spiritual classics informed by Scripture in our devotional practice.

We should look to signs that God makes available to his children. When doors close to a particular course of action, we should see in this the hand of God. The Psalmist implored, "Show me a sign of thy favor" (Ps. 86:17). At the same time, we are not to put God to a test by demanding signs of our own choosing, as Gideon did. In the long run we are to walk by faith and not by sight (2 Cor. 5:7).

We should also recognize that suffering will be an invariable consequence of an act of obedience to God's commandment. This is the suffering of faith, however, not of sin (cf. 1 Pet. 4:15, 16). "As servants of the Word," Jacques Ellul explains, "we must for its sake accept working with what revolts us, hurts us, and breaks our human hearts, for blind refusal is a disservice to the Word of God, and this Word declares forgiveness with judgment, not a judgment without pardon."[11]

Even when the motivations seem right and the consequences appear salutary, we should bear in mind that this may still not be God's will.[12] The road to hell is paved with good intentions. God wants us to walk in the darkness of faith, not by the light of reason. If a course of action seems too obviously right, it should be distrusted.[13] According to Proverbs, "There is a way that seems right to a man, but in the end it leads to death" (14:12 NIV). Thielicke says, "Even the Word of God which illumines my path is only a 'lamp to my feet' (Ps. 119:105) which lights up the next step; it is not a searchlight enabling me to see great stretches of the way that lies ahead."[14] "Trust in the Lord with all your heart," counsels the prophet, "and lean not on your own understanding; In all your ways acknowledge Him. And He shall direct your paths" (Prov. 3:5, 6 NKJV).

The will of God may not necessarily be the most heroic or daring thing to do. The healed demoniac was told to go home to his friends and family instead of following Jesus on the road (Mark 5:18, 19). What may be the humdrum cross of his choosing takes precedence over the often prestigious cross of our choosing.

The method here recommended is evangelical obedience rather than rational calculation. Thielicke describes its salient thrust: "We are forbidden to ask what the result will be when I keep this or that commandment, e.g., the command to do what is right even though the long-range possibilities of service seem thereby to be reduced if not shattered. We simply have to do what is right in the situation which is before us."[15] Nevertheless, the way of evangelical obedience may very well involve a creative compromise, and more will be said on this in the next section.

Once we enter into a personal relationship with Christ and grow in this relationship, we will come to know his voice. We will then be able to discriminate between the voice of our Master and other voices. We are told that the sheep recognize the voice of the Shepherd (John 10:4, 14).

We need to be convinced inwardly of the truth of God's word, and this is why the Holy Spirit was sent: to guide us to apprehend the truth and live according to it. The decision of faith is not an irrational step but a step informed by interior illumination. Paul declared, "Let every one be fully convinced in his own mind" (Rom. 14:5). The peace of God is the umpire that determines the will of God (Rom. 8:6).[16]

In judging whether the actions of another person are in accord with God's will, we have to be much more cautious. We can judge retrospectively on whether such a decision is in harmony with God's will, but rarely, if ever, can we know with full certainty at the time the decision is made. We can assess the personal effects and even the social consequences of a decision after it is made, but more often than not a considerable length of time must have elapsed before it is possible to make a valid appraisal.

Borderline Situations

The agony of ethical decision becomes especially acute in the so-called borderline situation. Not all ethical decision takes place in a context where moral codes no longer seem to apply, but all of our actions partake to a degree in the ambiguity of borderline situations.

In a borderline situation there is a conflict of life with life and also of truth with truth. Or between two goods or two evils. According to Jaspers, "borderline situations are those in which I cannot live without conflict and suffering, in which I take upon myself unavoidable guilt, in which I must die."[17] A borderline situation is one of extreme conflict. It often involves readiness to do wrong in order to prevent an incomparably greater wrong. Yet Thielicke warns that this must never be accepted as a moral principle, for it implies that the end justifies the means. He wisely cautions that our task is not to solve the borderline situation but to try to understand it and endure it. We must see it in terms of both "a fate which comes upon us" and "a guilt in which we are implicated."[18]

In this kind of situation, Christians sometimes find that they are moved toward actions that clearly defy moral convention. In Nazi Germany, many of the church's social missions falsified lists, forged death certificates, and used every kind of delaying tactic in order to protect the severely handicapped. Christians who were hiding Jews from their Nazi persecutors often lied in order not to betray a trust. Borderline situations are clearly manifest in biomedical ethics where the line between active and passive euthanasia is very thin indeed. Thielicke declares, "It is of the very nature of the borderline situation that it resists being pigeonholed in any larger or prior framework, and that it refuses to be subsumed under natural law."[19]

A borderline situation invariably involves compromise—not with the divine commandment but with the moral ideal, which is the goal of the divine commandment. But not all compromise is "creative"; it may also be destructive, and this kind of action is clearly out of bounds for the Christian. A destructive compromise occurs where the faith itself is denied or where greater evil may result. The German Christians, that congerie of groups within the German church in the thirties that sought to accommodate the faith to National Socialism, were guilty of a destructive compromise, since they diluted the faith in order to remain in the good graces of the government.

A creative compromise is one that leads toward the moral ideal rather than away from it. Treating heroin addicts with methadone is one example. Methadone is a synthetic narcotic drug not nearly as injurious as heroin. Those unable to break completely with drugs are given one that enables them to make some progress toward a dope-free existence. Salt I and Salt II might also be deemed creative compromises insofar as they are perceived as first steps on the way toward nuclear disarmament. Theodore Hesburgh's advocacy of laws that would severely restrict abortions but allow for some exceptions also reveals an effort toward a creative compromise that takes into consideration the realities of the cultural situation. Paul's admonition to women to keep silent in the churches was a kind of creative compromise, since it signified a temporary solution to a problem that was getting out of hand, that is, worship services constantly being interrupted by women glossolalists (1 Cor. 14). It is an open question whether Jesus compromised with his own ideal of nonresistance when he sent out his disciples with purse and sword (Luke 22:35–38).[20]

A creative compromise can be embarked upon only when it is based on the divine commandment. The divine commandment contains two aspects: the ideal or goal toward which the Spirit of God would direct us and the concrete steps toward this goal. Just as God's permissive will leads to his ultimate or perfect will, so a creative compromise will hopefully lead toward the fulfillment of the great commandment of love toward God and neighbor.

The creative compromise in conflict situations is not an accommodation to evil but an acceptance of a solution that falls short of the ideal of love. This solution nonetheless has God's sanction and is therefore covered by justifying grace. In conflict situations Christians are never called to compromise their faith; they may, however, be called to let go of their ideals in order to be obedient to God's commandment.

Karl Barth and Reinhold Niebuhr differ somewhat in the way they assess the actions of a Christian in a conflict situation. For Barth the divine commandment is always a choice for the good.[21] Niebuhr claims that Christian action in the social arena is generally the lesser of two evils. In my judgment, while obedience to the divine commandment is always good and never evil, in a conflict situation it will involve us in acts that fall short of the goal toward which God beckons us. There is no sin in our obedience insofar as it is truly obedience, but there is sin in what accompanies our obedience.

Because both the divine promise and the divine commandment often contravene the moral consensus of the civil community, it can be said that in one sense they stand beyond the polarity of good and evil. What God commands is the good, but this cannot always be reconciled with what the moral ethos calls the good. If we could dictate to God the nature of the good, then God would be in our power and not vice versa. "The Christian message stands beyond good and evil," says Bonhoeffer, "and that must be the case, for should the grace of God be made dependent upon the extent of man's good or evil, the basis would be laid for a claim of man upon God, and in this way God's sole power and glory would be assailed."[22]

The Risks of Holiness

The call to holiness involves a venture fraught with peril as well as with promise. To strive after holiness (Heb. 12:14) often entails the sacrifice of moral respectability, of material security, of health, even of life itself. To follow Christ into the tribulations and dereliction of the world means to become vulnerable to contamination by the world. It means to be exposed to temptation, to become prey to the world's delusions, though it does not necessarily mean to fall into sin.

Christians are not saints who remain above the things that afflict humanity but sinners struggling for integrity and fidelity in the midst of the shame and darkness of the world. Christians are sinners, but justified sinners, for their trust and hope are in Jesus Christ, who gives them the strength to endure and overcome, who guides them by his Spirit toward the goal of perfection in faith and love. Christians are sinners who are moving toward holiness, but they never claim to have arrived at perfect holiness in this life. Paul wrote: "Not that I have already obtained this or am already perfect; but I press on to make it my own, because Christ Jesus has made me his own" (Phil. 3:12).

The will of God contravenes conventional wisdom, and this is why it is so easily misunderstood. It is frozen into a formula or law that can be mastered and controlled by reason. Or it is dismissed as a figment of human imagination or a product of human bias. The divine commandment negates the common morality even while it fulfills the deepest intent of this morality. Too often we confuse the will of God with what society or our peer group expects us to do. It is well to note that the early Christians were accused of both immorality and atheism because the claims of their faith could not be reconciled with the syncretism and latitudinarianism of that time.

Søren Kierkegaard referred to the "teleological suspension of the ethical."[23] By this he meant that the spiritual goes beyond the merely ethical even while it embodies the supremely ethical. What characterizes the religious stage of life, he argued, is not conformity to the ideal of

the good but suffering in the name of Christ. Kierkegaard's decision
to break his engagement with Regina, whom he truly loved, was made
out of a commitment to live exclusively for the kingdom of God in a
state of celibacy and lent credibility to his protest against a domesticated church.[24] His decision appeared to contradict moral propriety,
since he had gone back on his word, and its purpose did not have
moral value in the minds of his contemporaries. Yet in retrospect we
can say that it is highly probable that he was being obedient to the will
of God, since the witness he made through his life and prolific writings
has proved to be a powerful source of renewal for the church in the
twentieth century.

Kierkegaard pointed to Abraham's sacrifice of his son Isaac (Gen.
22:1–14) as an example of the teleological suspension of the ethical.[25]
In my judgment, Abraham was called not so much to break the moral
law as to place the divine promise in jeopardy, the promise to make
of his descendants a mighty nation.[26] Child sacrifice was relatively acceptable in the social milieu of the time, but the sacrifice of one's divinely appointed vocation to be a father of a great people was indeed
a heavy burden.[27] This story illustrates the willingness of Christ to place
his church in jeopardy. His people are sent out as sheep amid wolves
(Matt. 10:16). Yet to make sure they are not utterly consumed, God
offers his own Son as the Lamb to be slain for the sins of the world.

Rahab's lie to the king of Jericho in order to protect the Israelite
spies (Josh. 2) is celebrated in the Bible as an act of heroism (Heb.
11:31; James 2:25). One can say that Rahab was honored not because
she lied but because she heeded the command of God to preserve the
life of the two spies. She was honored despite her lie, which was covered by the righteousness of faith. Yet her obedience involved the act
of lying, and a consistent legalist cannot accept this.

Elisha's deception of the company of blind Syrian soldiers who were
led toward the Israelite camp where they were captured (2 Kings 6) is
another illustration of a creative compromise. Was this only the practice
of the martial art of mental reservation (as John Murray suggests), or
was this a conscious and deliberate ruse to mislead but done out of
fidelity to the divine command?

Elisha's cursing of the boys who jeered at him presents still greater
problems for those who seek to measure all actions in the light of universal moral principles, such as fidelity, honesty, or love. We read that
two bears came out of the woods and tore to pieces forty-two of the
boys (2 Kings 2:23–25). Such a story points to the severity of God's
judgment on those who mock the aged or one of God's prophets, but

this is an offense to liberal theologians who see God only in terms of love and not also of holiness and wrath.[28] The incident reminds us that it is God who gives life, and it is God who takes away life.[29]

Gideon, who marched against the tens of thousands of Midianites with only three hundred men armed with nothing but torches and trumpets (Judges 7), can justly be accused of placing his men in grave peril, thereby sinning against moral law as well as ignoring all military wisdom. Yet the biblical author makes clear that Gideon was acting out of obedience to God's commandment, and the fact that the Midianites were routed lends credibility to this interpretation.

The Bible also gives examples of acts of self-destruction that seem to have the divine sanction.[30] When Samson pulled down the pillars of the hall in which the Philistines were celebrating, killing himself as well as his captors, this appears to involve both self-murder and the murder of many presumably innocent people, including children (Judg. 16:23–31). Jonah's pleading with the sailors to toss him overboard in order to assuage the divine wrath and the sailors' compliance can hardly be reconciled with traditional moral wisdom, including that of the Judaeo-Christian tradition (Jon. 1:12–16). Queen Esther placed her life on the line when she went to the king's inner court in order to plead for her people, the Jews, fully aware of the law that all who approached the king without express invitation would be put to death. The only exception was if the king held out his golden scepter, thereby sparing the intruder's life. Heeding the entreaties of her father Mordecai, Esther made the venture of faith: "I will go to the king, which is against the law; and if I perish, I perish" (Esther 4:16 NKJV).

Our moral sensibilities are also challenged by Elijah's prayer that it might not rain for three years (cf. 1 Kings 17:1; Luke 4:25; James 5:17), which meant starvation and financial ruin for many people. Here we are dealing not with self-destruction but certainly with the destruction of human life, though whether this is innocent life is another question.

All these stories remind us that God's commandment against killing protects life, but it does not enthrone life. It was given to preserve life, but not to idolize life. Life is something good, but it is not unconditionally sacred in the biblical perspective. Human life proceeds from God and is designed to give glory to God. Since it is a gift from God, life must be respected and may be taken only for the sake of life.

The most striking example of a biblical figure who appeared to live above the law was Jesus himself. Contrary to what was considered proper and morally decorous, Jesus left his parents, broke with his disciples (who shared the Zealot vision of a worldly kingdom), fraternized with publicans and sinners, and willingly went to death on a cross. He disobeyed his parents by teaching in the temple (Luke 2:41–45). He drove the moneychangers out of the temple with a whip (Matt. 21:12, 13), thereby apparently contradicting the message of nonresistance that he came to give. He healed people on the Sabbath and permitted his disciples to pick grain on that day and was therefore accused by the Pharisees of breaking the Sabbath law. His retort was that the Sabbath was made for man and not man for the Sabbath (Mark 2:27, 28). Did Jesus himself break the commandment against killing by laying down his life as a sacrifice for sin?

In the Middle Ages Francis of Assisi (d. 1226) illustrated the risks that attend obedience to the divine command. The son of a wealthy merchant draper, he lived a carefree, frivolous life in his early years. Then one day, while in the church at San Damiano, he heard the voice of Christ say, "Francis, repair my falling house!" Taking the words literally, he took a bale of goods from his father's warehouse and sold it in order to repair the crumbling church. Because he had not obtained his father's permission (his father was away at the time), this began a rupture in their relationship. Because of his enthusiastic fervor, his commitment to a life of poverty as an itinerant evangelist, his father finally denounced him as a thief and a madman and disinherited him. Francis did repay what he had stolen from his father, but his commitment to his Lord took precedence over his adherence to codes of moral law and convention.

The patron saint of Switzerland, Nicholas of Flüe, is another intrepid spirit with whom moralists have immeasurable difficulty. After serving in two wars, he married a farmer's daughter, who bore him ten children. He became both a successful farmer and a respected figure in his community. But then in 1465 he suddenly retired from public life, protesting in this way against an unjust decision in a local law court. Two years later with his wife's consent he left his family to embrace the eremetical life. The remaining nineteen years of his life were spent in a mountain cottage where he subsisted solely on Holy Communion. Predictably, his friends and relatives expressed indignation over his extraordinary decision, but he blithely disregarded their admonitions. As a religious hermit, be became noted for his wisdom and was visited by scores of people seeking counsel. He was instrumental in preventing a civil war between the urban and rural cantons by drawing up a peace plan that saved the unity of Switzerland. Nicholas was a bold and earnest spirit, but it is not easy to reconcile his decision to leave his wife and ten children and retire to a mountain cottage with the canons of moral propriety.

In the sixteenth century, Martin Luther defied his father's wishes by entering the Augustinian monastery at Erfurt, where he lived a life of exemplary piety and rigorous devotion. But after being called as a professor of biblical studies at the University of Wittenberg, he discovered the evangelical doctrine of justification by faith as he pondered over Paul's Epistle to the Romans in the monastery tower. Unable to keep this discovery to himself, he soon found himself at odds with the leaders of his order as well as with the ruling establishment of the Roman Catholic church. He was finally compelled to sever ties with his order as well as with the church and subsequently married a former nun. He betrayed his father's trust and later broke his monastic vows; yet he followed a norm higher than moral and religious law, namely, the law of the Spirit of life, which is not a law imposed on conscience but on the contrary one that sets the conscience free. Luther was bold enough to say that all laws ought to be broken if they conflict with the demands of faith and love.

Luther's advice in the Peasants' War has often been attributed to stubbornness and shortsightedness rather than wisdom. What is important to understand is that Luther had two stances. His first counsel was to reprimand the nobles for their greed and insensitivity while at the same time urging the peasants to cease their violence. When he saw that the revolt was getting out of hand and throwing the whole country into anarchy, Luther encouraged the nobles to crush the revolt by force. Yet their barbarities and cruelties appalled him, and he seemed to have second thoughts about the counsel he gave them.[31] He argued against the nobles that true justice is compassionate rather than vengeful. Luther favored a police action against the peasants when they would not turn from their rebelliousness, but he was adamantly opposed to indiscriminate slaughter, even though his own intemperate language may have played a baneful role in the beginning of the counterattack of the nobility.

When John Calvin retired to Strasbourg after suffering harassment and much humiliation in Geneva, he remarked that he would sooner die a hundred times than shut himself up again in that hell of torment. When some years later he was asked to return to Geneva to resume his pastoral role, after much agonizing he finally consented, in order not to be of "those who have more care for their own ease and profit than for the edification of the church."[32] Calvin's life is an admirable testimony that the practice of holiness entails risking comfort and security for the sake of the gospel.

In our century we can point to Dietrich Bonhoeffer, who joined a resistance group in Nazi Germany that eventually planned to assassinate Hitler in order to bring peace to Europe. Though previously a pacifist, Bonhoeffer was prepared to sacrifice the principles of pacifist ideology in order to be obedient to what he believed was a divine call. Admitting that he was involved in wrongdoing in the civil sense, he nevertheless felt guided by a higher law. After being captured and imprisoned, he had an opportunity to escape but decided to remain with his fellow prisoners in order to spare his family from possible retribution. Bonhoeffer did not make tyrannicide into a universal principle, but he did believe that he was being obedient to the divine commandment by pursuing this particular path.

Another example in modern times of a warrior of faith who seemed to rise above moral convention was C. T. Studd. Converted at one of Dwight L. Moody's evangelistic crusades in England, he had labored for some years on the mission field in China and India when he heard the call of God to serve in the interior of the Congo in Africa.[33] At the age of fifty-two and already in poor health, he left for his destination against the advice of both his doctor and his friends and family, returning to England on only two brief occasions in the remaining years of his life. His decision cannot be justified on the grounds of morality, but it can be seen to be the will of God in the light of the amazing fruit of his missionary work in Africa.

What these stories tell us is that an action may be suspect or even wrong according to the accepted standards of morality and yet not be reckoned as sin in the sight of God if it has his blessing and sanction. What God wills is the supremely moral, but this is not always in harmony with the expectations of either the church or the wider society.

In the Christian view, God is at work in evil bringing good out of evil. He does not will evil, but he enables his people to persevere and overcome in the midst of tribulation and distress. Even guilt can be a blessed thing (felix culpa) if it causes one to hunger and thirst for righteousness (Augustine).

The ethics of responsible decision that I uphold could be construed as an evasion of the divine mandate, but my position is that genuine ethical decision entails risks. One of these risks is to be denounced as immoral, and this indeed was a charge leveled against our Lord as well as against many of the great saints of the church through the ages. The divine command is not self-evident or axiomatic. Sometimes it can only be discovered through the agony of prayer and a diligent searching of the Scriptures. It will always stand in tension, if not in conflict, with our personal desires as well as with the expectations of the community in which we live.

In short, holiness in the biblical sense is not the same as moral uprightness as this is understood by the pillars of society. Holiness means to be separated by God from the world for a special vocation. It indicates nearness to God, transparency to the divine, rather than a rigid adherence to a moral code. To strive for holiness means to strive for the vision of God, but this is something other than seeking for ethical perfection. The holy man or woman lives in the freedom of the new life in Christ. That person has been emancipated from the restrictions of law in order to fulfill the spirit of the law.

The Ideal versus the Actual

God calls us to strive for the perfect good, but he also calls us to decide for the best attainable. The perfect good is a transcendent ideal; the best that is available is a proximate good. It is the difference between the abstract best and the concrete good, between ultimate and penultimate goals. God's ultimate will is the ideal of perfect love. His permissive will is what leads to this ideal in the concrete situation. An action may well fall short of this ideal and yet prepare the way for it. The task of ethics is to determine the presently attainable as well as the highest.

The best action in a given situation is not necessarily the most loving. Yet we are called to bring love into our actions. God wills the highest, but he also wills the "best"—the presently possible among imperfect alternatives. Sometimes he wills a course of action that proves to be a compromise with his perfect will. What may be the "right thing to do" considering the circumstances is not necessarily a fully righteous alternative. Yet God wills that we move beyond the best under the present circumstances to the highest.

The mature in faith can distinguish between good and evil (Heb. 5:14). If we abide in Christ, we will recognize his voice and heed his command. His call and not the quality of our response justifies our actions. We must never claim righteousness as a result of our decision. As Christians, we are moving toward righteousness. We are on the way to becoming righteous, but we are not yet righteous in fact.

Our obedience does not deserve God's approval because it is always mixed with impure motives and accompanied by imperfect consequences. After we have done all that is commanded, we must still confess that we are unworthy servants (Luke 17:10). As Luther put it, "A righteous man sins in all his good works."[34] We must therefore repent of our virtues as well as of our vices. Even when we are obedient to God's commandment, we need the cleansing blood of Christ (Kohlbrügge).

Our task, then, is to steer clear of the dual dangers of irresponsibility and irrelevance on the one hand and using unlawful means to secure a just order in society on the other. Even the pacifist must ask forgiveness for being implicated in the guilt of the nations. We have a perfect goal and a perfect criterion but an imperfect means.

The way of the cross that we walk is but a feeble approximation of the road to Golgotha that Christ walked. Sacrificial love in its full dimension is present only in his act of obedience. Our acts are always mixtures of neighbor love and carnal ambition.

My quarrel with Moral Rearmament is that it regards the four absolutes (love, honesty, purity, unselfishness) as simple possibilities that can be attained by an act of the will.[35] I see these absolutes as ideals we can strive toward, but never perfectly realize. The proper attitude of the Christian is therefore one of penitence toward a holy God and hope for a merciful God.

In ethical decision God will not let us be tested beyond our endurance and will always provide a way of escape (1 Cor. 10:13; 2 Peter 2:9). But this way of escape is not a fully righteous alternative except for those who are without the stain of sin. God will not allow us to fall into bondage to sin in our moral engagements, but he nevertheless sometimes calls us into situations where we may very well stumble into sin.

The law of God is "holy, righteous, and good" (Rom. 7:12 NIV), but we always fall short of the infinite requirement that the law contains. God's commandment is good, but man's action is always tainted by sin even when its aim is obedience.

This does not mean that we do not know the will of God but that we do not know the will of God perfectly. It is not our obedience that is a sin in conflict situations but what goes with our obedience. Even when we do our best, we are not doing our best in the spirit of perfect love. Can there be a fully righteous act if there is not a fully righteous person who is the author of the act? We are therefore justified not by our works but only by faith in Christ's righteousness, which covers our sinfulness.

God's call is not that we disengage ourselves from the world but that we serve God and our neighbor in the world (John 17:15–18). The Christian life is not the pristine purity of innocence but the marred purity of responsible involvement in the world for the sake of the glory of God. Hegel rightly criticized the latter-day pietistic ideal of "the beautiful soul" that "lives in dread of staining the radiance of its inner being by action and existence and to preserve the purity of its heart, . . . flees from contact with actuality."[36] Hegel substituted, however, not the suffering servant who identifies with the travails of the oppressed but the world-historical individual who tramples upon the weak and afflicted in order to realize worldly ambition. The ideal of the suffering servant was powerfully reaffirmed by the French Roman Catholic theologian Maurice Blondel: "One must be involved, at the risk of losing everything, one must be compromised."[37]

Bonhoeffer championed the "man of freedom" who "values the necessary deed more highly than a clear conscience or the duties of his calling, who is ready to sacrifice a barren principle for a fruitful compromise."[38] This "man of freedom" is not the one who aspires to the highest but the one who descends to the lowest, for the presence of God is experienced in the midst of oppression and dereliction. Paradoxically, one is given a foretaste of the glory of God in the hell of the despair of people in need.

We are to be in the world but not of the world. Yet active engagement on behalf of our brothers and sisters in the world entails decisions that are often tainted by mixed motives and marred by questionable consequences. Such a perception should not, however, lead to inaction or quietism. If we act in fidelity and penitence, we can be assured that Christ is with us, that our sins are covered by the grace of God.

Moralists are quick to find fault with Luther's advice to Philip Melanchthon: "Be a sinner and sin boldly, but believe even more boldly and rejoice in Christ, who is victor over sin, death and world. We must sin so long as we are what we are; this life is not the dwelling place of righteousness, but we look for new heavens and a new earth in which righteousness dwells."[39] Luther was not advocating antinomianism, but he was recommending that we act with boldness despite the fact that as sinners we will be sinning even in our actions of obedience. We should go ahead if God calls us, knowing that our sins are covered by Christ's righteousness. Luther was not implying that sin is justified because it is an inevitable element in every person's life. He simply meant that we should not lose heart if we are involved in sins because we know that Jesus Christ is victor over every sin and that his blood wipes our slate clean.

Sometimes we must choose between two ways, both of which involve sinning, but one of which is more acceptable than the other.[40] In 1 John we are reminded that there is a sin that is mortal and one that does not lead to death (5:16, 17). Reinhold Niebuhr speaks of an equality of sin and an inequality of guilt. Not every sin is accompanied by the same horrendous consequences. This kind of distinction is also affirmed by Bonhoeffer: "There are heavier sins and lighter sins. A falling away is of infinitely greater weight than a falling down. The most shining virtues of him who has fallen away are as black as night in comparison with the darkest lapses of the steadfast."[41]

As Christians, we are to act in the world to give glory to God, even if our actions may involve us in sin. Sometimes we have to flee the world as did Lot. This situation is present when society is beyond repair, when there is no hope of turning it around. Yet those who flee are not exempt from sin. They cannot take pride in their actions but must simply thank God for giving them a true perception of the situation, which can only be attributed to his free grace.

Occasionally Christians even have to break with the institutional church, particularly when it is so pervaded by the world that it ceases to be the church. We should take this drastic action, however, only when the church itself forces us to it. Sometimes the commandment of God will call us away from public worship if this worship is not done in spirit and in truth. Kierkegaard toward the end of his life ceased to attend the public services of worship in order to demonstrate his opposition to a secularized church.[42] On his death bed he refused Holy Communion on the grounds that the state church no longer embodied the holy catholic faith. Kierkegaard's protest against the church was for the sake of the church, for his objective was to arouse the church to self-reform.

In traditional Christian spirituality, the three types of discipleship are the active life (pursuing a secular vocation in the world), the contemplative (or monastic) life, and the mixed life (the religious life in the world). It has been a matter of debate which of these is superior. What should be kept in mind is that all three entail sin. Sin is not in the way but in the person, and this is why even those who embrace the contemplative life need to look to Christ as their Savior from sin as well as their Pattern and Example.

Jesus Christ is the one in whom the will of God is fully embodied and exemplified. He is the only one who has fully obeyed God's will. It is his righteousness that justifies us, for his righteousness alone is perfect. His righteousness is the ground and goal of the Christian life.

To know the will of God for our lives, we must look not to an abstract ideal but to his life, death, and resurrection. Christ is not only the pinnacle of human perfection but the source of the spiritual wisdom that enables us to discern the "good" in our situation. We must also look to him for the victory that enables us to overcome and for the pardon that cleanses us of every sin on the way to the higher perfection.

John Calvin cogently points us to the ground of our hope and obedience:

> Our hope is in no other save in Thee,
>   Our faith is built upon Thy promise free;
> Come, give us peace, make us so strong and sure,
>   That we may conquerors be and ills endure.[43]

The way of the cross is the way of nonretaliation, but this does not necessarily mean submission to evil. It may very well entail resistance to evil but one that is united with love and a refusal to retaliate in kind. The way of the cross cannot be reconciled with the terror of war, because our own security rather than the glory of God inevitably becomes the paramount concern, and hatred always prevails over love in armed conflict. To take up the sword in defense of the rights of the oppressed does not necessarily mean wilful participation in the terror of war. It could simply mean wielding the sword in the line of duty as a police officer, prison guard, or state executioner. It might also involve taking part in an assassination attempt on a mad dictator (as in the case of Bonhoeffer). Jesus Christ may call us into a situation where armed conflict and lethal violence are inevitable, but we must be obedient to the divine imperative even where sin is unavoidable.[44]

Presumption and Humility in Ethical Decision

The ethical stance I uphold goes beyond both relativism and absolutism. Although God's commandment is absolutely binding, it is always directed to a particular situation. Moreover, we only apprehend it within a particular historical and cultural matrix.

The two dangers to guard against are gnosticism and agnosticism. We should not rush into a precarious situation as though we had divine perception; on the other hand, we must not shirk our responsibility on the grounds that we have no light whatever to guide us. We must not be agnostic and hold that God's Word and will are basically unknowable. We have to act on the light that is given to us. We are

moving toward a perfect knowledge of the will of God, but we now
have a partial knowledge, and we must stand on it. Our theology is a
theologia viatorum (theology of wayfarers), not a *theologia beatorum* (theology of the blessed in heaven).

We must not boast that we know the will of God, since such knowledge is not a virtue or achievement. At the same time, we should be
bold to confess that God has revealed his will to us. Otherwise we
walk in complete darkness, but Christians walk in the light (Eph. 5:8,
9).

If our conscience is informed by the Word of God, we must remain
true to this inner light even when social pressures propel us in another
direction. I agree with the Roman Catholic theologian Bellarmine:
"Conscience is above all other human courts, and if we are of good
conscience we ought not to fear and will not be condemned by God
even though all men, who do not see the heart, judge what is done
very differently."[45]

Even in times of dereliction and tribulation, we can know as Christians that God is acting and moving in our midst. The darkness of the
world cannot extinguish the light of God's presence. We should be able
to confess with the Psalmist, "I know, O Lord, that Your judgments
are right, and that in faithfulness You have afflicted me" (Ps. 119:75
NKJV; cf. Heb. 12:3–11).

We must be humble in our claim to knowing the will of God, but
not equivocal. We must venture forth boldly on the basis of the light
given to us, but we must not be presumptuous in claiming to know
more than what is revealed to us. We do not have a pipeline to God,
but God has a pathway to us—Jesus Christ.

Our faith in Christ is something that cannot be taken for granted
but must be renewed daily. For as Barth perceives: "Our faith as an
act of our own spontaneity is notoriously enmeshed in the corruption
of our decision. That my faith is accepted as true faith is something
that again I can only believe—believe as I believe in the miracle of the
divine mercy."[46]

We should not empty God's will or God's word of its conceptual
content. Yet this conceptual content goes beyond what is explicitly
stated in the Bible, even though it includes this. God's word is the light
that the Spirit brings to us through the written text but related to the
existential situation in which we find ourselves. The situation is not a
norm for our decision, but it is the field in which our decision takes
place.

The will of God is more a goal than a present possession. We are moving toward the will of God insofar as we are faithful to the light given to us, but we cannot claim we are actually living in conformity to his will. On occasion, we receive a special commission from God, a word of prophecy or a word of wisdom, and then we must proclaim this with certainty and power. The Old Testament prophets were not averse to introducing their exhortations with "Thus saith the Lord."

All people have to some extent the sense of a moral order, the sense of an "I ought." The divine commandment, on the other hand, is rightly perceived only by the eyes and ears of faith. We all have some intimation of the criteria for the moral life, but only faith can lay hold of God's specific command.

We have to follow the light we have, and this means that we do not remain in the darkness. Our perception of the will of God is relative, but it can still be a true perception. Now we walk by faith; but then we shall know even as we are known (1 Cor. 13:12; 2 Cor 5:7).

God's commandment is absolute, but our perception and formulation of it are relative. Ethical norms can never be absolute in the sense that they are unrelated to and independent of anything else. They can be absolute in the sense of being unconditionally binding.

In an ethical decision we must take into consideration motives and consequences, but we do not finally base our decision on these alone or even on these primarily. Yet they are not to be excluded. Consequentialism errs by focusing on immediate consequences and losing sight of long-term consequences. It can also be faulted for claiming to know too much about the specifics of the outcome of a decision, which are often hidden from sight and understanding.

It is not true that anything can be said to be the will of God. We have objective criteria given to us in Scripture, such as the Decalogue and the Sermon on the Mount. That which dishonors the name of God or Jesus Christ and that which causes irrevocable injury to our neighbor are manifestly not the will of God.[47]

We must not claim that everything that comes to pass is the will of God. We are called to decision and obedience, not to resignation. The Providence of God must not be confused with the Fate of pagan speculation. In the first case God's will is realized through our free decision and obedience. In the second case the outcome of our decision is determined by forces beyond and outside our control.

Not everything that happens is the express will of God. Some things God does not will, but he permits them to happen. God does not cause evil, but he brings good out of evil. He is Lord of both the light and the darkness, but the latter has reality only because it is negated by his will.

God accomplishes his purposes through our freedom but also despite our freedom. Sometimes he causes our lives to prosper despite our misuse of this freedom. The divine predestination is realized through our faithful response to his grace but also through the desolation wrought by unbelief.

The "man of freedom" is the one who ventures boldly into the darkness of the world knowing that Jesus Christ is victor and that his word is the only ground for hope and certainty. The one who has been liberated from the fears and doubts that sin produces is ready to face the challenges and trials of life. Such a person does not meekly submit to intimidation by the world but goes forth to conquer the world through the power that comes from the living God (Rom. 8:37–39).

What distinguishes people of faith from people of the world is that the former try to subordinate their desires and goals to God's word, which often cannot be reconciled with the classical virtues of temperance, courage, wisdom, and justice. The way of the cross means the death of worldly ambition and the surrender of any claim to worldly happiness. Luther put it very dramatically: "Not the work which you choose, not the suffering you devise, but the road which is clean contrary to all that you choose or contrive or desire—that is the road you must take."[48]

The way of the cross is the way of obedience to Jesus Christ. Ideally, it will entail nonresistance to anyone seeking to bring about our ruin. In some situations, however, it may call for nonviolent resistance, especially where the freedom to practice our religion or the life of our neighbor is at stake. In some *very exceptional* circumstances, it may even involve taking up the sword in defense of the rights of others.[49] In all cases, our motivation must be a sincere desire to serve God and neighbor above our own welfare, and our ultimate reliance must be on the sword of the Spirit, the Word of God.

Our bearing of the cross can at the most be a broken approximation of the way Christ walked. We are sinners, and therefore our choices will always be marked by a certain amount of ambiguity and self-deception. The way of the cross is perfectly embodied and demonstrated only in the life and death of Jesus Christ, but through the power of his Spirit we as justified sinners can move towards his cross. By his grace, our obedience can be made to correspond to his obedience, but it cannot duplicate or re-present it. It can point to his way and to his work, but it cannot add to what he has merited for us. Our cross can be a sign and witness of his cross and therefore can be used by the Spirit to draw the despairing to the One who alone can pardon and overcome sin.

Notes

1. A case could be made that James's references to the gospel as "the law of liberty" and "the royal law" roughly correspond to what Paul describes as "the law of the Spirit of life in Christ Jesus." For the continuity between James and Paul see Bo Reicke, *The Epistles of James, Peter, and Jude* (New York: Doubleday, 1964), pp. 3–10, 29, 34.
2. See Bonhoeffer, *Ethics*, p. 38.
3. Not all ethical decision involves agony, to be sure, for much of the Christian life consists in a daily doing of God's commandment with little conscious reflection, since his Word gives light to our conscience. Yet where God's will is not obvious, where we are confronted by what appear to be two wrongs or two rights, we then must wrestle with the Lord in prayer. Even when God freely grants us the guidance of his Spirit in the decisions of life, there remains a certain tension between our will and that of our heavenly Father.
4. Teresa nonetheless preferred spiritual directors who were without education but still good and holy over those who were only half-educated, for the latter can do the soul much harm. St. Teresa of Avila, *A Life of Prayer*, ed. James M. Houston (Portland, Oreg.: Multnomah, 1983), p. 11.
5. Bonhoeffer, *Ethics*, p. 136.
6. Cf. Hannah Whitall Smith: "In all doubtful things you must stand still and refrain from action until God gives you light to know more clearly His mind concerning them. Very often you will find that the doubt has been His voice calling upon you to come into more perfect conformity to His will; but sometimes these doubtful things are only temptations, or morbid feelings to which it would be most unwise for you to yield, and the only safe way is to wait until you can act in faith." *The Christian's Secret of a Happy Life* (Old Tappan, N.J.: Fleming H. Revell, 1966), p. 73.
7. Bonhoeffer also counsels: "Do and dare what is right, not swayed by the whim of the moment. Bravely take hold of the real, not dallying now with what might be. Not in the flight of ideas but only in action is freedom." *Ethics*, p. 15.
8. Cited in Gerhard Ebeling, *Introduction to a Theological Theory of Language*, trans. R. A. Wilson (Philadelphia: Fortress, 1973), p. 17.
9. We must at the same time affirm that God has spoken and continues to speak to his people through dreams and visions. But these must always be weighed in the light of the teaching of the prophets and apostles in Holy Scripture. We should never set our hope or trust in these things. The Franciscan mystic Peter of Alcántara gives a salutary warning: "Do not seek revelations, marvels or extraordinary things, but rather those things which our Lord teaches in his Gospel and which Holy Church declares unto you. The devil often transforms himself into an angel of light in these strange things." Also cf. Teresa of Avila: "The highest perfection does not consist in feelings of spiritual bliss nor in great ecstasies or visions nor yet in the spirit of prophecy, but in bringing your will into conformity with that of God." Quoted in *The Wisdom of the Spanish Mystics*, ed. Stephen Clissold (New York: New Directions Books, 1977), pp. 61, 62, 76.
10. *John Wesley's Forty-four Sermons*, 12th ed. (London: Epworth, 1975), p. 428.
11. Jacques Ellul, *The Meaning of the City*, trans. Dennis Pardee (Grand Rapids: Eerdmans, 1970), p. 76.
12. According to Bonhoeffer, "Precisely when the action arises from the purest motives,

when the most pious and selfless deeds are performed, the danger is especially great that this is the ungodly antithesis to the will of God which resembles the will of God to the point of being entirely indistinguishable from it, but which springs from a man's own knowledge of good and evil, from his disunion with God." *Ethics,* p. 48.

13. Cf. Thomas à Kempis: "Not every feeling that seems good is at once to be acted upon, nor is every feeling that runs contrary to your inclinations to be immediately rejected. It is sometimes necessary to restrain even your good intentions and endeavours, lest by over-eagerness your mind becomes distracted; lest by lack of discipline you cause offense to others; or lest you suddenly become confused and upset by the opposition of others." *The Imitation of Christ,* trans. Leo Sherley-Price (Harmondsworth, Baltimore: Penguin Books, 1959), pp. 105–106.

14. Thielicke, *Theological Ethics* 1: p. 614.

15. Ibid., p. 615.

16. While Pat Robertson and his 700 Club associates also use this language, I contend that an act may be in accord with God's will even when the experience of the peace of God is absent.

17. Quoted in Thielicke, *Theological Ethics* 1: p. 580.

18. Ibid., p. 596.

19. Ibid.

20. See chap. 14, p. 293.

21. It is interesting to hear Barth's answer to some Hollanders who during the war asked him whether it was ever right to lie to the occupying Germans: "Do it—but not with a bad conscience. If you have a bad conscience, then do not do it. But if you must lie in the name of justice, then do it. No dirty hands here!" *Karl Barth's Table Talk,* p. 79. See also note 40.

22. Dietrich Bonhoeffer, *No Rusty Swords,* trans. Edwin H. Robertson and John Bowden (New York: Harper & Row, 1965), p. 41.

23. See Søren Kierkegaard, *Fear and Trembling,* trans. Walter Lowrie (New York: Doubleday, 1954), pp. 64–77.

24. See Vernard Eller, *Kierkegaard and Radical Discipleship,* pp. 207–208, 235–248.

25. On Francis Schaeffer's criticism of Kierkegaard's interpretation of Abraham's sacrifice see Harold O. J. Brown, "Kierkegaard's Leap or Schaeffer's Step?" *Christianity Today* 28, no. 18 (Dec. 14, 1984): p. 82. Schaeffer argues that Abraham was called not to make a leap of faith (as Kierkegaard would have it) but simply an act of trust, confident that God would remain faithful to his promises even though this was not evident at the time. Schaeffer points to the words of Abraham as he departed with Isaac: "I and the lad will go yonder and worship, and come again to you" (Gen. 22:5 KJV). In my opinion, both Brown and Schaeffer tend to downplay the agony in ethical decision so that faith becomes a "reasonable" or "plausible" conclusion rather than a life-and-death decision. It should be noted that Kierkegaard held that Abraham believed without doubting, but he believed what was manifestly an absurdity to reason. *Fear and Trembling,* pp. 27, 36, 46, 47.

26. For Yoder's helpful discussion of Abraham's sacrifice see *The Politics of Jesus,* pp. 80–81.

27. The saga tells us that the angel of the Lord stopped Abraham in time, since he had proved his willingness to give up his only son to the Lord. Then Abraham saw a ram caught in a thicket by its horns and presented it as the burnt offering in place of his son.

28. Liberal theologians who interpret biblical history in terms of the evolution of moral consciousness regard such a story as reflecting a primitive morality of the Old Testament. For a current attempt to appraise the Bible in the light of an evolutionary philosophy see Gerd Theissen, *Biblical Faith: An Evolutionary Approach,* trans. John Bowden (Philadelphia: Fortress, 1985). Theissen writes that the God of Jesus is conceived of no longer as "a devastating power," as with John the Baptist and the Old Testament, but now as a "gracious father" (p. 113).

29. Raymond Calkins has these pertinent comments: "A careful reading of the text . . . will show us that Elisha did not himself summon the bears. He was not that kind of man. Thus understood, the story, however dreadful, has its sharp significance. The irreverence, lawlessness, hoodlumism of youth are sure to result in moral disaster. The bears that came out of the woods are the symbol of that inevitable retribution which overtakes vicious behavior. The boys of this story are the prototype of thousands of youth today. . . . Lawless youth may not be torn asunder by bears, but they are rent by passions, devoured by appetite, until their characters and careers and all their hopes for happy, useful living are destroyed." *The Interpreter's Bible,* vol. 3 ed. George Arthur Buttrick, Walter Russell Bowie, and Paul Scherer (New York: Abingdon, 1954), p. 197.

30. Just as not all acts of taking the life of another human being are murder, so not all acts of self-destruction are suicide in the theological sense. There is a marked difference between killing oneself to end it all and laying down one's life for one's neighbor out of obedience to God's commandment. The first is born out of desperation and rooted ultimately in disbelief in God's goodness and mercy. The second has its roots in fidelity to God's promises. The deaths of Saul and Judas are examples in the Bible of suicide in the sense of self-murder. The death of Samson, on the other hand, is an example of self-sacrifice out of fidelity to God.

31. See H. G. Haile, *Luther* (New York: Doubleday & Co., 1980), pp. 156, 284, 347.

32. Quoted in Georgia Harkness, *John Calvin: The Man and His Ethics* (Nashville: Abingdon, 1958), p. 20.

33. See Norman P. Grubb, *C. T. Studd: Cricketer & Pioneer* (Fort Washington, Pa.: Christian Literature Crusade, n.d.).

34. *Luther's Works,* ed. George W. Forell (Philadelphia: Muhlenberg Press, 1958), p. 83.

35. Many of those who follow Moral Rearmament (formerly known as the Oxford Group movement) claim to have reached moral perfection. They would do well to heed this apostolic admonition: "If we say we have no sin, we deceive ourselves, and the truth is not in us." (1 John 1:8).

36. G. W. F. Hegel, *The Phenomenology of Mind,* 2d ed., trans. J. B. Baillie (London: George Allen & Unwin, 1961), p. 666.

37. Quoted in John Macquarrie, *In Search of Humanity* (New York: Crossroad, 1983), p. 141.

38. Dietrich Bonhoeffer, *Prisoner for God,* ed. Eberhard Bethge, trans. Reginald Fuller (New York: Macmillan Co., 1954), p. 15.

39. See *Luther's Correspondence,* trans. and ed. Preserved Smith and Charles M. Jacobs, 2 vols. (Philadelphia: Lutheran Publication Society 1913–1918), 2: p. 50. For an evaluation of Luther's remarks see Thielicke, *Theological Ethics* 1, pp. 503, 504.

40. Yoder observes that while Barth does not use the phrase "lesser evil," he does actually hold to this concept, since he regards war as always evil, and yet sometimes we have to choose the way of war in order to overcome still greater evils, such as "consistent contempt for and violation" of human rights. Yet we can act in good conscience knowing that even in our killing we will not be judged as murderers. We are involved in evil, but because of God's commandment we need have no guilt. See John Howard Yoder, *Karl Barth and the Problem of War* (Nashville: Abingdon Press, 1970), p. 83.

41. Bonhoeffer, *Ethics,* p. 65.

42. Eller, *Kierkegaard and Radical Discipleship,* pp. 24, 25.

43. From Calvin's hymn, "I Greet Thee, Who My Sure Redeemer Art," in *Psalter Hymnal* (Grand Rapids: Board of Publications of the Christian Reformed Church, 1976), p. 503.

44. The use of the sword is involved in discipleship under the cross only as something provisional, only as something that must be left behind as we seek means more in accord with the law of the kingdom of God.

45. Cited in Barth, *Ethics,* p. 484.

46. Ibid., p. 103.

47. The Reformers attributed the terrible things that happen in the world to the secret will of God as opposed to his revealed will. From my perspective, such events have their basis in God's negation rather than his affirmation or positive will. Injuries to our neighbor that may have the permission of God are to be explained as falling short of the perfect will of God. Anything that causes irrevocable or permanent damage to another person is always opposed to the perfect will of God, since he wishes no one to perish (2 Pet. 3:9; Ezek. 18:23).

48. Cited in Bonhoeffer, *The Cost of Discipleship*, p. 83.

49. God's blessing on people of faith taking up the sword should be interpreted more as a divine permission than a divine commandment in that it signifies a divine accommodation to the sinful situation of mankind. Just as God permitted divorce because of the hardness of the hearts of his people (Matt. 19:8), so he may permit the sword to be wielded by his people—but never for the defense of the Word or the kingdom, only to secure order with justice.

CHAPTER 12

God the Civilizer

The major advances in civilization are processes that all but wreck the societies in which they occur.

ALFRED NORTH WHITEHEAD

If we believe that the Spirit of God is the only fountain of truth, we shall neither reject nor despise the truth itself, wherever it shall appear, unless we wish to insult the Spirit of God.

JOHN CALVIN

It would seem that the more civilized we become the more incapable of maintaining civilization we are.

F. S. C. NORTHROP

Religion does not merely criticize one form of civilization or another but casts doubt upon civilization itself and upon humanity, because it casts doubt upon man.

EMIL BRUNNER

I suppose there never will be a Christian civilization, I suppose there never will be a civilization with which a sensitive soul ought not to feel itself in conflict.

REINHOLD NIEBUHR

If humanity was created in the image of God and if God has revealed himself to humanity for its salvation in Christ, there are immense consequences for the creation itself. In spite of the impression that some evangelicals occasionally leave, Christianity is not about pie in the sky. The Christian faith is based in transcendent realities, but its implications appear immanently in creation. "God was in Christ," the apostle said, "reconciling the *world* to himself" (italics mine) (2 Cor. 5:19). Put another way, God wants to save souls, but souls in factories, offices, farms, and the unemployment office, souls with their different amounts of money, souls engaged in the scientific enterprise as well as in political activity, souls in bedroom and boardroom, souls on the playing field, souls in the domestic order, and so on.

Theologians have long pondered what it means for God, as another aspect of his being, to be a civilizer, a restorer of the world he has made. The discussion in this chapter draws upon that history of theological interpretation to outline several important issues attendant to the divine restoration of the world. It explores the relationship between religion and culture, sacred history and human history, creation and redemption, human culture and the kingdom of God. It also makes the argument that God works to restore civilization primarily through the church, an argument that I set out abstractly before applying it directly to the conditions in which we now live. Karl Barth's insights have proved especially helpful to me in this area of theological reflection.

Definitions: Christ and Culture

To assess the complex and intricate relationship between Christ and culture, we need to keep in mind that much depends on the definitions we use. By *Christ* I mean neither the historical Jesus of liberalism nor the eternal Christ of mysticism but the Jesus Christ of biblical faith. It is God's self-revelation in Christ that comprises the divine side of this polarity. By *culture* I mean the sum total of the creative accomplishments of a given people. Or it could be defined as the intellectual, pragmatic, and social expression of a particular metaphysical orientation.[1]

Civilization I understand as a higher stage of human achievement, associated with great art, literature, and philosophy. This agrees very much with standard definitions, as in *The American Heritage Dictionary:* "an advanced stage of development in the arts and sciences accompanied by corresponding social, political and cultural complexity."[2] The work of civilizing is the cultivation of skills and attitudes that enable one to function creatively in social interaction. As I use the terms, culture and civilization are virtually synonymous.

In his pivotal study *Christ and Culture* H. Richard Niebuhr maintains that culture represents the pinnacle of human achievement.[3] It is thus concerned with the realization and conservation of human values. Culture embodies a world of values because human achievements are always directed toward higher ends. He also reminds us that culture is invariably pluralistic because any one civilization contains a wealth of often conflicting values.

All human culture is secular to some degree because it belongs to the age (*saeculum*) in which it exists and necessarily reflects the spirit of that age (*Zeitgeist*). A culture can at the same time be religious in that it may be engrossed not only with penultimate but also with ultimate concerns. A religious culture in this sense is more of a threat to the church than a culture that remains merely secular, for it is then tempted to absolutize cultural goals and values. Karl Barth reminds us that Christian faith frees culture from all absolutism: we are called to appreciate but not deify the human.

I have thus far presented a sociological understanding of culture. But it can also be defined theologically. In this sense *culture* is the task appointed to humans to realize their destiny in the world in service to the glory of God. Or it can be said to be the sphere that yields images parabolically of God and his kingdom (Barth). Barth regards culture as something worthwhile on its own level because it is the divinely appointed means for men and women to realize their humanity. "What else is civilization than the endeavour of man to be man, and therefore to bring honour and to set to work the good gift of his humanity?"[4] Indeed, "the term *culture* connotes exactly that promise to man: fulfillment, unity, wholeness within his sphere as creature, as man."[5] In Anabaptist circles, on the other hand, one detects a profound mistrust of cultural pursuits; culture is here seen as "the institutionalization of structured unbelief and sin."[6]

Paradoxically, culture can be said to be both a human achievement and a divine gift. It is the result of both human dexterity and divine grace. God gives the motivation and inspiration; human cultural achievements are the answer to this divine call. The grace that undergirds and adorns cultural achievements is the grace of preservation, however, not the grace of redemption. God acts to preserve humanity even in its sin and folly. And God rewards humanity for its creative contributions to human welfare and justice, even though such efforts fall far short of the perfect righteousness that God demands.

The motivation to realize our creative potential comes from God, but our striving for fulfillment is invariably corrupted by sin. Culture is not only a tribute to human sagacity and ingenuity but also a monument to human pride. It represents not only a flowering of human creativity but also its distortion. Indeed, the flowering of human culture aggravates rather than ameliorates the human predicament.

Patterns of Interaction

The particular strategy for Christians in meeting the challenges and threats of the secular culture will no doubt vary depending upon the historical situation (*Sitz im Leben*) in which the church exists. In some situations, where the culture has become irretrievably idolatrous, the church must sound the call to separation. Flight rather than fight is then the strategy with divine sanction, even though this kind of withdrawal must always be carried out for the sake of a return at a later time and on a deeper level. In other situations where the forces of good are not so completely overwhelmed by the forces of evil, the Christian might well work for reform so that the present civilization could be humanized.

For considerations of the Christian stance over against culture, the typology offered by H. Richard Niebuhr in *Christ and Culture* is very helpful.[7] Niebuhr suggests that Christians have approached the larger world (that is, culture) from one of five ideal types: "Christ Against Culture," a position whereby people of faith try to divorce themselves from the world in all of its vanity; "Christ of Culture," which accommodates the gospel to what the world values most dearly; "Christ Above Culture," which attempts to forge a synthesis between eternal values and the wisdom of the world; "Christ and Culture in Paradox," a dualistic stance in which believers are active in the world but not confident about success in bringing it captive to Christ; and "Christ the Transformer of Culture," where believers attempt to shape the world in every particular according to the norms of Scripture and Christian tradition.

Niebuhr's "Christ-of-culture" position identifies the highest values of the culture with the substance of faith and thereby represents an ignominious accommodation to the spirit of the age. Niebuhr finds cultural Christianity in the Gnostics, Abelard, Schleiermacher, and Ritschl. On the contemporary scene, I believe it can be detected in liberationist, process, and feminist theologies, as well as in the new religious right.[8] For each of these groups, some value from the culture molds, informs, and even determines the shape of faith.

Those who espouse a "Christ-against-culture" stance, by way of contrast, sound the call to separation from the evils, allurements, and compromises of the world. The Christian is impelled to live a life in conscious opposition to the values, claims, and practices of a culture supposedly under the sway of the powers of darkness. H. Richard Niebuhr discusses in this connection the monastic tradition as well as Tertullian and Tolstoy. I would add that this tendency also shows up in Menno Simons, Jacob Amman, Jacob Hutter, Eberhard Arnold, John Nelson Darby, and, in our day, the French Reformed iconoclast Jacques Ellul and the founder of the Catholic Worker movement, Dorothy Day (though several of these manifest a strong conversionist motif as well).[9]

Those who view Christ as being "above culture" try to do justice to the cultural quest for wisdom and truth but contend that it can be fulfilled only in Christ. Their aim is to correlate the fundamental questions of the culture with the answer of Christian revelation. They therefore strive for a theology of synthesis, with cultural expectations subordinated to Christian concerns. We see this strategy at work in Clement of Alexandria, Thomas Aquinas, and, in our day, Paul Tillich, whose theology had not been significantly developed at the time Niebuhr wrote.[10]

The "Christ-and-culture-in-paradox" position is dualistic in that the Christian is said to belong to two realms (the spiritual and temporal) and must live in the tension of fulfilling responsibilities to both. Both the apostle Paul and Martin Luther are listed in this category. An important representative of this tradition in our time is Reinhold Niebuhr (curiously overlooked), who was especially alert to the ironies accompanying life lived simultaneously in the divine and human spheres.[11]

Finally, we have those who uphold what Niebuhr calls "Christ-transforming-culture." These are the people who try to convert the values and goals of secular culture into the service of the kingdom of God. In their thinking, Calvary must be fulfilled in Pentecost. The author includes in this category the Gospel of John, Augustine, John Calvin, John Wesley, Jonathan Edwards, and F. D. Maurice, the Christian Socialist in nineteenth-century Britain whose views nonetheless transcended a narrow ideological vision.

In my opinion, Karl Barth is closest to the conversionist mentality, since he presses for a transformation of the cultural vision in the light of the divine promise and commandment. At the same time, this approach is drastically modified in his theology because he refuses to identify any cultural achievement with the coming kingdom of God. The righteousness that we as Christians are called to effect is not the divine righteousness of the kingdom, which God alone can enact, but a purely human righteousness that nonetheless corresponds with and is determined by this higher righteousness. Barth on occasion appears to uphold a cultural Christianity when he endorses the values of democratic socialism as most nearly approximating the values of the kingdom of God.[12] At the same time, he could just as well be regarded as a separationist because of his deep-seated conviction that the demands of the gospel always run counter to the hopes and expectations of the culture. Christians will always be standing against the stream of what is popular and acceptable for the time.[13]

For Barth, Jesus Christ is the humanizer of culture. It is through his grace, which is always redemptive and never simply preservative, that men and women can move toward a more just and humane society.[14] God alone is Renewer, Reconciler, and Sanctifier, but God is Civilizer only in conjunction with human efforts toward a better world. God makes us his covenant partners in fashioning a society that will redound to his glory. He enables us to realize our vocations to be signs and witnesses to Jesus Christ.

My own position with regard to the Niebuhr typology is, like Barth's, closest to the conversionist ideal. Yet I believe that "Christ-transforming-culture" must always be united with "Christ-against-culture" in order to maintain the transcendent character of the claims of the gospel over cultural goals and expectations. What Niebuhr has given us is a valuable heuristic tool, but neither his categorizations nor mine are to be taken as dominical classifications. What they do set up is a grid useful for making more searching judgments regarding the stances that Christians over the centuries have assumed toward culture.

Religion and Culture

A consideration of Niebuhr's types raises the more general question of the precise relation between religion and culture. It is generally agreed in both theology and the social sciences that this relationship is inseparable and indissoluble. Tillich put it well when he declared that culture is the form of religion, and religion is the substance of culture.[15] Every culture has its genesis in a spiritual and moral vision, and every religion seeks a cultural incarnation. Religion is the wellspring of culture; culture is the social embodiment of religion. Culture is the bearer of religion; religion is the ground and goal of culture.

A culture can deny or cover up its metaphysical undergirding and thereby become secularized. Yet even in this state, it cannot remain insulated against religious and moral claims. On the contrary, it will then most likely invest its forms and ideals with religious and moral significance. A culture closed to the transcendent will find the locus of the sacred in its own creations.

For Tillich, the church and culture are within, not alongside each other.[16] The kingdom of God includes both even while it transcends both. The erosion of religion betokens the secularization of the culture, but no culture, he claims, can exist in a metaphysical vacuum. When God is dead, the gods are reborn, and Christianity is once again confronted by idolatry.

Christianity is both a religion and a cultural phenomenon, but in addition it is anchored in a divine revelation. The Christian faith bears witness to a God who infinitely transcends human culture and religion even while entering into cultural and religious activity. This is the God who judges as well as blesses human accomplishments, even those done in the name of Jesus Christ. God's self-revelation in Christ might well be regarded as the crisis or judgment of both religion and culture (Barth).

At their best, both culture and religion can be a sign and witness of the redemptive action of God, which occurs in them but does not arise from them. Cultural and religious activity can be parabolic of the coming kingdom of God.

Conflicting Views on History

The Christ-culture problem can be clarified by considering how theologians assess the meaning of history. Here, too, there are many discordant voices. For Reinhold Niebuhr history is a perennial tragedy—the story of human hubris and divine nemesis.[17] Such seminal thinkers as Hegel, Tillich, and Moltmann view human history as the unfolding of divinity and therefore are inclined to be optimistic with regard to its final outcome. For process theologians such as Wieman, Meland, Whitehead, and Hartshorne, the trajectory of human history and culture signifies the realization of the creative process toward a more complex and humane social order, however checkered its course may be. In the thought of Augustine, Calvin, and Luther, history is best understood as a perpetual battleground between two kingdoms, light and darkness. In the theology of Karl Barth, history is the drama of the ongoing encounter between an aspiring humanity and the living God of the Bible, who both casts down and raises up kings and empires.

Drawing mostly from the latter thinkers, I suggest that history is the story of human vanity and creativity in conflict with the omnipotence of God, to which every culture bears witness in some way or other (Acts 14:17). This conflict must be seen in the light of a wider and deeper struggle—that between the devil, the adversary of God and humanity, and the God of Jesus Christ. The devil is superior to humankind but drastically inferior to God, but he is permitted to work his destruction in the world for a time and then only to further the purposes of God to bring healing and deliverance to all peoples. God makes even the "wrath of men" to praise him (Ps. 76:10; cf. Exod. 9:16;

Rom. 9:17), and in this way his work of civilizing and humanizing goes on even in the midst of chaos and disorder.

While I cannot go along with Barth that all human history is sacred history, I do believe God is working in all history—though preservatively, not redemptively. Only where the living God, the God who revealed himself in Jesus Christ, is acknowledged as Savior and Lord do we find the sphere of redemption in history. Yet all of history moves toward the goal of the kingdom of God, since eventually the whole of humankind will be brought under the redemptive rule of Jesus Christ.

The meaning of the world, too, is brought more sharply into focus in light of these conflicting approaches to human culture. For Reinhold Niebuhr, the world is most accurately portrayed as a tower of Babel in which our infinite possibilities are time and again subverted by our sin. Tillich, on the other hand, sees the world as the sanctuary of divinity, the latent church in which the Spiritual Presence is hidden rather than manifest. The Unconditioned, he says, "can be recognized in the cultural and natural universe," but this natural knowledge yields at the most the fundamental question of human existence, for which the Christian revelation is the answer.[18] In Calvin's view, the world is the theater of the glory of God, the sphere in which God's glory is advanced even in the midst of human destruction, as well as in human liberation. For Barth the world is the field of the redemptive action of God, but it is not the source of his redemptive activity. According to Thomas Aquinas, the kingdom of nature is fulfilled and perfected in the kingdom of grace.

As I see it, the world is the locus of the pilgrimage of faith, the crucible or place of probation where the people of God are tested and prepared for eternity. It is not a prison from which we need to escape (as in Gnosticism). Nor is it a ladder by which we can ascend to heaven with the assistance of grace (as in classical Christian mysticism). Instead, it is the arena in which people, all people, are summoned to work out their vocation to be servants and heralds of the one Lord and Savior, Jesus Christ. We prove our fidelity to this high and holy calling by bearing fruit that proceeds from repentance (Matt. 3:8–10; Acts 26:20).

Creation and Redemption

The role of the Christian in human culture is best understood against the background of the doctrines of creation and redemption. The approach of evangelical theology will be somewhat different from that of other theological traditions. There are those who see creation as essentially a preparation for redemption and redemption as the elevation and fulfillment of creation (Aquinas, Tillich, Brunner, Rahner). Nature is the precondition for grace, and grace is the perfection of nature.[19] Others have been inclined to view redemption as basically the completion of creation—even as a further or higher stage of creation.[20] In Schleiermacher's thought, the appearance of Christ "is to be regarded as a preservation . . . of the receptivity, implanted in human nature from the beginning and perpetually developing further, which enables it to take into itself such an absolute potency of . . . God-consciousness."[21] According to Moltmann, the divine kenosis begins at creation and reaches its fulness in the incarnation.[22] For those standing in the Gnostic tradition, on the other hand, redemption is an escape from creation.[23] This stance is reflected in those evangelical sectarians who say that this is Satan's world rather than God's. Mystics whose affinities are with Neoplatonism (pseudo-Dionysius, Meister Eckhart, Simone Weil) view redemption as the transcendence of creation.

In refreshing contrast Karl Barth, who here represents evangelical theology at its best, sees creation for the sake of redemption.[24] Redemption, moreover, brings about the renewal of a creation that has been marred by human sin. It entails the regeneration of human nature, which is in effect a new creation (2 Cor. 5:17). "Redemption is more than creation, more also even than (as Schleiermacher thought) the completion and crown of creation. God's creation needs no completion. It was and is complete. But we can lose that completeness of creation, and we *have* lost it. It must be restored to us inalienably, by forgiveness and renewal."[25]

While revelation enables us to perceive the beauty and perfection of creation, Barth contends, it also awakens us to the depth of the corruption of creation by human sin. Creation is good in its own right and as such displays the beneficence and power of God, but its telos or goal is to prepare the way for redemption as a higher good, which occurs not because of the defectiveness of creation but because of its abuse. For Barth the covenant that God makes with humanity in Jesus Christ is "the goal of creation and creation the way to the covenant."[26]

Building upon Barth, one can say that redemption signifies the dawning of a wholly new reality that satisfies the yearnings of creation but negates the hubris of a creation sundered from its ontological moorings.[27] The possibility of this new reality lies not in creation but in a divine intervention in human history.

I further agree with Barth that creation can be rightly understood only from the perspective of redemption. The buried and forgotten truth of God in creation is only brought to light in the awakening to faith in God the redeemer. We can truly appreciate the work of God as civilizer only when our eyes are opened to his glorious work of redemption in Jesus Christ.

Reformed theology has been accustomed to making the distinction between common and saving grace. The first signifies the general grace by which God preserves mankind from being destroyed by its own sin and rekindles within mankind the desire to transcend itself in works of creative achievement. Saving grace is the work by which God transforms the human lust for power into the generosity of love. Calvin himself did not use the term "common grace," but he alluded to a general grace (*gratia universalis*) that upholds human culture and mitigates the effects of human sin. The concept of common grace is not in the Bible as such, but it has a biblical basis (cf. Matt. 5:45; 7:11; Luke 11:13; John 1:9; Acts 14:17; 17:26–28; James 1:17).

The danger in this distinction lies in separating the two activities of God, thus creating the impression that God calls only a select few to salvation. This distinction can be maintained so long as we hold that God's preservative work is for the sake of his redeeming work. God's civilizing activity leads to and is confirmed by his redemptive activity.

From his own perspective, Emil Brunner shows that he appreciates this truth: "The first thing is always what God wills as Creator; but— even apart from our sin—it is not the last. For He wills to lead the Creation out beyond itself, into the perfecting of all things. God does not preserve the world simply in order to preserve it, but in order that He may perfect it."[28]

Theology, both Catholic and Protestant, has often made the distinction between the kingdoms of nature, grace, and glory. For Thomas Aquinas, there is always a leap between the stages; they do not unobtrusively blend into one another. In biblical understanding, God's grace and glory are the source and goal of nature. God the Reconciler precedes God the Civilizer. Before the foundation of the world, God has chosen us to inherit the crown of eternal life (Matt. 13:35; John 17:24; Eph. 1:4; 1 Pet. 1:20). Before there was a cross in human history, there was a cross in the heart of God (2 Tim. 1:9, 10; 1 Pet. 1:20; Rev. 13:8). Jesus Christ, the new Man, precedes Adam, the primal man. From the perspective of eternity, redemption is prior to creation, though, to be sure, on the plane of human history redemption occurs after creation.

Human Culture and the Kingdom of God

Such considerations raise the larger question about the fascinating and enigmatic relationship between human culture and the kingdom of God. Culture may be regarded as a sign of the kingdom but not the seedbed. The kingdom of God breaks into culture, but culture does not lead to the kingdom. The kingdom is not an extension or flowering of the culture, but culture can be a parable of the kingdom. Barth puts it very well: "The Church will not see the coming of the kingdom of God in any human cultural achievement, but it will be alert for the signs which, perhaps in many cultural achievements, announce that the kingdom approaches."[29]

The discontinuity between culture and the kingdom becomes more evident when we consider the gulf between the righteousness of the kingdom and social justice. According to Tillich, human culture at its best is characterized by proportional justice, but the kingdom of God is marked by transforming justice, where justice is united with love.[30] Luther contrasted civil and spiritual righteousness, insisting that the latter, which transcends civil obligation, is characteristic of the new social order inaugurated by Jesus Christ, where love and forgiveness prevail. It is the difference between the common morality and the morality beyond morality—creative compassion. Whereas human decency and fairness are the marks of a genuinely humane culture, holy love pervades the kingdom of God. Bonhoeffer acutely perceived the radical newness of the kingdom when he declared, "God has founded his church beyond religion and beyond ethics."

Divine grace is both the elevating force in human culture and the creative source of the kingdom of God. This is why Barth could contend that the foundation of a genuinely free culture is not human potentiality but the freedom of God.[31] We are made free to realize human potential on the basis of divine grace. In the power of this grace we can strive for human righteousness, though this must always be distinguished from the divine righteousness that belongs to the kingdom of God. Yet the social righteousness that we can bring about under the impact of his grace can be a provisional reflection and foreshadowing of the perfect righteousness of the kingdom. This is why Barth could say, "The action of those who pray for the coming of God's kingdom and therefore for the taking place of his righteousness will be *kingdom-like*, and therefore on a lower level and within its impassable limits it will be *righteous* action."[32]

I concur with Barth that both church and state are under the rulership of Jesus Christ. Jesus Christ is Lord because he is not only Creator along with the Father but also Redeemer through his decisive and world-shattering victory over the principalities and powers of darkness.[33] This is why both church and state can be signs of the kingdom of God. The state can even be envisioned as an analogue to the kingdom of God, since this kingdom is a new social order, "the city of the living God" (Heb. 12:22), not simply an assembly for worship. The essence of the state is not violence or power but justice, or power in the service of justice. To be sure, the state is given as a restraint on sin, but it is also the sphere in which justice can be realized. The human righteousness realized in the state corresponds to the higher righteousness of the kingdom, but there is still a discontinuity. It is the difference between the force of law and freedom in love. Unfortunately, some states spurn their divinely given mandate and arrogate power to themselves, ruthlessly suppressing the hopes and wants of their citizens. A Christian does not owe obedience to a state that has become demonic (cf. Acts 5:29; Rev. 13).

The role of social legislation is not only to preserve order in society but to make secure the rights of all, especially the rights of the oppressed. Yet social legislation has its limits: it can alter human behavior, but it cannot change human nature. The state can legislate against immorality and thereby curb the rapacity of its citizens, but it cannot make people more loving. It can make people law-abiding but not God-fearing. The key to social reformation is wrought by the Spirit of God in the awakening to faith in Jesus Christ. A society can only advance toward greater justice when it contains within it a church that reminds it of a higher claim and a higher morality, a church that functions as an agent in bringing people a new life orientation and the spiritual gifts that enable them to realize this orientation in their thoughts, words, and actions.

The Two Kingdoms

The relationship between human culture and the kingdom of God must be assessed in the light of the cosmic conflict between the kingdom of God and the demonic kingdom of darkness. This last is anticultural because it fosters disorder and anarchy. It is also the fulcrum of inhumanity because it denigrates and defaces the human.

Augustine dramatized the human situation in his famous depiction of two cities arrayed against one another: that of the world, ruled by the devil, and that of God.[34] The city of God advances in the world through its earthen vessel, the holy catholic church. Indeed, Augustine speaks of a building up of the kingdom through the Word and the sacraments. At times he virtually equates the kingdom and the church, though for the most part he keeps the two distinct. Augustine gives us a "realized eschatology": the kingdom of God is realized now in history and is therefore engaged in mortal combat with the principalities and powers that presumptuously strive to control human destiny.

This contradition between the two kingdoms was underscored by Martin Luther, who interpreted world history in light of an apocalyptic conflict between two cosmic powers, culminating in a momentous final struggle.[35] The kingdom of Christ is an island of light in a world still under the domain of the demonic powers of darkness. The world will not be flooded by light until a new divine intervention at the end of history when Christ will come again—this time as triumphant king rather than suffering servant. Christ is Lord of both church and world by virtue of his role in the creation, but he is Savior only where his rule is acknowledged in the hearts of men and women. Luther also referred to the two governments of church and state; both of these are vulnerable to penetration by the powers of darkness, just as both can be vehicles of the kingdom of God.

John Calvin's eschatology is more optimistic, looking forward to the triumph of the kingdom of God over the kingdoms of this world within earthly history. This is not, however, a total or unqualified triumph which will not come until the eschaton, but a gradual seizure of power; hence there is a postmillennial motif in Calvin. His ideal was a holy community in which both church and state cooperate in fashioning a social order where the glory of God is served in every area of life.[36] Both church and state are under the revealed law of God; the church interprets this law to the state, and the state in turn applies this law to the life of society. The holy community is not itself the kingdom of God, which is fundamentally a spiritual kingdom, but it can be a means by which the kingdom of God is extended in the world. Indeed, Calvin was adamant that as humans transformed by grace we can extend and advance the kingdom of God through the preaching of the Word, prayer, church discipline, the sacraments, and works of social service.

Reflecting a quite different orientation is Reinhold Niebuhr, who upholds a transcendental eschatology.[37] The kingdom of God is depicted as a transcendental ideal beyond history, calling into question every human expectation and achievement. Niebuhr sees world history as the story of human hubris and divine nemesis, and while the kingdom gives meaning and purpose to human endeavor, there can never be a realization of the kingdom by means of human endeavor. The kingdom is always coming, but it is never here. It is a religio-moral ideal by which we can measure our progress toward a higher degree of justice and mutual love. The kingdom impinges on history, but it never becomes incarnate in history. Its reality can be momentarily experienced when individuals are grasped by the power of sacrificial love, but it can never be identified with any cultural movement or achievement.[38]

While Niebuhr does not envision any cosmic conflict between two opposing spiritual kingdoms, he does affirm the polarity of the kingdom of the world and the kingdom of God. Although the first stands in contradiction to the second, it also points beyond itself to this higher kingdom in which it finds both its fulfillment and negation.

Yet another perspective comes from Paul Tillich, whose eschatology is both transcendental and inner-worldly, with the accent on the second, especially in his earlier years.[39] The kingdom of God, in his view, has two dimensions: it is both inner-historical and eternal. The kingdom is not only above history but also within history. In addition, there is a "demonic kingdom," signifying not simply a deficiency of the good but a corruption of the creative dynamic at work in all things. Tillich called for a theology of synthesis in which the fundamental questions and highest values of the culture are brought into a working relationship with the demands and ideals of the kingdom of God. In contrast to the dialectical theology, Tillich saw hope and promise in cultural endeavor and achievement. From his perspective, the kingdom of God is being realized wherever people are awakened to the reality of the New Being, which appears in all genuinely prophetic figures and movements. The Spiritual Presence can also be encountered in great art, literature, and philosophy insofar as they throw light upon the human condition.

Even in the so-called dark periods of history when demonic forces seem ascendant, Tillich was insistent that the creative power of being was at work making all things new. Whereas Barth viewed the experience of defeat and despair, the economic collapse, and rising social conflict following the First World War as a crisis in the history of European civilization, a divine judgment on the nations, Tillich regarded this unsettling time as a *kairos*, a promise of new beginnings.

Nothwithstanding his dour appraisal of current events, Barth's writings exude a holy optimism. He breaks with theological tradition by insisting that the triumph of Jesus Christ over the powers of darkness was so definitive and final that Christ is even now Lord and Redeemer of all creation. This is what Moltmann aptly calls the doctrine of the royal or kingly lordship of Christ.[40] Christ is even now the center of both state and church. The church is under the knowledge of Christ, the state under the power of Christ. It is the responsibility of the church to remind the state of its true nature and mission—to establish justice for the poor and oppressed.

Yet we are not being fair to Barth if we fail to take seriously his belief that the demonic kingdom of darkness, which spawns anarchy and disorder, is still very much alive. Though it has been divested of its power ontologically, it still wields power through deception. This is why he can refer to the lordless powers that continue to rule as rebels and usurpers. Christ has indeed demolished the demonic powers that have held the world in subjection, but until this fact is generally recognized they will continue to wreak havoc. Barth can speak at the same time of a world fully reconciled to God in Jesus Christ and of a "still unredeemed world."

Though very much influenced by Barth, Jürgen Moltmann has swerved in another direction.[41] Moltmann basically takes a positive view of culture, though he is also acutely aware of the lingering shadow over cultural achievements—that of exploitation and oppression. The division he sees in history is between the oppressors and the oppressed, and this is why Moltmann belongs in the larger circle of liberation theology. Following Hegel, he contends that all human history is taken up into the history of God. There is hope in history because God is acting in human conflict, bringing good out of evil, transmuting suffering into joyous expectation. Culture has revelatory promise because it is the medium through which the Absolute Spirit unfolds itself in history. He even says that the coming of the redeeming kingdom rests partly "in the potentialities and powers of the world religions."[42]

Whereas Barth's emphasis is on the finished work of Christ, Moltmann gives us a "theology of hope" for a world still groaning in travail, still waiting for the promised redemption. What Jesus Christ gained for us is the promise of a new world, but we still wait for its fulfillment. But we can do more than wait: we can join the human struggle for liberation and thereby pave the way for the kingdom. For Moltmann, the lordship of Christ is realized wherever the hungry are fed, the naked are clothed, and unjust rulers are dethroned. Indeed, the lordship of Christ takes effect only where it is acknowledged and realized in acts of compassion, service, and social action.

Moltmann envisages the kingdom of God as a kingdom of freedom, a world free of exploitation and oppression. His eschatological hope is "the humanizing of man," "the socializing of humanity," and "peace for all creation." Although we can prepare the way for the kingdom through politics, God himself will bring in his kingdom in his own time. Yet we can cooperate with the Spirit of God in building a just society and bringing peace to all creation.[43] We can thus anticipate and facilitate the coming of the kingdom. The real presence of God is experienced wherever there is release from economic or political captivity, bread for the hungry, and security for the disinherited. The goal of liberation is "the ultimate dignity of man."[44]

I see in Moltmann a mixture of the "Christ-transforming-culture" and "Christ-of-culture" positions. He calls for the transformation of the social order even through revolution, but he betrays an unwarranted dependence on Hegelian and Marxist philosophy in the attempt to render the Christian hope intelligible and credible to an age in the throes of turmoil and upheaval. He loses sight of the transcendent and otherworldly dimensions of the kingdom of God, so that in his effort to do justice to the millennial promises of Scripture he transmutes the kingdom into a this-worldly practopia.[45] The Christian hope "is not directed towards 'another' world, but towards the world as it is changed in the kingdom of God."[46]

God as Civilizer and Reconciler

The cultivation of the arts and sciences would not be possible apart from the work of God as Civilizer. It is God who educates and enlightens so that people can realize their potentialities for culture and wisdom. It is God who leads people beyond provincialism and tribalism into a social existence that makes room for human sublimity.

Yet the benefits of civilization mean little unless we maintain a deepening communion with God. We must not forget that God is Reconciler and Sanctifier as well as Civilizer. Unless his reconciling and regenerative work takes place in our lives, we will be prone to resist and deny the light of God in nature and conscience that makes civilization possible.

Cicero contended that justice is necessary for order in society, but Augustine maintained that piety, the fear of God, takes precedence over both justice and order. Unless people learn to know and fear their Creator and Lord, their efforts to build a just society will ultimately be self-defeating. Sanctity is necessary before education, for otherwise people will misuse the skills and knowledge they acquire. Repentance is necessary before there can be genuine peace among peoples.

No enduring civilization or culture, in the highest meaning of the terms, is possible apart from the light of the gospel and the leaven of the church. It is the church that provides the spiritual and metaphysical foundation for culture, and it is the Spirit working through the gospel who endows people with the motivation and power to pursue peace and justice.

Our goal as Christians is not the Christification of the universe, as Teilhard de Chardin contends, nor is it simply humanization, as Barth and Bultmann sometimes seem to say; instead, it is Christianization in the sense of bringing people into a saving relationship with Jesus Christ. We cannot realize our humanity in the way God intended until we come to a right knowledge of the living God and what he has done for us in Jesus Christ.

What I am calling for is not an imperial church, which imposes its peculiar beliefs upon an unwilling people, but an obedient church, which tries to live in the light of God's promise and in fidelity to his commandment. The weapons of the church are spiritual: the Word of God, prayer, and works of mercy. It is not by law or coercion that people are brought into the kingdom but by the preaching and hearing of the Word of God and by deeds of love.

Today, as in the past, what the world needs is a prophetic, not a triumphal, church. Such a church will see itself as the moral monitor of the state, not as a state within the state. It will serve as the conscience of the state, not a power structure wielding a club over the state.

Our protest, as Christians, is not against the secular culture, for culture should have a certain autonomy, but against secularism, the enthronement of cultural values and ideas. The church combats idolatry when it brings the law of God to bear upon human pretension through its preaching and teaching.

A prophetic church should also be contrasted with a servant church, whose preeminent concern is to meet human need, to alleviate social ills. We must never forget that the mandate of the church is to bring the good news of salvation through the cross and resurrection of Christ to a dying and lost humanity; in so doing it will help to satisfy the deepest of all human needs—peace and reconciliation with God. The servant church carries out its witness by Christian presence rather than by the kerygmatic proclamation. The prophetic church will insist that deeds accompany words, but it will labor in the realization that the key to the new creation is the gospel united with the Spirit.

In opposition to certain strands within Protestant liberalism, we must insist that the church of God is neither a humanitarian agency nor an ethical culture society. Instead, it is the social embodiment of the new reality of the kingdom of God. Its gospel is neither the social gospel nor the privatistic gospel of interior peace but the biblical gospel of reconciliation and redemption through the atoning work of Christ on the cross and his glorious resurrection from the grave. Such a gospel, however, has far-reaching social and political implications.

Karl Barth has said that the Christian is called to be a *witness* rather than either a *crusader*, one who tries to set the world right, or a *monk*, one who withdraws from the fray in order to realize personal spiritual pursuits.[47] Yet this same theologian acknowledges that Christians are free to join, even to initiate, crusades as well as to embrace monastic-type vocations as long as their primary aim is to hold up Jesus Christ before a sinful and ailing world and their trust is not in their own efforts but in divine grace.

The church has a spiritual mission and a cultural mandate. Its primary goal is to bring the glad tidings of reconciliation and redemption to all races and nations, but it is also responsible for teaching people to be disciples of Christ in the very midst of the world's plight and dereliction.

Church and state should be separate regarding specific roles and obligations, but both should be seen as under the rulership of Jesus Christ. The church must generally refrain from dictating to the state, but it can be a goad that spurs the state to fulfill its obligations to the poor and disinherited.

At its best, the church should be a leaven that turns the world in a new direction by changing attitudes and ideas, by altering hopes and goals. It is not primarily a battering ram that breaks down the walls that keep culture intact, though on occasion it may have to assume this role as well.

The church of God is basically not anticultural but transcultural. It is not iconoclastic but transformative. Its aim is not to tear down but to refocus. In the Christian perspective, human culture should not be overthrown or uprooted but relativized and demythologized.

Worldliness, not civilization, should be seen as the main foe of the gospel. Civilization is something to be appreciated, even celebrated, but worldliness is something to be spurned and combated. Christianity, says H. Richard Niebuhr, rejects "the ascetic and romantic efforts to solve life's problems by flight from civilization."[48] Our Lord does not call us out of the world but sends us into it—though to conquer, not to succumb (cf. John 17:15–19). Worldliness takes the form of both ideological deformation and pusillanimous conformation to the values and goals of secular culture.

The overriding issue today is idolatry. People are tempted to absolutize cultural forms and ideals instead of treating these things as means to a higher end. The higher the level of civilization, the greater the peril of culture idolatry. According to H. Richard Niebuhr, "The temptation to idolatry and lust is the greater the more man is surrounded by the works of his own hands."[49]

By far the most insidious type of idolatry is elevating to divine status the religious ideals, values, and practices that find general acceptance within a culture. With his usual perspicuity, Barth observed, "Godlessness appears in a worse form in religion than it does in theoretical atheism, for here it does not make open confession as it tries to do in atheism, but thinks it has sought and found a positive substitute for what is lacking."[50]

The older Protestant liberalism did not fully consider how easily cultural achievements can become towers of Babel that foster confusion or new Molochs that hold people in servile subjection. In some quarters, civilization was even regarded as the condition for apprehending the truth of faith. "Christianity," declared Lynn Harold Hough, "has a great stake in the recovery of the civilized mind. The modern preacher confronts a major task in the remaking of the mind of his congregation. When minds become civilized, they can understand the Christian message."[51] The gospel is here reduced to the wisdom of the world.

The church today is confronted by various temptations. On the left, there are those who are all too ready to identify the cause of human liberation with salvation and movements of liberation with the kingdom of God. We should bear in mind that a great many social idealists were attracted to the program of the German Christians, that segment within the German church in the thirties that sought to accommodate the gospel to National Socialism.[52] They, too, protested against our profit-loving, capitalistic civilization, but their substitute was not a proletarian but a National Socialist utopia.

On the right, we have those who hold that America as the New Israel has a destiny to be a light to the nations. I heard a TV evangelist proudly declare, "It is religion that has made America strong." But when religion is appreciated primarily for its social utility instead of for its truth, we have succumbed to a secularist mentality.

We should not try to establish a self-consciously Christian nation in which Christian symbols are invoked to justify social policy or sanctify imperial ambition. Instead, we should press for a just nation—but one informed by a Christian life- and world-view. Our goal is a nation steadily becoming more Christianized and therefore more humanized, but we must never presume that any nation in this aeon can be wholly or even genuinely Christian. There is a difference between a nation suffused with Judeo-Christian values and a nation that actively promotes the dogmatic beliefs and practices of a particular church. Our membership as Christians is not in the New Israel as a Christian America but in the New Israel as a spiritual church.

The demands of the gospel impel us to strive for a nation characterized by justice and caring; yet such a nation cannot come into being unless it is grounded in and nurtured by piety—reverence for the living God. Piety is never the outcome of social planning, though it provides the fabric for social order. True religion is something interior, not something that needs to be exhibited. True religion cannot be enforced by civil law, but it ought to be respected by civil authority.

Richard Neuhaus has complained of a growing metaphysical vacuum in the public arena of life, which he describes as the "naked public square."[53] There is considerable merit in his charge, but the remedy is not a civil religion, much less a popular or folk religion."[54] Instead, our nation needs to rediscover the culture-transcending vision of Jonathan Edwards, Lincoln, and Melville or, as in Britain, of Wilberforce or Gladstone, a vision that keeps alive the infinite distance between the holy God and man the sinner.[55]

Our choice today is between a prophetic religion and a culture religion. The first is anchored in a holy God who infinitely transcends every cultural and religious form that testifies to him. The second absolutizes the cultural or mythical garb in which God supposedly meets us. A prophetic religion will keep a nation humble but at the same time hopeful, knowing that its destiny is in the hands of a living and sovereign God. A cultural religion makes a nation vain and ultimately foolish, tempting it to yield to the deception that the gods are in its power and service.

We must steer clear of both a theocracy, where the church actively wields political power, and a rationalistic, egalitarian democracy, where the voice of the people is equated with the voice of God. Democracy in the Christian context is based on the axiom that all people are equal before God: all are created in his image and all have sinned and fallen short of his glory. Liberal democracy, on the other hand, which has its roots in the Enlightenment, is based on the infinitive value of humanity. We need today a democracy anchored in theonomy, in which ultimate authority is assigned to the living God rather than to the nation or religious institution. A truly theonomous culture acknowledges that only the God revealed in the sacred history of the Bible is sovereign and that besides the civil law there is a higher law to which all people are subject.

Yet we should keep in mind that a democratic society under the moral law is not yet the kingdom of Christ, nor is its justice to be confounded with the righteousness of the kingdom. At the same time, a just society is not possible apart from the providential and superintending work of God, which preserves people from their own worst natures and prepares them for faith in Jesus Christ. A righteous state is not possible apart from the redemptive work of God in Jesus Christ, which gives such a state a viable spiritual center and a righteous nucleus that will make it more sensitive and knowledgeable concerning the needs of the poor and oppressed in its midst.

Christians as citizens of the state are obliged to work for justice, meaning equity or fairness, as a penultimate ideal. As members of the body of Christ, we are called to herald the coming of his kingdom, which is not of this world (John 18:36). Justice is made possible by God's universal grace; the righteousness of the kingdom is made possible by the grace revealed in Jesus Christ.

The Christian lives between the times, between the collapse of the kingdom of this world and the dawning of the messianic kingdom of Christ. We can earnestly seek for this kingdom, but we cannot create it. We can herald it, but not procure it. We can prepare the way for it by the preaching of the Word in the hope that God may deign to work in conjunction with our broken and feeble witness.

Our divinely appointed task is to be witnesses and servants of the Word. But it is also incumbent on us to be doers of justice, since our witness must be in deed as well as word (Rom. 15:18). Through our prayers and godly lives we can hasten the day of the Lord, though we cannot force the hand of God (cf. Acts 3:19–21; 2 Pet. 3:11–12). Our efforts may be used by God to call attention to his kingdom, to deepen our yearning for his kingdom. But they are not the necessary means by which God brings in his kingdom.

The criterion for social justice is divine justification, the act of unmerited forgiveness made available to us in Jesus Christ. The evidence for our justification is a commitment to social justice.

The coming of the kingdom of God involves the elevation and transformation of human culture. But it also brings about the negation and purification of cultural achievements. Human culture is elevated through the conversion of the attitudes and expectations of its people. It is negated through a divine judgment on its idolatrous trust in its own accomplishments and panaceas.

Because our values and attitudes need to be constantly refashioned and overturned by divine grace, the kingdom of God might well be described as a "permanent revolution."[56] What is important to understand is that even the regenerate or the elect need to be converted and renewed by grace. Even their values and expectations are suspect, for they too are sinners, though the power of sin is, for the most part, checked in their lives.

The hope of the world rests on God as Civilizer, Reconciler, and Redeemer. God's work of civilizing presupposes and is carried forward on a new level by his work of reconciliation and redemption. His civilizing work is done for the sake of his reconciling and redeeming work.

The perfect social order, the kingdom of God, should be welcomed as a new social order that displaces the old. By no means is it to be seen as the crystallization or maturation of the old. Nor does it build upon the old. At the same time, it fulfills the quest for meaning and purpose and the hope of justice and peace that pervade the old. What has genuine value is taken up into the kingdom of God and made to serve his glory.

The perfect social order is a goal, not a present possession. But it can be anticipated now in fellowships of outgoing love and missionary concern that exist within and apart from the institutional church. The *koinonia* is a visible and poignant sign of the *parousia*, when Christ shall come again to claim his own and to set up the kingdom that shall have no end.

Notes

1. For the integral relation between culture and world views see Stackhouse, *Creeds, Society, and Human Rights*.
2. *American Heritage Dictionary* (Boston: Houghton Mifflin Co., 1982), p. 277.
3. Niebuhr, *Christ and Culture*.
4. Karl Barth, *The Humanity of God*, trans. Thomas Wieser and John Newton Thomas (Richmond: John Knox, 1960).
5. Karl Barth, "Church and Culture," in *Theology and Church*, trans. Louise Pettibone Smith, intro. Thomas F. Torrance (New York: Harper & Row, 1962), p. 343.

6. Hauerwas, *Vision and Virtue*, p. 206. Hauerwas is here purportedly describing John Howard Yoder's position. Yoder clarifies his position in *The Priestly Kingdom: Social Ethics as Gospel* (Notre Dame, Ind.: University of Notre Dame Press, 1985) where he argues that Christian discipleship does not necessarily involve separation or abdication of responsibility for the governance of society.

In a recently published study of the Anabaptist luminary Michael Sattler, C. Arnold Snyder makes a convincing case that Sattler's spirituality is much closer to the tradition of Benedictine monasticism than to the mainline Protestant Reformation. *The Life and Thought of Michael Sattler* (Scottdale, Pa.: Herald, 1984).

7. Niebuhr's typology should be treated as a heuristic tool and not as a definitive judgment on the landscape of theology. I am well aware of the criticisms of this typology, but I have not found the suggested alternatives any more enlightening. Fundamentalists have faulted Niebuhr for placing them in the Christ-of-culture camp (though their disclaimers are not convincing), and some Anabaptists have been uncomfortable with being labeled separatists or anticultural. I have difficulty with Niebuhr's contention that the consistent transformationist will be a universalist. Yet granting certain limitations in the way Niebuhr develops his typology, I nevertheless find it exceedingly helpful in the kind of analysis I am undertaking here. In delineating this typology, I shall try to give a fresh interpretation and not simply summarize the author's views.

8. While liberationists and feminists in particular are intent on reforming society, they identify with particular cultural ideologies that claim to speak for the oppressed and thereby end up in a Christ-of-culture position.

9. One can discern both conversionist and separatist motifs in Eberhard Arnold, founder of the communalistic Society of Brothers. Arnold says that Christians should not expend their energies in trying to convert the old order into the service of the new. Instead, we should labor in the hope of the dawning of an entirely new kingdom that stands in contrast to "the crumbling world-city which we must now finally leave." At the same time, he insists that "the garden must be won back for God," though "God himself will conquer and rule it." Our task is to accept and rejoice in his rule. See Emmy Arnold, ed., *Inner Words for Every Day of the Year* (Rifton, N.Y.: Plough Publishing House, 1975), pp. 57, 48.

10. Although there are conversionist and dualistic strands in Tillich as well, he is a theologian of synthesis par excellence. His typology of autonomy, heteronomy, and theonomy cannot be understood except in this light.

11. In his later years, Reinhold Niebuhr became increasingly open to the social ethic of revolutionary Calvinism with its vision of a transformed society. See "The Problem of a Protestant Social Ethic," *Union Seminary Quarterly Review* 15 (Nov., 1959): pp. 1–11. In my judgment, the Lutheran dualistic outlook (with its polarities of love and justice, the spiritual and temporal, eternity and history) remained dominant in his thinking even toward the end of his life.

12. It was only in his early, liberal phase and in his last phase that Barth sought to ascertain a correspondence between a socialist society and the kingdom of God. In his second phase, that of dialectical theology, he was adamant that the kingdom of God stands in judgment over all cultural and political activity. He remained convinced, even in his later years, that socialism as an ideology contradicted the kingdom of God, but he was sympathetic to socialism as a concerted attempt to fashion a more humane society.

13. Barth writes that in their zeal for the honor of God, Christians will always find themselves in conflict with the principalities and powers of the age. Barth, *Christian Life*, pp. 206–7.

14. Barth would not speak of Christianizing social structures, since they already belong to Christ by virtue of his victory over the principalities and powers of the culture. Yet they need to be humanized so that they can reflect and bear witness to the cosmic victory of Christ.

15. See Paul Tillich, *Theology of Culture*, ed. Robert C. Kimball (New York: Oxford Uni-

versity Press, 1978); idem, *The Protestant Era*, trans. James Luther Adams (Chicago: University of Chicago Press, 1948), pp. 55–65; idem, *Political Expectation*, ed. James Luther Adams (Macon, Ga.: Mercer University Press, 1981), pp. 1–39; and James Luther Adams, *Paul Tillich's Philosophy of Culture, Science, and Religion* (New York: Harper & Row, 1965).

16. Tillich, *Theology of Culture*, p. 51.
17. See Niebuhr, *Moral Man and Immoral Society*, p. 256; idem, *Beyond Tragedy* (New York: Charles Scribner's Sons, 1937), pp. 186, 193, 224; and idem, *Discerning the Signs of the Times* (New York: Charles Scribner's Sons, 1946), pp. 57–72. See also John D. Barbour, "Niebuhr Versus Niebuhr: The Tragic Nature of History," *The Christian Century* 101, no. 36 (Nov. 21, 1984): pp. 1096–99.
18. Tillich, *Theology of Culture*, p. 26.
19. According to Troeltsch, "The ethic of civilization of St. Thomas according to the principle: *'Gratia praesupponit et perficit naturam,'* contains all the principles of modern Catholicism." Troeltsch, *Social Teaching of the Christian Churches* 1: p. 420.
20. Schleiermacher, who exemplifies this position, differed from Aquinas in that he regarded redemption as basically the maturation of creation, whereas Thomas contended that there is a yawning gap between the two that can only be bridged by divine grace bestowed sacramentally from above. While Schleiermacher saw religion ennobling everything that is, Thomas saw religion as perfecting and purifying human cultural endeavor. For Thomas culture is ultimately transcended in the contemplation of God.
21. Friedrich Schleiermacher, *The Christian Faith*, ed. H. R. Mackintosh and J. S. Stewart (New York: Harper & Row, 1963), 2: p. 368.
22. Jürgen Moltmann, *The Trinity and the Kingdom*, trans. Margaret Kohl (San Francisco: Harper & Row, 1981), p. 118.
23. See Kurt Rudolph, *Gnosis*, ed. Robert McLachlan Wilson (San Francisco: Harper & Row, 1983).
24. While Walter Kasper also speaks in this fashion and claims this is the position of the classical theologians of the church, including Augustine and Aquinas, he means a nature that is deficient apart from the perfecting grace of redemption. The emphasis is quite different in Barth, who contends that creation is complete in itself but needs to be restored because of human sin. Kasper takes issue with Barth's condemnation of natural theology and the *analogia entis*. See Walter Kasper, *The God of Jesus Christ*, trans. Matthew J. O'Connell (New York: Crossroad, 1984), pp. 74–76, 97–98.
25. Barth, "Church and Culture," *Theology and Church*, p. 347.
26. Barth, *Church Dogmatics* III, 1, p. 97.
27. Cf. "Revelation is not creation nor the continuation of creation. It is a mysterious new work of God upon creation." Quoted in Hans Urs von Balthasar, *The Theology of Karl Barth*, trans. John Drury (New York: Holt, Rinehart & Winston, 1971), p. 108.
28. Brunner, *The Divine Imperative*, trans. Olive Wyon (Philadelphia: Westminster, 1947), p. 214.
29. Barth, "Church and Culture," *Theology and Church*, p. 344.
30. Tillich, *Theology of Culture*, pp. 143, 144.
31. See Robert J. Palma, *Karl Barth's Theology of Culture* (Allison Park, Pa.: Pickwick Publications, 1983).
32. Barth, *Christian Life*, p. 266.
33. I hold that Jesus Christ is Lord of this world de facto and Redeemer of the world de jure. He does not become Redeemer in fact until he is accepted in faith as Savior and Lord. Yet he rules in such a way as to direct people to his redemption, which becomes concrete and tangible in the community of faith and love.
34. Augustine, *The City of God, The Basic Writings of Saint Augustine*, ed. Whitney J. Oates (New York: Random House, 1948), vol. 2.
35. See Jürgen Moltmann, "Luther's Doctrine of the Two Kingdoms and Its Use Today," in *On Human Dignity*, trans. M. Douglas Meeks (Philadelphia: Fortress, 1984), pp.

61–77; and Althaus, *Ethics of Martin Luther,* trans. Robert C. Schultz (Philadelphia: Fortress, 1972), pp. 50–53.

36. For Ernst Troeltsch's brilliant exposition of Calvin's concept of the holy community, see Troeltsch, *Social Teaching of the Christian Churches* 2: pp. 590–602.

37. See Reinhold Niebuhr, *Interpretation of Christian Ethics;* idem, *Reflections on the End of An Era* (New York: Charles Scribner's Sons, 1934); idem, *The Nature and Destiny of Man,* 2 vols. (New York: Charles Scribner's Sons, 1951); and idem, *Christian Realism and Political Problems.*

38. Niebuhr describes the pure sacrificial love, which is the essence of the kingdom of God, as an "impossible possibility" in that it cannot be deliberately willed by individuals, but it can take place in human life and experience when we are opened to the grace of God by faith. It can never be a political strategy, but it can be an object of hope that lends meaning to human existence and history. *Interpretation of Christian Ethics,* pp. 123–36.

39. See Paul Tillich, *Systematic Theology* (Chicago: University of Chicago Press, 1963), 3: pp. 297–423.

40. See Moltmann, *On Human Dignity,* pp. 79–96. According to Moltmann, Christ now reigns not as triumphal king but as the crucified one. His power is that of vicarious or suffering love. For a critique of Barth's universal Lordship theory from the perspective of Lutheran confessionalism, see Walter Künneth, *Der Christ als Staatsbürger: Eine Ethische Orientierung* (Wuppertal: Brockhaus, 1984), pp. 38–43.

41. See Jürgen Moltmann, *Theology of Hope,* trans. James W. Leitch (New York: Harper & Row, 1965); idem, *The Church in the Power of the Spirit,* trans. Margaret Kohl (New York: Harper & Row, 1977); idem, *The Trininty and the Kingdom* (1981); idem, *The Crucified God,* trans. R. A. Wilson and John Bowden (New York: Harper & Row, 1974); idem, *Religion, Revolution and the Future,* trans. M. Douglas Meeks (New York: Charles Scribner's Sons, 1969); idem, *Hope and Planning* (New York: Harper & Row, 1971); and idem, *On Human Dignity.*

42. Moltmann, *The Church in the Power of the Spirit,* p. 163.

43. Moltmann, *On Human Dignity,* pp. 113–31.

44. Moltmann, *Crucified God,* pp. 317–40.

45. Moltmann views transcendence in terms of the future into which we are raised. *The Church in the Power of the Spirit,* p. 287.

46. Ibid., p. 164.

47. Barth, *Christian Life,* pp. 197–201.

48. H. Richard Niebuhr, Wilhelm Pauck, and Francis P. Miller, *The Church against the World* (Chicago: Willett, Clark & Co., 1935), p. 126.

49. Ibid.

50. Barth, *Christian Life,* p. 129.

51. Lynn Harold Hough, *The Civilized Mind* (New York: Abingdon, 1937), p. 58.

52. See Niebuhr, Pauck, and Miller, *Church against the World,* p. 144.

53. Richard John Neuhaus, *The Naked Public Square* (Grand Rapids: Eerdmans, 1984).

54. Richard Pierard accuses Neuhaus of advocating a civil religion, though he acknowledges that Neuhaus would deny this. Richard V. Pierard, "Hankering for a Civil Religion," *New Oxford Review* 52, no. 6 (July–August, 1985): pp. 26–28.

55. For a brilliant study of the loss of this transcendent vision in American culture see John Patrick Diggins, *The Lost Soul of American Politics* (New York: Basic Books, 1984).

56. H. Richard Niebuhr, *The Kingdom of God in America* (Chicago: Willett, Clark & Co., 1937), p. 179.

CHAPTER 13

The Ideological Temptation

Do not conform any longer to the pattern of this world, but be transformed by the renewing of your mind.

ROMANS 12:2 NIV

We must all preach *to* our age, but woe to us if it is our age we preach, and only hold up the mirror our time.

P. T. FORSYTH

The decisive seat of evil in this world is not in the social and political institutions . . . but simply in the weakness and imperfection of the human soul itself.

GEORGE KENNAN

Today . . . we must guard ourselves from the temptation of accepting either a philosophy of revolution or a philosophy of reaction.

KARL BARTH

It is wrong to assume that the highly informed citizen is more capable. Rather, he is drowned in current events, thus becoming an easy prey for propaganda and the very symbol of the political illusion.

JACQUES ELLUL

The Ideological Spell

Like the false prophets in ancient Israel, today's self-styled prophets are giving misleading counsel to both church and state. On the one hand, we find those who hail the Sandinistas as the shining hope of Latin America and the contras as political criminals allied with the discredited Somoza regime. On the other, we hear those who label the Sandinistas as agents of an international Communist conspiracy and portray the contras as freedom fighters comparable to the early American revolutionaries. Again, there are those who urge support for the sanctuary movement in which churches open their doors to illegal refugees from Central American countries listed by our State Department as friendly, such as El Salvador and Guatemala. On the opposite side are those who accuse the sanctuary movement of being duped by left-wing propaganda designed to embarrass the Reagan administration. Such persons seem oblivious to the right-wing death squads in various Central American nations that have been given virtually free rein to silence all dissent.

On the subject of peace, we are also bombarded by discordant voices. The Ban the Bomb movement calmly assures us that peace can become a reality by the virtual unilateral dismantling of our nuclear arsenal. The Peace through Strength movement calls for shoring up our nuclear defense as the only way to maintain the balance of power in a precarious world. Both sides see human ingenuity and diligence as the key to peace.[1]

In the area of economics, we find those who contend that prosperity lies in the unfettered market and that economic ruin has its source in unwarranted interference by big government in the private sector. Poverty is traced to indolence and apathy rather than to exploitation by corporations. Their opponents argue that only by state regulation of the means of production can justice be ensured for all classes in society.

While there is some truth in all these viewpoints, they also betray a narrowing of vision that accounts for their often naive and simplistic solutions to social and political problems. The confusion in their counsel derives from what I call the ideological spell, the blurring of one's perceptions by an uncritical identification with a particular social cause. An ideology paints the world in black and white and allows for no greys. It therefore loses sight of the ambiguous and uncertain character of all human enterprises.

Christian faith can ill afford to align itself with any ideology lest it lose its anchor in the transcendent. When we hear that the "evil empire" is the Soviet Union, for example, we as Christians must remind world leaders that the ultimate evil empire exists within all of us, that it cuts through both West and East, right and left. I am not suggesting that Christians can remain aloof from the social struggle and must refrain from making relative judgments concerning the right and wrong in any social conflict. But in their judgments they must keep in mind that all human endeavor lies under the divine judgment, that before God no one's hands are clean.

Faith and Ideology

Surely one of the most pressing issues in theology today is the enigmatic relation between faith and ideology. Does faith in the living God revealed in Jesus Christ need an ideological framework in order to relate to the practical issues of the time? Should faith enter into an alliance with an ideology in order to maintain its relevance? Can the truth of faith be brought into the service of a strategic goal without losing its redemptive impact and power?

The concept of ideology has a long history in Western civilization,[2] but ever since Marx and Engels it has come to represent a false consciousness that distorts the realities of the cultural and religious situation.[3] It connotes a bias rooted in cultural and economic factors that prevents people from seeing the whole of reality.

An *ideology* might be defined as an orientation toward life and the world that serves to advance the interests of a particular class or group in society. It presents a picture of the world that gives legitimacy to the cultural values and goals it holds most dear. While its focus is on social-empirical reality, the workaday life in the world, it colors one's understanding of every aspect of life. It generally arises as a protest against some social wrong or as a reaction to some perceived threat to social order.[4]

An ideology is invariably reductionistic. By giving simplistic answers to difficult problems, it hides or ignores the complexity and ambiguity of the situation. It therefore constricts rather than broadens one's social vision.

Whereas pure philosophy is engaged in the dispassionate pursuit of truth, ideology connotes an attempt to bend truth to practical ends. By contrast, theology places the emphasis on obedience to the truth.

Characteristic of all ideology is its reliance on propaganda rather than dialogue to achieve its ends. While it may give lip service to an open investigation of the facts, the results are already predetermined. An ideology serves to disguise "real abuses and replaces rational arguments by an appeal to emotion."[5]

Ideologies in effect function as substitute salvations, since the knowledge they purport to give is redemptive insofar as it provides "existential hope and guidance."[6] An ideology is also inclined to be totalistic in that its claims penetrate every area of human existence and it can tolerate no alternative view of reality.

Reinhold Niebuhr is one theologian who has been ready to acknowledge the ideological taint in human reasoning.[7] He maintains that no religion or political system is exempt from this taint; even the vision of those who champion the rights of the oppressed is vulnerable to ideological distortion. The task of theology is to recognize the ideological temptation and always to struggle against it. According to Niebuhr, ideology has its source not simply in finiteness or ignorance but in people's inveterate tendency to justify self-interest, thereby making it appear identical with the common good.[8] Thus ideology betrays the mystery of a corrupted will, which presents an insuperable difficulty to rationalist philosophy and sociology.

This is certainly not the prevailing position on the current theological scene. Liberation theologian Juan Luis Segundo believes ideology to be salutary and necessary, since every religious community needs a conceptual system that organizes and directs practical human life.[9] An ideology becomes stifling and oppressive only when it is divorced from a transcendent religious faith. Elisabeth Schüssler-Fiorenza concludes that theology will always serve certain interests, and therefore it "has to reflect and critically evaluate its primary motives and allegiance." If it is to be on the side of the poor and oppressed, it has "to abandon its so-called objectivity and . . . become partisan."[10]

My position is closer to Niebuhr's. I see a fundamental contradiction rather than a congruity between ideology and faith. Whereas faith calls for the criticism of reality in the light of eternity, ideology critiques reality on the basis of a social theory. Faith questions all human presuppositions and assumptions;[11] ideology demands a blind adherence to particular assumptions about man and society. Faith seeks understanding and reconciliation between opposing parties in society; ideology tries to crush all those who stand in the way of human progress. Faith is an opening of one's inward eyes to the action of God in history that brings an end to the existing world order; ideology is a vision of the triumph of human ingenuity in building a new world. Faith recognizes that truth can make its own way in the world; ideology sees the efficacy of truth dependent on human strategy and technique. Faith is content to wait for the full disclosure of truth; an ideology claims a premature possession of truth. Faith makes use of ideas as aids in understanding the mystery of God's self-revelation in Christ; an ideology regards ideas as tools in social engineering. Faith's concern is the regeneration of the human spirit; the overriding concern in ideology is the restructuring of society.

Segundo is right that every ideology has a religious or metaphysical basis. Yet upon close examination this most often proves to be a religion rooted in cultural aspirations and is therefore to be contrasted with the faith that comes to us by revelation. Both faith and religion are generally dismissed by ideologies of the left as obstacles to human liberation, since they turn people's attention away from the agonizing issues of this world to some other world. Ideologies of the right, on the other hand, are usually very open to religion, which they see as buttressing the interests of the classes in power. From this perspective, religion is valued for its social utility, but not for its truth. Religion becomes a sacred canopy that legitimates "human social arrangements by projecting them as our sacred and cosmic frame of reference."[12]

In our day ideologies are coming more and more to reflect tribalistic loyalties rather than class interests per se. When people give their ultimate allegiance not to class but to race, nation, or ethnic heritage, then an ideology takes on an entirely different complexion. Its basis is no longer the hope of economic betterment but the vision of ethnocentric unity and identity. We see this new thrust in ideology in pan-Arabism, Polish nationalism, Russian hegemonism, Zionism, black African tribalism, Christian Nationalism in South Africa, and communalism in India. I believe that class interests will always be present to some degree in any ideology, but the stirrings of racial or national consciousness may be far more significant in our time.[13]

One should keep in mind that not all people associated with a particular ideological camp are ideologues. That is, there are undoubtedly many who have only a tangential relationship to an ideology and are therefore not fully committed to its social program. Others may once have been under the spell of an ideology but are now breaking away through disillusionment with its promises. An ideologue, by contrast, is totally committed to an ideological vision and is therefore impervious to the persuasive power of reason. Not all card-carrying Communists, for example, are hard-nosed ideological Marxists, nor are all feminists committed unreservedly to the goals of feminism as an ideology. It is important to make such distinctions if we are to combat ideology successfully in the present age.

Types of Ideology

Among the ideologies competing to be king of the hill in our time, perhaps none is producing more dismay in the academic establishment than conservatism. This train of thought, which by all accounts has made dramatic strides in recent years, vigorously upholds free enterprise, regional autonomy, and rugged individualism.[14] The entrepreneur takes the place of the saint as the model of the "new man." The laws of the marketplace are practically equated with the laws of God.

Conservatism in its American form has its sources in classical liberalism, Social Darwinism and transcendentalism. Among its luminaries are Adam Smith, David Ricardo, Charles de Montesquieu, Edmund Burke, Thomas Jefferson, John Locke, Ralph Waldo Emerson, Herbert Spencer, and Alfred Marshall. In our day, it is defended in varying degrees by such provocative and scintillating writers as Russell Kirk, George Gilder, Ayn Rand, Milton Friedman, Irving Kristol, Patrick Buchanan, Michael Novak, William Safire, and William Buckley.[15] Emerson voiced the credo of this ideology when he asserted: "Wealth brings with it its own checks and balances. The basis of political economy is non-interference. The only safe rule is found in the self-adjusting meter of demand and supply. Do not legislate."[16]

In this orientation, bourgeois acquisitiveness is generally applauded, indicating as it does the desire to better one's condition by diligent application. The happy result will be "the improvement of *everyone's* condition."[17] According to Adam Smith, the laws of supply and demand united with business acumen will inevitably lead "to the greatest number and quality of goods at the lowest price for the greatest number of people."[18]

Ideological conservatives give primacy to economic freedom, believing that this will result in a world where material wants and needs are satisfied to the highest degree possible. The liberation they eulogize is freedom from governmental control and regulation. The principal sinners are the big spenders. Poverty stems from slothfulness and limited social horizons rather than the exploitation and oppression of workers by big corporations. Among the enemies that need to be combated, none is so sinister as the misguided idealists who in the name of social equality try to impose a system of progressive taxation upon the public so that the industrious are penalized for the sake of those who will not pull their own weight.

Though ideological conservatism embraces the economic system of free enterprise capitalism, the latter must not be confused with the former. An economic theory as such is not an ideology, but it may lend itself for use by an ideology, which is inspired by a mythological vision of a perfect society or new social order. Ideology emerges when penultimate concerns are elevated to the level of ultimacy.

While the consistent conservatives seek not only economic but also religious and political freedom, a number of conservatives associated with the new populism call for government regulation of private morality. One can detect growing tensions between those who decry government intervention in all areas of life and those who favor it in the area of morals.[19]

Reinhold Niebuhr gives this caustic criticism of modern ideological conservatism:

What is usually now defined as "free enterprise" is a form of economic organization which rests upon a physiocratic theory, which is consistently secular and naturalistic. It erroneously assumes that the ambitions of men are contained within the bounds of what is called "nature"; it erroneously believes that the desires of men are chiefly economic and essentially ordinate and that the market place is a sufficient instrument for the coordination of all spontaneous human activities.[20]

In opposition to classical liberalism, now called conservatism, there has arisen especially since the Depression years the ideology of welfare liberalism. While continuing to affirm faith in human progress and perceiving the hope of the human race in primarily economic terms, it calls for state regulation of the means of production to overcome the disparity between rich and poor.[21] It does not wish to stifle human initiative, but it sees the public good as taking precedence over individual prosperity. The social planner is more highly regarded than the entrepreneur. The benevolent government takes the place of the unfettered market as the source of human well-being. The orientation of welfare liberalism is collectivist and statist. Justice and equality have priority over economic freedom.

Welfare liberalism draws its support not only from disinherited minorities and the working class but also from what Peter Berger and Richard Neuhaus call the "new class." These are the people who favor increased governmental intervention in all aspects of society. Their aim is to create a new kind of individual—one who is other-directed rather than inner-directed and is sensitive to the needs of those less fortunate in society. A great many of these people, who have upward mobility on the economic scale, are employed in the rapidly growing public sector of society and are therefore dependent on government aid for their livelihood. They generally belong to the teaching and service professions, as opposed to the business and farming interests, which are likely to throw their support to ideological conservatism. Neuhaus aptly calls them a "new elite," since they "make a living by minting and marketing the metaphors by which they think society should be ordered."[22] Whereas the bourgeois values of the old elite were based on the production and distribution of material goods, "the new class produces and distributes symbolic goods—knowledge and enlightenment."[23]

Welfare liberalism might be considered a transitional stage between conservatism and socialism. Both welfare liberalism and socialism in its modern phase are to be seen as reactions to the supposed inequities and injustices spawned by capitalism.

It is socialism that has given the modern world the captivating vision of a classless society where all inequity and exploitation are eradicated. Socialism advocates state ownership of the means of production and state control of the means of distribution for the sake of the welfare of the masses. Corporations, which allegedly create and exploit the poor, need to be abolished if social justice is to become a tangible reality. Protesting against the concentration of wealth in the hands of a few (as in capitalism), socialists favor the distribution of wealth to the whole populace.

Socialism has its intellectual roots in the writings of Jean-Jacques Rousseau, Karl Marx, Friedrich Engels, Louis Blanc, Ferdinand Lassalle, Eduard Bernstein, Leon Trotsky, and Nikolai Lenin.[24] The most consistent type of socialism is Marxist-Leninism, which upholds a proletarian dictatorship as the necessary means to attain an equitable distribution of goods in society. Socialism has also taken democratic forms, for example, in the British Labor Party and the socialist parties of France, Germany, the United States, and Scandinavia.[25] As in the case of classical liberalism, socialism has been embraced by a significant number of Christian theologians, among them Frederick Denison Maurice, Leonhard Ragaz, Paul Tillich, Friedrich-Wilhelm Marquardt, and the early Reinhold Niebuhr.[26]

Socialism seeks the breakup of hierarchy and the leveling of authority. It champions free medical aid and universal education. Yet it places its faith in a socially enlightened elite of welfare planners, who may be democratically elected or who may be compelled to seize power by military force. The socialist state is collectivist, but its purported aim is not the extension of power as an end in itself but power in the service of justice. Its purpose is the amelioration of the misery of the masses for whom it speaks.

By its very nature, socialism is utopian, since it envisages a social order free from strife and exploitation, one that can be ushered in by legislation, even by violent revolution. Socialism can be criticized for its unwavering and unsubstantiated faith in the innate goodness of humanity and its blindness to the corrupting influence of centralized power. Like both classical and welfare liberalism, socialism is an Enlightenment creed: its hope is in the infinite possibilities resident in the human soul rather than in a divine promise to redeem humankind from its iniquity. It presupposes a belief in human perfectibility and inevitable human progress, both of which patently conflict with the biblical understanding of the inevitability of tragedy in history because of human sin.

Harboring many of the same utopian illusions, feminism also divides humankind between the oppressed and the oppressors. It is best understood as an ideology for the liberation of women from oppression and exploitation by a sexist and patriarchal society.[27] The adversary in feminism is not monopolistic corporations nor the military-industrial complex (though these generally remain objects of stricture) but the patriarchal life-and world-view that presumably holds women in a subordinate or inferior position. Feminists loudly complain that women are the most oppressed of all segments of society, since they are systematically kept from the reins of power. Like socialists, feminists are intent on breaking up hierarchy in social relationships. With socialists and welfare liberals, they zealously throw their support behind affirmative action legislation designed to ensure for minorities equal opportunity in job selection and an equal voice in business decisions.

Feminists are inclined to see the traditional family as a prime obstacle to women's liberation. In place of the traditional family where the man is considered the sole head and breadwinner, feminists promote the egalitarian family where decisions are mutually agreed upon and where each party is free to pursue his or her own career.

Authority is rooted in the experience of women who have been made aware of their status as oppressed persons in a male-dominated world. Men who can empathize with this experience are welcomed as comrades in the quest for a more just society. Feminists are inspired by the vision of a holistic humanity where men and women work together in harmony as equals.

In order to achieve their ends, feminists advocate consciousness-raising—the art of cultivating sensitivity to the needs and plight of the oppressed. Consciousness-raising must take place in public education, and this is why feminists are so intent on rewriting texts to make sure that women's history is not neglected and that inclusive language is always used.

One cannot properly understand feminism without some comprehension of its adversary—partriarchalism.[28] Patriarchalism is the ideology that legitimates patriarchy, the rule of man over woman and children. It is both an ancient and a modern ideology and is by no means monolithic. In its classical form, it holds that man is the sole head of the family as well as its provider and protector. Human relationships are understood in terms of hierarchy in which the headship of man in the family is analogous to the lordship of kings and feudal barons. The main role of woman is to bear and raise children and to comfort and satisfy her husband. According to Aristotle, "ruling-class Greek males are the natural exemplars of mind or reason, while women, slaves, and barbarians are the naturally servile people, represented by the body and passions, which must be ruled by the 'head.' "[29] Women and children are the property of the husband and father and therefore have no rights of their own. In medieval civilization, classical patriarchy was humanized to a degree, but the male was still regarded as the norm of humanity.[30] Indeed, it was commonly held that only man is created directly in the image of God and that woman participates in this image only by being joined to man. Patriarchalism was also evident in Reformation Protestantism, which valued woman chiefly for her capability to bear male heirs and thereby ensure the perpetuation of property and the family name.[31] Both Calvin and Luther transcended this mentality at times, but they nevertheless still thought in hierarchical and dualistic terms when describing human relationships. Patriarchalism was more successfully challenged in Puritanism, Pietism, and Quakerism, where the woman was depicted as a partner in ministry and the door was opened for women to assume positions of spiritual leadership.

It is interesting to ascertain how ideology colors one's understanding of basic Christian truths. In patriarchalism God is the kingly Lord who arbitrarily elects some to salvation and others to damnation. In feminism God is the creative force within us that enables us to realize our human potential. For patriarchalism sin is rebellion against authority, thereby preparing the way for anarchy. For feminism sin is the exploitation of the poor and powerless and acquiescence to this exploitation. Whereas patriarchalism sees the chief sin as pride, feminism views the principal sin as passive resignation to social evil.[32] In patriarchalism salvation lies in childlike faith in an almighty Father. In feminism salvation is to be found in the rediscovery of authentic humanity and in assertiveness in the cause of equality.

This ideological polarity becomes especially evident in the current abortion controversy. Because feminism upholds female autonomy, it naturally supports the free choice position on abortion. Because patriarchalism accentuates the reproductive role of women, it generally supports the right-to-life position.[33]

One ideology that belongs peculiarly to the twentieth century is fascism.[34] Fascism draws upon various intellectual sources, including neo-idealism, vitalism, activism, and the cult of the hero. It was profoundly influenced by such philosophical luminaries as Nietzsche, Carlyle, Pareto, Sorel, and Herbert Spencer, the philosopher of Social Darwinism. While classical liberalism stresses property rights and modern welfare liberalism and socialism focus on human rights, fascism's emphasis is on national rights. While modern liberalism celebrates diversity and pluralism, fascism seeks a state that is racially and ethnically homogeneous. Whereas welfare liberalism and socialism are committed to social planning, fascism protests against creeping bureaucracy and rational controls. Although it advocates a strong centralized state, it sees this state personified in a charismatic leader who becomes a father figure to the masses. Ideally it seeks an alliance of government with big business and big labor in a corporate state for the purpose of creating a homogeneous national unit.

While a fascist state is authoritarian, what differentiates it from a military dictatorship is its ability to provide an ideology that gives people a sense of national destiny, an incentive to perform feats of often heroic proportions. In a system that places national honor and security above all else, the main enemies are minorities that are unwilling or unable to assimilate. But threats abroad are by no means ignored. In foreign policy fascism is likely to be adventurist and expansionist, for it recognizes that national and racial survival are contingent on taking the offensive against unfriendly states and peoples.

Unlike classical liberalism, welfare liberalism, and socialism, all of which have their roots in the Enlightenment, fascism draws from the age of Romaniticism, which celebrates the irrational and the heroic. Violence is seen as more efficacious than rational persuasion, even as redemptive. Fascism triumphed in Nazi Germany and in Italy under Mussolini, but fascist ideas have also found a lodging in Spain under the Falangists, in Argentina under the Peronists, and in South Africa under the Christian Nationalists.

Because of our democratic heritage with its tolerance of divergent opinions and life-styles, fascism would seem to have little hope of success in America. Yet if our country should ever sink into a severe depression with inflation and unemployment out of hand and if racial and ethnic minorities at the same time became more vocal in the demand for full equality, I could perceive a situation in which people might turn to a charismatic figure who would promise social and national security at the price of giving up elemental freedoms. An upsurge in xenophobia could create a climate of receptivity to a fascist scenario. The American brand of fascism might well give eloquent praise to the ideals and values associated with democracy and capitalism, but in actuality it would crush these ideals in the attempt to forge a national consensus.[35]

Just as socialism and welfare liberalism have a certain affinity with feminism, uniting in their call for federal laws combating discrimination and supporting affirmative action, so fascism appears to be congruous with patriarchalism. But appearances can be deceptive. Even though defending traditional family values in its rhetoric, in practice it subordinates the family to the all-powerful state. Its opposition to abortion is rooted not in a respect for life but in a desire to perpetuate the *Volk*, or people, on which the national security state rests.

One final ideology should be mentioned: technological liberalism, in which both property rights and human rights are subordinated to technological growth. We need to recognize that pragmatists and technocrats can be just as ideological as new rightists and leftists. The vision of a technological practopia is the emerging ideology of the center, and it could be argued that it is slowly but surely replacing both the traditional, patriarchal ideal of a stratified society and the Marxist ideal of a classless society. It may well signify a partial synthesis of the opportunity state of classical liberalism and the welfare state of modern liberalism. We should pay serious attention to Pope John Paul II's condemnation of an "ideology of technology," which imposes "the primacy of matter over spirit, of things over the human person, of the technical over the moral."[36]

Still other ideologies could be included in this discussion: scientific positivism, monarchism, anarchism, pacifism, gay liberationism, vegetarianism, syndicalism, and so on. Several of these (as well as some of those discussed) represent branches of the metaideology—secular humanism. We should bear in mind that ostensibly religious movements like fundamentalism, evangelicalism, and Catholicism can also become ideologies if their aim is to perpetuate a cultural ethos rather than bring a divine Word of hope and judgment to a despairing humanity.

Ideology and Mythology

Behind every ideology is a mythology, an imaginative projection of human hopes and aspirations on the plane of history. A mythology connotes a vision of reality set forth in primal symbols that give meaning and purpose to human existence. Such a vision is rooted in a cultural faith that is invariably idolatrous, for it means enthroning cultural values and ideals.

Adam Smith's perception of reality is less empirical than mythological.[37] Nature is personified as a beneficent force that makes use of impersonal mechanisms and laws. This "Invisible Hand," as Smith called it, should not be interfered with by governmental authority. God becomes the "Conductor of the Universe" and the "great Physician of Nature." Smith's ideology is rooted in the Enlightenment myth of preestablished harmony. It was naively believed that the free interplay of egoisms effects a harmony or congruity between competing interests that redounds to the good of the human race as a whole.

Similarly, the so-called scientific materialism of Karl Marx proves to be based on a mythopoetic vision of reality that can be accepted only by faith, since it lacks sufficient empirical corroboration.[38] Marx envisaged a kingdom of freedom that would signalize the liberation of the impoverished masses from the tedium of producing the bare minimum necessary for survival. He perceived human history evolving according to a materialistic dialectic from feudalism to capitalism to communism. This proletarian utopia or classless society is the mythical construct that has given Marxists the motivation to struggle against the moneyed classes in power, sometimes against almost insuperable odds. History is interpreted in the light of the class struggle, but the working class will inevitably triumph because this triumph is ordained by history itself. Marxism is actually a secularized form of postmillennialism, since the millennial promises of peace and brotherhood are to be fulfilled within history.

National Socialism was also motivated by a myth—the eternal creative power working within nature and history that drives peoples of various origins to unity and identity with their own kind.[39] Every race, it was said, has its soul and every soul its race. The cardinal sin was mongrelization, the mixing of superior and inferior races. History was seen in terms of an ongoing conflict between "good blood," representing creativity and light, and "bad blood," the symbol of parasitism and darkness. The Teutonic destiny was the triumph of the soul of the Germanic race over inferior peoples, a triumph that is not the automatic result of evolution but the prize of heroic effort. Thus the hope of Germany was held to rest upon the realization of folkic consciousness, which would solidify the recovery of national unity and purpose. The vision of the Third Reich corresponds to the third age of the Spiritual Franciscan Joachim of Floris (d. 1202), in which peace and harmony would be restored to the nations. Joachim's influence is also conspicuous in Karl Marx's dialectic of history.

Even the modern technological state has its myth: the "Third Wave"—the practopia of the electronic-computer society, which is now being ushered in by the communications revolution.[40] Just as the industrial state supplanted the agricultural state, so it in turn will be superseded by the computer state (reminiscent again of Joachim's three stages of history). The distribution of knowledge will characterize the new age, just as the production and distribution of material goods marked the industrial age. Bureaucracy will give way to ad-hocracy, the fast-moving kinetic organization of the future. The deadening uniformity of the industrial age will be replaced by diversity and opportunity. The spirit of the entrepreneur will be reborn as corporations encourage individual initiative. Participatory democracy will supplant representative democracy. The "associative man" will take the place of the "organization man"; the former participates in managerial decisions even at the highest level instead of simply carrying out decisions made by an industrial-managerial elite. The principal struggle today is between the progressive forces representing the Third Wave and the conservative and reactionary forces represented by the Second Wave, and this struggle overshadows class and racial conflicts in our time. An emphasis on free will contrasts the Third Wave mythology with the historical determinism of dialectical materialism.[41]

At the risk of oversimplification, one could say that the underlying myth that has shaped the ideologies of Western society is evolution, which here encompasses not simply biological but moral and spiritual evolution. Progress toward a yet unrealized paradise on earth becomes an irreversible principle in human history. This is the myth that inspired the Enlightenment, and it persists today—in classical liberalism or conservatism, welfare liberalism, socialism, fascism, feminism, and the new technological liberalism.

The primordial myth that has shaped the East is reincarnation. This is the myth behind Hindu communalism, which accounts for the caste stratification in India and Nepal and explains why the accent is placed on resignation to Fate rather than revolution against the oppressor classes (as in Marxism).[42] The myth of reincarnation also dominates in Buddhist countries where the ideal is not social transformation but equanimity attained through detachment from the discords and sufferings of life.

It is important to recognize that ideologies are not equal. Some are closer to Judaeo-Christian values than others, although they all contain thrusts that contravene a transcendent religious faith. Most of us would agree with Reinhold Niebuhr that the idolatry of democratic liberalism is far less noxious than the idolatries of modern secular totalitarianism, which have subjugated large parts of Europe and the Third World.[43] At the same time, we need to take seriously Barth's warning that ideologies that seem congruous with the Christian outlook on life and the world are more seductive to earnest Christians and therefore more of a threat to the integrity of Christian faith.

Ideology and Heresy

Alliances with ideologies have often been the occasion for heresy in the church. *Heresy* here refers to a refocusing of the Christian message and mission so that the claims of the gospel are muted or downplayed. Whenever the church is tempted to align itself with an ideology, the way is paved for the emergence of some heresy or faith aberration.

The church is led to seek ideological support and undergirding for various reasons. First, there is the apologetic concern, which moves the church to appeal to the cultured despisers of religion. Again, a church often becomes more intent on institutional survival than on commitment to the great commission. It then is led to curry favor with vested interests in society, especially those that wield political power. Finally, class bias is always present in the quest for a homogeneous membership. Church growth experts tell us that a church prospers when it is culturally and ethnically homogeneous, but a move in this direction solidifies the ideological cast of the church.

The role of ideology in promoting heresy throws light upon the sociological sources of heresy. H. Richard Niebuhr has made a convincing case that the proliferation of denominations and sects in the United States has its roots in class affiliation more than in doctrinal disagreements.[44] Whenever class becomes the key to theological or ecclesiastical identity, this is a sure sign of the encroachment of ideology in the domain of the church.

An ideological intrusion into faith invariably results in the resymbolization of God, Christ, and salvation. God may still be confessed as Father, Son, and Holy Spirit, but new symbols loom more significant: Divine Providence, the ground of being, the Primordial Matrix, the Creative Process, the power of the future, the all-determining reality, the Unconditioned, and so on.

Ideology is as evident in traditional orthodoxy as in liberalism. We need to give serious consideration to the complaint of feminists that patriarchal ideology has colored the traditional conceptions of God, Christ, the church, and male-female relationships. The medieval theologians' contention that woman was created primarily for procreation and not for spiritual and intellectual companionship evinces a shift away from the biblical vision to an ideological perspective that teaches male supremacy. Behind this ideological bias is the biblical-classical synthesis in which Hellenistic ideas were incorporated into the Christian life- and world-view without sufficient discrimination.

The impact of the ideology of classical liberalism upon current expressions of orthodoxy, both Catholic and Protestant, is also indisputable. When Christians, who ostensibly believe in salvation by grace alone, try to give divine sanction to such ideas in the political and economic realm as "God helps those who help themselves" and "prosperity is the reward for diligence," an ideological bias is at work. The incongruity between classical Christian orthodoxy and ideological liberalism is especially noticeable in this interpretation of Adam Smith: "Although we should never love ourselves at the expense of others, for this would be unjust, we should nonetheless realize that love of our neighbor will not improve us nearly as much as loving ourselves and our dignity."[45] Even though the classical liberals generally considered themselves Christian, they nonetheless were accustomed to refer to God not by the anthropomorphisms of biblical faith but by such superlatives as "Author of Nature," "Director of Nature," "Conductor of the Universe," "all-wise Architect," and "Parent of the Human Race."

An ideological thrust is also apparent in what Karl Barth calls "Neo-Protestantism," that movement within Protestant theology bent on forging a synthesis between traditional faith and the ideals of the Enlightenment. Theologians commonly associated with this endeavor include Schleiermacher, Ritschl, Bushnell, Harnack, Herrmann, and Troeltsch.

The ideological complexion of Schleiermacher's thought is often overlooked by both his friends and critics. Yet it can be shown that Schleiermacher presented a sacred canopy for the newly arising Prussian bourgeoisie.[46] By identifying Christianity with the movement of civilization and by viewing the fulfillment of citizenship as an activity in the kingdom of God, he gave religious sanction to the cultural values and aspirations of those who claimed to be "enlightened." His concerns sometimes acquired a truly prophetic dimension, especially when he labored for social welfare as a right, not a charity, and for shortening the hours of work. At the same time, he applauded the virtue of political order in the form of the state. Toward the end of his life he exulted:

Since the peace of Tilsit we have made tremendous progress, without revolution, without houses of parliament, even without freedom of the press. But always the people with the king, and the king with the people. Wouldn't one be out of one's mind to think that we would make more progress with a revolution? For my part, I'm very sure always to be on the side of the king when I'm on the side of the intellectual leaders of the nation.[47]

I think it would be fair to Schleiermacher to say that while he favored social amelioration, his message contained nothing socially revolutionary. After careful study, Frederick Herzog concludes that Schleiermacher "was explicating the human being and experience of the rising Prussian bourgeoisie. The liberal theologian thus usually defines as religiously possible what is possible for the bourgeois human being and experience." "If we copy his approach," Herzog asks, "will we not inevitably have to be loyal to the same class?"[48]

The ideological character of Protestant liberal thought is even more pronounced in Ernst Troeltsch. Troeltsch perceived the inseparability of religion and culture, recognizing that religion will reflect cultural motifs and values even though in its origin it transcends them. This situation did not distress him: "Religion becomes a power in ordinary life only by taking up civilisation into itself and giving it a special direction. But it always itself remains distinct from this civilisation; it is always more a formative than a creative force."[49] No religion can be understood apart from its historical and cultural matrix. Every religion is acted upon and shaped by historical and cultural forces that thereby relativize as well as contextualize it. Religious ideas are powerless until they are objectified in social institutions; but once they assume cultural forms, they become culturally conditioned.

According to Troeltsch, we can affirm the validity of Christianity for those who live in European civilization, but we must allow for the fact "that other racial groups, living under entirely different cultural conditions, may experience their contact with the Divine Life in quite a different way."[50] He saw the development of religion as rooted in race more than in class: "The great religions might indeed be described as crystallizations of the thought of great races, as these races are themselves crystallizations of the various biological and anthropological forms."[51] Troeltsch was willing to aver that Christianity "stands or falls with European civilization."[52] No wonder that he came to understand the mission of the church in terms of "the promulgation of the world of religious ideas of Europe and America in intimate association with the extension of the European sphere of influence."[53]

To Ernst Troeltsch, perhaps more than any other theologian, we owe the discovery of the historical and cultural character of religious ideas and institutions. Ideas can be rightly evaluated only in the light of their place in history (*Sitz im Leben*). Troeltsch is the theologian of historicism, but in celebrating the contingency and individuality of religious ideas he was unable to combat successfully the ideological subversion of these ideas. As a zealous patriot during the First World War, he exulted in the German military machine: "The army is flesh from our flesh and spirit from our spirit; our salvation lies in its hands."[54] After the war he maintained an ambivalent attitude toward the Jewish minority in Germany in face of a rising rightist movement that promoted anti-Semitism. Despite the need to rebuild Germany's national culture, Jews, he said, could never be authentic spiritual leaders in this enterprise but only "zealous commentators and clever transcribers of German leadership."[55] Troeltsch's theology reflects the loss of nerve of the German bourgeoisie concerning the universality and normativeness of its religious and ethical heritage.[56]

Probably the most outstanding example of ideological infiltration into the Christian faith is to be found in the story of the German Christians, that group within the German Protestant church in the late twenties and thirties that sought an accommodation of the faith to National Socialism.[57] Barth regarded the German Christian movement as the sorry culmination of culture Protestantism begun by Schleiermacher in the early nineteenth century. In order to show their support for the National Socialist revolution, the German Christians reconceived the gospel as a divine call to create a new social order unfettered by the constrictive taboos of the past. Discipleship was interpreted in terms of manly heroism. In the more radical circles, God was envisioned as the Soul of the Germanic race, the Creative Spirit within the nation or *Volk*. According to the German Christian Gerhard Kittel, the proclamation of the gospel is always codetermined by the historical moment in which the church and nation find themselves.[58] Karl Barth attacked the German Christians for appealing to a second source of revelation besides Holy Scripture, namely, the political and cultural ethos.

The German Christian movement gradually joined forces with the racial mysticism of the new pagan religions in Germany, but many moderates would not go this far. Hermann Rauschning declared: "There was no necessity for the 'German Christian' movement to end in neo-paganism or an empty pantheism. . . . The Christian message could and should be associated with the elements of nationalism and socialism."[59] The question remains: Can the gospel ever be used to support nationalistic or socialistic aspirations without ceasing to be the gospel of our Lord Jesus Christ that stands in judgment over all cultural ideology?

In our nation, ideological coloration is conspicuous in the positive-thinking movement, which holds that people can improve their station in life by tapping into the pool of unlimited power or the realm of unbounded possibility. The key to mastery over nature is an alteration

in attitudes. Because mind is the basic reality in the universe, our political and economic fortunes are tied to the kind of perspective we
have toward life and the world. This movement has its spiritual roots
in Transcendentalism and is part of the neo-Transcendentalist or New
Thought constellation. One critic complains that the Transcendentalists
(Emerson, Alcott, Thoreau) privatized virtue by making private character rather than the public good the chief concern of the American
people.[60]

Its uncritical acceptance of health, wealth, and prosperity as legitimate moral and spiritual goals has made the positive-thinking movement on the whole impervious to the suffering and dereliction of the
underclasses of society as well as to the plight of the Third World peoples. A new attitude toward wealth, not a redistribution of wealth, is
regarded as the cure for poverty. Economic poverty is said to have its
basis in a poverty of mind or spirit, and until the latter is remedied
nothing can be done for the former. The class character of this movement is incontrovertible. It is no surprise that it draws its main support
from the affluent classes in society. Here we see how religion becomes
a cloak for hiding from the harsh realities of the world, a subtle means
of eschewing social responsibility to those in material need.

Process theology, another powerful influence on the American
scene, also has an ideological cast. By viewing God as a creative agency
in the universe or even as the universe in its creative dimension rather
than Almighty Lord and Creator, the process movement reconceives
God in terms of the democratic experience. The hierarchical dualism
between God and humanity is overcome as God becomes a fellow suf-
ferer who needs our help just as we need his. Together we seek to
create a new world where rational persuasion will triumph over the
use of force. The key to meaningful existence is no longer supernatural
conversion but "creative interchange." Process theologian Charles
Hartshorne regards the appeal to an infallible divine revelation as anti-
democratic because it anachronistically calls for submission to an external authority instead of finding truth through dialogue and consensus.[61] The salient values of liberal democracy—freedom, autonomy,
relativity, and pluralism—are all championed by process theologians.

Feminist theology, too, has an unmistakable ideological slant.[62] It is
patently tied to the women's revolution in society, which insists on
equal pay for equivalent work and presses for the liberation of women
from male domination. God becomes the Empowering Matrix (Rosemary Ruether) that enables both men and women to realize their full

potential as sons and daughters of a new age in which sexual differences are no longer a barrier to economic and political advancement as well as to spiritual leadership. The immanentalistic bent of feminist theology is tied to its reconception of God as the vital force within nature rather than as Sovereign King or Lord.[63] Feminist theology converges with process theology at many points, for both mirror the new wave of democratic egalitarianism that seeks to eradicate all hierarchy in human relationships.

Liberation theology, which is the parent movement of feminist theology, is unashamedly ideological in character. It identifies with the social needs and aspirations of the disinherited and disenfranchised of society on the grounds that God has a preference for the poor. The "poor" in the Beatitudes are equated with the economically or materially deprived rather than those who are poor in a spiritual sense. Capitalism and colonialism are exposed as the main enemies, and the hope of society is said to lie in a kingdom of freedom that will be introduced only through the travail of a social revolution. Conversion is reinterpreted as raising one's consciousness to the sufferings and plight of the poor.

Among the new metaphors for God in liberation theology are "the power of the future," "the ever open horizon leading to creativity and historical initiative," "the courage to struggle," "the event of self-liberating love," and "the dynamic of history." The only true God is the God of the disinherited, a God who consigns the rich and powerful to damnation. The privileged classes bow down before wealth, power, and comfort, the gods that sanctify imperial ambition and the exploitation of the poor. One liberationist avows: "There can be no true faith if these false gods are not destroyed. This is the central problem: in order to believe in God we must first disbelieve in the gods that we have contrived; we must begin by being atheists."[64]

Although it purports to speak for the poor, liberation theology can actually be shown to appeal to the sons and daughters of the middle and upper-middle classes who have become disillusioned with the pressures for upward mobility and the unadulterated worship of mammon that characterize these circles.[65] Not a few of these people identify vicariously with the poor without themselves making significant financial sacrifices. In fact, some unwittingly profit from the misery of the poor, which provides an agenda for teachers in state universities and seminaries and also accounts for the livelihood of those who administer welfare aid subsidized by the government. This is not to deny that an increasing number of sensitive souls, particularly in Third World countries, have identified with the poor to the extent of giving up their possessions and living as one of them.

Several decades ago, H. Richard Niebuhr shared some prophetic insights on the ideological temptations that would confront the church: "Looking to the future, the danger of the church lies more in a readiness to adjust itself to new classes, races, or national civilizations than in refusal to accept them. This moment of crisis, between a worldliness that is passing and a worldliness that is coming, is the moment of the church's opportunity to turn away from its temporal toward its eternal relations and so to become fit again for its work in time."[66]

Finally, we need to look at the new religious right as still another flagrant example of ideological subversion in the church. The new religious right, which is well represented in the electronic church, gains a large measure of its support because of its appeal to the national and cultural ethos. Its attempted synthesis of the American Way of Life and Christian faith results in a message that lacks the cutting edge of the biblical gospel and waters down the cost of discipleship in a technological society. While exuding commendable loyalty to the traditional family, it bases its defense of traditional familial and economic values on the supposition that people who support such values are more productive citizens. The right to property, which has an eighteenth-century flavor, is given religious sanction. "Ownership of property," says Jerry Falwell, "is biblical. Competition in business is biblical. Ambitious and successful business management is clearly outlined as a part of God's plan for His people."[67] Gary North is confident that *"long-term economic growth is a sign of God's blessing on His people."*[68] Long-term poverty, on the other hand, *"is always a sign of God's curse. The so-*called underdeveloped societies are underdeveloped because they are socialist, demonist, and cursed."[69] Similarly, Rousas Rushdoony declares, "A free economy allows the deserving to get out of the slums, and there has always been an exodus of those with character."[70] Merlin Carothers defends capitalism over communism on the basis of a pragmatic criterion: "As soon as the Communists are in power, they give men burdens ten times greater than they had before. The capitalist says, 'I will give you nothing; but I will show you a way to work whereby you can receive everything you need.' This perhaps is not the quick easy solution, but it is the one that works."[71]

Capitalism as an economic system may present both problems and promise for well-meaning Christians, but it is not in itself inimical to Christian faith. When it takes the form of an ideology, however, it becomes a dire threat to faith. H. Richard Niebuhr's words are still relevant: "Capitalism in its contemporary form is more than a system of ownership and distribution of economic goods. It is a faith and a way of life. It is faith in wealth as the source of all life's blessings and as the savior of man from his deepest misery. It is the doctrine that man's most important activity is the production of economic goods and that all other things are dependent upon this."[72]

The new religious right not only tries to justify unlimited technological growth on the basis of a free market economy but also bestows a quasi-divine sanction on America's founding documents that virtually amounts to a second source of revelation. It believes, moreover, that by providing a strong military defense we are fulfilling a religious duty. The way is thereby prepared for a national security state in which human rights are subordinated to the quest for national honor and security in the face of real or imagined dangers at home and abroad.

Christians in particular should rejoice in the blessing of living in a free country that has protected human liberties in the past. Yet we should not close our eyes to the many violations of human freedoms that mar our national history, particularly against such minorities as blacks and Native Americans.[73] Nor should we delude ourselves that "America is the most unselfish of all nations" (Woodrow Wilson) or that "America is great because America is good" (Dwight D. Eisenhower). National greatness is seldom if ever based on the moral character of its people (for all are sinners before God) but instead on the undeserved blessing of a gracious God (cf. Deut. 8:17; 9:4). America has indubitably been given a special role as a defender of freedom against totalitarianism, but this does not mean that America is a New Israel with a manifest destiny to be a light to all the nations—an imperial nation-church.[74]

Nationalism in America has deep roots in the equation of American cultural and national ideals with the kingdom of God. With the rise of the new right, it is fashionable in academic religious circles to bewail the dangers of this amalgamation. Yet we must not swing to the other extreme of blaming America for all the world's ills or of seeing the principal enemy today as American imperialism. Richard Neuhaus sounds this needed cautionary note:

The trinity of Christianity—America—civilization may have been naive and discredited, but probably no more so than the current bureaucratized obeisance to the trinity of Christianity—third world—revolutionary justice. They may both be instances of backstopping Christian truth by demonstrating its utility to some other end, but at least the first version engaged American Christians "where they live" and resulted in more than memos for a revolution, the noise of prophetic assemblies, and pervasive feelings of failure and guilt.[75]

Toward the Recovery of a Prophetic Church

The church in our time can only become truly prophetic when it awakens to the reality of the ideological temptation. Only when it successfully begins resisting the beguiling promise of ideological support will it be free to speak the Word of God with power and boldness.

Our task today is to deideologize the church's self-understanding of its mission and to demythologize the myths of the secular culture that lie behind the current ideologies. We must take the way of Kierkegaard over Grundtvig, who sought to incorporate elements of Norse mythology into the thought and life of the church of Denmark.[76] We must side with Barth over Emanuel Hirsch, Gerhard Kittel, and other German Christians who appealed to new words from God in nature and history that amounted to a second source of revelation besides Holy Scripture. In our day we must stand firm against both the rightist mythology of manifest destiny, which sanctions American imperial ambition, and the utopian socialist mythology of the classless society as the culmination of historical evolution. We must also resist the centrist mythology of the Third Wave practopia in which the hope of humanity is pinned on the seemingly innocuous but actually deadly alliance of unlimited technological growth with democratic consensus.

There have been various suggestions for overcoming the ideological temptation. Karl Mannheim advocated a more refined sociology of knowledge as the way to rise above ideological thinking.[77] Nietzsche favored a nihilistic stance that would break through the fog of mass opinion to a new morality beyond good and evil.

I concur with Reinhold Niebuhr that the only viable way of combating ideology is to place our faith in a God who infinitely transcends human culture, even though he condescends to our level in a self-disclosure through historical events.[78] For only in moments of faithful recollection and prayerful self-transcendence can we gain a vision of the world that judges rather than confirms ideological self-interest. Not that we can ever be completely successful: our transcendence of ideology can only be partial, since we are not only people of faith but also people who belong to a particular cultural matrix in human history. Even Christians, Niebuhr reminds us, cannot wholly escape the vicious circle of ideological reasoning, and this is why we must be continually self-critical as well as critical of ideological deformation of the culture and the church. We must never be too sure of our own perceptions and interpretations of the truth even while we confess that there is a transcendent or absolute truth that both measures and judges all human claims to finality. Our hope on this earthly pilgrimage is to be known by God rather than to comprehend the mysteries of God (cf. 1 Cor. 8:1–3; Gal. 4:9).

The church can only become independent of the claims and norms of cultural religion when it abandons its pusillanimous acquiescence to the strident demands of Trojan elements in its midst and boldly acknowledges the reality of a God who is not the product of cultural imagination but who contradicts and judges this imagination. H. Richard Niebuhr has put it so well: "The church's declaration of independence can begin only with the self-evident truth that it and all life are dependent upon God, that loyalty to him is the condition of life and that to him belong the kingdom and the power and the glory."[79]

As a first step toward a genuinely prophetic stance, the church must again become profoundly aware of the wide gulf between the kingdom of God and cultural movements of reform and revolution. The bane of the Social Gospel movement was that it virtually identified the cause of social justice with the claims of the kingdom of God, falling into the delusion that the kingdom of God could be ushered in through social legislation and education. Liberation theology perpetuates this deceptive vision, giving it a revolutionary flavor.

I agree with Barth that we can neither build nor inaugurate the kingdom of God but we can bear witness to the kingdom that already exists in the remnant of the faithful in all churches, though it remains hidden and is yet to be revealed to the whole creation. We can seek and pray for the kingdom, but we cannot create it or procure it. How disconcerting for us to realize that despite our vast skills and dynamism, we must leave the coming of the kingdom to the Lord. For the kingdom, says Barth, is "God's own action, which does not merge into the best of human action, for example, that of Christian faith or the Christian church, which does not mingle with it, let lone identify itself with it, which remains free and independent over against it, and which in its purity and freedom is God's gracious, reconciling, and finally redeeming action."[80]

How untidy and inefficient this seems to the streamlined American mind! H. Richard Niebuhr shows that the idea of the kingdom of God underwent a metamorphosis in American religious thought that irretrievably compromised the original Puritan vision. For the Puritans the "kingdom of God was not something to be built or to be established nor something that came into the world from without; it was rather the rule which, having been established from eternity, needed to be obeyed despite the rebellion against it which flourished in the world."[81] In our time, by contrast, Niebuhr contends, "The kingdom of God in America, so regarded, is the American kingdom of God; it is not the individualization of a universal idea, but the universalization of the particular. It represents not so much the impact of the gospel upon the New World as the use and adaptation of the gospel by the new society for its own purposes."[82]

In our quest for the reform of the church, we must go beyond the insights of the Reformation and even of Pietism and Puritanism. Whereas the Reformers rightly discerned that the two practical marks of the church lacking in their time were the preaching of the Word of God and the right administration of the sacraments, the Pietists and Puritans added to these (either explicitly or implicitly) the marks of fellowship *(koinonia)* and mission. Without the fellowship of love and missionary concern for the spiritually lost, we still do not have the church in its fulness. In our time, I believe that the emphasis should be on still another mark of the church—social inclusiveness. In an age when churches are becoming divided on the basis of ideological or class affiliation, we should boldly affirm that the holy catholic church is not yet fulfilled until it constitutes a fellowship that transcends racial, class, and ethnic barriers (cf. Eph. 2:14–16). The false ideology of the church growth movement must be combated. By no stretch of the imagination can cultural and racial homogeneity be conceived as an ideal that belongs to the horizon of biblical faith. Doubtless it makes for a smooth operation, reducing the possibility of church members making waves. But efficiency and comfort do not seem to have been among Jesus' priorities.

The choice today is between a prophetic church and a merely cultural church. The first is anchored in an infallible divine revelation in history; the second appeals to the aspirations and hopes of the culture in which it finds itself. In a cultural church, religion is appreciated for its social utility, for the psychic and cultural benefits it provides, rather than for its truth. In a prophetic church, religion moves us to surrender the illusions and pretensions of the culture and to live only by the promises in Holy Scripture.

It is not only liberal Christianity but evangelical Christianity that has become vulnerable to ideological subversion. Evangelicals today tend to rely on slogans (such as biblical inerrancy and the four spiritual laws) rather than on hard study of the theological and social implications of the gospel.[83] The virtues of the technological society—utility, productivity, and efficiency—are uncritically accepted by most evangelical churches and seminaries. We should heed Nathan Hatch's timely admonition:

By continuing to exploit what they do best, reaching people at large, and continuing to abdicate what they pursue awkwardly, the life of the mind, evangelicals must sooner or later face the specter of Pyrrhic victory. The vitality of evangelical life does little to reverse the pervasive secularization of American thought—a current that undercuts the foundation while evangelicals are admiring the fine job of decorating being done on the third floor.[84]

Hatch appropriately cites Charles Malik's observation at the dedication of the Billy Graham center in Wheaton, Illinois: "If you win the whole world and lose the mind of the world, you will soon discover you have not won the world. Indeed it may turn out that you have actually lost the world."

One serious problem is that when evangelicals do apply themselves to current intellectual issues, they often join liberals in relying on natural theology as a support for or supplement to God's self-revelation in Jesus Christ, thus opening the door to a cultural form of Christianity. We need to discern the hand of God in the times (Matt. 16:3 KJV) as well as the Word of God in Scripture, but it is only in the light of the latter that we can do the former. Once we mute the folly of the gospel by appealing to the wisdom of the culture we are on the way to a compromised Christianity. George Hunsinger underscores the danger of building a theology on natural or cultural norms: "The trajectory of natural theology leads from the Christ who is not supreme to the Christ who is not sufficient and finally to the Christ who is not necessary."[85]

We must not shirk our responsibility to reexamine the integral relation between ideological alliances and natural theology. Indeed we may be entering a confessional situation (*status confessionis*) when the church will have to reaffirm the integrity of the gospel in the face of ideological deformations. The task today is to try to locate the theological error behind the myriad social evils and injustices around us.

Francis Miller paints a dour picture of modern Protestantism: "Having won their liberty from enslavement to the Roman hierarchy, Protestants are now in process of being enslaved by their respective national cultures and it remains to be seen whether their last estate may not be worse than their first."[86] Protestant churches, he says, no longer have a common ground of unity, and because they no longer teach truths equally valid for people everywhere, they "cannot be regarded as reliable witnesses to the Christian faith."[87]

Miller perceives a new national religion emerging out of American culture that is more pervasive than either rightist or leftist ideology. Such a religion "expresses the most characteristic ethical and spiritual aspects of that culture. It is empirical in its approach to religious truth. It sets great store upon human ideals and human values. It is profoundly concerned with the realization of these ideals and values in social relations. It is essentially humanitarian in its outlook on life. It is the champion of personality. And it has a vivid sense of world mission."[88] How alluring some of these phrases sound, and yet how remote they are from the biblical perspective on life and the world!

A prophetic church will find itself at odds with both civil religion and popular cultural religion. It will see through the appeal to traditional values and to the national heritage, for its God cannot be used to promote either a national spiritual revival or an egalitarian cultural ideal realizable by social legislation and education. It will champion a transcendent religion that does not simply shore up human values but gives primacy to the kingdom of God.[89]

Democracy at the Crossroads

As Christians, we should seek not only the prosperity of the church but also the health of the nation. Our concern should be not only the evangelization of the world but also the advancement of justice in the world. Although Christianity is not contingent on the existence of democratic institutions, it is more congruous with representative democracy than with alternative forms of government where power is concentrated in the hands of an elite. Therefore, Christians have a stake in maintaining a viable democracy in our time.

This is not an easy task. Democracy as we know it is not in a robust state at present. Tillich has observed that democracy has "definite historical presuppositions without which it cannot work. It presupposes a large amount of natural harmony and conformity. . . . If the harmonistic foundation of a democratic system disappears, the democracy breaks down."[90] Today, democratic principles are eroding as competing ideologies—totalistic in orientation—struggle to fill a growing spiritual vacuum.

Ideological deformation imperils not only the church but also the nation. When a nation falls under the sway of an ideology, which brooks no opposition and relies on propaganda to achieve its ends, the people will surely suffer. A nation that succumbs to the ideological spell is bound to become disrespectful of minorities (both racial and religious). It is also liable to become idolatrous, trusting in its own ideals and achievements.

America, G. K. Chesterton observed, is "a nation with the soul of a church." It is a nation shaped by religiously based values, and it is these values, strongly adhered to by the fathers of our country, that have given our people a sense of cohesion and direction. Now because of the inroads of secular humanism and nihilism, this moral consensus is breaking down, and we are left with what Richard Neuhaus calls a "naked public square."

The values that have constituted the sacred canopy for American culture are for the most part derived from both the Enlightenment and the Reformation, but the former is dominant. Sidney Mead speaks of America's two religions: the religion of the Republic and the religion of the denomination.[91] Whereas the first tends to be inclusive and humanitarian, the second is divisive and sectarian. Mead contends that we need a renewal of the civil religion of the founding fathers if America is to survive as a viable democratic state.

Richard Neuhaus also calls for the restoration of a sacred canopy that can give moral legitimacy to the American enterprise.[92] His vision converges at various points with Mead's, though the two men come out of quite different denominational backgrounds and represent basically different theological thrusts.[93]

While I also see national purpose linked to a religio-cultural matrix, I am uncomfortable with assessing religion in terms of its cultural utility, its capability of stabilizing and revitalizing culture. Neuhaus, too, objects to this kind of utilitarianism, but the way he develops his thesis sometimes gives the impression that this is precisely what he favors. I contend, moreover, that in forging an alliance between religion and culture, we may end in giving dubious moral sanction to national policies that may openly conflict with the imperatives of the gospel. We dare not forget that the Word of God cannot be used to buttress national aspirations, that it always stands in judgment over a religio-cultural ethos as well as national policy. Neuhaus speaks favorably of the Constantinian synthesis in which church and state were reconciled under the Emperor Constantine. Yet such a synthesis may well contain the seeds of dissolution of religious particularity and of a genuinely prophetic witness on the part of the church. It may well be the first step toward the transmutation of Christianity into a culture religion. Neuhaus argues for "a symbiosis between the nation with the soul of a church and the church with the soul of a nation."[94] The danger is that a symbiosis of this kind may make the church socially respectable and the nation morally invulnerable to criticism.

A democracy needs a moral and metaphysical basis, but only one that is culturally and religiously transcendent. The Word of God can neither be identified with the principles or values that inform and legitimate a nation nor be equated with a particular political program or policy. Some form of civil religion is inevitable in a nation such as ours, but this kind of religion must never be confused with Christianity.

What makes democracy especially attractive to evangelical Christians is that it is a form of government that allows the church freedom to proclaim the Word of God. If church and state become too tightly interwoven, the state may try to dictate to the church what its proclamation should be. On the other hand, if they remain too far apart, the association may unravel, with the state dismissing the church as an institution pertaining only to the individual or private area of life.

I have noted that democracy in its American form has two principal sources: the Enlightenment on the one hand and Puritanism and religious nonconformism on the other. This accounts for the tensions within our democracy as well as for its ambivalence toward religion. The Enlightenment grounds democracy in natural rights (in the Stoic tradition), whereas Puritanism sees the source of democracy in the freedom of the people of God.[95] The Enlightenment tends to be both elitist and egalitarian, holding that only an enlightened few can ensure equality for all. Puritanism, on the other hand, is suspicious of both radical egalitarianism and elitism. It questions the first because of the tendency to blur the lines between God and humanity, divine revelation and human opinion. It opposes the second because it believes that all people remain sinners before God, whatever their efforts at education and enlightenment. The only safeguard that is relatively dependable is a system of checks and balances by which one group or person is prevented from amassing absolute power.[96] This is why Puritanism and religious nonconformism supported representative democracy, which provided for representatives of the people freely chosen and continuing in office only for a time. Whereas a major strand within the Enlightenment was prone to perceive the voice of the people as sovereign, the Reformation and Puritanism upheld only the living God as sovereign, and consequently could never place absolute trust in the people or nation.

Today, two types of democracy are struggling for supremacy. The first is a mass egalitarian democracy, collectivist in orientation, locating the source of all sovereignty in the nation-state.[97] The second is a representative or republican democracy, inimical to centralized power and favoring a government under the revealed law of God. In the latter, while government relies on the consent of the governed, moral law does not so derive, and this is why government is *under* this higher law rather than its source.[98]

With the dissipation of the doctrine of original sin and the erosion of the sense of a divine ruler over the nations, there has been an upsurge in sentiment for radical egalitarian or participatory democracy in which democratic consensus is seen as the measure of moral and religious truth. A democracy that does not have to give an account to a higher law or power is likely to construct God in its own image and to sanction only that kind of morality conducive to social cohesion and stability. The general will of the collectivity replaces the sovereign will of God as the overarching criterion for national life. Those ideologies that sanctify and crown cultural achievement will be rewarded, whereas voices that call into question cultural norms and goals will either be ignored or silenced.

Such a scenario is more than a lugubrious variant of the Orwellian theme. It stems from a grim recognition of the ominous signs around us. We live today in a climate of rising nationalism and ethnocentrism. The myth of manifest destiny united with a fixation on technological growth is preparing the way for a new authoritarianism that seeks to use public opinion to sanctify cultural and national goals. In this climate pluralism no longer means tolerance for a wide variety of opinion but intolerance of any particularist claim to truth that calls into question the reliability of the democratic consensus or the sovereignty of the general will.[99]

Democracy can only be a Christian option when it is acutely aware of the limitations of human power and authority and when it is motivated by a vision that transcends as well as negates human culture. If it falls under the spell of either radical egalitarian ideologies or nationalistic mythologies, it drifts from its metaphysical moorings and may well sink under the pressure of an emerging totalitarian ethos.

In this perilous time, one commentator warns:

The myth of manifest destiny, when joined to the myth of scientific progress, endangers the spiritual and physical health of individuals and societies. Bluntly put, we must stop thinking of ourselves as God's chosen people and think more about our opportunities and obligations among the community of nations. We are not an innocent and inspired people; like all the earth's folk, we are tired and treacherous but also capable of the sublime and sensitive. Only when we grasp the chastisement of divine justice and the guidance of divine will on our work can we hope to participate in redemptive purpose.[100]

Behind the moral crisis of our civilization is a spiritual malaise associated with both the loss of faith in a transcendent, living God, Creator and Judge of the world, and the emergence of ideologies or political salvations that strive to fill the growing metaphysical vacuum. When God is dethroned, he will most certainly be replaced by constructs of an idolatrous human imagination.

Democracy can endure and flourish only when it is united with what Tillich calls "the Protestant principle," the protest against absolutizing the finite.[101] The best hope of democracy lies in a church that is free to make this kind of prophetic protest, for in this way we are kept from both national and religious idolatry. Democracy is not a panacea for human ills but merely a palliative that allows us to mitigate some of them. It is not the kingdom of God on earth, as some liberal clergy would have us believe, but a tentative experiment in human relations that points beyond itself to the God who is ruler and Lord of all peoples.[102]

Democracy is made possible because God's kingdom limits all human power. Democracy is necessary because human power is inevitably corrupted by sin and therefore needs to be curbed and regulated.[103] Democracy is most vital when the ideologies and mythologies that it permits to flourish are debunked and exposed by men and women whose faith is not in a this-worldly utopia but in a kingdom not of this world that relativizes all human endeavor and achievement.

The hope of both church and nation rests in a genuinely religious revival—not one that blesses and sanctifies national or imperial ambition—but one that directs us to a God who stands over and against both culture and religion. To be authentically evangelical, this revival must call both our leaders and our people to national repentance, to a grace-given willingness to subject all our agendas, petty and grandiose alike, to the searing scrutiny of the Word of God.[104] There is no other way that the will of God can be discerned anew for our time. In no other way can we know the joy of witnessing the breaking in of the new reality of the kingdom, which God grants in this life to all those who believe and obey.

Notes

1. Against the peaceniks, Christians who seek to be instructed primarily by the wisdom that comes from God would not dispute the horrendous evil that nuclear

THE IDEOLOGICAL TEMPTATION

weapons portend, but they would question the reliance on a strategy of love to avert war. Nor would they reject out of hand the arguments of the "realists" that peace has been maintained through a strong defense in the past, but they would insist that nuclear weapons are not commensurable with traditional weaponry and that this creates a different ethical situation.

2. For the history of the concept of ideology, see Hans Barth, *Truth and Ideology*, trans. Frederic Lilge (Berkeley and Los Angeles: University of California Press, 1961).

3. Paul Tillich aptly describes ideology as "concealment." At the same time, he reminds us that an ideology does not represent conscious falsification, for "if this were the case, ideologies would not be very dangerous. But they are dangerous precisely because they are unconscious and are therefore objects of belief and fanaticism." *The Protestant Era*, trans. James Luther Adams (Chicago: University of Chicago Press, 1948), pp. 169–70.

4. When Kenneth Minogue in *Alien Powers: The Pure Theory of Ideology* (New York: St. Martin's, 1985) avers that all ideologies are forms of revolutionary praxis, I must disagree. There can be ideologies that seek to shore up existing institutions as well as those that try to overthrow them. If we define an ideology as an explanation of social-empirical reality that serves to reinforce certain vested interests in society, we can see how this can apply to the right as well as to the left. Even ideologies on the right are intent on remolding society—but in the light of the conservative agenda.

5. Hans Küng, *Does God Exist?* trans. Edward Quinn (New York: Doubleday, 1980), p. 124.

6. Peter L. Berger and Hansfried Kellner, *Sociology Reinterpreted* (New York: Doubleday Anchor Books, 1981), p. 144.

7. See Niebuhr, *Christian Realism and Political Problems*, pp. 75–94; and idem, *The Nature and Destiny of Man*, 2 vols. (New York: Charles Scribner's Sons, 1951), 1: pp. 194–97.

8. Niebuhr has aptly described ideology as "a compound of ignorance and dishonesty." *Faith and History* (New York: Charles Scribner's Sons, 1949), p. 161.

9. Juan Luis Segundo, *Faith and Ideologies*, trans. John Drury (Maryknoll, N.Y.: Orbis Books, 1984).

10. Elisabeth Schüssler-Fiorenza, "Feminist Theology as a Critical Theology of Liberation," in *Woman: New Dimensions*, ed. Walter J. Burghardt (New York: Paulist Press, 1977), p. 40.

11. Cf. Ellul: "Faith is a terribly caustic substance, a burning acid. It puts to the test every element of my life and society; it spares nothing. It leads me ineluctably to question all my certitudes, all my moralities, beliefs, and policies. It forbids me to attach ultimate significance to any expression of human activity." *Living Faith*, p. 111.

Faith questions even its own presuppositions and assumptions, but only in order to clarify and reclaim them. The truth of faith can be maintained only through an unceasing struggle to lay hold of this truth.

12. Elizabeth Dodson Gray, *Patriarchy as a Conceptual Trap* (Wellesley, Mass.: Roundtable, 1982), p. 72. See also Peter L. Berger, *The Sacred Canopy* (New York: Doubleday, 1967).

13. Kim Il Sung, leader of the People's Democratic Republic of Korea, has averred: "The homeland is a veritable mother for everyone. We cannot live or be happy outside of our homeland. Only the flourishing and prosperity of our homeland will permit us to go down the path to happiness. The best sons and daughters of our people, all without exception, were first of all ardent patriots. It was to recover their homeland that Korean Communists struggled, before the Liberation, against Japanese imperialism despite every difficulty and obstacle." Quoted in Nicholas Wolterstorff, *Until Justice and Peace Embrace* (Grand Rapids: Eerdmans, 1983), p. 120. Wolterstorff comments that communist states are not expected to depend on appeals to national loyalty.

14. Cf. Adam Smith, *Wealth of Nations;* (reprint, New York: Penguin Books, 1983); Herbert Spencer, *Social Statics* (1851 reprint, New York: Kelley, 1969); idem, *The Man Versus the State* (Indianapolis: Liberty Classics, 1982); Ludwig von Mises, *Liberalism in the Classical Tradition* (Irvington-on-Hudson, N.Y.: Foundation for Economic Education; San Francisco: Cobden Press, 1985); George Gilder, *Wealth and Poverty* (New York: Basic Books, 1981); Alexander H. Shand, *The Capitalist Alternative* (New York: New York University Press, 1984); Russell Kirk, *The Conservative Mind* (New York: Avon, 1973); William F. Buckley, Jr., *Up From Liberalism* (New York: Stein & Day, 1985); Jeffrey Hart, *The American Dissent: A Decade of Modern Conservatism* (New York: Doubleday, 1966); Irving Kristol, *Two Cheers for Capitalism* (New York: Basic Books, 1978); idem, *Reflections of a Neoconservative* (New York: Basic Books, 1983); Harry V. Jaffa, *American Conservatism and the American Founding* (Durham, N.C.: Carolina Academic Books, 1984); Guy Sorman, *The Conservative Revolution in America* (Chicago: Regnery, 1985); and Robert Nisbet, *Conservatism: Dream and Reality* (Minneapolis: University of Minnesota Press, 1986).

15. Conservative economic theory is given Christian sanction by theologians Harold Lindsell in his *Free Enterprise: Judeo-Christian Defense* (Wheaton, Ill.: Tyndale House, 1982); John Jefferson Davis in his *Your Wealth in God's World* (Phillipsburg, N.J.: Presbyterian & Reformed, 1984); and Ronald H. Nash in his *Social Justice and the Christian Church* (Milford, Mich.: Mott Media, 1983). See also Gary North, *An Introduction to Christian Economics* (Nutley, N.J.: Craig Press, 1973); idem, *Unconditional Surrender: God's Program for Victory* (Tyler, Tex.: Geneva, 1981); and Franky Schaeffer, ed., *Is Capitalism Christian?* (Westchester, Ill.: Crossway Books, 1985).

16. Quoted in Diggins, *Lost Soul of American Politics,* p. 201.

17. Kristol, *Reflections of a Neoconservative,* p. 165.

18. Stackhouse, *Creeds, Society and Human Rights,* p. 115.

19. Barry Goldwater, William Safire, and the Libertarians, all of whom champion individual liberty, find themselves at odds with groups like Moral Majority, which seek to bring Judeo-Christian values to bear on personal and family life.

20. Niebuhr, *Christian Realism and Political Problems,* p. 97. For the influence of the Physiocrats on modern capitalism see Henry Higgs, *The Physiocrats* (New York: Langland, 1952).

21. For books that defend welfare liberalism see Tom Hayden, *The American Future,* rev. ed. (New York: Washington Square, 1982); John Rawls, *A Theory of Justice* (Cambridge, Mass.: Harvard University Press, 1971); John Kenneth Galbraith, *American Capitalism* (Boston: Houghton Mifflin Co., 1956); idem, *The Affluent Society* (Boston: Houghton Mifflin Co., 1954); idem, *The New Industrial State* (Boston: Houghton Mifflin Co., 1963); and idem, *Economics and the Public Purpose* (Boston: Houghton Mifflin Co., 1973). Welfare liberalism is anticipated in the writings of Thomas Paine and John Stuart Mill. See Jacob Oser, *The Evolution of Economic Thought* (New York: Harcourt, Brace & World, 1963). Mill is also appreciated by conservatives, for example, Michael Novak, *Freedom with Justice* (San Francisco: Harper & Row, 1984), pp. 81–107.

22. Neuhaus, *Naked Public Square,* p. 239.

23. Ibid.

24. See Harry W. Laidler, *History of Socialism* (New York: Thomas Y. Crowell Co., 1968); Leslie Derfler, *Socialism Since Marx* (New York: St. Martin's, 1973); and Albert S. Lindeman, *A History of European Socialism 1918–1933* (New Haven: Yale University Press, 1983).

25. See especially J. Ramsay MacDonald, *The Socialist Movement* (New York: Henry Holt & Co., 1911); and Michael Harrington, *Socialism* (New York: Saturday Review Press, 1970).

26. See Paul Tillich, *The Socialist Decision,* trans. Franklin Sherman (New York: Harper & Row, 1977); and John R. Stumme, *Socialism in Theological Perspective: A Study of Paul Tillich 1918–1933* (Missoula, Mont.: Scholars, 1978). Tillich's early ideological commitment to socialism is reflected in this statement: "Only socialism can make

certain that the unlimited possibilities for technical domination of the world that have been created in the bourgeois period will remain under human control and will be employed for the service of humanity." *Socialist Decision*, p. 161.

On Barth's attitude towards socialism see Friedrich-Wilhelm Marquardt, *Theologie und Sozialismus* (Munich: Chr. Kaiser Verlag, 1972); George Hunsinger, *Karl Barth and Radical Politics* (Philadelphia: Westminster, 1976); and Eberhard Jüngel, *Karl Barth, a Theological Legacy*, Trans. Garrett E. Paul (Philadelphia: Westminster Press, 1986), pp. 82–104. In my judgment, Barth, in contrast to Tillich, was never an ideological socialist.

27. For representative books on feminist ideology see Betty Friedan, *The Feminine Mystique* (New York: McGraw-Hill, 1971); idem, *The Second Stage* (New York: Summit Books, 1981); Germaine Greer, *Sex and Destiny* (New York: Harper & Row, 1984); Carolyn G. Heilbrun, *Toward a Recognition of Androgyny* (New York: Alfred A. Knopf, 1973); Simone de Beauvoir, *The Second Sex*, trans. and ed. H. M. Parshley (New York: Bantam Books, 1970); Mary Daly, *Beyond God the Father* (Boston: Beacon, 1973); Rosemary Radford Ruether, *Sexism and God-Talk* (Boston: Beacon, 1983); Elisabeth Schüssler-Fiorenza, *In Memory of Her* (New York: Crossroad, 1983); and Marilyn French, *Beyond Power: On Women, Men and Morals* (New York: Summit Books, 1985).

28. For seminal books on the conflict between patriarchalism and feminism, see Kate Millett, *Sexual Politics* (New York: Doubleday, 1969); and George Gilder, *Sexual Suicide* (New York: Bantam Books, 1975). Whereas the first critiques patriarchalism, the second generally defends the traditional cultural ethos. It is important in this discussion to distinguish between *patriarchy* and *patriarchalism*. The first term refers to a mode of human relationship, whereas the second signifies an ideology that legitimizes this relationship.

Other pertinent books are Steven Goldberg, *The Inevitability of Patriarchy* (New York: William Morrow & Co., 1974); Harriet Holter, ed., *Patriarchy in a Welfare Society* (New York: Columbia University Press, 1984); Rosalind Coward, *Patriarchal Precedents* (London: Routledge and Kegan Paul, 1983); Daniel Amneus, *Back to Patriarchy* (New Rochelle, N.Y.: Arlington House, 1979); Elizabeth Dodson Gray, *Patriarchy as a Conceptual Trap*; and Gerda Lerner, *The Creation of Patriarchy* (New York: Oxford University Press, 1986).

29. Rosemary Radford Ruether, *Sexism and God-Talk*, p. 79. See also Aristotle, *Politics*, bk. 1, chap. 5.

30. See Ernst Troeltsch, *The Social Teaching of the Christian Churches*, 3d impression, trans. Olive Wyon (New York: Macmillan Co., 1950), 1: pp. 287–88. See also Kari Elisabeth Borresen, *Subordination and Equivalence: The Nature and Role of Women in Augustine and Thomas Aquinas* (Lanham, Md.: University Press of America, 1981).

31. See Robert M. Kingdon, "The Reformation and the Family," *On the Way* 2, no. 2 (Winter 1984): pp. 12–25; Steven Ozment, *When Fathers Ruled: Family Life in Reformation Europe* (Cambridge: Harvard University Press, 1983); and Jean-Louis Flandrin, *Families in Former Times: Kinship, Household, and Sexuality in Early Modern Europe* (New York: Cambridge University Press, 1979).

32. For Calvin, by contrast, the fundamental sin is unbelief; pride and sloth are manifestations of this deeper sin.

33. This is not to deny that there are genuine theological and biblical reasons for favoring the right-to-life position.

34. See Salo Baron, *Modern Nationalism and Religion* (New York: Harper, 1947); Edward Shillito, *Nationalism: Man's Other Religion* (Chicago: Willett, Clark & Co., 1933); Eric Voegelin, *Die Politischen Religionen* (Stockholm: Bermann-Fischer Verlag, 1939); Trygve R. Tholfsen, *Ideology and Revolution in Modern Europe* (New York: Columbia University Press, 1984), pp. 105–31; A. James Gregor, *The Ideology of Fascism* (New York: Free Press, 1969); Stanley G. Payne, *Fascism: Comparison and Definition* (Madison: University of Wisconsin Press, 1980); Ernst Nolte, *Three Faces of Fascism*, trans. Leila Vennewitz (New York: Holt, Rinehart & Winston, 1966); and John Weiss, *The Fascist Tradition* (New York: Harper & Row, 1967).

282   FREEDOM FOR OBEDIENCE

35. On the new style of fascism that might prosper in America, see Bertram Gross, *Friendly Fascism: The New Face of Power in America* (New York: M. Evans & Co., 1980).
36. In an address in Ciudad Guayana, Venezuela. *Des Moines Register,* Jan. 30, 1985.
37. See Robert Brank Fulton, *Adam Smith Speaks to Our Times* (Boston: Christopher Publishing House, 1963).
38. See Robert C. Tucker, *Philosophy and Myth in Karl Marx* (Cambridge: Cambridge University Press, 1961); Sergei Bulgakov, *Karl Marx as a Religious Type* (Belmont, Mass.: Nordland Publishing Co., 1979); Leonard P. Wessell, Jr., *Prometheus Bound: The Mythic Structure of Karl Marx's Scientific Thinking* (Baton Rouge: Louisiana State University Press, 1984); and Karl Marx, *Capital, The Communist Manifesto and Other Writings of Karl Marx,* ed. Max Eastman (New York: Modern Library, 1932).
39. See Houston Stewart Chamberlain, *The Foundations of the Nineteenth Century* (New York: John Lane, 1911); Alfred Rosenberg, *Der Mythus des 20. Jahrhunderts* (Munich: Hoheneichen-Verlag, 1934); idem, *Race and Race History and Other Essays,* ed. Robert Pois (New York: Harper & Row, 1971); Adolf Hitler, *Mein Kampf* (New York: Reynal & Hitchcock, 1939); Albert Richard Chandler, *Rosenberg's Nazi Myth* (Ithaca, N.Y.: Cornell University Press, 1945); Hermann Rauschning, *The Conservative Revolution* (New York: G. P. Putnam's Sons, 1941); and Rohan D'O Butler, *The Roots of National Socialism* (New York: E. P. Dutton & Co., 1942).
40. See Alvin Toffler, *The Third Wave* (New York: Bantam Books, 1981). Other significant works heralding a humanized technopolis in which the mastery of nature rests on the mastery of mind include Alvin Toffler, *Future Shock* (New York: Random House, 1970); Jean-François Revel, *Without Marx or Jesus,* trans. J. F. Bernard (New York: Doubleday, 1971); John Naisbitt, *Megatrends* (New York: Warner Books, 1982); John Naisbitt and Patricia Aburdene, *Reinventing the Corporation* (New York: Warner Books, 1985); Marilyn Ferguson, *The Aquarian Conspiracy* (Los Angeles: J. P. Tarcher, Inc., 1980); Theodore Roszak, *Person/Planet: The Creative Disintegration of Industrial Society* (New York: Doubleday, 1978); and idem, *Unfinished Animal: The Aquarian Frontier and the Evolution of Consciousness* (New York: Harper & Row, 1975). All these authors are egalitarian, iconoclastic, optimistic, and futuristic. They celebrate what is called the new American revolution, a transformation in consciousness which is destined to change the world. Marilyn Ferguson describes the Aquarian conspiracy as neither leftist nor rightist but as "a kind of Radical Center" (*Aquarian Conspiracy,* p. 228). The ideological character of this "conspiracy" is reflected in this remark of John Vasconcellos: "We need to see to it that our institutions, including government, become peopled by those who share our struggle, our vision about this human transformation" (*Aquarian Conspiracy,* p. 234).
41. Cf. Toffler: "The responsibility for change . . . lies with us. We must begin with ourselves, teaching ourselves not to close our minds prematurely to the novel, the surprising, the seemingly radical" (*Third Wave,* p. 443). At the same time, he can say: "We live in the final, irretrievable crisis of industrialism. And as the industrial age passes into history, a new age is born" (ibid., p. 115).
42. See Stackhouse, *Creeds, Society, and Human Rights.* Other Indian religions that strongly adhere to karma and reincarnation are Sikhism, Jainism, and Buddhism.
43. Niebuhr, *Christian Realism and Political Problems,* p. 98.
44. H. Richard Niebuhr, *The Social Sources of Denominationalism* (New York: H. Holt & Co., 1929).
45. Daniel A. Dombrowski, "Adam Smith's *The Theory of Moral Sentiments* and Christianity," *American Benedictine Review* 35, no. 4 (Dec. 1984): p. 429.
46. For an in-depth treatment of the ideological and mythological character of Schleiermacher's thought, see Yorick Spiegel, *Theologie der bürgerlichen Gesellschaft: Sozialphilosophie und Glaubenslehre bei Friedrich Schleiermacher* (Munich: Kaiser Verlag, 1968). Spiegel maintains that the myth of the inevitability of the hidden hand and the model of exchange and reciprocal action played a determinative role in Schleiermacher's theologizing. See also Dieter Schellong, *Bürgertum und christliche Religion: Anpassungsprobleme der Theologie seit Schleiermacher* (Munich: Kaiser Verlag, 1975). For

an able, though not altogether convincing, defense of Schleiermacher against the charge of cultural accommodation, see Richard Crouter, "Schleiermacher and the Theology of Bourgeois Society: A Critique of the Critics," *The Journal of Religion* 66, no. 3 (July 1986), pp. 302–323.

47. Quoted in Frederick Herzog, "Birth Pangs: Liberation Theology in North America," *The Christian Century* 93, no. 41 (Dec. 15, 1976): p. 1123.

48. Ibid., pp. 1122–1123. See also Frederick Herzog, "Schleiermacher and the Problem of Power," in *Justice Church* (Maryknoll, N.Y.: Orbis Books, 1980), pp. 55–71.

49. Ernst Troeltsch, *Protestantism and Progress*, trans. W. Montgomery (Boston: Beacon, 1958), p. 176.

50. Ernst Troeltsch, *Christian Thought: Its History and Application*, ed. Baron F. von Hügel (New York: Meridian Books, 1957), pp. 55–56.

51. Ibid., pp. 58, 59.

52. Ibid., p. 54.

53. Ernst Troeltsch, *Die Mission in der modernen Welt* (1906). Cited in Robert J. Rubanowice, *Crisis in Consciousness: The Thought of Ernst Troeltsch* (Tallahasee, Fla.: University Presses of Florida, 1982), p. 35.

54. Cited in Rubanowice, *Crisis in Consciousness*, p. 103.

55. Ibid., pp. 126, 127.

56. For a sympathetic treatment of Troeltsch as a representative of culture-Protestantism, see George Rupp, *Culture-Protestantism: German Liberal Theology at the Turn of the Twentieth Century* (Missoula, Mont.: Scholars, 1977).

57. See Arthur Frey, *Cross and Swastika: The Ordeal of the German Church*, trans. J. Strathearn McNab (London: Student Christian Movement Press, 1938).

58. See James Bentley, *Martin Niemöller* (New York: Free Press, 1984), pp. 92–130; and Robert P. Ericksen, *Theologians Under Hitler: Gerhard Kittel, Paul Althaus and Emanuel Hirsch* (New Haven: Yale University Press, 1985).

59. Rauschning, *Conservative Revolution*, pp. 255, 256.

60. Diggins, *Lost Soul of American Politics*, p. 228.

61. Charles Hartshorne, *Omnipotence and Other Theological Mistakes* (Albany, N.Y.: State University of New York Press, 1984), pp. 5, 6.

62. See Colin Grant, "Feminist Theology Is Middle Class," *Encounter* 45, no. 4 (Autumn 1984): pp. 393–402.

63. Cf. Dorothee Sölle: "God is our capacity to love . . . the spark that animates our love." *The Strength of the Weak: Toward a Christian Feminist Identity*, trans. Robert and Rita Kimber (Philadelphia: Westminster, 1984), p. 138.

64. Victorio Arayag, "The God of the Strategic Covenant," in Pablo Richard, et al. *The Idols of Death and the God of Life*, trans. Barbara E. Campbell and Bonnie Shepard (Maryknoll, N.Y.: Orbis Books, 1983), p. 111.

65. One of the ironic paradoxes in Latin American nations is that although the theological schools of Roman Catholic and mainline Protestant denominations are generally dominated by liberation ideology, the poverty-stricken masses are increasingly turning to Pentecostalism.

66. Niebuhr, Pauck, and Miller, *Church Against the World*, pp. 11, 12.

67. Jerry Falwell, *Listen, America!* (New York: Doubleday, 1980), p. 12.

68. North, *Unconditional Surrender*, p. 162.

69. Ibid., p. 163.

70. Rousas J. Rushdoony, *The Foundations of Social Order* (Nutley, N.J.: Presbyterian and Reformed, 1972), p. 224.

71. Merlin Carothers, *Praise Works!* (Plainfield, N.J.: Logos, 1973), p. 161.

72. Niebuhr, Pauck, and Miller, *Church Against the World*, p. 128.

73. For a catalogue of the crimes of the United States of America against the American Indian nations see Dee Brown, *Bury My Heart at Wounded Knee* (New York: Holt, Rinehart & Winston, 1970).

74. See Albert K. Weinberg, *Manifest Destiny: A Study of Nationalist Expansionism in American History* (Baltimore: John Hopkins University Press, 1935); and Robert Jewett,

The Captain America Complex: The Dilemma of Zealous Nationalism (Philadelphia: Westminster, 1973).

75. Neuhaus, *Naked Public Square*, p. 237.
76. Gruntvig held that an awakening of national consciousness was necessary for the vitality of the Christian religion. For a penetrating discussion of the glaring contrast between Kierkegaard's prophetic Christianity and Gruntvig's cultural Christianity see John W. Elrod, *Kierkegaard and Christendom* (Princeton, N.J.: Princeton University Press, 1981).
77. For Reinhold Niebuhr's criticisms of Mannheim see Niebuhr, *Faith and History*, p. 161; idem, *Nature and Destiny of Man* 2: pp. 237, 238.
78. See Niebuhr, *Nature and Destiny of Man* 1: pp. 194–202; 2: pp. 214–20. Tillich's prescription for overcoming ideology is similar: it is only when the paradox of the justification of the sinner by a holy God is understood and accepted that "all ideologies are destroyed." *Protestant Era*, pp. 170, 171.
79. Niebuhr, Pauck, and Miller, *Church Against the World*, pp. 149–50.
80. Barth, *Christian Life*, p. 240.
81. H. Richard Niebuhr, *Kingdom of God*, (New York: Willett, Clark & Co., 1937), p. 56.
82. Ibid., p. 9.
83. I am here taking issue not with the doctrine of biblical inerrancy but with the widespread tendency to use this as a slogan in order to silence discussion.
84. Nathan O. Hatch, "Evangelicalism as a Democratic Movement," *The Reformed Journal* 34, no. 10 (Oct. 1984): p. 16.
85. George Hunsinger, "Barth, Barmen and the Confessing Church Today," *Katallagete* 9, no. 2 (Summer 1985): p. 23.
86. Niebuhr, Pauck, Miller, *Church Against the World*, p. 84.
87. Ibid., p. 89.
88. Ibid., pp. 103, 104.
89. My position converges at several points with that of Richard Quinney, who calls for a transcendent religion of the kingdom of God "with its own public morality that will guide us in our social, economic, and political formations in the earthly kingdoms of the world." *Providence: The Reconstruction of Social and Moral Order* (New York: Longman, 1980), p. 75. Quinney, however, believes that Paul Tillich's vision of a theonomous culture provides this kind of transcendent direction. I agree with Barth that only the living Word of God, the incarnate Jesus Christ, can be this transcendent criterion, and this Word always calls into radical question the cultural and religious quest. Quinney ties the hope of a theonomous culture too closely to religious socialism. As a result, religion becomes the ground and goal of cultural endeavor rather than a word from the beyond, pointing to a kingdom not of this world. Quinney says that "in the struggle for religious socialism we hope to recover our wholeness, to heal our estrangement from the source of our being" (p. 98). But does not biblical faith teach that only God can overcome this alienation and that he has done so in his reconciling work in Jesus Christ? When Quinney astoundingly declares that "in the creation of a socialist culture . . . we redeem ourselves as human beings on this earth" (p. 95), he undercuts the central teaching of Christian faith that only God in Christ redeems. The hope of the world therefore rests not on the struggle for a religiously based socialism but on the proclamation of the advent of Christ and the promise of his second advent.
90. Tillich, *Protestant Era*, p. 243.
91. Sidney E. Mead, *The Nation With the Soul of a Church* (New York: Harper & Row, 1975).
92. Neuhaus, *Naked Public Square*.
93. Neuhaus tends to give more particularity to the spiritual and moral ethos by speaking of the normativeness of our Judeo-Christian tradition and of "the promises and judgments revealed in the Biblical story." Hunsinger regards Neuhaus's option as

a variation of civil religion: "Most of the time his preferred religious vocabulary is of the deracinated type which speaks nebulously of 'the transcendent,' 'experiences of the absolute' and other assorted nonentities." Hunsinger, "Barth, Barmen and the Confessing Church Today," p. 21.
94. See ibid., p. 22. Note that this is Hunsinger's description of Neuhaus's position.
95. According to Nichols, "In both Church and State the primary motive of Puritan democracy was less to claim equal rights, or to fulfill one's personality as such—which was simply sin—than to fulfill certain specific and inalienable religious duties." James Hastings Nichols, *Democracy and the Churches* (Philadelphia: Westminster, 1951), p. 37.
    Barth says: "I do not like the notion of individual rights, with the idea that the State must protect the right of individuals. The State must protect the *freedom* (not 'liberty,' which is a strange Latin word) of man, which means also responsibility." *Karl Barth's Table Talk*, ed. John D. Godsey (Edinburgh: Oliver & Boyd, 1963), p. 77.
96. I heartily agree with James Packer: "Since in this fallen world, as Lord Acton put it, all power corrupts and absolute power corrupts absolutely, the separation of powers and the building of checks and balances into executive structures will limit the dangers of corruption, even if such procedures for restraint will never eliminate them entirely." "How to Recognize a Christian Citizen," in *The Christian As Citizen*, ed. Kenneth Kantzer (Carol Stream, Ill.: *Christianity Today*, 1985), [pp. 4–8], p. 7.
97. Note that the Declaration of the Rights of Man of the French Revolution says, "The source of all sovereignty resides essentially in the nation." Alfred Cobban, *A History of Modern France* (New York: George Braziller, 1965), Bk 1, p. 165. According to Albert Sorel, the object of the Enlightenment philosophers was not to abolish the state "but to take possession of it. It was not a question of reducing its omnipotence to the gain of individual liberty, but of using this omnipotence to constrain the citizens to receive the baptism of the new religion." *Europe and the French Revolution*, trans & eds. Alfred Cobban and J. W. Hunt (New York: Doubleday, 1971), p. 102.
    On the totalitarian thrust of "direct democracy" and utopian social planning see J. L. Talmon, *The Origins of Totalitarian Democracy* (London: Secker and Warburg, 1952); Karl Popper, *The Open Society and its Enemies* (London: Routledge and Kegan Paul, 1945); and Roland Huntford, *The New Totalitarians* (New York: Stein & Day, 1972).
98. Many of the early representatives of liberal democracy, including Montesquieu, Adam Smith, John Locke, and Thomas Jefferson, all appealed to a higher law than civil law. See Gottfried Dietze, *Liberalism Proper and Proper Liberalism* (Baltimore: John Hopkins University Press, 1985). Dietze says that threats to "proper democracy" seem to be "motivated by egalitarian, socialist thinking" (p. 255). In the modern period, "Madison's ideas were increasingly replaced by those of Rousseau" (p. 233). In my judgment, by calling into question an authoritative divine revelation in history, liberal ideology was not able to maintain the sense of the reality of a universal moral law. The moral ethos of society cannot be severed from its metaphysical moorings without itself collapsing.
99. Both Rousseau and John Dewey appealed to "the general will" or "the public spirit" as the final criterion for truth. Rousseau is the inventor of what has come to be known as "guided democracy." See Lester G. Crocker, *Rousseau's Social Contract* (Cleveland: Press of Case Western Reserve University, 1968).
100. Kenneth L. Vaux, "Crisis in Science and Spirit," *The Christian Century* 102, no. 4 (Jan. 30, 1985): p. 104.
101. Tillich, *Protestant Era*, pp. 161–81, 192–205.
102. For a devastating critique of the confusions of modern religious liberalism in this area, see H. Shelton Smith, *Faith and Nurture* (New York: Charles Scribner's Sons, 1941).
103. Cf. Reinhold Niebuhr: "Man's capacity for justice makes democracy possible; but

man's inclination to injustice makes democracy necessary." *The Children of Light and the Children of Darkness.* (New York: Charles Scribner's Sons, 1944), p. xi.

104. That the call to national repentance has solid biblical precedent is documented in Jacques Ellul, *The Meaning of the City,* trans. Dennis Pardee (Grand Rapids: Eerdmans, 1970).

CHAPTER 14

The Folly of War

I will listen to what God the Lord will say; he promises peace to his people . . . but let them not return to folly.

PSALM 85:8 NIV

Religion is to be defended not by putting to death, but by dying; not by cruelty, but by patient endurance; not by crime, but by faith.

LACTANTIUS

In the long run, the sword will always be conquered by the spirit.

NAPOLEON

There is a constant struggle between good and evil going on in the world, and the battleground is the heart of man.

FEODOR DOSTOEVSKY

There is one problem only today, and that is the problem of murder. All our disputes are vain. One thing alone matters, and that is peace.

ALBERT CAMUS

Philosophical Perspectives on War

In the history of philosophy, war is often viewed as an imperfect means of resolving social disputes among nations, but it is seldom condemned as an incontrovertible evil. What is disturbing is the number of philosophers who celebrate war as an opportunity to display courage and manly valor.

The pre-Socratic philosopher Heraclitus contended that Homer was wrong in saying, "Would that strife might perish from among gods and men!" If that prayer were answered, Heraclitus feared, civilization, indeed the universe, would disintegrate, for "War is the father of all and the king of all; and some he has made gods and some men, some bond and some free. . . . We must know that war is common to all, and strife is justice, and that all things come into being and pass away through strife."[1]

We find similar sentiments expressed in modern times. According to Nietzsche: "War and courage have done more great things than charity. Not your sympathy, but your bravery hath hitherto saved the victims."[2] Hegel regarded war as necessary to the ethical health of a nation; by imposing its will on other peoples a nation strengthens its own will to be. William James saw war as one of the humanities, an art that produces art, providing "new outlets for heroic energy."[3] At the same time, war occurs because of the interminable presence of evil in the world. "The recourse to war must be expected to continue as long as organized evil, outrage, oppression, terrorism themselves continue."[4]

The tradition of Heraclitus and the ancient Greeks reappears in our century in Teilhard de Chardin, who celebrated war as a catalyst of purification in humanity's evolutionary ascent. War is necessary for the greatness of a nation as it struggles to realize its divinely appointed destiny in history. Although war breeds suffering and despair, it also affords an opportunity for God to bring good out of evil. Teilhard regarded the dead and wounded of Hiroshima as "unavoidable sacrifices on the road toward fulfilling the duty of pushing evolution forward."[5] On the early nuclear tests, he remarked, "Despite their military setting, the recent explosions at Bikini . . . announce the coming of the spirit of the earth."[6] Regretting that his priestly status relegated his service in the armed forces to that of a medical orderly, he felt that "he would be 'more priestly' as a member of the fighting force, with a grenade in his hand or behind a machine gun."[7]

A less sanguine view is to be found in the Russian philosopher Nicolas Berdyaev, who condemned war as a positive evil, though not necessarily the greatest of evils. While regarding war as a tragedy rather than a moral or cultural advance, he contended that to try to detach oneself from war after it has started is dangerously misguided.

Once a war has begun and can no longer be stopped, the individual must not throw off its burden or give up his share of the common responsibility; he must take upon himself the guilt of the war for the sake of higher ends, but he must feel the tragedy and the inevitable horror of it. War is a part of man's destiny and this is why it repels the Christian conscience which resists destiny. War is retribution. And it must be accepted in an enlightened spirit, as all other trials of life.[8]

He could even say that in the darkness of the sinful world war "may prove to contain an element of light and be a source of heroism and nobility."[9]

It remained for Mahatma Gandhi to condemn war unreservedly and to offer a concrete alternative to war—nonviolent resistance. Gandhi believed that oppressed peoples can ultimately gain their rights through the exercise of soul-force rather than military force. He envisaged a strategy that employed the weapon of *satyagrapha* (the union of love and truth), which could prove invincible against entrenched powers of depotism. "Do not fear," he counseled, for "he who fears, hates, he who hates kills. Break your sword and throw it away, and fear will not touch you. I have been delivered from desire from fear *so that I know* the power of God."[10] Gandhi's philosophy has had a perceptible influence on a number of Christian thinkers and statesmen, including Martin Luther King, Jr., Thomas Merton, Dorothy Day, Charles Fager, and Jim Wallis.

War in the Bible

In the biblical perspective, war is always evil, for it patently conflicts with God's will and purpose for his creation. It involves killing the body, which in the New Testament is called "the temple of God" (1 Cor. 3:16, 17; 6:19; 2 Cor. 6:16). It merits divine retribution: "Whoever sheds the blood of man, by man shall his blood be shed; for God made man in his own image" (Gen. 9:6; Lev. 24:17; Ezek. 7:23, 24; 22:4; 35:6). God will not listen to the prayers of a people whose "hands are full of blood" (Isa. 1:15;[11] cf. Isa. 59:3; 2 Chron. 24:20–22; Matt. 23:34–35). Our Lord admonished one of his disciples who tried to defend him by the sword, "Put your sword back into its place; for all who take the sword will perish by the sword" (Matt. 26:52; cf. Ps. 37:14, 15; Isa. 33:1; Rev. 13:10).

In the biblical as opposed to the classical view, war is not the product of a deficiency in being or understanding but has its origin in the perverse inclination of the heart (cf. Jer. 17:9; James 4:1, 2: Sirach 28:8–12). It springs not from weakness or ignorance but from an inborn lust for power. It signifies an assault of nonbeing upon being, an attack upon God's good creation.

War is also portrayed as folly, indeed, as the height of folly (cf. Eccles. 9:18; Pss. 68:30; 120:7; Nah. 3:1–4).[12] We stumble into war because we are blind to our limitations (2 Kings 14:8–10; 2 Chron. 16:9). We fondly presume that we can control events that lead to war and that war precipitates. But war is something that controls us, in fact destroys us. The later biblical prophets would tend to agree with the Greek tragedian Euripides: "Whom the gods destroy, they first make mad."

War cannot be understood apart from the biblical doctrine of sin, the hardness of heart that breaks communication between people and leads them ever deeper into the abyss of isolation and fear. Sin is the rapacious desire to control and to possess. The Epistle of James leaves little doubt on the subject: "What causes wars, and what causes fightings among you? Is it not your passions that are at war in your members? You desire and do not have; so you kill. And you covet and cannot obtain; so you fight and wage war" (4:1, 2).

Sin is characterized by irrationality (Barth) or absurdity (Berkouwer). Barth describes it as an "ontological impossibility," for although humanity is created in God's image, sin nevertheless happens inexplicably and repeatedly. The Bible does not offer a rational solution to the problem of evil, including human sin, but it does point to a cosmic resolution, God's reconciling act in Jesus Christ by which humanity can recover its freedom to live as God intended.

Even though the Bible presents war as an attack upon God's creation, God is nevertheless pictured as permitting and occasionally even sanctioning war because of sin. Sin is always the immediate cause of war (cf. Jer. 11:22; Ps. 78:62; Hos. 10:9; James 4:1, 2), but God is at work in war bringing good out of evil. God uses war to discipline and chastise a rebellious people. God punishes people by the sword for their iniquities (Jer. 16:4; 18:21; Amos. 9:10; Ezek. 26:11; 2 Chron. 29:9).

Biblical religion also condemns the dependence of nations on armaments (cf. Pss. 33:16, 17; 44:6; 60:10–12; Isa. 31:1–3; 37:23–36; Hos. 10:13, 14). In the Old Testament, those who rely on armaments in preparation for war invariably incur God's wrath. God may order certain wars in order to humble a proud people or to bring down an idolatrous people, but sin is still present in these wars, and therefore they fall drastically short of the perfect will of God. War is the rod of God's anger, not the sign of his mercy. War expresses God's judgment on sin, not the grace that overcomes sin. War is what God does with his left hand, by which he chastises sinners, not his right hand, by which he justifies and redeems sinners. War is his alien work, not his proper work. The sixth commandment, "You shall not kill," expresses God's opposition to war as well as to murder.

War is always evil because sin is always present in war. Indeed, sin is accentuated in war. It comes to fruition in war, even if war has God's secret sanction. Because its immediate cause is sin, it brings with it the penalty of divine judgment. Because of blood on his hands, David was not permitted to build the temple, even though the wars he engaged in presumably had God's blessing (1 Kings 5:3; 1 Chron. 22:8).

The holy wars of the Old Testament have been an enigma to many Christians, since they appear to have been commanded by God against the pagan peoples whom Israel confronted in fulfilling its divine mandate to take possession of Canaan. First, it should be said that the removal of godless people by the sword indicates God's permissive will, not his ultimate will, which is that no one should perish (cf. Ezek. 18:23, 32; 2 Pet. 3:9). Second, the concept of the holy war is in accord with the vision of the higher prophets that abominable sins merit destruction and annihilation. Again, the children of Israel in their subjugation of the pagan occupants of Canaan have to be seen as instruments of the wrath of God, not servants of his love. The Old Testament prophets were given only a partial understanding of the meaning of the holy war, but they did correctly interpret the will of God for their time.

Finally, one must consider that in the holy war the dependence of the people must be on God, not on weapons of destruction. This is the abiding truth in this concept, which has profound implications for both church and nation through the ages. In the holy war it is actually God who wages war and brings about victory. His people are only instruments of his avenging and purifying work, even witnesses to what he accomplishes for them and sometimes despite them. Pharaoh was defeated not by arms but by the waters of the Red Sea. Gideon was victorious over the Midianites, but his small band was armed only with trumpets, pitchers, and torches so that the glory was given only to God. At the sound of the trumpets the walls of Jericho collapsed (Josh. 6:20). Philistia was overpowered by a lad with a sling shot (1 Sam. 17). Sisera was defeated by a hammer and tent peg (Judg. 4:17–24). Sennacherib, king of Assyria, was forced to retreat after a mysterious affliction sent by God decimated his army (Isa. 37:36, 37).

In the holy war of the Old Testament, God does not so much fight *with* Israel as *for* Israel. In the prophetic development of this concept, Israel's role became increasingly passive, leaving the direction of history in God's hands (cf. Isa. 30:3–5, 15, 16; 31:1–3). The Psalmist says, "With God we shall do valiantly; it is he who will tread down our foes" (Ps. 108:13; cf. Ps. 37:14–17). Moses counsels the children of Israel: "Fear not, stand firm, and see the salvation of the Lord, which he will work for you today; for the Egyptians whom you see today, you shall never see again. The Lord will fight for you, and you have *only to be still*" (italics mine) (Exod. 14:13, 14; cf. Isa. 31:4–9). This vision of God as the sole deliverer is also present in Hosea 1:7: "I will have pity on the house of Judah, and I will deliver them by the Lord their God; I will not deliver them by bow, nor by sword, nor by war, nor by horses, nor by horsemen."

In the New Testament, the idea of the holy war is radially transformed. The holy war is now envisaged in terms of spiritual combat and is to be fought with spiritual weapons. Military metaphors abound, but this is a spiritual conflict with the powers of darkness (cf. Eph. 6:10–20). In the Old Testament, such wars were believed to be battles between Yahweh and the pagan gods. In the New Testament, the holy war is waged between Jesus Christ and Satan. In the Old Testament holy war, the elect people of God offered the enemy as a human sacrifice to God. In the New Testament holy war, we offer ourselves as sacrifices to God. Our weapons are now spiritual—the Word of God, which is the sword of the Spirit; prayer; fasting; and preaching. It is in the name of Jesus that we cast out demons.

The sixth commandment in its original meaning indubitably referred to murder, not war. But in the light of the wider biblical witness, it came to mean an injunction against all intentional killing of human beings. Since bloodshed invariably takes place in war, the commandment came more and more to be applied against war, and this is especially true of the community of faith in the apostolic and patristic ages.

In its deepest meaning, the commandment against killing is a command to preserve life, though not to enthrone life. It does expressly forbid the taking of innocent life, that is, murder. Yet murder is inextricably bound up with war and always accompanies war. Murder, of course, is a legal as well as a moral concept; it indicates the deliberate or premeditated killing of another human being. The Old Testament civil laws fell short of the standard of perfection required by Jesus, who forbade even murderous thoughts against others (Matt. 5:21, 22). To kill in the name of Christ and in order to advance the kingdom of Christ is expressly forbidden by Jesus (Matt. 26:52, 53). Yet sometimes we have to take up the sword in order to preserve life, and this is permitted in the Bible but as something that pertains to the passing aeon, the world of sin and darkness, not to the new age of the kingdom of God. Since we belong to the old age as well as to the new, we act in two roles: as responsible citizens of the state, which can only maintain itself by force, and as ambassadors of the kingdom of Christ, which maintains itself solely by works of faith and love.

The ethic of Jesus expressed in the so-called Sermon on the Mount

was given to disciples, not to nations. If the radical ethic of nonresistance were applied directly to nations, it would mean the end of all
civil government. Yet the church, which is under this higher command,
can be a guide to the nations. It is the moral monitor or conscience of
the state. In Romans 13 the power of the state to wield the sword is
expressly acknowledged by Paul; at the same time, the sixth commandment is vigorously reaffirmed. The principle of nonresistance or
no retaliation can be a goal or ideal in the social arena but never a
political strategy.

The commandment of God is not the very same for persons and
for nations. Nor is it the very same for Christians and for non-Christians. Yet there will always be a correspondence or continuity between
the will of God for the church and the will of God for the nation. There
will be a broken similarity but never a radical disjunction between what
God wills for his people as the body of Christ and what he wills for
the nations of the world, which are necessarily either non-Christian or
pre-Christian.

Although it unequivocally upholds the way of peace, the New Testament does not teach an absolute pacifism. Jesus used physical force
and a whip to drive out the traders from the temple (John 2:14, 15),
but there is no mention of killing. He forbade the use of the sword to
defend or advance the kingdom of God (Matt. 26:52; Luke 9:54–56),
but he did not condemn the enforcement of Mosaic law by the sword
(Mark 7:10).[13] This latter text must be treated with caution, however,
since it appears that Jesus was trying to expose the inconsistencies of
the Pharisees.

A more difficult text, where Jesus urges his disciples to buy a sword
(Luke 22:36), has been the subject of considerable debate. Many scholars contend that he was speaking symbolically. When the disciples
came to him with two swords, he said, "Enough of this" (Luke 22:38
GNB), and abruptly broke off the conversation. Was he asking them to
rely on the sword of the Spirit, which is the Word of God (Eph. 6:17)?
Or did his request that they buy a sword indicate that he was giving
up on his disciples for their folly and stubbornness of heart? Surely,
one reason for this command was that Old Testament prophecy might
be fulfilled (Luke 22:37).

When soldiers came to John the Baptist asking, "What shall we
do?," he replied, "Rob no one by violence or by false accusation and
be content with your wages" (Luke 3:14). He gave no hint that the
soldiers should leave the army. John's eyes, of course, were not yet

opened to the full implications of the new reality that is the kingdom of God, and yet the author of the Fourth Gospel does not question the role of the soldiers in this context.

In the Synoptic Gospels, a Roman centurion is praised for his faith (Matt. 8:5–13; Luke 7:1–10), and another, stationed at the cross, confesses that Jesus is God's Son (Matt. 27:54; Mark 15:39; Luke 23:47). Cornelius, who was a soldier, is presented as the church's first gentile convert (Acts 10). To be sure, he was only a babe in Christ and had not yet been instructed in discipleship. Yet there is no suggestion that military service is incompatible with the Christian faith, though there is no endorsement of it either.[14]

Paul demanded his rights as a citizen and accepted the protection of the Roman army when his life was threatened (Acts 22, 23). Yet his message signaled the end of the old order. His own conversion was from the way of violence to the way of the cross, from reliance on the sword to reliance on love.

In the Book of Revelation, the faithful remnant are portrayed as overcoming the powers of evil not by the sword but "by the blood of the Lamb and by the word of their testimony" (Rev. 12:11). Nevertheless, in this same book Christ is depicted as making war on the nations with a heavenly army and ruling over them with a "rod of iron" (Rev. 12:5; 14:19, 20; 19:11–21). Yet this war is won simply by the power of the word that goes forth from his mouth, the fiery word of wrath and condemnation (cf. Rev. 19:15; 2 Thess. 2:8; Isa. 11:4; Job 4:9). Moreover, the warfare that Christ wages is only to prepare the way for the eternal peace of the kingdom of God, which the church anticipates by its reliance on the cross rather than the sword.

The final biblical position seems to be that force is defensible to preserve law and order in society, but another strategy is called for in the kingdom of God. The use of the sword belongs to the governing authority, for there can be no order or justice without coercion (Rom. 13).[15] The state may wield the sword only because of the continuance of sin, though its role pertains to the old age that is passing away, not the new age of the kingdom. War may be entered into only as a last resort, only when all other means have failed. It is not something we embrace joyously but something we fall into because of human sin and obstinacy. Our dependence must always be on God (Luke 12:5), never on weapons or entangling alliances. War falls drastically short of the ideal of the righteousness of the kingdom. It belongs to the old aeon which is passing away. It can be tolerated in certain instances, but it will finally be superseded. Some wars are absolutely forbidden by God because of the unnecessarily cruel and barbaric means employed (Amos 1, 2). In the new age people "will beat their swords into plowshares and their spears into pruning hooks. Nation will not take up sword against nation, nor will they train for war anymore" (Isa. 2:4 NIV; cf. Mic. 4:3).

It should be recognized that the condemnation of war in the Old Testament is not as clear as might be desired. While the prophets did denounce the false security that weapons and foreign alliances might provide (cf. Isa. 30:1–7; 31:1–3; 36:6; Jer. 17:5), their arguments often seem to be based on the futility of war rather than its immorality.[16] Some passages that imply disapproval of massacre and bloodshed (1 Sam. 25:31–33; 1 Chron. 28:3) may be rooted in ritualistic rather than moral concerns. The Old Testament authors did not always see that war is something that God tolerates rather than expressly desires for his people. Nor did they adequately grasp the deeper implications of the holy war, a war waged by God for Israel instead of by Israel for God.

At the same time, it is remarkable how often peace is celebrated and war is questioned by the prophets. The people who "delight in war" shall be scattered (Ps. 68:30). A "wonderful future" is foretold for "the man of peace" (Ps. 37:37 LB). Salvation is pictured as the embracing of righteousness and peace (Ps. 85:10). The altar that Gideon built at Ophrah is named "The Lord is Peace" (Judg. 6:24 NIV). The prophetic texts that herald the end of war in the new age show that war is excluded from God's final purpose for his creation (Isa. 2:4; 11:6–10; 32:17–18; Hos. 2:18; Zech. 9:10; Ps. 72:3, 14; Mic. 4:2–4).

Significantly, in the New Testament, the apostles after Pentecost tended to follow the path of nonresistance laid down by our Lord. Like their Master, they too frequently fled from threats of death (cf. Acts 8:1, 4; 9:25, 30; 14:6; 17:10–14). When they were cornered by their adversaries, they did not offer tangible resistance but let themselves be taken (Acts 4:3; 5:26, 41; 21:30–33). They were put to death without any visible show of opposition (Acts 7:54–60; 12:2–5). Their reliance was not on the sword but on the grace and love of the living God.

The Early Church Period

Until the time of Constantine (fourth century), the early church generally refused to support war. Christians were discouraged from serving in the armed forces partly because this entailed a pledge of homage to the emperor but even more because it involved the shedding of blood.[17] Tertullian opposed military service on both grounds, but especially the second. He concluded that Jesus "by disarming Peter, disarmed all soldiers."[18] Cyprian complained, "If a murder is committed by an individual, it is called crime; but if it is committed on the State's order, it is called courage."[19] Origen considered war to be inspired by demons and argued that the prayers and disciplined lives of Christians were of more value to the state than service in the army.

The early church produced a number of martyrs for the kingdom of peace. Maximilian in the third century refused to be inducted and was put to death. He confessed: "I cannot serve in the military, I cannot commit a sin. I am a Christian." Martin of Tours (fourth century) was also a celebrated witness for peace. After his conversion while he was still in the Roman army, he asked to be discharged, believing his commitment to Christ to be incompatible with further service as a soldier. To prove his sincerity, he offered to face the enemy on the next day with no arms except a cross.[20]

Even after the victory of the Christian emperor Constantine and the Edict of Milan (313), which gave toleration to Christians, most of them remained largely aloof from military service. This was due less to a reluctance to perform idolatrous immolations than to a desire to rely on spiritual weapons rather than the sword.[21]

Toward the end of the fourth century, a number of theologians, such as Basil, Athanasius, and Ambrose, conceded that killing might be justified if it was for the sake of the common good or in defense of the true religion. Augustine (d. 430) believed that while it is impermissible for Christians to act in self-defense, we are required to defend our defenseless neighbor.

Yet even in the later patristic period and into the Middle Ages, war was considered something that carries the taint of sin, something that has to be repented of before God. While Basil admitted that killing in war is not the same as murder, he advised that "nevertheless perhaps it would be well that those whose hands are unclean abstain from communion for three years."[22] In the Western church, soldiers who killed were barred from Holy Communion for ten months. Priests whose hands were tainted with blood could not offer mass apart from a rite of cleansing. In France and Germany in the first half of the eleventh century, the Truce of God limited the time for military operations. There was to be no fighting on holy days or from Advent through Epiphany. The Peace of God limited those involved in war by increasing the category of the exempt. At a council in Winchester, England, in 1076 it was decreed that anyone who killed another human being should do penance for a year.[23]

In the later Middle Ages, a double standard in religion emerged in which those dedicated to the religious life were under a special obligation to imitate the nonviolence of Christ. Committed to the counsels of perfection (poverty, celibacy, obedience), such persons were expected to live only by the cross and not by the sword. Thomas Aquinas argued that clerics and bishops should not fight because "warlike pursuits . . . hinder the mind very much from the contemplation of Divine things."[24]

Pacifists trace the change in the church's attitude toward war to the accommodation with the state at the time of Constantine. In exchange for recognition, the church gave its support to the state in its use of coercion to maintain justice and order. Lasserre believes that this "Constantian heresy" was responsible for the emergence of a facile optimism concerning the state, a readiness to uphold the state as "beneficient protector of order," whereas previously it had been portrayed as a principality or power that needed to be demythologized and dethroned.[25]

Christian Approaches to War

In the history of the Christian church, it is possible to distinguish various, often conflicting, approaches to the problem of war. All of them have some basis in biblical faith, but several indicate a noticeable accommodation to classical thought.

First, there is the crusade. In this view, a state may initiate a war to protect the faithful or advance the faith. Or a war may be waged to preserve Christian civilization or Judaeo-Christian values. Those who perpetuate this kind of war seek and claim the blessing of God. This view has some continuity with the holy war of the Old Testament. But the notion of a war in defense of true religion is explicitly forbidden by Jesus (Matt. 26:52; Luke 9:54–56; John 18:36).

Seemingly oblivious to this injunction, the medieval church threw its support behind the Crusades designed to protect the passage of pilgrims to the Holy Land and also liberate the Holy Land from Moslem control. The crusade mentality was also responsible for the forcible suppression of heresy at home. The shameful campaigns against the Cathari in France were carried out with papal blessing.

Although allowing for the right of the state to wield the sword, Luther adamantly opposed the idea of war as a crusade. He resisted the papal demand for a new crusade against the Turks on the grounds that God's kingom cannot be defended by the sword. He also opposed rebellion against civil order by those having no authority to wield the sword.

While Calvin recognized the legitimacy of a holy war, he noted that the divine permission for such a war in the Old Testament was "far distant from perfection," explicable only as a concession to the "ferocity" of the Jews.[26] On the whole, Calvin argues for restraint and humanity in war. Even though he allows for revolt against an unjust king on the part of the lower magistrates, he counsels Christians to suffer oppression patiently; they should even be ready to forfeit their possessions should their case be lost in the civil courts. Love for our enemies excludes a desire for vengeance but not the prayer that God may take vengeance upon them in his own way and time.

The idea of the crusade was revived by the Puritans who virtually elevated the Old Testament to the same level as the New. Thomas Sutton declared, "Every good member of Christ must turn soldier, and become a defender of the faith."[27] A war could be justified if it had a holy cause, including the overthrow of false or idolatrous worship. At the same time, the Puritans cautioned against indiscriminate violence, the shedding of innocent blood.

Defenders of the idea of war as a crusade inspired by devotion to Christ or to religious values—Bernard of Clairvaux (whose preaching sparked the Second Crusade against the Moslems); Henry Bullinger in the sixteenth century; the Puritans Oliver Cromwell, William Gouge, Thomas Sutton, and Thomas Barnes—have notable successors in our day—Francis Schaeffer and Harold O. J. Brown.[28]

The crusade proves to be a profound distortion of the Christian mission. More often than not, it stems from the false assumption that people can be forced into the kingdom by the sword. It is prone to dismiss the enemy as beyond the pale, and this is why the code of humanity soon collapses.[29] Its appeal is invariably to the Old Testament rather than the New, and the plain teachings of Jesus are blithely disregarded. The crusade, moreover, impedes the possibility of a magnanimous peace.

An approach seemingly more consonant with the spirit of the gospel is that of the just war. Here the intent is not to glorify but to humanize and limit war. This position signifies an accommodation of Christian faith to the realities of power, and derives in part from classical philosophy. Indeed, it was Plato who first gave formulation to the code that came to be called the "just war." According to him, it is permissible for a nation to defend itself, but the conquered should not be enslaved. In this perspective war may not be an ideal solution, but it still may be necessary. There is always evil in war, but war itself may not be an unmitigated evil. The word "just" is used in a relative sense and indicates the possibility of greater justice through the waging of war. War may be the lesser of two evils. It might be less evil than slavery, irreligion, or anarchy, for example. God appointed the state to wage war in order to protect people from these greater evils. A text often appealed to by just war theorists is Rom. 13:4: "He does not bear the sword in vain."

The just war theory was first delineated by Augustine and then expanded by Thomas Aquinas and later Catholic theologians (Suarez, Bellarmine, Cajetan) as well as Protestants.[30] In this view, a war is just or lawful if its aim is to procure justice and if the means used in waging war are just. The means must be appropriate to the ends sought, namely, justice with order. The good they accomplish must outweigh the evil they create. Such means always exclude the indiscriminate killing of noncombatants. Again, a war must be undertaken only as a last resort and must be sanctioned by legitimate authority. Moreover, there should be a reasonable expectation of success. Among the advocates of the just war theory in our day are Paul Ramsey, Arthur Holmes, William V. O'Brien, David Hollenbach, and Reinhold Niebuhr.

Besides the pacifists, Pannenberg is a major critic of this concept. No war is just, according to Pannenberg, for every war involves unspeakable crimes against God. It is a fiction that a war can be kept within certain moral limits once it has broken out. "It is possible to oppose the self-righteousness of the parties to a war only when the attribute of righteousness is denied to war absolutely and without exception."[31] At the same time, he believes that there may be good grounds for a nation to defend itself by taking up arms against an unprovoked attack and even "for anticipating an attack that is certain to come."[32]

The pacifist tradition in the church probably goes back to the apostolic age, but what should be recognized is that pacifism exists in more than one form. There is an existential or practical pacifism, which regards nonviolent resistance as a substitute for war in some situations. It is possible to adhere to the just war theory and still be a pacifist in the modern situation where nations are threatened by total war. Then there is the dogmatic or absolute pacifist position, which holds that under no circumstances may Christians take up the sword in defense either of themselves or of their neighbors. Although some of these absolute pacifists acknowledge that the state has the right to wield the sword, they insist that Christians cannot take part in this particular dimension of the state's duties. All violence is evil and is therefore to be avoided.

Reinhold Niebuhr has been the most consistent critic of pacifism in modern times. He argues against the pacifists that the source of evil is not violence but ill will.[33] While some pacifists make a place for non-violent resistance, Niebuhr points out that this still falls short of the ideal of nonresistance, which we see in the suffering love of Jesus, who willingly went to the cross with hardly any protest.

Among the luminaries associated with the strategy of pacifism are Tertullian, Lactantius, Origen, Count Leo Tolstoy, Menno Simons, Jacob Hutter, George Fox, and Eberhard Arnold. In our day we can mention Dale Aukerman,[34] John Howard Yoder, Dale Brown, Jim Wallis, Ron Sider, Gordon Zahn, Peter Maurin, Dorothy Day, Jacques Ellul, Jean Lasserre, and Stanley Hauerwas.

My principal reservation about pacifism is that it tends to substitute the principle of nonresistance for the divine commandment. It also blurs the distinction between the role of Christians as ambassadors of the kingdom and their role as responsible citizens of the state, which is based on coercion. It is prone to equate all force with violence (this is particularly true of Ellul) and thus lose sight of the fact that force can be a restraining action and, unlike violence, need not be out of rational control. Pacifism all too easily makes the gospel into a new law, as is evident in Lactantius and Tolstoy. Christianity must never be reduced to the law of love, for it is essentially a gospel of grace.

At the same time, pacifism need not be moralism or ethicism. It could be rooted in a profound understanding of the implications of the divine promise and the divine commandment. I can see a biblical basis for pacifism as a symbolic witness by committed individuals and groups rather than as a strategy for nations. But can the use of force also be a witness for peace in some situations? Is force never commanded by God, even in police action?

In Karl Barth's theology, we see an opening toward pacifism, though, at least in his earlier years, he disclaimed the pacifist label. In contradistinction to a dominant strand in pacifism, Barth sought to ground his position in the total biblical witness, not just in the teachings of Jesus. He argued that war is not the essence of the state (as Brunner would have it) but an abnormal condition that turns the state from its true purpose—to maintain peace with justice. The state must make use of power, but this is its alien work, not its proper work. War is a devastating eruption of human rapacity and lust for power and should always be viewed with abhorrence by the church. Barth criticized both liberal theologians like Herrmann[35] and conservatives like Adolf Schlatter for downplaying or ignoring the enormity of the horror of war.

Yet Barth argued that war may nevertheless be sanctioned by God in a borderline or exceptional situation—where a nation must fight to preserve its historical existence within its own boundaries. Even this cannot be a casuistic principle, for a nation's historical existence may have to be sacrificed if God should so demand it. Barth saw war as an emergency operation that is nevertheless attended by evil of horrendous proportions. A nation may embark on such a venture in order to preserve a cultural heritage that has the blessing of God and is under attack by the powers of darkness. Even worse than war is the rule of the evil spirit of conscious falsehood and deliberate injustice.[36] Once Christians hear the divine commandment for war, they must enter war with a clear conscience, knowing that in their killing they are not murderers but forgiven sinners.

For Barth, war is the exceptional case (Grenzfall), but he also had serious doubts that in the climate of today, when nations are armed with weapons of mass extermination, there can ever be an occasion where God would give his blessing to war. In his later years, Barth came very close to embracing a nuclear pacifism that disallowed the Christian from participating in war. Even in his earlier period he upheld the need for conscientious objection as a witness to the gospel of peace and believed that the church should press the state to permit this kind of exemption from military service.

Finally, we should consider the view that war is a fateful tragedy, unavoidable for nations because of the perpetual clash of egoisms and values. Tillich speaks of "the tragic destiny of nations" and of civilizations involved in "tragic hubris." Leaning upon the Greek understanding of tragedy, he sees the hallmark of the tragic as being doomed to self-destruction by aspiring to human greatness.[37] Yet Tillich insists that the struggle for existence is characterized not only by the tragic (the state of being blind) but also by the demonic (the state of being split).[38] When nations see themselves as the center of the universe, as the locus of the sacred, they are guilty not just of tragic hubris but of folly born of demonic self-aggrandizement.[39]

Reinhold Niebuhr also perceives the tragic element in life and war, but he insists that Christianity transcends tragedy, for it offers the resolution of tragedy, namely, the cross of Christ. The cross reveals that

what seems to be an inherent defect in life is really a defect within
man himself, the defect of sin, which signifies a misuse of human freedom. For Niebuhr war is more pitiful than tragic, because the attempt
by nations to overreach themselves has its roots much more in weakness than in strength, in desperation than in an aspiration to grandeur.
He nevertheless sees a perennial tragic element in the conflicts of life—
the inevitable corruption of our most creative endeavors and highest
ideals. In his view, the truly tragic heroes in war are not those who
resolutely heed the call to duty but those who boldly plunge into war
recognizing their common humanity with its intended victims.[40]

Other theologians who occasionally use the language of fate or tragedy to express the human predicament include Helmut Thielicke,[41] Paul
Althaus, Nicolas Berdyaev, Stanley Hauerwas, and Jacques Ellul. This
general stance was already anticipated in Augustine: "War and conquest are a sad necessity in the eyes of men of principle, yet it would
be still more unfortunate if wrongdoers should dominate just men."[42]

I empathize with this position without fully endorsing it. I see war
as a compound of the pitiful and the tragic, for it is based on stubbornness and folly as well as on the prideful arrogation of power that
always invites divine retribution. War is not simply a matter of fate but
also, and above all, of human guilt. When we recognize and deplore
our involvement in this guilt, we begin to rob war of its character as
fateful tragedy (Thielicke).[43]

War is always an evil, but it may also become inevitable, particularly
where one nation is bent on aggression against another. Yet it is not
an absolute necessity, for we are not pawns in the hands of fate. At
the same time, we can pass the point of no return—where God withholds his grace and leaves us to the destiny we have chosen and inherited. Thus, the tragic vision has a place even within the Christian
perspective. Yet this vision is filtered through the lens of biblical spirituality, which is shaped not only by a provisional pessimism but also
by an ultimate optimism, because it acknowledges that human destiny
is in the hands of a God who is beneficient even in his judgments.

When a nation becomes entrapped in a scenario leading to war, all
of its people are affected. Christians cannot remain uninvolved, but
they are also free to register a protest against the drift toward war.
Violence is the law of nature (Ellul), but Christians are required to stand
against this. They are called to be signs of the new aeon, which is not
subject to the law of violence. The kind of pacifism espoused here is
an eschatological one, oriented to the breaking in of the new age of
the kingdom.

Yet when violence sweeps a country, Christians regrettably will be caught up in this violence even when they try to swim against the stream. If they fight, they must do so only in a spirit of penitence, with an uneasy conscience (Reinhold Niebuhr) rather than with a good conscience.[44] Likewise, those Christians who opt for pacifism should bear witness to peace only in the spirit of penitence, knowing that they could well be benefiting by the engagement of their fellow citizens in defense of their country.

Christians who feel they must resist the policy of their nation in its military preparations or engagements should try to give a visible witness for peace, but they will see this witness as mainly symbolic. Not paying taxes or not registering for the draft cannot alter social policy, but it can remind the state of a higher law. Ceasing to work in munitions factories can also be a powerful sign of resistance, though it is debatable whether such action can deflect a state from its war policy. Serving as noncombatants in the armed forces is still contributing to the war effort.

Christians who decide to resist their country's war policy are still to see the state as ordained by God for the purpose of maintaining law and order. If they break the laws of the state by refusing to serve in the armed forces or by refusing to pay taxes to support the war effort, they should then be prepared to accept the penalty the state imposes, whether it be paying a fine, incarceration, exile, or even death. In this way they continue to show their respect for the state.

As I see it, war is something abominable in the sight of God and can never merit his justification or blessing. I reject the contention of Boettner (among others) that altruism can be maintained in war, that it is possible for sinful human beings to fight without hate. At the same time, I believe that the principle of love can be present in the execution of war, restraining people from atrocities.

What makes me open to the position that views war as the tragic denouement of folly and pride is that it candidly recognizes the evil in war and the necessary implication of even pacifistic Christians in communal guilt.[45] It would rarely if ever see war as a divine commandment, though it could regard it as a divine permission, as a concession to human weakness and sinfulness. This approach makes a place for pacifism as a witness to the kingdom, but not as a social strategy that can take the place of coercion in maintaining justice and order in the state. It supports efforts to humanize warfare, as in the just war tradition, but it does not believe that war can ever be humanized to the degree that it can be considered "just" either in the eyes of God or in the light of the judgment of moral law. Moreover, it holds that the Christian must be a witness for peace even in the midst of war, even in service on the battlefield, and this means that the Christian will come to be suspect in the eyes of those in charge of the war. I have more to say about this later in this chapter.

I have already taken note of the view that regards war as a cathartic purification, belonging to the glorious destiny of nations in the unfolding of creative evolution or the dynamic of history. We find this stance in Teilhard de Chardin and Hegel, but it is also present in another form among liberation theologians, who consider wars of liberation necessary for the realization of the dialectic of history culminating in a proletarian utopia or classless society. Through such wars, it is believed, oppressed peoples can gain self-determination and freedom from exploitation. In my opinion, any view that exalts war or that sees war as a creative passage to a renewed earth fails to do justice to both the Old Testament depiction of war as a divine judgment on the nations and the New Testament call to Christian discipleship, which entails overcoming evil with good (Rom. 12:21).

The Problem of Total War

Humankind finds itself in a new and horrifying situation—the threat of total war. A war waged by weapons of mass extermination—nuclear, biological, chemical—would mean irreparable loss of life and incalculable damage to modern civilization. Such a war would stand apart from all other wars in that it could only be carried on by immoral means. Weapons of mass extermination are qualitatively different from swords and guns, even from pinpoint bombing, because no distinction is made between military targets and civilian populations. Such weapons kill indiscriminately and affect even the lives of the unborn. Moreover, those who survived would find the ecological balance in nature irretrievably altered. A war fought with these monstrous weapons would have unthinkable consequences; it would result in the slow, torturous death of hundreds of millions of people.

Nuclear weapons that have a first-strike capacity give a nation a certain advantage, but they also make the horror of a preemptive or preventive war more enticing. Yet whether a nation that initiated such a ghastly scenario could survive in our day is extremely doubtful, for there is no guaranteed way of blocking mass retaliation by the opposing nuclear power.

The fact is a nation cannot use these weapons, either offensively or defensively, without ensuring its moral destruction and very probably its physical destruction as well.[46] Their only value would seem to lie in deterrence, but the very threat to use weapons of this magnitude is sufficient to erode the moral fabric of a nation.

This kind of war is impermissible for the Christian because it is impossible to trust and believe in a God of love and to use weapons that injure and disfigure the helpless and innocent.[47] This kind of war cannot be reconciled with the traditional idea of the just war, since it employs unjust means and can only result in mass terror rather than in justice. Such weapons are a far cry from the trumpets, pitchers, and torches used by Gideon in the Old Testament. They differ qualitatively from swords and guns, and also from pinpoint bombing aimed at military targets. The principle is the same as the genocidal bombing of Warsaw and Rotterdam by the Nazis and the saturation bombing of Dresden by the Allied forces toward the end of the Second World War.[48] All of these acts were aimed primarily at civilian populations and were designed to inspire terror.[49] There is also a marked similarity to the chemical warfare employed by the Americans in Vietnam and now by the Soviets in Afghanistan.

In seeking to ensure the security of their peoples by nuclear stockpiling, nations are elevating themselves to the position of God, fondly imagining that they can control the prodigious power of these weapons. Trust in such weapons presupposes an overweening trust in ourselves. Only a nihilistic state could use such weapons, a state that was a law unto itself. In Job 4:18 (KJV) we read that the Lord charged his angels with folly. The nations of our time are inviting a similar judgment, for their actions can be explained only on the basis of folly and blindness.

It is well to note that the Old Testament prophets condemned certain nations not for engaging in war but for the immoral and inhumane manner in which they conducted war (cf. Amos 1, 2; 2 Chron. 28:9–11; Hos. 1:4). There is a palpable gulf between legitimate self-defense and the genocide of civilian populations. There is a pronounced difference between pinpoint bombing of military targets and the indiscriminate fire bombing of the aged, women, and children.

I cannot follow traditional pacifists in trying to convert the enemy through love. Love is not a "weapon at our disposal" (Gandhi). It is a divine gift, not a human attainment. Yet nonviolent resistance born out of faith in the God who is love may be feasible in some circumstances. It might even be the key to combating a totalitarian government. It was successfully employed by the Norwegians in resisting their Nazi occupiers, who tried to remold the churches and schools in that country, and also by the Danes and Bulgarians, who defied Hitler's edict to surrender their Jewish populations to the Nazis.[50] It was also effective against the Russians at the beginning of the Hungarian revolution. But when the Hungarians resorted to force, the revolution was quickly put down by Soviet tanks. By means of nonviolent tactics, the Solidarity movement in Poland has effectively prevented the communization of Polish society, even though the state remains officially communist.

People today are constantly confronted by the slogan, "Would you rather be Red than dead?" But for the Christian, this is not the proper question. Helmut Gollwitzer gave this adroit answer: "Rather Red and dead than a murderer."

The appropriate attitude for Christians in this ominous situation is one of confession. We need to forsake our sin and the sin of our nations and look to Christ who chose to be killed rather than to kill. We need to lay hold of the resources in the Christian faith in order to survive as people of faith and integrity in the perilous times in which we are living.

This does not mean taking refuge in simplistic solutions. I cannot agree with Father Theodore Hesburgh that we can hope to put an end to the nuclear armaments race because we are "free and intelligent."[51] Nor do I concur with Harvey Cox that "we must believe that people will respond to reason and love. We have to believe that about the Russians. We have to believe it about the Iranians."[52]

The source of war and strife in the world lies in the bondage of humanity to the power of sin. The predisposition to evil within the human heart proves to be stronger than any inclination to good. People need to be delivered from the grip of the powers of darkness that hold them in bondage, and this deliverance has to come from without. Christians have been blessed by being given the knowledge of the hope of humanity—God's act of reconciliation and redemption in Jesus Christ. Eberhard Arnold put it very succinctly: "Lasting peace can be brought about only by Him who is immortal and eternal. It can never be established by earthly powers. Only the infinite power of God can build up unity and keep peace."[53]

This is not an invitation to quietism. Pope John Paul II in a speech to the United Nations University in Hiroshima in February 1981 spoke like a latter-day prophet: "Humanity *must* make a moral about-face. . . . From *now on*, it is *only* through a *conscious choice* and through *deliberate policy* that humanity can survive."[54] Yet his words could be a prescription for desperation unless we see that our choice for peace is made possible only through the power that comes to us through God's choice for us to be his sons and daughters. The key to a new world lies not in new strategies of peacemaking but in repentance and faith in the living God.

The Church Under the Cross

The challenge to Christians is to work for disengagement from the cold war between the superpowers. We must press for a drastic reduction in the nuclear arsenal of all nations. We must warn against the idolatrous dependence on these weapons, evident in both West and East, and the arrogant presumption that we can control them. We must also protest against the identification of Christianity with the cause of the West.

With the bumptiousness born of considerable technological achievement, we delude ourselves into thinking that nuclear weapons can ensure the peace of the world, when this peace actually rests upon God's continuing forbearance with a sinful human race. Deterrence at best can be tolerated only as a holding action, an action that might prepare the way for nuclear disarmament. But even when understood in this way, it is not justified in the sight of the living God. This is not only because of the idolatrous trust it evokes but also because the very threat to use these monstrous weapons against another people already places us under divine judgment.

Will Christian political action today involve overt resistance to the government? The peace movement within and outside the churches is increasingly taking the stand that the central institutions of our society are so corrupted by militarism that resistance in the form of both non-cooperation and confrontation becomes necessary.[55] Among the kinds of resistance advocated are withholding of taxes earmarked for military purposes; underground sanctuary and railroad strategies for assisting Central American refugees; vigils, marches, and demonstrations at military-related installations; boycotts of businesses involved in armaments production; and resistance to draft registration. Although violent acts of resistance are not categorically ruled out, the strategy commanding most support is nonviolent resistance that seeks "engagement, confrontation and transformation." According to these peace activists, the time has come for civil disobedience to a government fast becoming a national security state.[56] Christian resistance requires political involvement and political action. Building a mass movement of tax resisters is one strategy advocated. Enlisting church support for occupational withdrawal from nuclear weapons factories is another. Occasionally liberation theologians are commended for reminding us that Christian discipleship must be embodied in the concrete historical situation that is given to us.

The peace movement, at least within the churches, manifests a genuine Christian concern, and some of its declarations have a prophetic ring. Yet what is disquieting is that little if anything is said about individual or national repentance, prayer, preaching, and evangelism. Instead we are left with the impression that our hope lies in political strategies of overt resistance to state authority. Our government is often criticized for its belligerent attitude toward Nicaragua, but the mounting persecution of the church in that country is conveniently ignored or underplayed. A church under the cross will indeed embody the way of peace in its own life and conduct, but should it engage in open confrontations with civil authorities that might precipitate violence? Here again Christians must search their own souls to make sure they are doing God's will and not simply succumbing to group pressure.

The church of Jesus Christ must speak out against evil on all sides, the evil of totalitarian communism as well as the evil of the nuclear armaments race. Pope John Paul II, who somehow succeeds in transcending ideology to a greater extent than Protestant church leaders, has repeatedly said that peacemaking is required on both sides. The fact that the other side continues to place its hope and confidence in weapons of mass extermination, however, does not compel us to follow a similar suicidal path.

In these critical times, the church has the duty to proclaim the divine commandment, which is always in support of peace, and urge nations to place their trust in divine providence. Its role must be prophetic, and this will necessarily have political implications. Christians as citizens of the state are obliged to implement the divine command in their personal lives and in their political involvement.

What is called for today are statesmen as well as prophets. The former are those with the power and practical wisdom to alter social policy in the light of the divine commandment. We need Christians in governmental office, even in positions of military authority, to stem and possibly reverse the drift toward nuclear war through an inspired creative imagination united with political power. It is not only the divine commandment we must consider but also the concrete steps by which we can make progress toward fulfilling this commandment, steps that have the divine permission.

Christians in all walks of life should be active in peacemaking. Our

Lord declared, "Blessed are the peacemakers, for they shall be called sons of God" (Matt. 5:9). We cannot create peace, but we can be witnesses to his peace. We cannot assure the security of our nation even by our prayers, but we can be a leaven within our nation as instruments of the peace of God. In our peacemaking activities we need to be reminded that "unless the Lord builds the house, its builders labor in vain. Unless the Lord watches over the city, the watchmen stand guard in vain" (Ps. 127:1 NIV).

The peace of God is a mystery hidden from the eyes of the "natural man." The only peace the world can know is either an uneasy armistice or a Roman peace, one imposed by a superior power on another. The peace of the world is a peace won through strife (Augustine). But the church is called to herald a new kind of peace, based on the reconciliation of all peoples in Jesus Christ. This is the peace that "passes all understanding" (Phil. 4:7). This kind of peace is a gift from God and is given only to penitent peoples and nations. It can, moreover, be taken away when peoples begin to trust in themselves, in their own ingenuity and wisdom (Jer. 16:5).

Christians may indeed work in the secular peace movement, but their motivations and goals, their world-view, will set them apart from their fellow workers. They will not, for example, make self-preservation an absolute principle. They will resist death in all of its manifestations, including abortion, infanticide, and euthanasia. They will appeal primarily not to fear but to the victory of Christ over the principalities and powers of darkness.

The Christian answer to the threat of nuclear or chemical-biological war will entail diligence in peacemaking, but peace means more than the mere absence of war and strife. Peace in the biblical sense signifies *shalōm*, a wholeness that includes reconciliation with our neighbor and justice.[57] Christians will press for justice for all peoples as a means of eliminating conflict before it erupts, correcting conditions that might lead to rancor and strife. They will announce God's commandment against weapons of mass extermination and try to present in their own lives a peaceable alternative. They will be zealous in preaching the gospel of regeneration, in the knowledge that only a reborn heart, a new vision of God and the world, can bring people closer to the reality of peace in our time. They will vigorously employ the prayer of intercession, realizing that only God by his Spirit can move the world toward a more durable peace for this age.

Indeed, a bona fide Christian witness for peace will be noticeably different from secular versions. First, the focus will be on reconciliation between opposing parties rather than striving for a consensus for the purpose of united action. Second, the appeal will be to the divine promise and the divine commandment over secular wisdom, including that of the social sciences. Third, the emphasis will be on personal regeneration rather than social reformation. Christians are obliged to work for social reform, yet without ever forgetting that their efforts will be in vain if the spiritual change is lacking. It follows that personal and national repentance will be valued over political alterations. Only through such repentance will we gain the creative imagination to perceive alternatives to the way the nations are going. It is imperative that we as a people sense the utter hopelessness of our situation and then turn to God in contrition, seeking his wisdom and guidance. Both the ideological right and left strive for a rational solution to world conflict.

Fourth, peace will be acknowledged as a gift from God rather than a human achievement. It is God who makes peace in our borders (Ps. 147:14; 2 Chron. 14:6; Isa. 26:12), and it is God who takes away such peace (Jer. 16:5). Consequently, Christians will depend far more on prayer than on politics to advance the cause of peace. Prayer is not a substitute for action but the highest action, for it is through prayer that we gain discernment and motivating power. Finally, our appeal will be to the victory of Christ rather than to the fear of the devastating consequences of war.[58] To fear the devastation that these weapons can wreak above all else is to place our fear in these weapons. The biblical way is to place our fear in God (Isa. 8:12, 13; Matt. 10:28; Heb. 10:31), who is more powerful even than the atomic bomb.

As I have already indicated, war takes on the character of a tragic drama on the stage of history, and political maneuvering cannot reverse a slide toward catastrophe once a nation has passed the point of no return. Yet war is a fateful tragedy only in a qualified sense, for we are not pawns in a chess game, acted upon by powers beyond our control. War is a tragedy not in the sense of a fated necessity but in the sense that it becomes practically inevitable when unruly passions gain ascendancy over reason and people become blinded to both their limitations and their presumption.

The tragic dimension of life is the dark side of human existence that carries with it the element of inevitability. The disaster that befalls us could have been avoided if we had only acted differently, but the fact is we did not act differently. Christian faith speaks of the law of retribution that is not irreversible but inevitable if repentance is lacking. The Greek tragedians referred to the nemesis that invariably follows hubris, which is heightened rather than lessened when accompanied by an open acknowledgement of our personal implication in the tragic unfolding of events.

War is not a tragic necessity as the Greeks understood this, but it has the earmarks of tragedy. The tragic is the darkness in human life characterized by the ineluctable downfall of supposedly well-intentioned people and precipitated by some corrosive flaw in their personality or some destructive force in their life. For Christians this tragic flaw is hardness of heart, idolatrous pride. Its prime manifestation is folly; indeed, folly and hardness of heart are closely related, as can be seen in Pharaoh's ambivalent response to Moses (Exod. 5–12).

War is an absurdity even more than a tragedy. It happens even though it could have been avoided. Because it is avoidable, it is inexcusable. From the human standpoint, the descent into chaos may indeed be irreversible, but God can turn even hopeless situations around. In the biblical view, God is over Fate, whereas in the Greek view Fate is even more powerful than the gods. Man may be powerless to halt the tragic course of events leading to war, but God is never powerless.

War is not an accident in human history precipitated by mistaken judgment or the caprice of some leader or group. It occurs when God withholds his grace in the face of the repeated defiance of his will, and therefore war becomes inevitable. Unless the people listen, God will give them up to the stubbornness of their hearts. Yet, the way of repentance is still open (Ps. 81:8–14). In war we see both the outpouring of divine wrath and the tragic unfolding of the human lust for power. War signifies the divine judgment on human sin as well as the final, terrifying outcome of human iniquity.

The deployment of nuclear weapons for deterrence against attack is not justifiable from a Christian point of view, since it carries the threat of the total obliteration of another people. At the same time, it could be tolerable if it were treated as a staying action designed to give time to both sides to come to an agreement on arms reduction. The trouble is that instead of deterring would-be aggressors, it makes them only more fearful and actually accelerates the arms race. There is a real question whether nuclear deterrence is illusory, for the more nuclear weapons systems multiply throughout the world, the greater the chances of accidental conflagration.

While total unilateral disarmament would very likely have a destablizing effect, even to the point of precipitating war, Christians should nevertheless support unilateral initiatives for peace that involve a willingness to make more than token concessions. In the political arena Reinhold Niebuhr still has words of wisdom: "If the democratic nations fall, their failure must be partly attributed to the faulty strategy of idealists who have too many illusions when they face realists who have too little conscience."[59] Yet Niebuhr himself acknowledged that a too consistent realism leads finally to despair. We should endeavor to maintain the hope that God is at work in history reversing the self-destructive proclivities of peoples and nations.

The nuclear armaments race today presents us with a dilemma that is rationally insoluble. Yet this does not mean that some kind of resolution is not historically feasible. God's grace may open to us new possibilities that reason has hitherto been unable to fathom. New alternatives become visible when we seek the will of God in prayer. Yet these alternatives will remain hidden from us unless we acknowledge the evil of nuclear and biochemical weapons, unless we confess as a people that we are involved in sin. Our nation has yet to repent of the atomic bombing of Hiroshima and Nagasaki, which was indeed a dark day in the history of our nation and of humanity.

Christians must not be political quietists, relying exclusively on prayer and fasting. We can press for unilateral initiatives for peace and bilateral disarmament in stages. We can urge governments to make a place for selective conscientious objection in their civil codes. We can encourage people to disengage themselves from employment in nuclear armaments factories. We can seek a church-supported rather than state-supported military chaplaincy.

The world today faces an uncertain future. Should we as Christians try to be a leaven in a society steadily becoming more secularized and callous? Or should our strategy be a flight to the desert, withdrawal from the political and cultural arena in order to prepare for a deeper penetration into the secular enclave at a later time? We need today a fresh vision as well as a new demonstration of the power of the kingdom of God.

The key to peace in our time lies in the Prince of Peace, Jesus Christ. It behooves us to acknowledge him not only as Savior but as Lord and Master and follow him wherever he might lead us. The church of Jesus Christ will always be on the side of peace, not war, on the side of the oppressed, not the powerful. It will know that until Christ comes again, there will always be "wars and rumors of wars" (Matt. 24:6), but that through the gift of the Spirit to the church, Christians can exert a leavening influence on the nations, thereby making possible some strides toward peace within earthly history.

Our situation may well become like that of the church in the crumbling Roman empire. We may have to see ourselves as a creative minority in a culture slipping irrevocably into chaos. The stance of the Christian may have to be creative noncooperation with the powers of our age, but there should be no recourse to violent revolution.

We are entering an era when all war may come to stand under the interdiction of God.[60] In a society where moral norms are collapsing and war itself can be waged only in a spirit of lawlessness, it may be that the church will have to resume its role as a church under the cross, a church in constant conflict with the secular state.

In our gullibility, we are prone to think that those who have been illustrious defenders of the moral values of the West are necessarily on the side of the angels. It is well to note that Winston Churchill was seriously considering "drenching" the German cities with poison gas in retaliation for the Nazi bombing of London. He deemed it "absurd to consider morality on this topic when everybody used it in the last war without a word of complaint from the moralists of the church."[61] He was finally dissuaded by his advisors who told him that such an action might prompt an even more deadly German retaliation. Besides authorizing the destruction of Hiroshima and Nagasaki, President Truman also toyed with the idea of unleashing nuclear bombs against the Chinese in the Korean war.[62] In the Second World War we witnessed the obliteration bombing of Dresden and Tokyo and in the Vietnam war the napalm bombing of open villages as well as the generous use of chemical defoliants like Agent Orange.[63] All of these methods of terror and genocide are out of bounds in the light of God's moral law.

Should our churches declare themselves to be peace churches and utter an unconditional repudiation of war in all of its modern forms? Can a nation ever be called to be pacifist, or is pacifism only a strategy for individuals? Scripture does give us the example of Jeremiah advising the king of Judah to lay down his arms and surrender to the Babylonians rather than try to resist on the basis of an alliance with Egypt (Jer. 38:17–28). I personally believe that God would have us move toward a disarmament in stages. Atomic bombs will never be completely destroyed because we have atomic knowledge. We are in the Einsteinian era and will never be able to return to the Newtonian era (Arthur Cochrane).

As the world faces a possible nuclear holocaust, both Christians and non-Christians need to develop a will never to use these weapons. But the will to say no—uncompromisingly and irrevocably—to weapons of mass extermination can come only from divine grace. We must pray that God will make his awesome presence known to unbelievers as well as to believers, that he will fill the people of the world with at least a servile fear of his might and majesty and at most with a holy dread.

Our hope lies in God alone, not in human ingenuity or heroism. In the case of the non-Christian, the motivation will be fear of the devastation these weapons can bring. But in addition, there will be, at least to some degree, a nagging fear of the judgment of a holy God, whom the unbelieving world has some intimation of even in its denial of his existence. In the case of the Christian, the motivation will be reverence for God's commandment.

Appendix on the Warrior God and the God of Peace

Liberal theologians are inclined to contrast the God of war portrayed in the Old Testament with the God of peace in the New. The Catholic Bishops' Pastoral Letter on War and Peace (May 1983) betrays the same misconception, for it suggests that the idea of the Warrior God belongs to an earlier period in the evolution of religious consciousness.[64] But this is to misunderstand the unity of the God of war and the God of peace. The main thrust of the holy wars is to remind us that it is God who carries out retribution against his enemies, that vengeance belongs to him alone (cf. Deut. 32:35; Ps. 35; Rom. 12:19; Heb. 10:30). The Catholic bishops acknowledge that the God of war is in the Book of Revelation, but they regard this as an eschatological conflict beyond history. I see this book as presenting the whole panorama of sacred history beginning with the incarnation of Christ. The God of the Bible is one of both holiness and love, of judgment as well as mercy. He raises up kings and empires by his grace and brings them down by his wrath. The unity of the God of war and the God of peace lies in the biblical insight that God's wrath is but a form of his love, that his judgments are exercised for the sake of his mercy (cf. Hos. 6:1; Isa. 30:26; 38:15–17; Ps. 60:1–5; 99:8; Rom. 11:25–36).

It is, moreover, precisely in the cross of Christ that God's wrath as well as his righteousness is most dramatically revealed. When Paul declared that "the wrath of God is revealed from heaven against all ungodliness and wickedness of men" (Rom. 1:18), he was very probably referring to the righteousness of Jesus Christ mentioned in verse 17. Barth convincingly argues that these verses belong together, that verse 18 does not speak of a prior revelation of God but of the one revelation in Jesus Christ.[65] God has acted decisively and irrevocably to bring about peace between peoples and nations by taking upon himself the retribution for sin in the person of his Son. His wrath and judgment against sin was born by Jesus Christ, who has broken down "the dividing wall of hostility" (Eph. 2:14) that separates Jew and Gentile by creating one new people united in their faith in him. Our Lord has taken away the enmity between God and a rebellious human race by taking this enmity upon himself.[66] "Every record of the debt that we had to pay" has been cancelled, having been nailed to the cross (Col. 2:14 JB). By removing the penalty for sin, he also brought down the devil, whose power rests on God's condemnation of the sinner (cf. Col. 2:15).

Yet the efficacy of this atoning sacrifice is blocked in peoples' lives by their tenacious refusal to acknowledge the reality of the cross and resurrection victory of Jesus Christ. We have been set free for obedience to the imperatives of the gospel, but this freedom must be seized in faith if we are to live as the reconciled and as reconcilers, if we are to be "more than conquerors through him who loved us" (Rom. 8:37).

Notes

1. John Burnet, *Early Greek Philosophy*, 4th ed. (London: Adam & Charles Black, 1930), pp. 136–37.
2. *The Philosophy of Nietzsche*, intro. Willard Huntington Wright (New York: Random House, Modern Library, 1927), p. 48.
3. Jacques Barzun, *A Stroll With William James* (New York: Harper & Row, 1983), p. 172.
4. Ibid., p. 173.
5. Ernst Benz, *Evolution and Christian Hope*, trans. Heinz G. Frank (New York: Doubleday, 1966), p. 232.
6. Quoted in Ibid.
7. Ibid., p. 231.
8. Nicolas Berdyaev, *The Destiny of Man*, 3d ed., trans. Natalie Duddington (London: Geoffrey Bles, 1948), p. 201.
9. Ibid., p. 200.
10. Quoted in Jacques Ellul, *Violence*, trans. Cecelia Gaul Kings (New York: Seabury Press, 1969), p. 173.
11. Some scholars see this verse as a stricture on blood sacrifice only, but more likely it condemns sacrifices offered by people who have committed violence against others. See Edward J. Young, *The Book of Isaiah* (Grand Rapids: Eerdmans, 1965), 1: pp. 69–70.
12. On the close relation of folly and sin see Ps. 85:8 NIV; Isa. 19:13; Prov. 18:6; 2 Sam. 15:31; 2 Kings 14:8–10; Jer. 4:19–22; Eccles. 7:25; 9:17, 18).

    Psalm 85:8 (see introductory quotes) is especially interesting, for here peace (*shalōm*) is expressly contrasted with folly, which leads to strife and unrest. In this section of the psalm, the worshipers may have been addressed by a prophet of peace, who points to the way out of the strife and unrest that trouble the nation (A. A. Anderson). At a time of crisis in their faith, they were tempted to fall back into folly, that is, into sin or prideful self-confidence and lose the inheritance of their promise (Artur Weiser). But God himself intervenes and revives the people by his word. According to most commentators, this Psalm is probably postexilic, referring to a period shortly after the return from the exile when the nation was troubled by strife, privations, and bad harvests.

Matthew Henry offers these perceptive comments on Psalm 85:8: "To those, and those only, peace is spoken, who turn from sin; but, if they return to it again, it is at their peril. All sin is folly, but especially backsliding; it is egregious folly to turn to sin after we have seemed to turn from it, to turn to it after God has spoken peace. God is for peace, but, when he speaks, such are for war." *An Exposition of the Old and New Testament* (New York: Fleming H. Revell, n.d.), vol. 3, Psalm 85:8.

13. On the basis of this and, even less plausibly, several other texts, José Miranda holds that Jesus was committed to violence in advancing the cause of the kingdom. *Communism in the Bible*, pp. 75–78.

14. See Victor Paul Furnish, "War and Peace in the New Testament," *Interpretation* 38, no. 4 (Oct. 1984): p. 377.

15. While Reformed and Anabaptist traditions agree that the use of the sword is necessary to maintain order in society, they differ on whether Christians can ever occupy positions in government where the use of force is necessitated. Anabaptists deny that Christians themselves can ever wield the sword or be a party to decisions where the sword must be used.

16. See Jean Lasserre, *War and the Gospel*, trans. Oliver Coburn (Scottdale, Pa.: Herald Press, 1962), pp. 60–61.

17. See Roland Bainton, *Christian Attitudes Toward War and Peace* (Nashville: Abingdon, 1960), pp. 73–74, 77–84.

18. Lasserre, *War and the Gospel*, p. 183.

19. Quoted in ibid., p. 172. See Saint Cyprian, *To Donatus*, in *Treatises*, trans. and ed. Roy J. Deferrari (New York: Fathers of the Church, 1958), chap. 6, p. 12. Cyprian cites 2 Tim. 2:4: "No soldier fighting in God's service entangles himself in the anxieties of this world, thereby enabling himself to be free to please Him who enlisted him." *The Letters of St. Cyprian of Carthage*, trans. G. W. Clarke, (New York: Newman, 1984), vol. 1, 1:1, p. 51.

20. Bainton, *Christian Attitudes*, pp. 88–89.

21. Ibid., pp. 77, 78.

22. Ibid., p. 78.

23. Ibid., p. 109.

24. Thomas Aquinas, *Summa Theologica*, II-II, 40.2. trans. Fathers of the English Dominican Province (London: Burns Oates & Washbourne, 1916) vol. 9, p. 505. cf. II-II, 64.4, vol. 10, p. 202.

25. Jean Lasserre, *War and the Gospel*, p. 130.

26. Timothy George, "War and Peace in the Puritan Tradition," *Church History* 53, no. 4 (Dec. 1984): p. 494.

27. Ibid., p. 500.

28. See Harold O. J. Brown, "The Crusade or Preventive War," in *War: Four Christian Views*, ed. Robert G. Clouse (Downers Grove, Ill.: InterVarsity, 1981), pp. 151–68. Brown defines a crusade "as a war waged to remedy a past atrocity, especially one recognized as such for spiritual or religious reasons" (p. 156).

29. See Bainton, *Christian Attitudes*, p. 243.

30. See Roger Smith, "The Witness of the Church," in *Nuclear Weapons—A Catholic Response*, ed. G. E. M. Anscombe et al. (New York: Sheed & Ward, 1961), pp. 103–22.

31. Wolfhart Pannenberg, *Ethics*, trans. Keith Crim (Philadelphia: Westminster, 1981), p. 169.

32. Ibid., p. 168.

33. Niebuhr, *Moral Man and Immoral Society*, p. 170.

34. See Dale Aukerman, *Darkening Valley* (New York: Seabury, 1981).

35. Barth quotes Wilhelm Herrmann: "War itself is neither Christian nor unchristian, neither moral nor immoral. In certain historical circumstances it is the imperative expression of human nature as this has developed with civilisation to political life." *Church Dogmatics*, vol. 4, 4, p. 457.

36. See John Howard Yoder, *Karl Barth and the Problem of War* (Nashville: Abingdon, 1970), p. 83.

37. Paul Tillich, *Systematic Theology* (Chicago: University of Chicago Press, 1951), 1: p. 254.

38. Paul Tillich, *Systematic Theology* (Chicago: University of Chicago Press, 1963), 3: pp. 92–94, 102, 103.

39. Tillich fails to explore the concept of folly in relation to war and the demonic, preferring instead to speak of "demonic hubris." Yet because he ties the demonic so closely to the irrational, his view and mine tend to converge in this area. For Tillich the demonic signifies forces both creative and destructive that emerge out of the unconscious, "fateful expressions of the eruption of the depths." James Luther Adams, *Paul Tillich's Philosophy of Culture, Science, and Religion* (New York: Harper & Row, 1965), p. 232. Those under the spell of the demonic succumb to an "unbroken enthusiasm" that deprives them of "critical insight and critical utterance." Paul Tillich, "Open Letter to Emanuel Hirsch," in *The Thought of Paul Tillich*, ed. James Luther Adams et al. (San Francisco: Harper & Row, 1985), p. 365. It is doubtful that Tillich would claim that all war is demonic, though he would probably say that the demonic is always present in war.

40. Reinhold Niebuhr, *Beyond Tragedy* (New York: Charles Scribner's Sons, 1937), p. 158.

41. Thielicke takes pains to disassociate himself from the tragic-naturalistic interpretation of history. See *Theological Ethics*, ed. William Lazareth (Philadelphia: Fortress, 1969), 2: pp. 437–43.

42. Augustine, *The City of God*, vol. 4, chap. 15. Cited in *The Challenge of Peace: God's Promise and Our Response*, 4th printing (Washington, D.C.: United States Catholic Conference, 1984), p. 27.

43. Thielicke, *Theological Ethics* 1: p. 602.

44. Insofar as Christians are obedient to God's commandment, they need not have an uneasy conscience because they know they are doing what God wills. Yet at the same time, because they are disobedient even in their obedience, their conscience will be troubled, for they know that they are falling short of all God demands of them.

45. Because this general position embraces such a wide variety of viewpoints, I am here giving my own interpretation, which some, but not necessarily all, of the theologians mentioned in this section would support. For more on the tragic character of war, see pp. 310–11.

46. Thielicke sees the choice as between physical destruction, if we use the bomb, and moral destruction, if we submit to communism. *Theological Ethics* 2: p. 482. Yet he fails to recognize that using the bomb will also entail our moral destruction.

47. Arthur Cochrane gives this prophetic warning: "The threat and exercise of the means of mass extermination in waging war is blasphemy against God the Creator, Preserver and Redeemer of human life and is sin against the creature for whom Christ died and rose again. It defeats the very purpose for which war may lawfully be waged, and a State which employs such means becomes (in this respect) a nihilistic State by the indiscriminate destruction of the evil and the good, the just and the unjust, the defenseless and the armed, the living and those not yet born." "Mass Extermination As a Means of Waging War," in *The Mystery of Peace* (Elgin, Ill.: Brethren Press, 1986), p. 168.

48. In modern times it remained for the Nazis to revive and perfect the horror of genocide, the wholesale destruction of civilian populations. Their nihilistic policies led to the annihilation of Lidice and the barbaric obliteration bombing of Warsaw, Rotterdam, and Coventry. While the allies initially condemned these crimes, they resorted to similar methods as the war progressed. Hitler lost the war, but the spirit of Hitler triumphed, since the methods he sanctioned became normative in modern warfare. One is here reminded of Nietzsche's aphorism: "Be careful when you fight the dragon, lest you become a dragon."

49. In Cochrane's opinion, the bombing of Dresden was primarily motivated by a desire for vengeance. *The Mystery of Peace*, pp. 134, 149.

50. Ronald J. Sider and Richard K. Taylor, *Nuclear Holocaust and Christian Hope* (Downers Grove, Ill.: InterVarsity, 1982), pp. 238–45.

51. "Is There A Crisis in the Catholic Church?" Transcript of the Firing Line Program, Jan. 15, 1984 (Columbia, S.C.: Education Communications Association, 1984), p. 17. To do justice to Father Hesburgh he also spoke of the need for prayer and fasting.

52. In his *Religion in the Secular City* (New York: Simon & Schuster, 1984) Harvey Cox contends that the hope of a new world rests on "contemplative intelligence," which brings together the wisdom of the sages and scientific knowledge. See pp. 58, 59, 220.

53. Quoted in Emmy Arnold, ed., *Inner Words*, (Rifton, N.Y.: Plough Publishing House, 1975), pp. 117–18.

54. Quoted in Knut Willem Ruyter, "Pacifism and Military Service in the Early Church," *Cross Currents* 32, no. 1 (Spring 1982): p. 63.

55. See, for example, Dana Wilbanks, *Presbyterians and Militarism: Does Peacemaking Now Require Resistance?* (A mimeographed study document offered to the General Assembly Advisory Committee on Peacemaking in 1985, Guadalajara, Mexico, 1984.) See also Dana W. Wilbanks and Ronald H. Stone, *Presbyterians and Peacemaking: Are We Now Called To Resistance?* (New York: Advisory Council on Church and Society, 1985); and Ronald H. Stone and Dana W. Wilbanks, *The Peacemaking Struggle: Militarism and Resistance* (Lanham, Md.: University Press of America, 1985).

56. Vernard Eller, who regards himself as a biblical pacifist, criticizes those he calls the "peace zealots" in his own denomination (the Church of the Brethren), for singling out America and the West as the principal enemies and discreetly overlooking the sins of the Communist and Third World countries. See his *Towering Babble* (Elgin, Ill.: Brethren Press, 1983), pp. 77–101.

57. See Nicholas Wolterstorff, *Until Justice and Peace Embrace* (Grand Rapids: Eerdmans, 1983).

58. Cf. Jonathan Schell, *The Fate of the Earth* (New York: Alfred A. Knopf, 1982).

59. Cited in James Reston, "Kennedy in the Middle on German Debate," *New York Times*, Oct. 25, 1961, sec. 36.

60. This is Arthur Cochrane's thesis in *Mystery of Peace*, pp. 149–50.

61. James Warren, "Which War Moral—Poison Gas or Atom Bomb?" *Chicago Tribune* Aug. 7, 1985, sec. 5.

62. See Paul Johnson, *Modern Times* (New York: Harper & Row, 1983), p. 451.

63. An editorial in the *New Republic* comments: "What surprises and shocks in the Vietnam case is the now clear-cut revelation of what can befall an unfortunate rice-thatch village that happens to be located in a Viet Cong controlled zone: apparently, regardless of whether it is inhabited by civilians or not, it is subject to total obliteration. . . . War never descended to *that* kind of barbarity at least in Western Europe, where aircraft would not attack villages and where even the Nazi destruction of such rural communities as Lidice in Czechoslovakia, Oradour in France, or Stavelot in Belgium, remain odious exceptions to be remembered forever." *New Republic* 155, no. 8 (Aug. 27, 1966): p. 6. This is not to overlook the barbarities of the other side in this war, including the inhumane treatment of prisoners. Communist atrocities in Indochina following the war, including the wholesale murder of hospital patients in their beds and the systematic destruction and expulsion of ethnic minorities, are amply documented by Paul Johnson in *Modern Times*, pp. 654–58.

64. *The Challenge of Peace: God's Promise and Our Response*, pp. 10–14. For my critique of the Pastoral Letter see Donald G. Bloesch, "The Catholic Bishops on War and Peace," *Center Journal* 3, no. 1 (Winter 1983): pp. 163–76.

65. Karl Barth, *Church Dogmatics* IV, 1, pp. 392–93.

66. Cf. Thomas Aquinas: "In fulfilling the Old Testament symbols, he killed the hostility that had arisen through the law between the Jews and the Gentiles. But the hostility that existed between God and men through sin, he killed in himself when he blotted out sin through the death of the Cross." *Commentary on Saint Paul's Epistle to the*

Ephesians, trans. Matthew L. Lamb (Albany, N.Y.: Magi Books, 1966), p. 108. Here we see that it is precisely the Warrior God who has made it possible for real peace to come to the world.

A Selected Bibliography*

Adams, James Luther. *Paul Tillich's Philosophy of Culture, Science and Religion.* New York: Harper & Row, 1965.

Althaus, Paul. *The Divine Command; A New Perspective on Law and Gospel.* Translated by Franklin Sherman. Philadelphia: Fortress, 1966.

———. *The Ethics of Martin Luther.* Translated by Robert C. Schultz. Philadelphia: Fortress, 1972.

Aquinas, Thomas. *Treatise on the Virtues.* Translated by John A. Oesterle. Notre Dame, Ind.: University of Notre Dame Press, 1984.

Aristotle. *The Ethics of Aristotle: Nicomachean Ethics.* Translated by J. A. K. Thomson. New York: Penguin, 1976.

Augustine, *The City of God.* Introduction by Thomas Merton. Translated by Marcus Dods. New York: Modern Library, 1983.

Barbour, John D. *Tragedy as a Critique of Virtue.* Chico, Calif.: Scholars Press, 1984.

Barth, Karl. *The Christian Life.* Translated by Geoffrey W. Bromiley. Grand Rapids: Eerdmans, 1981.

———. *Church Dogmatics* II, 2; III, 4. Edited by G. W. Bromiley and T. F. Torrance. Edinburgh: T. & T. Clark, 1957, 1961.

———. *Community, State and Church.* Introduction by Will Herberg. New York: Doubleday, 1960.

———. *Ethics.* Edited by Dietrich Braun; Translated by Geoffrey W. Bromiley. New York: Seabury, 1981.

Battaglia, Anthony. *Toward a Reformulation of Natural Law.* New York: Seabury, 1981.

Bennett, John C. *The Radical Imperative.* Philadelphia: Westminster, 1975.

Berdyaev, Nicolas. *Dream and Reality.* Translated by Katherine Lampert. New York: Macmillan Co., 1951.

Biéler, André. *The Social Humanism of Calvin.* Translated by Paul T. Fuhrmann. Richmond, Va.: John Knox, 1964.

Bloesch, Donald G. *The Christian Life and Salvation.* Grand Rapids: Eerdmans, 1967.

---

*The books listed focus for the most part on theoretical rather than practical ethics.

Böckle, Franz. *Law and Conscience*. Translated by M. James Donnelly. New York: Sheed & Ward, 1966.

———. *Fundamental Moral Theology*. Translated by N. D. Smith. New York: Pueblo Publishing Co., 1980.

Bonhoeffer, Dietrich. *The Cost of Discipleship*. Translated by R. H. Fuller. New York: Macmillan Co., 1959.

———. *Ethics*. Edited by Eberhard Bethge and translated by Neville Horton Smith. New York: Macmillan Co., 1965.

———. *Letters and Papers from Prison*. Edited by Eberhard Bethge and translated by Reginald Fuller. New York: Macmillan Co., 1953.

Bonino, José Míguez. *Toward a Christian Political Ethics*. Philadelphia: Fortress, 1983.

Bornkamm, Heinrich. *Luther's Doctrine of the Two Kingdoms*. Translated by Karl H. Hertz. Philadelphia: Fortress, 1966.

Brown, Dale W. *Biblical Pacifism: A Peace Church Perspective*. Elgin, Ill.: Brethren, 1986.

Brunner, Emil. *Christianity and Civilization*. 2 vols. New York: Charles Scribner's Sons, 1948–49.

———. *The Divine Imperative*. Translated by Olive Wyon. Philadelphia: Westminster, 1947.

———. *Justice and the Social Order*. Translated by Mary Hottinger. New York: Harper & Brothers, 1945.

Cadoux, C. John. *The Early Christian Attitude to War*. New York: Seabury, 1982.

Calvin, John. *John Calvin's Sermons on the Ten Commandments*. Edited and translated by Benjamin W. Farley. Grand Rapids: Baker, 1980.

Carnell, Edward John. *Christian Commitment*. Grand Rapids: Baker, 1982.

Childress, James F., and John Macquarrie, eds. *The Westminster Dictionary of Christian Ethics*. Philadelphia: Westminster, 1986.

Clouse, Robert G., ed. *War: Four Christian Views*. Downers Grove, Ill.: InterVarsity, 1981.

Cochrane, Arthur C. *The Mystery of Peace*. Elgin, Ill.: Brethren, 1986.

Cooper, John W. *The Theology of Freedom: The Legacy of Jacques Maritain and Reinhold Niebuhr*. Macon, Ga.: Mercer University Press, 1985.

Cox, Harvey, ed. *The Situation Ethics Debate*. Philadelphia: Westminster, 1968.

Craigie, Peter C. *The Problem of War in the Old Testament*. Grand Rapids: Eerdmans, 1978.

Cunningham, Robert L., ed. *Situationism and the New Morality*. New York: Appleton-Century-Crofts, 1970.

Curran, Charles E. *Directions in Fundamental Moral Theology*. Notre Dame, Ind.: University of Notre Dame Press, 1985.

———. *Moral Theology: A Continuing Journey*. Notre Dame, Ind.: University of Notre Dame Press, 1974.

Daly, Mary. *Gyn/Ecology: The Metaethics of Radical Feminism*. Boston: Beacon, 1978.

D'Arcy, M. C. *The Mind and Heart of Love*. 2d rev. ed. New York: Henry Holt, 1954.

Diggins, John Patrick. *The Lost Soul of American Politics*. New York: Basic Books, 1984.

Dodd, C. H. *Gospel and Law.* Cambridge: Cambridge University Press, 1951.

Dunphy, William. *The New Morality.* New York: Herder & Herder, 1967.

Elert, Werner, *Law and Gospel.* Translated by Edward H. Schroeder. Philadelphia: Fortress, 1967.

Eller, Vernard. *Kierkegaard and Radical Discipleship.* Princeton, N.J.: Princeton University Press, 1968.

――――. *King Jesus' Manual of Arms for the Armless.* Nashville: Abingdon, 1973.

――――. *The Promise: Ethics in the Kingdom of God.* New York: Doubleday, 1970.

Ellul, Jacques. *The Ethics of Freedom.* Translated and edited by Geoffrey W. Bromiley. Grand Rapids: Eerdmans, 1976.

――――. *Living Faith.* Translated by Peter Heinegg. San Francisco: Harper & Row, 1983.

――――. *The Political Illusion.* Translated by Konrad Kellen. New York: Alfred A. Knopf, 1967.

――――. *The Politics of God and the Politics of Man.* Translated by Geoffrey W. Bromiley. Grand Rapids: Eerdmans, 1972.

――――. *Violence.* Translated by Cecelia Gaul Kings. New York: Seabury, 1969.

――――. *To Will & to Do.* Translated by C. Edward Hopkin. Philadelphia: Pilgrim, 1969.

Erickson, Millard J. *Relativism in Contemporary Christian Ethics.* Grand Rapids: Baker, 1974.

Fitch, Robert. *Of Love and of Suffering.* Philadelphia: Westminster, 1970.

Fletcher, Joseph. *Situation Ethics: The New Morality.* Philadelphia: Westminster, 1966.

Forde, Gerhard O. *The Law-Gospel Debate.* Minneapolis: Augsburg, 1969.

Forell, George W. *Ethics of Decision.* Philadelphia: Muhlenberg Press, 1955.

――――. *History of Christian Ethics.* Vol. 1. Minneapolis: Augsburg, 1979.

Fourez, Gérard. *Liberation Ethics.* Philadelphia: Temple University Press, 1982.

Fried, Charles. *Right and Wrong.* Cambridge: Harvard University Press, 1978.

Fromm, Erich. *Man for Himself.* New York: Holt, Rinehart and Winston, 1947.

Fuller, Daniel P. *Gospel and Law.* Grand Rapids: Eerdmans, 1980.

Furnish, Victor P. *The Love Command in the New Testament.* Nashville: Abingdon, 1972.

――――. *Theology and Ethics in Paul.* Nashville: Abingdon, 1968.

Gaffney, James. *Moral Questions.* New York: Paulist, 1975.

Gallagher, John. *The Basis for Christian Ethics.* New York: Paulist, 1985.

Geisler, Norman. *Ethics: Alternatives and Issues.* Grand Rapids: Zondervan, 1971.

――――. *Options in Contemporary Christian Ethics.* Grand Rapids: Baker, 1981.

Gilder, George. *Wealth and Poverty.* New York: Basic Books, 1981.

Gill, Robin. *A Textbook of Christian Ethics.* Edinburgh: T. & T. Clark, 1985.

Graham, W. Fred. *The Constructive Revolutionary: John Calvin and His Socio-Economic Impact.* Richmond, Va.: John Knox, 1971.

Grisez, Germain. *The Way of the Lord Jesus: Christian Moral Principles* Vol. 1. Chicago: Franciscan Herald, 1983.

Grisez, Germain, and Russell Shaw. *Beyond the New Morality: The Responsibilities of Freedom.* Notre Dame, Ind.: University of Notre Dame Press, 1974.

Gustafson, James M. *Ethics From a Theocentric Perspective.* 2 vols. Chicago: University of Chicago Press, 1981–1984.

————. *Protestant and Roman Catholic Ethics.* Chicago: University of Chicago Press, 1978.

Gula, Richard M. *What Are They Saying about Moral Norms?* New York: Paulist, 1982.

Gutiérrez, Gustavo. *A Theology of Liberation.* Translated by Sister Caridad Inda and John Eagleson, Maryknoll, N.Y.: Orbis Books, 1973.

Hall, Robert T. *The Morality of Civil Disobedience.* New York: Harper Torchbook, 1971.

Hancock, Roger N. *Twentieth Century Ethics.* New York: Columbia University Press, 1974.

Happel, Stephen, and James J. Walter. *Conversion and Discipleship.* Philadelphia: Fortress Press, 1986.

Häring, Bernhard. *Free and Faithful in Christ.* Vol. 1. New York: Seabury, 1978.

————. *The Law of Christ.* 2 vols. Translated by Edwin G. Kaiser. Westminster, Md.: Newman, 1964–65.

Harrelson, Walter. *The Ten Commandments and Human Rights.* Philadelphia: Fortress, 1980.

Harries, Richard, ed. *Reinhold Niebuhr and the Issues of Our Time.* Grand Rapids: Eerdmans, 1986.

Hauerwas, Stanley. *Against the Nations.* Minneapolis: Winston-Seabury, 1985.

————. *Character and the Christian Life.* San Antonio, Tex.: Trinity University Press, 1975.

————. *Vision and Virtue.* Notre Dame, Ind.: University of Notre Dame Press, 1981.

Hebblethwaite, Brian. *Christian Ethics in the Modern Age.* Philadelphia: Westminster, 1982.

Hengel, Martin. *Victory Over Violence: Jesus and the Revolutionists.* Translated by David E. Green. Philadelphia: Fortress, 1973.

Hennig, Kurt. *God's Basic Law.* Philadelphia: Fortress, 1969.

Henry, Carl F. H. *Christian Personal Ethics.* Grand Rapids: Eerdmans, 1957.

Hershberger, Guy F. *War, Peace, and Nonresistance.* Scottdale, Pa.: Herald, 1946.

Herzog, Frederick. *Justice Church.* Maryknoll, N.Y.: Orbis Books, 1980.

Hildebrand, Dietrich, and Alice von Hildebrand. *Morality and Situation Ethics.* Chicago: Franciscan Herald, 1966.

Holl, Karl. *The Reconstruction of Morality.* Edited by James Luther Adams and Walter F. Bense. Translated by Fred W. Meuser and Walter R. Wietzke. Minneapolis: Augsburg, 1979.

Hollenbach, David. *Nuclear Ethics: A Christian Moral Argument.* New York: Paulist Press, 1983.

Holmes, Arthur F., ed. *War and Christian Ethics.* Grand Rapids: Baker, 1975.

Hornus, Jean Michel. *It Is Not Lawful for Me to Fight.* Translated by Alan Kreider and Oliver Coburn. Scottdale, Pa.: Herald, 1980.

Houlden, J. L. *Ethics and the New Testament.* New York: Oxford University Press, 1977.

Kaiser, Walter C., Jr. *Toward Old Testament Ethics.* Grand Rapids: Zondervan, 1983.

Kant, Immanuel. *The Metaphysics of Morals.* Translated by John Ladd. Indianapolis: Bobbs-Merrill Co., 1965.

Kierkegaard, Søren. *Either/Or*. Translated by David F. Swenson and Lillian Marvin Swenson. Princeton, N.J.: Princeton University Press, 1949.
———. *Works of Love*. Translated by Howard and Edna Hong. New York: Harper, 1962.
King, Martin Luther, Jr. *Strength to Love*. New York: Harper & Row, 1963.
Lasserre, Jean. *War and the Gospel*. Translated by Oliver Coburn. Scottdale, Pa.: Herald, 1962.
Lehmann, Paul. *Ethics in a Christian Context*. New York: Harper & Row, 1963.
Lester, William. *The Transfiguration of Politics*. New York: Harper & Row, 1975.
Lewis, C. S. *The Four Loves*. New York: Harcourt, Brace & World, 1960.
Lochman, Jan Milič. *Signposts to Freedom*. Translated by David Lewis. Minneapolis: Augsburg, 1982.
Long, Edward L. *Conscience and Compromise*. Philadelphia: Westminster, 1954.
———. *A Survey of Recent Christian Ethics*. New York: Oxford University Press, 1982.
Lovin, Robin W. *Christian Faith and Public Choices: The Social Ethics of Barth, Brunner and Bonhoeffer*. Philadelphia: Fortress, 1984.
Luther, Martin. *Christian Liberty*. Edited by Harold J. Grimm and translated by W. A. Lambert. Philadelphia: Fortress, 1970.
McCann, Dennis P. *Christian Realism and Liberation Theology*. Maryknoll, N.Y.: Orbis Books, 1981.
McClendon, James William, Jr. *Ethics: Systematic Theology*, vol. 1 Nashville: Abingdon, 1986.
McCormick, Richard A. *Notes on Moral Theology 1965 Through 1980*. Lanham, Md.: University Press of America, 1981.
McInerny, Ralph. *Ethica Thomistica: The Moral Philosophy of Thomas Aquinas*. Washington, D.C.: Catholic University of America Press, 1982.
MacIntyre, Alasdair C. *After Virtue: A Study in Moral Theory*. Notre Dame, Ind.: University of Notre Dame Press, 1981.
Macquarrie, John. *In Search of Humanity*. New York: Crossroad, 1983.
———. *Three Issues in Ethics*. New York: Harper & Row, 1970.
Mannheim, Karl. *Ideology and Utopia*. Translated by Louis Wirth and Edward Shils. New York: Harcourt, Brace and Co., 1966.
Marrin, Albert, ed. *War and the Christian Conscience*. Chicago: Henry Regnery, 1971.
Maston, T. B. *Biblical Ethics: A Survey*. Cleveland: World Publishing Co., 1967.
Meilaender, Gilbert C. *The Theory and Practice of Virtue*. Notre Dame, Ind.: University of Notre Dame Press, 1984.
Merton, Thomas. *Conjectures of a Guilty Bystander*. New York: Doubleday, 1966.
Milhaven, John Giles. *Toward a New Catholic Morality*. New York: Doubleday, 1970.
Miranda, José P. *Marx and the Bible*. Translated by John Eagleson. Maryknoll, N.Y.: Orbis Books, 1974.
Moltmann, Jürgen. *On Human Dignity: Political Theology and Ethics*. Translated by M. Douglas Meeks. Philadelphia: Fortress, 1984.
———. *Religion, Revolution and the Future*. Translated by M. Douglas Meeks. New York: Charles Scribner's Sons, 1969.

Monden, Louis. *Sin, Liberty, and Law.* Translated by Joseph Donceel. New York: Sheed & Ward, 1965.

Mott, Stephen Charles. *Biblical Ethics and Social Change.* New York: Oxford University Press, 1982.

Muelder, Walter G. *Moral Law in Christian Social Ethics.* Richmond, Va.: John Knox, 1966.

Murchland, Bernard. *The Dream of Christian Socialism.* Washington, D.C.: American Enterprise Institute for Public Policy Research, 1982.

Nelson, James B. *Moral Nexus.* Philadelphia: Westminster, 1971.

Neuhaus, Richard John. *The Naked Public Square.* Grand Rapids: Eerdmans, 1984.

Niebuhr, H. Richard. *Christ and Culture.* New York: Harper, 1951.

―――. *The Kingdom of God in America.* Chicago: Willett, Clark & Co., 1937.

Niebuhr, H. Richard, Wilhelm Pauck, and Francis P. Miller. *The Church Against the World.* Chicago: Willett, Clark & Co., 1935.

Niebuhr, Reinhold. *Christian Realism and Political Problems.* New York: Charles Scribner's Sons, 1953.

―――. *An Interpretation of Christian Ethics.* New York: Seabury, 1979.

―――. *Love and Justice.* Edited by D. B. Robertson. Philadelphia: Westminster, 1957.

―――. *Man's Nature and His Communities.* New York: Charles Scribner's Sons, 1965.

―――. *Moral Man and Immoral Society.* New York: Charles Scribner's Sons, 1932.

Nietzsche, Friedrich. *The Genealogy of Morals.* Translated by Horace B. Samuel. New York: Gordon, 1974.

Norman, Richard. *The Moral Philosophers.* Oxford: Clarendon, 1983.

Novak, Michael. *Freedom with Justice.* San Francisco: Harper & Row, 1984.

Nygren, Anders. *Agape and Eros.* Translated by Philip S. Watson. Philadelphia: Westminster, 1953.

O'Connell, Timothy E. *Principles for a Catholic Morality.* New York: Seabury, 1978.

Oden, Thomas C. *Radical Obedience.* Philadelphia: Westminster, 1964.

O'Donovan, Oliver. *Resurrection and Moral Order.* Grand Rapids: Eerdmans, 1986.

Ogletree, Thomas W. *The Use of the Bible in Christian Ethics.* Philadelphia: Fortress, 1983.

Outka, Gene. *Agape: An Ethical Analysis.* New Haven: Yale University Press, 1972.

Outka, Gene, and Paul Ramsey, eds. *Norm and Context in Christian Ethics.* New York: Charles Scribner's Sons, 1968.

Pannenberg, Wolfhart. *Ethics.* Translated by Keith Crim. Philadelphia: Westminster, 1981.

Piper, Otto A. *Christian Ethics.* London: Thomas Nelson & Sons, 1970.

Ramm, Bernard L. *The Right, the Good and the Happy.* Waco, Tex.: Word Books, 1971.

Ramsey, Ian T., ed. *Christian Ethics and Contemporary Philosophy.* New York: Macmillan Co., 1966.

Ramsey, Paul. *Basic Christian Ethics.* New York: Charles Scribner's Sons, 1950.

———. *Deeds and Rules in Christian Ethics.* New York: Charles Scribner's Sons, 1967.

———. *War and the Christian Conscience.* Durham, N.C.: Duke University Press, 1961.

Rauschenbusch, Walter. *Christianity and the Social Crisis.* New York: Macmillan Co., 1913.

Reist, Benjamin A. *Toward a Theology of Involvement: The Thought of Ernst Troeltsch.* Philadelphia: Westminster, 1966.

Rendtorff, Trutz. *Ethics.* Translated by Keith Crim. Philadelphia: Fortress, 1986.

Robinson, J. A. T. *Christian Morals Today.* Philadelphia: Westminster, 1964.

Robinson, N. H. G. *The Groundwork of Christian Ethics.* Grand Rapids: Eerdmans, 1972.

Rudnick, Milton L. *Christian Ethics for Today.* Grand Rapids: Baker, 1979.

Sanders, Jack T. *Ethics in the New Testament.* Philadelphia: Fortress, 1975.

Schnackenburg, Rudolf. *The Moral Teaching of the New Testament.* Translated by J. Holland-Smith and W. J. O'Hara. New York: Herder & Herder, 1965.

Schulweis, Harold M. *Evil and the Morality of God.* Cincinnati: Hebrew Union College Press, 1984.

Segundo, Juan Luis. *Faith and Ideologies.* Translated by John Drury. Maryknoll, N.Y.: Orbis Books, 1984.

Sellers, James. *Theological Ethics.* New York: Macmillan Co., 1966.

Sider, Ronald J. *Christ and Violence.* Scottdale, Pa.: Herald, 1979.

Sider, Ronald J., and Richard K. Taylor. *Nuclear Holocaust and Christian Hope.* Downers Grove, Ill.: InterVarsity, 1982.

Smedes, Lewis B. *Love within Limits: A Realist's View of I Corinthians 13.* Grand Rapids: Eerdmans, 1978.

———. *Mere Morality.* Grand Rapids: Eerdmans, 1983.

Smith, Adam. *Wealth of Nations.* Introduction by Richard F. Teichgraeber III. New York: Random House, 1985.

Spinoza, Baruch. *The Ethics of Spinoza: The Road to Inner Freedom.* Edited by Dagobert D. Runes. Secaucus, N.J.: Citadel, 1976.

Spohn, William C. *What Are They Saying About Scripture and Ethics?* New York: Paulist Press, 1984.

Spurrier, William A. *Natural Law and the Ethics of Love.* Philadelphia: Westminster, 1974.

Stackhouse, Max L. *Creeds, Society and Human Rights: A Study in Three Cultures.* Grand Rapids: Eerdmans, 1984.

Stob, Henry. *Ethical Reflections.* Grand Rapids: Eerdmans, 1978.

Storer, Morris B., ed. *Humanist Ethics.* Buffalo, N.Y.: Prometheus Books, 1980.

Stringfellow, William. *A Private and Public Faith.* Grand Rapids: Eerdmans, 1962.

Swomley, John M., Jr. *Liberation Ethics.* New York: Macmillan Co., 1972.

Tambasco, Anthony J. *The Bible for Ethics: Juan Luis Segundo and First-World Ethics.* Lanham, Md.: University Press of America, 1981.

Taylor, Richard. *Ethics, Faith, and Reason.* Englewood Cliffs, N.J.: Prentice-Hall, 1985.

Thielicke, Helmut. *Theological Ethics.* 2 vols. Philadelphia: Fortress, 1966–69.

Thomas, George F. *Christian Ethics and Moral Philosophy.* New York: Charles Scribner's Sons, 1955.

Tillich, Paul. *Love, Power, and Justice.* New York: Oxford University Press, 1954.

_____. *Morality and Beyond*. New York: Harper & Row, 1963.

_____. *Political Expectation*. Edited by James Luther Adams. Macon, Ga.: Mercer University Press, 1971.

_____. *The Protestant Era*. Translated by James Luther Adams. Chicago: University of Chicago Press, 1948.

_____. *The Socialist Decision*. Translated by Franklin Sherman. New York: Harper & Row, 1977.

Troeltsch, Ernst. *Christian Thought: Its History and Application*. Edited by Baron F. von Hügel. New York: Meridian Books, 1957.

_____. *The Social Teaching of the Christian Churches*. 2 vols. Translated by Olive Wyon. New York: Macmillan Co., 1950.

Vanderhaar, Gerard A. *Christians and Nonviolence in the Nuclear Age*. Mystic, Conn.: Twenty-Third Publications, 1982.

Weber, Max. *The Protestant Ethic and The Spirit of Capitalism*. Translated by Talcott Parsons. New York: Charles Scribner's Sons, 1976.

Westley, Dick. *Morality and Its Beyond*. Mystic, Conn.: Twenty-Third Publications, 1984.

Wheelwright, Philip E. *A Critical Introduction to Ethics*. New York: Doubleday, 1935.

White, R. E. O. *Christian Ethics*. Atlanta: John Knox, 1981.

Williams, Daniel Day. *The Spirit and the Forms of Love*. New York: Harper & Row, 1968.

Wingren, Gustaf. *Creation and Law*. Translated by Ross Mackenzie. Philadelphia: Muhlenberg, 1961.

Winter, Gibson. *Liberating Creation: Foundations of Religious Social Ethics*. New York: Crossroad, 1981.

Wolin, Sheldon S. *Politics and Vision*. Boston: Little, Brown, & Co., 1960.

Wolterstorff, Nicholas. *Until Justice and Peace Embrace*. Grand Rapids: Eerdmans, 1983.

Yannaras, Christos. *The Freedom of Morality*. Translated by Elizabeth Briere. Crestwood, N.Y.: St. Vladimir's Seminary Press, 1984.

Yoder, John Howard. *The Politics of Jesus*. Grand Rapids: Eerdmans, 1972.

Subject Index

Name Index

Scripture Index